MY TALISMAN
SELECTED LYRIC POETRY OF ALEXANDER PUSHKIN

ILLUSTRATED BY PUSHKIN'S OWN DRAWINGS

A BILINGUAL EDITION

TRANSLATED, WITH COMMENTARY,
AND A BIOGRAPHY OF PUSHKIN
BY
JULIAN HENRY LOWENFELD

GREEN LAMP PRESS
350 CENTRAL PARK WEST
NEW YORK, NY 10025
Tel. (212) 749-1434
Fax (212) 749-0821
www.AlexanderPushkin.com

© Julian Henry Lowenfeld 2003
All rights reserved.

No part of this publication may be translated, reproduced, or transmitted in any form or by any means, electronic or mechanical, including photocopy, recording, or any information storage and retrieval system now known or to be invented, without permission in writing from the publisher, except by a reveiwer who wishes to quote brief passages in connection with a review written for inclusion in a magazine, newspaper, or broadcast.

Library of Congress Cataloging Number: 2003108460
ISBN 0-094872-0-8
Printed in the United States of America

МОЙ ТАЛИСМАН

ИЗБРАННАЯ ЛИРИКА
А.С. ПУШКИНА

ИЛЛЮСТРИРОВАНА РИСУНКАМИ ПОЭТА
ДВУЯЗЫЧНОЕ ИЗДАНИЕ

ПЕРЕВОД, КОММЕНТАРИИ И БИОГРАФИЯ ПУШКИНА

ДЖУЛИАН ГЕНРИ ЛОУЭНФЭЛД

© *Джулиан Генри Лоуэнфэлд 2003*

НЬЮ-ЙОРК
ИЗДАТЕЛЬСТВО "ЗЕЛЕНАЯ ЛАМПА"
2004

ISBN 0-9748720-0-8

MY TALISMAN

SELECTED LYRIC POETRY
OF ALEXANDER PUSHKIN

ILLUSTRATED BY PUSHKIN'S OWN DRAWINGS
BILINGUAL EDITION
TRANSLATED, WITH COMMENTARY,
AND A BIOGRAPHY OF PUSHKIN
BY
JULIAN HENRY LOWENFELD

© Julian Henry Lowenfeld 2003

NEW YORK
GREEN LAMP PRESS
2004

www.ALEXANDERPUSHKIN.com

СОДЕРЖАНИЕ

Посвящение	i
Созерцание о Пушкине	iii
«Храни меня, мой талисман...»	vi
MY TALISMAN	1
A BRIEF BIOGRAPHY OF THE POET	22
I. ПЕСНИ МЛАДОСТИ	106
Певец	108
«Наперсница волшебной старины...»	110
Mon Portrait	112
Паж, или пятнадцатый год	114
Евгений Онегин, Глава 8 (Из неопубликованной версии)	116
Друзьям	122
В альбом Сосницкой	124
Дориде	126
Эпиграмма «На Аракчеева»	128
«Краев чужих неопытный любитель...»	130
Вольность. Ода	132
Тургеневу	138
Деревня	140
К Чаадаеву	144
II. ЮЖНЫЕ ИДИЛИИ	146
«Погасло дневное светило...»	148
«Увы, зачем она блистает...»	152
«Редеет облаков летучая гряда...»	154
Буря	156
Виноград	158
Гречанке	160
«В еврейской хижине лампада...»	162
«Я пережил свои желанья...»	164
«Умолкну скоро я. Но если в день печали...»	166
«Мой друг, забыты мной следы минувших лет...»	164
Птичка	166
Отрывок из путешествия Онегина	172
Ночь	182
«В твою светлицу, друг мой нежный...»	184
«Ночной зефир...»	186
«Пред испанкой благородной...»	188
«Под небом голубым страны своей родной...»	190
«Для берегов отчизны дальной...»	192
Заклинание	194
Узник	196
Демон	198
К морю	200

TABLE OF CONTENTS

Dedication	i
A Meditation on Pushkin	iii
Deliver me, My Talisman	1
MY TALISMAN	1
A BRIEF BIOGRAPHY OF THE POET	22
I. SONGS OF YOUTH	107
The Bard	109
My confidante of magical old times	111
My Portrait	113
The Page or My Fifteenth Year	115
Eugene Onegin, Chapter 8 (From the Unpublished Verses	117
To My Friends	123
In the Album of [the Actress] Sosnitskaya	125
To Dorida	127
Epigram about Arakcheyev	129
Of foreign lands an inexperienced lover	131
Ode to Liberty	133
To Turgenev	139
The Country	141
To Chaadayev	145
II. SOUTHERN IDYLLS	147
The day's last gleam fades out, is disappearing	149
Alas! Say, why is she so shining	153
The flying wisps of clouds are thinning, scattering far	155
The Storm	157
Grapes	159
To a Greek Girl	161
A lantern in a Jewish hovel	163
I have outgrown my aspirations	165
I will fall silent soon. But if, on days of sadness,	167
My friend, I have forgot all trace of passing years	169
A Little Bird	171
Fragment from Onegin's Journeys	173
Night	183
For one last time, my friend so tender	185
Night's soft breeze	187
By a noble señorita	189
Beneath the light blue skies of her own native land	191
Bound for your homeland's distant shoreline	193
Invocation	195
The Captive	197
The Demon	199
To the Sea	201

СОДЕРЖАНИЕ

III.	**МИХАЙЛОВСКАЯ ССЫЛКА**	206

«Ненастный день потух; ненастной ночи мгла...» 208
Талисман 210
Сожженное письмо 212
Желание славы 214
Сцена из Фауста 216
Зимний вечер 222
«Сват Иван, как пить мы станем...» 224
«Руслан и Людмила». Вступление 226
«В крови горит огонь желанья...» 228
Зимнее утро 230
К *** («Я помню чудное мгновенье...») 232
Признание 236
19 октября 238
Сцена XIII из «Бориса Годунова» 248
«Цветы последние милей...» 268
«Если жизнь тебя обманет...» 270

IV.	**ВИХОРЬ СУДЬБЫ**	272

Арион 274
И.И. Пущину 276
Послание в Сибирь 278
«Свободы сеятель пустынной...» 280
Анчар 282
19 октября 1827 г. 284
Ек. Н. Ушаковой 288
Эпиграмма на Ф. Булгарина 290
Три ключа 292
Вакхическая песня 294

V.	**РАЗДУМЬЯ**	296

«Каков я прежде был, таков и ныне я...» 298
Няне 300
«Весна, весна, пора любви...» 302
Вступление к поэме «Медный всадник» 304
«Город пышный, город бедный...» 310
«Счастлив, кто избран своенравно...» 312
«Я вас любил: любовь еще, быть может...» 314
Стихи, сочиненные ночью во время бессонницы 316
Цветок 318
26 мая 1828 г. 320
Воспоминание 322
Возрождение 324
«Когда порой воспоминанье...» 326

TABLE OF CONTENTS

III.	**RUSTIC EXILE: MIKHAILOVSKOYE**	207

A drizzly day's fizzed out; a drizzly night's dull haze — 209
The Talisman — 211
The Burnt Letter — 213
Wish for Glory — 215
Scene from Faust — 217
A Winter Evening — 223
Iván, dear coz', if we start drinking — 225
Prologue to Ruslan & Lyudmila — 227
My blood is blazing with desire — 229
A Winter Morning — 231
To *** ("A wondrous moment I remember") — 233
Confession — 237
October 19th — 239
Scene XIII from Boris Godunov — 249
The last late flowers are more dear — 269
If, perhaps, life should deceive you — 271

IV.	**THE STORMS OF FATE**	273

Arion — 275
To Ivan Ivanovich Pushchin — 277
A Message to Siberia — 279
In lonesome wasteland freedom sowing — 281
The Poison Tree — 283
October 19, 1827 — 285
To Yekaterina Nikolayevna Ushakova — 289
Epigram (on Faddey Bulgarin) — 291
Three Springs — 293
Bacchanalian Hymn — 295

V.	**MEDITATIONS**	297

The way I used to be, that way I still am now: — 299
To Nanny — 301
Oh spring, oh spring, oh time of love — 303
Prologue to The Bronze Horseman — 305
Town so gorgeous, town of beggars — 311
Oh, blessed he picked with choice capricious — 313
I loved you once, and still, perhaps, love's yearning — 315
Written on a Sleepless Night — 317
The Flower — 319
May 26, 1828 — 321
Remembrance — 323
Rebirth — 325
Sometimes when moody reminiscence — 327

СОДЕРЖАНИЕ

VI.	**В ПУТИ**	328
«Поедем, я готов; куда бы вы, друзья...»		330
Зимняя дорога		332
Телега жизни		334
Приметы		336
«Подъезжая под Ижоры...»		338
«Зима. Что делать нам в деревне?..»		340
Калмычке		344
Монастырь на Казбеке		346
«Не пой, красавица, при мне...»		348
«Зорю бьют... из рук моих...»		350
Делибаш		352
Туча		354
Предчувствие		356
«Чем чаще празднует Лицей...»		358
Бесы		362
VII.	**ОТ СЕРДЦА**	366
Мадонна (Сонет)		368
«Что в имени тебе моем?..»		370
«На холмах Грузии лежит ночная мгла...»		372
«Когда в объятия мои...»		374
Из «Сказки о царе Салтане»		376
«Нет, я не дорожу мятежным наслажденьем...»		382
Красавица		384
«Я думал, сердце позабыло...»		386
«Нет, нет, не должен я, не смею, не могу...»		388
«Пора, мой друг, пора! покоя сердце просит...»		390
«Я возмужал среди печальных бурь...»		392
«Когда б не смутное влеченье...»		394
«Простишь ли мне ревнивые мечты...»		396
VIII.	**И ЗАБЫВАЮ МИР...**	398
«Близ мест, где царствует Венеция златая...»		402
«Не дай мне Бог сойти с ума...»		404
Поэт		406
Эхо		408
Пророк		410
Поэту (Сонет)		412
Осень (отрывок)		414
«...Вновь я посетил...»		422
Из «Египетских ночей»		428
«Когда за городом, задумчив, я брожу...»		430
«Отцы пустынники и жены непорочны...»		432

TABLE OF CONTENTS

VI.	**ON THE ROAD**	329
Let's leave, I'm ready now! Wherever you, my friends		331
A Winter Road		333
The Cart of Life		335
Superstitions		337
Round Izhora I was riding		339
A country winter. What's to do here?		341
To a Kalmyk Girl		345
The Monastery of Mount Kazbek		347
Oh beauty, do not sing to me		349
Dawn drums sound...From my hand tips		351
Delibash (The Turkish Captain)		353
The Cloud		355
Foreboding		357
The more we do commemorate		359
Demons		363
VII.	**FROM THE HEART**	367
Madonna		369
What is there is my name for you?		371
Upon the Georgian hills there lies the haze of night		373
When in the grasp of my embrace		375
From *The Tale of Tsar Saltan*		377
No, I do not hold dear that pleasure so rebellious		383
Beauty		385
I thought my heart had long forgotten		387
No, no, it isn't right, I cannot, I don't dare		389
It's time my friend, it's time!		391
In mournful storms I have become a man		393
If not for something murky gnawing		395
Will you forgive my jealous reverie		397
VIII.	**AND I FORGET THE WORLD...**	399
Near lands where sovereignty of golden Venice rules		403
May God forbid I go insane		405
The Poet		407
The Echo		409
The Prophet		411
To the Poet (A Sonnet)		413
Autumn (A Fragment)		415
...I came back again		423
From Egyptian Nights		429
When past the city gates in wistful thought I roam		431
Our hermit fathers and our nuns blessed and blameless		433

СОДЕРЖАНИЕ

«Напрасно я бегу к сионским высотам...»	434
Из Пиндемонти	436
Элегия	438
«Брожу ли я вдоль улиц шумных...»	440
Памятник	442
Труд	444
«Евгений Онегин» (отрывки)	446
Глава I [Онегин] (отрывки озаглавлены Д.Л.)	448
Глава I [«Ах, ножки, ножки!..»]	458
Глава I [Онегин и Пушкин в Санкт-Петербурге]	464
Глава II [Ленский, Онегин, Татьяна]	474
Глава III [Татьяна с няней]	498
Глава III [Письмо Татьяны к Онегину]	508
Глава IV [Онегин и Татьяна в саду]	514
Глава V [Именины Татьяны]	528
Глава VI [Дуэль]	538
Глава VII [На ярмарке невест]	560
Глава VIII [Возвращение Онегина]	572
Глава VIII [Письмо Онегина к Татьяне]	586
Глава VIII [Окончание]	590
Очерк «Мой Талисман». Перевод на русский язык	610
Обращение к русскому читателю и примечание	632
Краткая биография поэта	634
Алфавитный указатель стихотворений на русском языке	710
Алфавитный указатель стихотворений на английском яз.	715

TABLE OF CONTENTS

In vain I seek to flee and climb up Zion's heights	435
From Pindemonte	437
Elegy	439
When through the noisy streets I wander	441
The Monument	443
Labor (Upon Completing Eugene Onegin)	445
EXCERPTS FROM EUGENE ONEGIN	447
Chapter I (Onegin) (Headings added by JHL)	449
Chapter I (The Pedal Digression)	459
Chapter I (Onegin and Pushkin in St. Petersburg)	465
Chapter II (Lensky, Onegin, Tatyana)	475
Chapter III (Tatyana and her Nanny)	499
Chapter III (Tatyana's Letter to Onegin)	509
Chapter IV (Onegin and Tatyana in the Garden)	515
Chapter V (Tatyana's Name-day Party)	529
Chapter VI (The Duel Between Lensky and Onegin)	539
Chapter VII (The Marketplace of Brides)	561
Chapter VIII (Onegin Returns)	573
Chapter VIII (Onegin's Letter to Tatyana)	587
Chapter VIII (Finale)	591
My Talisman (Russian translation)	611
For the Russian Reader	632
Short Biography of thePoet in Russian	634
Alphabetical Index of First Lines in Russian	710
Alphabetical Index of First Lines in English	715

ПОСВЯЩЕНИЕ

Прежде всего нужна благодарность. Когда мы забываем быть благодарными за то, что нам даровано, мы это теряем. Как Пушкин писал своему другу, поэту Жуковскому, «я бы предпочел слыть ветреным, чем неблагодарным».

Эта книга просто бы не оказалась сейчас в ваших руках, дорогие читатели, без моей любимой наставницы Надежды Семеновны Брагинской. Ее преданное поощрение, скрупулезная научность, блестящий пример безупречных стандартов, ее бескорыстные уроки литературы, сердечный подход к жизни самой, ее постоянная забота и доброта по отношению ко мне, ее чувство юмора — и изумления, ее бесконечная, заразительная любовь к Пушкину, терпение, вдохновение и удивительная вера в меня — всё сделало эту книгу возможной. Посвящаю ей эту книгу со всей моей любовью.

DEDICATION

Before all else thanks are due. If we don't remember to be thankful for our blessings, we have already lost them. As Pushkin wrote the poet Zhukovsky, "I would rather seem flippant than ungrateful."

This book would simply not be in your hands, dear reader, without my beloved teacher Nadyezhda Semyonovna Braginskaya. Her devoted encouragement, rigorous scholarship and selfless teaching, shining example of impeccable standards, her heartfelt approach to life itself, her constant care and kindness to me, her sense of humor – and of wonder, her tremendous, infectious love for Pushkin, her patience, understanding, inspiration, and amazing faith in me were all that made this book possible. I dedicate this book to her with all my love.

NOTE ON THE TEXT

To choose verse for just one book from ten volumes of consistent genius is a torturous task. Looking over my Table of Contents, I grieve for all the beauty I have had to exclude and keenly appreciate any scholarly criticism I may deserve over certain choices that may seem arbitrary. Many facets of Pushkin's protean genius could not be expressed in this book nearly as much as they should have been. More political and philosophical readers will, I hope, forgive my primary focus on the poet's incomparable love lyrics. But it seems to me Pushkin would understand.

Several scholars who were kind enough to glance at this manuscript before publication chided my inconsistencies in following the various systems of transliteration from the Russian Cyrillic. For example, I write "Tchaikovsky," but "Chaadayev," though both names in Russian begin with the Cyrillic letter "Ч". Two brothers devised the rival systems of Cyrillic transliteration: Sergey Yakobson and Roman Jakobson (and they couldn't even agree how to spell the family name). Abstaining in the ongoing academic fratricide may offend both brothers equally, yet I prefer picking the transliteration I like best in context, regardless of "system." Again, I daresay Pushkin would not have minded, in the spirit of Ralph Waldo Emerson's quip: "a foolish consistency is the hobgoblin of small minds." (Speaking of inconsistencies, there are, as with Shakespeare, various slightly different editions of the Pushkin canon. This book follows the USSR Academy of Sciences' Institute of Russian Literature (Pushkin House) official edition of Pushkin's complete works published in Moscow in 1962.

Yet I fear Pushkin would have indeed objected to my omission of the customary Russian patronymic in some cases in the biography, as do other Western biographers and commentators (Binyon, Feinstein, Edmonds, and Bayley). The omission is most grievous, perhaps, in referring to Pushkin's wife, Natalya Nikolayevna Goncharova, simply as "Natalya." To the more sensitive Russian ear not using the patronymic in naming another man's wife can be quite unforgivable familiarity — grounds for a challenge to a duel, in Pushkin's time. Yet this book is meant to cross the language barrier, to make Pushkin accessible to English-speakers. Patronymics tend to confuse those unfamiliar with them, and to introduce an extra degree of artificiality and distance antithetical to a true experience of Pushkin. Russian names are hard enough for foreigners as is; combining them with patronymics makes them even harder to remember, sometimes even for Russians. I refer scholars to Pushkin's joking rebuke to Gogol, in a letter dated August 25, 1831, "your Nadyezhda Nikolayevna, that is, my Natalya Nikolayevna, thanks you heartily for remembering her."

Above all — just enjoy this book! I value language with a punch over pedantry, and so deliberately avoid the academic mania for footnotes. A fruitless quest for arid exactitude is the bane of most scholastic prose. If at times I err on the side of liveliness — I make no apologies.

JULIAN H. LOWENFELD   AUTUMN 2003

ACKNOWLEDGEMENTS

Heartfelt thanks are due first and foremost to my dear friend David Roizin for his generous encouragement and support, and to Nadyezhda Semyonovna Braginskaya for insights and inspiration that were invaluable through all stages of my work. While writing this book, I have also been blessed with insights and kind assistance from many persons, including Viktoria Koff, Donald Fanger, Elena Dovlatova, Maxim Zhukov, Nelly Pogosova, Adelheid Christian-Zechner, Carlo Pierallini, Cosimo Calabró, Victoria Merkovich, Gifford Booth, David Wingrove. I also wish to acknowledge the effusive support I have received from Gregory Shields and Anna Simakova of NTV America, and Andrei Shuranov of Russian American Consulting Corporation. Their constant efforts to bring two great cultures together inspire all who know them.

A MEDITATION ON PUSHKIN

What good is poetry?
What good are songs when madmen capture power in the asylum? —
When books burn, and soon their readers?
With so much suffering in the world
How can melancholy dreamy spirits
Fight with an inferno? What is one man against an army,
One freak of kindness in a sea of hatred?

Too often the unthinkable is common,
Too casually the unspeakable slips from our lips;
Long for no "good old days"; the histories of this world
Prove over and over what Shakespeare knew too well:
"Humanity must perforce prey upon itself,
Like monsters of the deep."

The more I cease to disbelieve such things could happen,
The more that cruelty seems commonplace,
The more I'm numbed; there's no more left in me to feel or sleep,
The sun itself seems dark as it begins to rise,
The moon seems counterfeit,
Whatever stars gleamed through the anguished fog fade faster away,
Leaving neither day nor night,
Just a senseless, empty blight.

Just then, in my despair, I always turn to you,
"My very first and priceless friend"
(Whom I've never met, yet have carried so close to my heart
These many years of folly and self-doubting),
My high priest and my heretic,
My seer, my sage, my fool — my talisman:
I seek your portrait hung above my desk,
And look into your keen, warm, dancing eyes, and ask:
"What can a poem do against machine guns?
What verses about flowers hinder murders?
What right have we, the children of the few spared,
To steal joy from our grief
And treasure the pale warm gleam of morning
Denied to so many?"

You answer:
"One poet's longing brightens night's faint stars,
Provokes the nightingales to wake and sing.
One poet's longing,
One poet's gentle sobbing brings back spring!
One poet's listening deep within,
And singing into a blizzard, even a bit off key,
Sets off cathedral bells, cures numbness and soul-blindness,
Thaws mighty harbors, frees great rivers' flow,
Cracks the thickest ice in the coldest heart..."

What, warmest heart, was in your overpowering lightness,
So crystal clear yet deep as an enormous Lake Baikal of the soul,
Washing away the meaningless from the serene,
Leaving me keen and crying?
....Sometimes, like you, I've walked alone by the sea,
Felt its endless urging and churning crashing within me,
Wild wind in my hair, champagne-cold hissing foam chilling
And bracing, tugging the sand from beneath numbed toes,
And odd tears came from some temple of the sublime
And melancholy where you abided always...

I too have longed to flee from everyone who cannot hear
That sound of that sea, those waves of love, as you did!
And, taking comfort in my own oceanic language,
I've tried to help your bright sun at long last
Shine forth in another climate.
Where I've failed, the fault's all mine:
"...But here's
A partial, feeble rendering,
A pallid print of a live picture"...

Yet if, just slightly, sometimes, here and there,
Your warmth beams through the dark windows of a foreign language—
Springs like a small white flower, improbable and alone,
I saw once, stubborn in the crack of the concrete
On a pedestal of a forgotten monument to you,
In a wistful meadow, by an autumn wood,
By a lake in the blissful, misty middle of nowhere,

A MEDITATION ON PUSHKIN

If ever once this book helps someone smile,
Moves the disconsolate to stop and listen
To the true heart's silence,
That drinks in poetry like the waters of healing,
If ever once this book reveals your joy,
Then this "sacred sacrifice" of hours to you devoted,
Filched from vain pursuits, in search
Of an echo of your spark ineffable,
Will be but the first small token
Of what you've meant to me.

JULIAN LOWENFELD   AUTUMN 2003

Храни меня, мой талисман,
Храни меня во дни гоненья,
Во дни раскаянья, волненья:
Ты в день печали был мне дан.

Когда подымет океан
Вокруг меня валы ревучи,
Когда грозою грянут тучи,
Храни меня, мой талисман.

В уединенье чуждых стран,
На лоне скучного покоя,
В тревоге пламенного боя
Храни меня, мой талисман.

Священный сладостный обман,
Души волшебное светило...
Оно сокрылось, изменило...
Храни меня, мой талисман.

Пускай же ввек сердечных ран
Не растравит воспоминанье.
Прощай, надежда; спи, желанье;
Храни меня, мой талисман.

INTRODUCTION

MY TALISMAN

Deliver me, my talisman.
Deliver me from fear and fleeing,
Days of remorse and worry healing:
On a sad day you clasped my hand.

When rising by the ocean strand
The waves around me crash in pounding,
And when with lightning clouds are sounding,
Deliver me, my talisman.

Lost in seclusion, in strange lands,
In boredom's lull my bosom taming,
In the alarm of battle flaming,
Deliver me, my talisman.

You are my soul's own magic lamp,
You sweet and sacred trickery,
When you drop down, are flickering!
Deliver me, my talisman.

Wounds of the heart help me withstand
Forever; bad memories burn with fire!
Farewell, fond Hope; and sleep, Desire;
Deliver me, my talisman.

Alexander Pushkin: Self-portrait

Under Stalin's Terror, as millions died in prisons and camps, the Soviet secret police often made its daily quota of arrests at three in the morning, grabbing victims when they were surest to be groggy and unable to resist. Imagine for a moment being "back in the USSR" at this cruel time: the dread knock on the door, rude men crudely taking you away, without pity, without explanations. You'll probably never see home and family again...You've got just a few seconds before being swept into the merciless whirlwind of history...What do you do? The great Russian poetess Anna Akhmatova recorded how the last free act of countless Russians upon arrest was to clutch at a pocket book of Pushkin's poetry for solace on their fateful journeys.

Pushkin's poetry for many Russians is literally their talisman of hope. A dear friend of mine (now in England), during the height of the Cold War, risked his life fleeing through the bare strip of no man's land from East to West Germany—taking with him nothing but a small book of Pushkin's verse in his pocket. In World War II, countless such books were found on battlefields from the Arctic to the Black Sea, from the Volga to the Elbe, sometimes bloodstained, or pierced with bullet holes, or scarred by shrapnel. So literally close to their hearts — and so very deep in the depths of the celebrated "Russian soul" is Pushkin!

> Of heaven's realm on Earth a witness,
> With all within my soul on fire,
> I sang before the throne of goodness
> That warmth and beauty did inspire.
> And love and secret inner freedom
> Taught my heart hymns and honest tales.
> My voice, which never was for sale,
> Expressed the Russian people's yearning.

Pushkin's "love and secret inner freedom," that soul-freedom, that no worldly power can take away, have been the Russian soul's beacon of light in the darkness, its sacred talisman for all life's fateful journeys. Now (here and there–in Moscow, at least) the statues of Lenin have been torn down, as the statues of the Tsars were before them. It 's not clear what new statues—if any— will ever take their place on the empty pedestals of now-bankrupt ideals. But on more than 500 monuments to Pushkin throughout Russia, even on the bitterest, coldest days of winter, you will always find fresh flowers.

INTRODUCTION

Pushkin is Russia's most beloved and greatest genius. He is the very lodestar of the Russian culture and the creator of the Russian literary language. Gogol, Tolstoy, Dostoyevsky, Chekhov (the Russian literary geniuses best known in the West) and other great Russian writers all acknowledged themselves Pushkin's heirs and literary debtors. To Gogol, "Pushkin is an extraordinary phenomenon, perhaps the only true expression of the essential Russian spirit"; to Dostoyevsky, Pushkin was "the height of artistic perfection." Tolstoy wrote that he gained mastery of his craft by intense study of Pushkin's *Tales of Belkin*, and, wishing to praise Chekhov's genius, called him "Pushkin in prose." Indeed, it was from Pushkin that Chekhov acquired many of the qualities we now consider innately Chekhovian (deep, passionate emotions subdued with ironic intensity into a few words of unadorned, almost simple, stylistic perfection, an absence of any overt preaching, just sympathy and understanding). For Russian poets from Lermontov and Tyutchev to Bely, Blok, Mandelstam, Mayakovsky, Akhmatova, Tsvetayeva, and Yesenin, a deep devotion to Pushkin was something akin to and almost beyond religion. Pushkin is the "Prophet" of Russian literature, the giver of its law, its breadth, depth, richness of expression. In Russia, to this day, the poems of Pushkin still "burn people's hearts up with his word." Yet, while Russians revere Pushkin as English-speakers do Shakespeare, the West knows Pushkin far less well than it knows his literary heirs. The incomparable mastery of Pushkin's art has eluded translation, leaving even educated people in the West sometimes wondering vaguely whether perhaps Pushkin was Tchaikovsky's librettist. That would be like calling Shakespeare the "librettist" for various Verdi operas!

It is hard to describe Pushkin's magic to non-Russians. His genius in its sublimity compares with Mozart's: miraculous, prodigious feats of creativity, wrought with seemingly effortless, seamless grace, evocative power, warmth, wit, passion, sheer musicality, inventive rhythmic swing, and rhyming playfulness — and all imbued with a certain divine purity, a wisdom born of innocence, a childlike, direct, sweet, natural, vigorous, limpid, language — which is, alas, all the more mysteriously difficult to translate for its simplicity and clarity.

> If only everyone so felt the power
> Of harmony! But no! For then indeed
> The world could not exist. No one would think
> To bother for the lowly needs of living;

We'd all just lose ourselves in free creation.
So we're but few, we chosen happy idlers,
Who, of mere use neglectful and disdainful,
Are high priests of the One, the Beautiful.

These words, from Mozart's last speech in Pushkin's *Mozart and Salieri*, speak not only of Pushkin's own uniqueness but of the lonely relationship between a creative genius and the world around him. But how can English-speaking readers grasp something of the power of Pushkin's harmony? Nabokov's foreword to his own celebrated translation of *Eugene Onegin* voiced the just fears of many scholars:

> Can Pushkin's poem [*Eugene Onegin*], or any other poem with a definite rhyme scheme really be translated?...The answer, of course, is no. To reproduce the rhymes and yet translate the entire poem is mathematically impossible. But in losing the rhyme, the poem loses its bloom, which neither marginal description nor the alchemy of a scholium can replace.

Nabokov, therefore, chose to bequeath us as literal a translation as possible — apologizing in advance that "to my ideal of literalism I sacrificed everything (elegance, euphony, clarity, good taste, modern usage, and even grammar)..." Yet, with all due reverence for an incomparable stylist and scholar, such an entirely literal translation of Pushkin results in a lifeless specimen—neatly pinned, perhaps, to a label in a glass case by the master lepidopterist— but with none of the ineffable grace and beauty of a butterfly in flight.

To grasp Pushkin one must hear his musicality. Not just Tchaikovsky, but virtually all the great Russian composers — Mussorgsky, Rimsky-Korsakov, Prokofiev, Rachmaninoff, Glinka, and Glazunov, felt compelled to set his verse to music. The music is already there: it swirls in his sounds:

Snowstorm, gloom-filled, heavens drowning,
Wild the snowy whirlwind flies,
Sometimes, like a beast, it's howling,
Sometimes, like a child, it cries.

Pushkin was indeed one of the highest priests of the Pythagorean doctrine of the One, the Beautiful. The Pythagoreans, it is said, used to cure the sick with poetry, believing in the unique healing virtues of certain verses of the *Odyssey* and *Iliad* when read aloud in the proper way. Like Homer, Pushkin derives indescribable power as much from the sound—as from the sense—of his words, from their lilt, their swing, their magical incantation: their spell.

Yet the subtly inflected Russian language is infinitely richer in natural rhymes than English. Too many translators have veered from the Charybdis of "literality" to the Scylla of sacrificing Pushkin's natural unaffected language into impossibly stilted poses, just to fit into a given rhyme scheme. Various quite eminent scholars (Arndt, Johnston, Deutsch, and Falen, to name but a few) have produced fair rhyming translations, deserving of praise and respect. Yet Pushkin's majestic lightness is not easily conveyed. Too often Pushkin's Russian verses, so easy and magnificent in the original, come out even in good English translations with an incongruously comic effect derived from the forcing of the rhyme, like some Tin Pan Alley jingle, or at best W.S. Gilbert — but nothing like Pushkin. To avoid this, I have sometimes used approximate rhyme (as did Yeats or Dylan Thomas), rather than reaching for absurd synonyms just to get exact rhymes. This solves many problems: it gives the inner ear the assonance it craves, while saving the true meaning and freshness of the original. Yet another problem arises in the frequent disparity in the number of syllables between Russian and English synonyms. For example, let's look at the first quatrain of what is probably the most famous love poem in the Russian language. Literally, it says:

Я помню чудное мгновенье:	I remember a wonderful moment:
Передо мной явилась ты,	You appeared before me
Как мимолетное виденье,	Like a fleeting vision,
Как гений чистой красоты.	A genius of pure beauty.

But no literal translation captures the magic of this magical moment. Flaubert, given its literal translation by his friend Turgenev, is said to have remarked: "Il est plat, votre poète." ["He's flat, your poet"]. Magic requires "poetic license": it is better to add or omit a few words with loving caution, but keep the "swing," the Pythagorean talismanic power, the spell woven into the rhythm. Very slight liberties with the exact truth can be justified when they help reveal a higher truth:

A wondrous moment I remember:
Before me once you did appear;
A fleeting vision you resembled,
Of beauty's genius pure and clear.

Pushkin himself revelled in "poetic license" when translating. Most of the foreign verse he rendered into Russian "loses something in the original." Even Goethe, Ariosto, Shakespeare, and Chenier he treated not as holy writ to be reproduced word for word, but as themes to be played with as musicians improvise on given tunes. For example, look how Pushkin "translated" a poem by the obscure English country poet Brian Waller Procter, (1787 – 1874), known as Barry Cornwall.

Cornwall	"Translation" Translated
Inesilla! I am here!	I'm here, Inesilla,
Thy own cavalier	Your window beneath.
Is now beneath thy lattice playing;	While all of Sevilla
Why art thou delaying?	Embraces gloom's sleep.
He hath ridden many a mile	With valorous heart, here,
But to see thy smile.	In broad cloak I'm sheathed,
The young light on the	With sword and guitar, here,
Flowers is shining, but he is repining.	Your window beneath.

Pushkin cuts the "verbiage" and adds music; he turns us with him into Don Juan, transported to the Spain he dreamed of, where "Night's soft breeze/ blows easeful; clear/ and flowing/ foams/ Guadalquivir." Another of Pushkin's lifelong dreams was to visit Italy, "sacred to Apollo's grandsons." His works have over ninety quotations from Dante, Petrarch, Ariosto, and Tasso – in the original Italian. His love for Italian culture seems to have imbibed and incorporated the spirit of the Renaissance, the grand humanistic artistic philosophy expressed in Baldassare Castiglione's *Book of The Courtier*:

> But having considered often how grace is acquired (aside from those who have it from the stars), I find it a rule most universal which seems to me valid in practically all things human which are said or done...and that is to avoid, like the sharpest and most dangerous of shoals, affectation, and – to coin a new phrase perhaps – to use in all things a certain *sprezzatura* [nonchalance, lightness, disdain, detachment], which hides its own art, and

> shows all that is done and said to be effortless, almost without even thinking about it. From this I believe much grace is derived, because everyone knows the difficulty of performing things rare and difficult, such that ease therein engenders the greatest wonder, whereas, on the contrary, laborious forcing of oneself, and, as it might be said, dragging oneself by the hairs of one's head, shows the highest want of grace, and causes us to little appreciate it, no matter how grand it be. But that art is true indeed which does not appear to be art.

(*Il Libro del Cortigiano*, Book I, xxvi, my translation). Pushkin's works sparkle with this effortlessness artlessness, this ineffable *sprezzatura*. His poems confide in you like a best friend, fill your soul with warmth like the "amber glow" of the room in which he wakes his love on *A Winter Morning*. Yet there is something elusive about his love. Much stays veiled behind his glowing state of grace. Yet somehow, his verse seems to express that inexpressible, irrepressible, incomprehensible, so beloved and so-loving "Russian soul" — and make it universal. Dostoyevsky praised above all "Pushkin's universal sympathy."

The great Roman poet Terence wrote: "I will hold nothing human to be alien to me." Pushkin took this maxim to the max (as one might say in L.A.): "No one bores me — from a simple policeman all the way up to the Tsar." Fascinated by foreigners, he spoke 8 foreign languages, remaking the modern Russian tongue by sprinkling French, English, Italian, German, and Latin words into his works. He loved grand balls and the Frenchified lacey finery of the court, yet adored peasant fairs, and once taught a provincial governor's parrot to swear like a sailor — at an archbishop. He risked a hanging for *The Gavriliad's* "delightful blasphemy," and yet his "*Our hermit fathers*" is perhaps the most sublime prayer in verse ever written. Yet again, that same poet who had penned that prayer also wrote certain verses for stag-parties which still don't pass the censor…

Embracing all, rejecting none, he loved and wrote for both countesses and their maids. With kings and slaves alike, in palaces or jails, ballrooms or barracks, in the city, or in the country, in woods, fields, hills, mountains, ocean storms, and by tender little streams, by battlefields, graveyards, insane asylums, bordellos, gambling dens…the reader of this book will see Pushkin somehow at home everywhere, and yet everywhere keeping the keen curiosity of the outsider.

He celebrated "experience, son of bitter errors, and genius, friend of paradox." Pushkin's characters are always three-dimensional, right at home in what Coleridge termed "cognitive dissonance": duality is everywhere in Pushkin's work. The great Russian critic Vissarion Belinsky rightly called *Eugene Onegin* "an encyclopedia of Russian life." Yet it is also a poetic heart-to-heart talk between Pushkin's warring selves, dressed up as different characters. Pushkin's schoolmate, the poet Wilhelm Küchelbecker exclaimed: "Tatyana! — Why, she's Pushkin!" But another friend, the great Polish poet Adam Mickiewicz, taught in his lectures on Russian literature that in *Eugene Onegin* Pushkin had incarnated himself in Lensky and Onegin... Both bards were right; Pushkin was all his characters. Russian literature's grand tradition of compassionate objectivity, and of merciless detail suffused with warmth and soulfulness began, gloriously, with Pushkin.

In a letter whose perlustration by secret police earned "the sunshine of Russian poetry" exile and house arrest (for an offhand reference to "taking lessons in pure atheism"), Pushkin averred that he actually enjoyed reading the Bible. Or rather: "the Good Book's not bad, really, but the truth is I prefer Shakespeare or Goethe." Pushkin, indeed, was so impressed by Goethe's *Faust* that he composed a new *Scene from Faust* while in exile. Later he was very proud to be honored by Goethe with a present of a pen. Undoubtedly, in some ways the two poets were alike. Both Goethe and Pushkin essentially invented their respective languages' modern literary idiom. Both were Romantics; both were set to music by countless composers; both achieved what many consider the quintessential expression of their countries' souls. One might go so far as to say that each dramatized his county's virtues — and also flaws. Yet, while much admiring the "Muse of Weimar" (see illustration), Pushkin did not share Goethe's slightly didactic pragmatism, seen, for instance, in Goethe's *Wasser und Wein*:

Von Wasser allein wird man stumm.	From water alone speech is numb,
Das beweisen im Wasser die Fische.	Which is proved by the fish in the water.
Von Wein allein wird man dumm .	From wine alone one grows dumb
Das beweisen die Herren am Tische.	Which is proved by those gents' table chatter.
Und drum, um keines von beiden zu sein,	And — so that neither such state will be mine —
Trink ich mit wasser vermischt mein Wein.	With water diluted I drink my wine.

(My translation). 18 year old Pushkin reacted to his idol with a very different *Water and Wine* indeed:

INTRODUCTION

Pushkin's Portrait of Goethe

I love, when noontime's heat is blazing,
To suck the cool out from a stream.
And in a grove, secluded, shaded,
To watch the current dance and gleam.
When to the brim white wine is flowing
And foaming in our fateful bowls,
Who, friends, amongst you, aren't groaning,
Elated, eager in your souls?
But cursèd be that villain godless,
Who first should dare commit the crime,
Blinded, unbridled, and dishonored,
Oh woe! To mix with water wine!
Curse him through every generation!
So drink no more then! Fine! So be it!
Or mix the glasses in their places
And call cheap swill Château Lafitte!

Readers may be surprised by certain almost-macho, boyish strains in Pushkin's verse. In Pushkin, as in his other idol, Shakespeare, every character is strong — even when wavering. And whether happy or grieving, he seems ever sure of his masculinity, ever in touch with both the god and the impish little boy within. So at-one indeed with his own manhood is he that he freely celebrates the feminine in himself, even on occasion drawing himself as a woman. Perhaps his finest lines are about or for women. Another way of saying this is that Pushkin was always in love: not just with women, but with nature, art, and life itself. Being in love was to him as natural as breathing:

This heart again burns up with loving, because — why?
It simply cannot not be loving.

Pushkin once poked fun at himself in a note to a friend on the nature of first love, that his then-fiancée Natalya was "in parenthesis my one hundred and thirteenth love" (In parenthesis, various scholars mistake this sarcasm for a statistic, and one could probably find 113 clueless tomes inspired by just this one flippant remark). But there's no point losing sleep over everyone Pushkin might have slept with:

> My friends! What does it really matter
> Just where our idle heart gets rent?
> In ballrooms bright, smart box-seat chatter,
> Or in a nomad's wicker tent?

In truth Pushkin was always in love not just with the maid of the moment, but with the divine energy she evoked in him. Any woman he exalted was his Muse, was that spirit invoked by Goethe at the end of *Faust:* "*das Ewig-Weibliche*" (the "Ever–Feminine"). Pushkin's hymns to the Feminine attain a crystal purity that is somehow only deepend by his characteristically lighthearted and flippant attitude towards his own "light ease in suffering." His raging passions are no less intense for his self-deprecating, sly airiness, which seems forever smiling, even at the capriciousness of his own caprice.

I do not dare to seek your love.
It may be I have sinned so much,
My angel, I am not worth loving.
But just pretend it! Your look sweet
Sublimely says all things demurely!
Oh dear! It isn't hard to fool me!
I'm glad myself to be to be deceived!

Could someone truly "deceived" ever pen such lines? Yet in the foolish giddiness of falling in love, in a "crush," like a glass too much of wine, in *umilenie*, deeply moved affection, Pushkin found wisdom and communion with all humanity. He preferred raw love poems to odes, once even gently chiding a friend for writing verses that were too smart because: "All poetry should be — God forgive me — kind of silly!" Pushkin's solace, in dark times, is that of a friend who does not hide behind his genius. He jokes and winks at us, joys in his own foibles, and is fascinated by ours. He knows that in the end, only accepting and embracing each others' flaws do we graduate from effortless being in love to love itself, with its profound, mysterious contradictions. With exquisite intimacy, he even dares reveal the painful bliss of his own marital bedroom:

Pushkin as a woman watching Anna Petrovna Kern go by

Oh, with what tortured joy for you alone I pine
When you, at last yielding to lengthy supplication,
Give yourself tenderly to me without elation,
Feeling ashamed and cold, my joyousness within
But scarcely answering, and not feeling a thing.
Till livening with time, you too start thrilling,
Till more and more at last my flame you share unwilling.

Love — often openly erotic love — is the very fabric of Pushkin's *sprezzatura*. Yet being "all about love, and love, and love," Pushkin quite offended those who frankly wished he had been more political. Certain Soviet critics, notably the influential Vikenty Veresayev, and his school, practically condemned Pushkin for anti-Soviet behavior. In the dead language of *Pravda* editorials, Veresayev complained: "In political, societal, and religious questions, Pushkin was unreliable and infirm, and in various years full of internal contradictions" (So, according to Marx, was liberal capitalism). Thus, the very same Soviet propagandists who idolized the author of *The Prophet*, *The Poison Tree*, and a *Message to Siberia*, never really forgave the poet his sympathy not only for the jailed Decembrists who rebelled against the Tsar, but for their jailors as well (*"God help you all, my dear, dear, friends"*). Like Tsarist censors before them, they found unpatriotic his concern not only for the Russian soldiers on "our side," but also for the soldiers in the enemy camp. *Delibash, or The Turkish Captain* was the favorite poem of another great Russian poetic genius: Alexander Blok marvelled at its light, almost casual touch, its bare detail so perfectly conveying the profound senselessness of war. But Pushkin's rejection of fanaticism was nearly capital treason in an age of cruel ideals. In Veresayev's time, "ten years with no rights to correspondence" [the Stalinist euphemism for execution] was the common sentence for expressing sentiments like these:

I do not value much those rights hailed with such din
From which so many people's heads just seem to spin.
I don't complain and grouse about the gods' sharp practice,
Denying me sweet rights to argue about taxes,
Or make it hard for Tsars to war with Tsars.
It little riles me if the press is free to charge
And torment idiots, or tender censors' humors
Offend themselves in every ragsheet's rumors.

> Oh! Can't you see that all this is just "words, words, words?"
> By other, better rights my soul gets stirred;
> Another, better sort of freedom I am seeking.
> Depend upon the Tsar? Depend upon the people?
> Isn't it all the same? Who cares?

Both Tsars and commissars (supposedly representing "the people") were naturally quite offended by this. Thus Veresayev, like the censor-spy Bulgarin 100 years before him, went out of his way to claim to see "a striking difference between the live personality of the poet and its reflection in his works" — in other words, to deal with the inconvenient Pushkin by slandering him personally. Yet Pushkin's "better sort of freedom," the inner freedom of the soul, still sustains generations of Russians who have known no other liberty. Pushkin's teaching lies in never preaching. Pushkin, like Oscar Wilde, claims to know nothing except that "life is too important to be taken seriously." Hermann in his *Queen of Spades,* eyes life with Napoleonic ruthlessness and (near-Marxian) "calculation." But Pushkin laughs at "German" materialism. Instead he embraces the mysterious, the flippant, the quirky, the odd, the soulful, the feminine, the way of moods, the way of the moon:

The moon

> Your melancholy's without reason.
> You love with suffering and grieving;
> But woman's heart loves laughing, jokes.
> Look up! See, in the dark vault's distance,
> The moon so freely prances, preens,
> On all of nature she, in passing,
> Sheds equally capricious gleams.

> Though any cloud she'll notice brightens,
> And grows majestic with her hue—
> Just then on other clouds she lightens —
> And doesn't visit there long too.
> Who'll dare to bound her heavenly dancing?
> Who bids her stop, cuts off her range?
> Who'll give a maiden's heart commandments:
> "Love only one, and never change?"

Like love itself, the moon can be capricious and demanding.. In Pushkin's poems the moon usually brings sorrow with its dreaminess, and lonely grief with its beauty...that melancholy which Brazilians call "*saudade*" and Russians call "*toská.*" But to Pushkin, dreamy moonlit starlight was ever so much more precious than his place under the sun. Only the subtle gleam of the moon evokes that essence which day and night alike obscure. Only in soft starlight can the poet find his inner bliss:

> Near lands where sovereignty of golden Venice rules,
> A lone nocturnal gondolier his way plies through the pools.
> By evenstar's soft light, he — singing — turns his oars
> Of Reynald, Godfred, and Erminia — by their shores.
> He loves singing his song, for pleasure sings his story,
> Lacking all further plans, he sings heedless of glory,
> Of fears heedless, of hopes... Filled by the silent Muse,
> Above the waves' abyss with bliss his wake he hews:
> So, in this sea of life, where cruelly the tempest
> In darkening gloom to my lone sail grants no rest,
> Not minding what men say, I sing and I rejoice,
> Dreaming up secret poems with my secret voice.

Sometimes, though, his songs do not "rejoice" — especially in his last eight years, trapped in this "piggish Petersburg" (although "I love you, town of Peter's making"). The "chosen, happy idler" (whose friends nicknamed him "the Cricket" in his youth) soon chirped less, and mourned more, merged with a darker man, grieving, (*Remembrance*),fearing madness (*May God forbid I go insane*), and morbidly obsessed by death (*When past the city gates in wistful thought I roam*). Actually, that dark man was always present. "*I will fall silent soon*" and "*I have outlived my aspirations*" were written in cheerful days when he was still teaching parrots to swear at bishops, or chasing comely gypsy girls, or racing to fresh oysters. ("*And so I lived then in Odessa*").

Some blame his increasing gloom of later years on deep disillusionment with his wife, on jealousy over her flirtation (or worse) with a handsome French officer, Georges D'Anthès, who later killed him in a duel. Others blame the poet's growing frustration at the pompous, meretricious, stifling atmosphere of the imperial court, expressed in the last of his 78 letters to his wife: "Here, just being a decent human being is enough to earn one a scolding by the police...Why did the Devil let me be born in Russia — and with a soul and talent to boot?" A poet understands a poet, and Aleksandr Blok concluded: "Pushkin was killed not by D'Anthès' bullet, but by lack of air" for his free soul to breathe in. Much of his last years were spent accompanying his wife and her sisters to fancy balls, dressed as an imperial chamberpage, a flunkey of a court so cold, so focused on empty glitter, that it could not see its own most brilliant jewel. He would watch and brood as his wife flirted with men who were handsomer, richer, and more attuned to her selfish frivolity. To love her, and yet feel unloved by her, must have become ever more intolerable. Two years before his death he wrote:

> It's time, my friend, it's time! For peace the heart is calling.
> Day flies by after day, and every hour is tolling
> A bit of being away: together you and I
> Suppose that we will live — but see! but then — we die!
> There is no joy on earth, but there is peace and freedom:
> Long time of enviable fate I have been dreaming,
> Long time, I, tired slave, have dreamed of secret flight
> Unto a distant shrine of toil and pure delight.

And yet, who but the very freest spirit in an enslaved country dares call himself a "tired slave"? "Genius, friend of paradox," can joy in grief and mourn in happiness. Keats wrote "in the very temple of Delight/Veil'd Melancholy has her sovran shrine." For Pushkin, "my melancholy's bright" : his fundamentally playful, flirtatious attitude to life extended, in its way, even to flirtation with death. He once got in a duel insisting that a cafe orchestra play a mazurka instead of a Russian quadrille requested by some drunken officer. He let his opponent shoot first, unanswered at sixteen paces, then, since a snowstorm was swirling, gave his foe another chance to shoot at just twelve paces. His schoolmate Küchelbecker challenged him for a verse describing a hangover as feeling "Küchelbeckerish and bleary"; Pushkin refused to shoot, and, when his friend missed, extended his hand and said:

"Enough clowning around: let's go have tea." In yet another duel (later the plot of his short story *The Shot*) Pushkin let his opponent shoot at him while he stood calmly, eating a bunch of cherries. His foe exclaimed: "You stand up to bullets as well as you write!" Then they embraced. In *Delibash,* Pushkin advises: "Cossack, hey! Race not to battle." Yet in the only battle in which he himself ever took part, had to be dragged off the field, after seizing a lance from a slain Cossack—and charging. (No hobgoblins of foolish consistency troubled Pushkin!)

For all his courage, one wonders whether Pushkin himself noticed the uncanny similarities between the duel that killed him and the duel that killed his poet Lensky in Book VI of *Eugene Onegin*: a silly spat, provoked by the poet's jealousy over a frivolous society beauty who seems briefly attracted to a rake. Both duels took place at nearly the same date and time, with the same wintry scenery...In both duels the poet used the same Lepage pistols, and died when the rake shot first. Did Pushkin not, before his duel, reflect on Lensky's tragic ending? Why did Pushkin, so superstitious that he would turn his carriage around and ride home if a hare crossed his path, proceed, despite bad omens and a prophecy, to his fatal duel? Did he want to die?

> But, oh my friends, I do not want to die;
> I want to live, to think, suffer, and pine.

Yet it is said he left for his duel without a turquoise ring he usually wore for protection against violent death. Did he just forget? Was he tired of suffering and longing for release? Or is that story itself just a legend? We cannot unlock that secret now. We can only share his courageous readiness, his melancholy, light-hearted curiosity — even in the face of death itself:

> As I caress a child's head tender
> I think already: "Farewell" soon:
> To you my place I now surrender:
> For I must wither, you must bloom.
>
> Each day now, each year I'm amassing,
> I like to see off in my mind,
> Guessing the dates of my own passing,
> Trying the right one to divine.

> And where will fate send me my dying?
> In battle, wanderings, or waves?
> Or will the valley nearby lying
> Receive my ashes in its graves?

Certain Buddhists believe that the "higher self" chooses the time and manner of the soul's departure from the body. Musing and choosing how to die — would Pushkin, if those Buddhists are right, not find it somehow entirely meet to "meet his Maker" young and vigorous — because of love, and over a point of honor? It is a uniquely Pushkinian paradox: "my gift, like life, I frittered away heedless"; so in love with life was he that he was willing to cast it away lightly, at the drop of a glove, to march, like his unnamed hero in *The Shot*, meeting death's bitterness with the tart sweet taste of berries in his mouth. (Almost his very last words, by the way, were: "give me cloudberries").

Even at his saddest, some other part of him, a "friend," wryly stood back observing all with a certain sardonic affection. Even at Onegin's deepest, most lovelorn depression, he managed to joke:

> A very poet he resembled
> Alone in his dark corner, there,
> Watching the hearth blaze up and blare
> And purring, murm'ring "*Benedetta*"
> Or "*Idol mio*," to the flames threw
> His paper — or sometimes his shoe!

Being able to laugh at himself, Pushkin was ultimately an optimist. Unlike his literary heirs, famed for "more skies of grey/than any Russian play can guarantee," Pushkin dared to write happy endings—heresy to radicals whose over-politicized expectations demanded woe. Even his endings that aren't so happy easily could have been, as his beloved Tatyana laments, in her last rejection of Onegin:

> Yet happiness was there so nearly,
> So close by.

Nabokov shrewdly commented about the ending of *Eugene Onegin* that it is doubtful even just how final its unhappy "finale" really is:

> At the risk of breaking the hearts of all admirers of "Princess Gremin" (as the two bright minds that concocted Tchaikovsky's libretto dubbed [Tatyana]), I deem it necessary to point out that her answer to Onegin does not at all ring with such dignified finality as commentators have supposed it to do. Mark the intonations...the heaving breast, the broken speech, the anguished, poignant, palpitating, enchanting, almost voluptuous, almost alluring enjambments, a veritable orgy of run-ons, culminating in a confession of love that must have made Eugene's experienced heart leap with joy. And after those sobbing 12 lines — what clinches them? The hollow perfunctory sound of a pat couplet... shrill virtue repeating its cue!

Perhaps Nabokov goes too far. Pushkin was no Falstaff. To him, honor was no empty word, no "mere escutcheon" — honor was dearer than life, was art and love and freedom, all in one, and worth all. Still, Nabokov is right that ambiguity and irony pervade Pushkin's moral universe. He prefers observing to judging, presenting his characters choices, often metaphorized: forks in roads, corridors leading in different directions. Some choices are serious and some just flippant whims; all are fateful all the same. (Often mere whims are luckier; compare *The Snowstorm* with *The Queen of Spades*). He famously wrote in *The Queen of Spades*: "two fixed ideas cannot exist together in one moral space, just as two bodies cannot together occupy one and the same place in the physical world." But with his usual graceful ease, that law seems not to apply for him — just as quantum mechanics overrules classical physics on a fundamental level. Thus, simultaneously in his creations, Fate rules all, and things could have only turned out as they did. Yet, since man has free will, things could have turned out any way at all! Perhaps, as Schopenahauer said, "man has free will, but not the will to use it." At any rate, Pushkin's stories feel like life itself: choice and chance, in dance together, weave a seamless harmony, and, as if effortlessly, arrive at a bittersweet perfection, an ironic state of grace, higher in his works than what life's logic otherwise allows. And "I look through my bright tears and smile."

Alas, Pushkin himself never attained the choice he so dearly longed for, to "flee the rumor of the crowd" like another beloved Roman poet Horace, "for stillness pastoral"..."unto a distant shrine of toil and pure delight."

And yet the Tsar could only confine his movements; his heart remained free. Even brooding on death, he found transcendence and higher wisdom. One of Pushkin's final poems is based on Horace's great ode: *"Exegi monumentum."* In it, Horace took majestic pride in his enduring poetic legacy:

> I've built a monument that outlasts bronze,
> And looms up higher than the regal heaps of Pyramids,
> That nor the devouring rainclouds, nor the North Wind
> Blustering and impotent, nor row on row of years uncounted
> Midst the flight of Time can possibly destroy.
> Not all of me will die; much of me shall
> Escape the Temple of the Dead, through and through
> Growing in fresh praise, as long as the Pontiff shall
> Climb up the Capitol, with silent Vestal beside him.
> They'll say, where violent Aufidus roared its flood,
> And where King Daunus reigned in a land of peoples
> Bereft of water, that I, though sprung from lowness meek,
> First brought Aeolian song forth to the measures of
> Italian verse. Take then the lofty honors and rewards
> You've strived for and won me, and freely, with Delphic Laurel,
> Crown now, Melpomene, my hair.

Horace, Book III, Ode xxx (my translation; the Latin text is on p. 628).

Pushkin, millenia sadder than his Roman mentor, had no faith left in the tinsel of temporal power. No grace could be ever crowned on him by some pompous "*pontifex*," no empire could be depended upon to preserve the legacy of his soul. His crown came from the power of love, from the harmony of the god-man-boy in him with the "eternal feminine." Like love, grace comes from within, not on command of some Sun King. It lives, and gleams by itself — beneath the moon:

> No, I won't fully die: my soul, in sacred lyre,
> Will yet survive my dust, and, despite with'ring, thrive:
> I'll glorious be as long's in moonlit world entire
> One single bard is still alive.

In the end, all great poetry — especially Pushkin's — is always a monument to love, to that sacred weakness, the strongest force of all. Rome no longer rules the world, yet Horace is still here with us. Caesar's' Vestal Virgins are long gone, but not the verses they inspired... Just so, Pushkin's Tatiana (in her way too a vestal virgin, given away lovelessly to a fat crippled general) will ever be close to the hearts of millions...She and her beloved Eugene are like that unknown youth Keats comforted in his *Ode on a Grecian Urn*:

> Bold lover, never, never canst thou kiss,
> Though winning near the goal – yet, do not grieve;
> She cannot fade, though thou hast not thy bliss,
> For ever wilt thou love, and she be fair!

Portrait of the poet Horace

For that single poet in the "moonlit world entire," for that poet inside of all of us, we need Pushkin, a poet of poets, the poet of the Russian soul. We need his inspiring call "to sacred sacrifice," we need his courage, accepting hardship and exile over any compromise in the flawless integrity of his art. We need his serenity, his ability to smile into the abyss with the taste of berries in his mouth, disdainful of all Delphic laurels...

INTRODUCTION

We need his determined joy in the face of an unforgiving, uncomprehending world, his ease in turning mundane misery into divine grief, and his ease and contentment, perhaps greatest reward of all, in just being who he is, and thereby "waking up good feelings":

> And many years will I be favored with the people
> For waking up good feelings by my lyre's thrall,
> Because in my cruel age I praised and gloried Freedom,
> For mercy to the fallen called.
>
> The Lord's command, oh Muse, be ever heeding,
> Fear not offense and shame, care not for glory's rule,
> Take praise and calumny indifferently, not needing —
> And never argue with a fool.

Pushkin's undiluted voice is long overdue in the English language. May this book help those not blessed with knowing Russian to hear it, perhaps, for the first time. And may those readers already blessed with Russian, perhaps raised on his voice from childhood, please forgive me every time they cannot hear his incomparable grace in my English renderings, which, I am the first to admit, can never really do justice to the divine original.

Yet I hope that even Russian-speakers may catch in this book a different glimmer from the brightest star in their linguistic firmament, as a light shined from a new angle, sometimes, reveals hidden facets in a brilliant jewel. Though "of mere use neglectful and disdainful," Pushkin's poetry, like all great art, truly has magical healing power — the deep mysterious potency of a talisman, protecting and comforting our own souls' fateful journeys.

Julian Lowenfeld   Autumn 2003

Alexander Pushkin — Self portraits

A BRIEF BIOGRAPHY OF THE POET

"What is a poet? Someone who writes poems? Of course not. One is a poet not just because one writes poems, but one writes poems, harmonizing words and sounds—because one is a child of harmony— because one is a poet."
— Alexander Blok, The Poet's Mission

1799–1811 Childhood

Alexander Sergeyevich Pushkin was born in Moscow on June 6, 1799. (At least in the West it was. In Russia it was May 26, 1799, according to the Julian calendar used there till 1918; all further dates will be given as Pushkin himself experienced them, "in the old style"). The poet's father, Sergey Lvovich Pushkin, came from an illustrious, if impoverished, noble family. The poet's mother Nadyezhda Osipovna, née Gannibal, was called "*la belle créole*." Her black grandfather, Ibrahim Gannibal, had been kidnapped in childhood from Central Africa, sold by slave traders to the Turks, and then bought and sent as a "gift" to Tsar Peter the Great. Tsar Peter baptized the boy Abraham, raised him fondly, and, seeing his aptitude, made him his personal secretary, then sent him to study military engineering in France. Abraham became Russia's chief fortress builder, and wrote several textbooks in French on mathematics and fortification building. Proud of his African heritage, he chose his surname in honor of the great Carthaginian general Hannibal (Gannibal in Russian, which lacks a letter "h"). Twice decorated for valor, he retired *General en Chef* of the Imperial Russian Army. Empress Elizabeth, Peter's daughter, endowed him with estates, including Mikhailovskoye, in Pskov Province. And so a former slave became a Russian nobleman— himself the owner of 800 white slaves (serfs). Pushkin inherited many of his great-grandfather's African features: thick lips, somewhat frizzy hair, and tan-colored skin. He later kept an inkwell on his writing desk with a statuette of a Negro slave unloading cotton bales. And he often joked with defiant pride of being a "Moor":

> Why does your pencil so divine
> Attempt to draw my Moorish profile?

Poets and writers frequented the Pushkin home. One of the better-known poets was Pushkin's uncle Vasily Lvovich ("You are my uncle even on Parnassus," his nephew later wrote). Pushkin's father was known for his wit, his mainly French-language library, one of the best in Moscow, and for literary salons, in which he read Molière aloud, with aplomb and liveliness. Pushkin's mother was fond of reading

Sergey Lvovich Pushkin, the poet's father

Nadyezhda Osipovna Pushina, née Gannibal, the poet's mother

aloud to her children, and, in Pushkin's phrase: "Reading is the best teaching." If his family had not breathed with love for poetry, for the glories of European culture, and for Russian culture too, it is doubtful his genius would have developed as it did.

Yet most biographers and memoirists are critical of Pushkin's parents. "Sergey Lvovich was a tender father, but all tenderness shrank at spending money; he was extremely miserly," recalled Pushkin's friend Prince Peter Vyazemsky. The chance breaking of a little glass costing 35 kopecks sufficed to put him in a great rage all day, and "he never gave the slightest help to his son Alexander, in his entire life sparing him barely 500 rubles in notes—though in his own way he was very proud of his son's successes" wrote biographer Mikhail Semevsky. His mother is depicted as charming but neglectful and moody. "She could sulk for days, months, even years," one grandson recalled. In fairness, eight surviving children (of whom Pushkin was the second; five others died in infancy) would be hard for anyone to handle, though for some reason she favored the poet's younger brother Lev, and was noticeably unaffectionate with that *enfant terrible*, her restless, brilliant eldest son, Alexander. Some degree of connective warmth between the poet and his mother seems to have been attained only in their last few years of life. One senses in many of Pushkin's deepest love lyrics a grieving and yearning for the mother he missed in childhood. It does not seem coincidence that in a semi-autobiographic sketch, *A Russian Pelham*, the poet portrayed himself as motherless. And as to his father:

> My time under my father's roof has left nothing pleasant in my imagination. Father, of course, loved me, but didn't have the slightest interest in me, and left me to the care of various French tutors, who were constantly being hired and fired. My very first *gouverneur* was a drunkard, the second, though neither stupid nor uneducated, could fly into such rages that he once tried to murder me with a log for spilling a few drops of ink onto his waistcoat. The third, kept in our house for a whole year, was totally insane.

Modern notions of "hands-on parenting" were not in vogue then. *Au contraire*, benign neglect was considered *bon ton* and aristocratic; children "should be seen, not heard," routinely treated like all other household matters, ignored, or dealt with by mere servants. However he may have felt this lack of parental attention, unlike his contemporary Dickens, he rarely made childhood griefs his theme, although he did hint at it in some works. Instead he preferred just keeping a healthy distance from "his near and dear ones":

What does that mean, our near and dear ones?
Our near and dear ones are just these ones:
The ones we are obliged to kiss,
Caress, and love, and warmly miss,
Also, by custom and good cheer,
On Christmas we should pay them calls,
At least by mail should send them cards,
So all the rest of all the year
They will not think of us a mite...
And so, God grant them health, long life!

His brother Lev

Yet he wrote warm poems for his maternal grandmother Maria Alekseyevna and serf-nanny Arina Rodionovna, who once, out walking his pram in the park, got scolded by Tsar Paul I for forgetting to remove the boy's baby cap in the august presence of the Sovereign (an omen, perhaps, of problems to come). (See *My confidante of magical old times*, in which nanny transforms into a Muse). It was they who taught him Russian (back then the first language of much of the Russian nobility was French). He spent childhood summers in grandmother's country house in Zakharovo, near Moscow, by the ancestral lands of Tsar Boris Godunov. One senses the maternal warmth and affection given him by his nanny and grandmother merged in his perception with the sounds of the Russian language itself — and with great storytelling:

> Of Mamushka could I not say a word,
> Of nights mysterious made so bright by her
> In her old night-cap, and her threadbare gown
> Driving bad spirits off with prayers, frowns,
> Devoted, crossing herself o'er my bed?
> And then in whispers telling stories dread
> Of bandits, ghosts, the great Bová, the dead
> Who walked...Frozen in fear, with bated breath,
> I'd listen, shudder, hug my quilt to death,
> Could feel no more my toes, my feet, my head,
> The icon's candle in a lamp of clay
> Lit up her face and made its wrinkles play...

Even without dread tales, Pushkin seems to have had trouble sleeping at times. (See "*I can't sleep; fire's out, no light*" or *Remembrance*). Insomnia may be one of poetry's occupational hazards. One day when he was seven, Grandmother found him up before dawn, wandering the house entranced, saying: "I am writing poems." With his older sister Olga, he used to write and act various skits in verse. Pushkin's earliest surviving poem, in French, *bien sûr*, described the flop of his first world *première*:

> Tell me, why was *The Kidnaper*
> So roundly booed by the parterre?
> Alas, It seems its poor *auteur*
> Had kidnapped it from Molière.

Olga Sergeyvna, the poet's sister

Already — at the age of seven– we hear the first strains of Pushkin's voice: ironic detachment, self-deprecating wit, light-hearted, mischievous humor — masking, perhaps, a little sadness and inner loneliness... The truest portrait of Pushkin's boyhood may be his own description of Tatyana's girlhood in *Eugene Onegin*, Book II, xxv-xxix. He loved to read, to daydream, to lose himself freely for days in his father's vast library: Homer, Plutarch, Virgil, Ovid, Tacitus, Juvenal, Terence, Suetonius, Horace, Montaigne, Corneille, Racine, Molière, Beaumarchais, Laclos, St. Preux, Richardson, Sterne, Defoe, Diderot, Voltaire, Rousseau...young Pushkin devoured them all, while lapping up *bons mots* at his father's literary soirées. A French family friend exclaimed: "What an amazing boy! How quickly he grasps things! May this boy live and live; you'll see what will become of him!"

Between his mother's stories and his father's library, Pushkin's French became so fluent that his schoolmates at the Lycée would nickname him "the Frenchman." Indeed, the heady brilliance of his parents' French salon, mixed with grandmotherly singsong suckling in Russian folklore, uniquely endowed him to one day transform his language, and employ it as Peter the Great used his grand new capital, as a tool for Russia (in Pushkin's phrase) "to force a window free" to Europe. Pushkin's unique ability to straddle worlds, and feel effortlessly at home in two conflicting realities was a gift even of his infancy, for it is fair to call the "sunshine of Russian poetry" a true child of the French Enlightenment.

1811–1817 The Lycée

Originally his parents planned to send Pushkin to a French Jesuit school in St. Petersburg. But in 1811, Tsar Alexander I decided to found, in the pleasant suburb of Tsarskoye Selo, an elite academy (to which he donated his personal library) to be housed in the Summer Palace of the Tsars. Six years' continuous education (with no visits home or leaving school grounds allowed) were to be provided free of charge to young nobles destined for "highest office in the service of the state." Corporal punishment was forbidden–a rarity for that time. Vasily Pushkin, the poet's verse-writing uncle, brought his nephew to St. Petersburg for the entrance exam (spending the 100 rubles entrusted him by an aunt for the boy's spending money on a mistress, and never returning them). Pushkin passed, and, together with 29 other boys was officially inducted into the Lycée, on October 19, 1811, a date he'd revere all his life, and comemmorate in seven separate poems. No sooner was the imperial pomp of the inaugural ceremony over than all the boys ran out and got into a rousing snowball fight. From its founding, the Lycée and its close-knit students invoked in each other a spirit of boisterous boyish freedom, joy, deep friendship, competitive playfulness, joyous excess, and good humor, yet with an abiding reverence for a higher purpose in life, a devotion to love, art, and honor that came to be called "the spirit of the Lycée."

> My friends, how beautiful our union is!
> Eternal like the soul, it can't be broken.
> It withstands all, free, careless, and outspoken:
> Our links were formed by friendship and the Muse.
> Where'er we're cast by Fate, whate'er it's storing,
> Wherever happiness might let us roam,
> We're still the same: the whole world's strange and foreign,
> And Tsarskoye Selo is our true home.

Pushkin's friends from the Lycée, particularly the poets Anton Delvig and Wilhelm Küchelbecker, and Ivan Pushchin ("Jeannot"), later exiled as a Decembrist, remained for him beloved soulmates, pined for and cherished literally until his last moments on his deathbed.

The Lycée's curriculum was ambitious: "1. grammar: instruction in the Russian, Latin, French, and German languages; 2. moral sciences: introduction to religion, philosophy, ethics, and logic; 3. mathematics and physical sciences, algebra, physics, and trigonometry; 4. historical sciences: history of Russia and foreign countries, geography, and chronology; 5. foundations of literature: excerpts from the best authors, analysis, rules of rhetoric; 6. fine arts, gymnastics, calligraphy, drawing, dancing, fencing, horsemanship, and swimming..."

> We all did study (more or less so)
> Something or other at some time...

Had Pushkin taken it all seriously, maybe he'd have become, like Prince Gorchakov, first head boy, then one day, Heaven forbid, Chancellor of the Russian Empire. Yet the poet was influenced by some of his more liberal teachers. Kunitsyn, his professor of moral sciences, lectured against serfdom, and on behalf of "natural law" and the teachings of Adam Smith. And the French master was the brother of the French revolutionary leader Marat. The schoolboys vividly experienced Napoleon's invasion of Russia in 1812, the battle of Borodino, and the burning of Moscow, (at one point hurling away their French grammar books in protest, according to Pushkin's school friend Malinovsky).

> Remember: row on row went marching by;
> We said farewell then to our older bothers,
> Returned to Learning's canopy and grumbled,
> In envy of those lads who off to die
> Went marching past...

In his *Notes on Pushkin*, Ivan Pushchin remembered his best friend in those days:

> We all saw Pushkin was way ahead of us, had read many things of which the rest of us had never even heard, and had remembered all he'd read. Yet the best thing about him was that he never showed off or acted important as gifted people often do at that age. On the contrary, he held all learning to be nonsense, and was only ever busy trying to prove that he was a swift sprinter, or could jump over piled up chairs, or hurl a ball...

Pushkin indeed became a master fencer and rider, an avid swimmer and walker, a gymnast, even Russia's first lightweight champion in what was then known as "French boxing." Yet his poetic talents also did not pass unnoticed. His first publication, in 1814, came when his friends, as a prank, sent his manuscript of *To a Friend who Writes Poems* to the journal *Herald of Europe,* listing its author as "N.K.CH.P." (Pushkin backwards). In 1815, with his voice "ringing out youthfully," Pushkin declaimed his *Recollections of Tsarskoye Selo* at a Russian literature examination attended by Russia's most famous poet at the time, Gavriil Derzhavin. This got him so emotional that: "I don't remember how I finished reading; I don't remember where I ran away. Derzhavin was full of admiration, demanded to see me, wanted to embrace me...They looked for me, but couldn't find me."

But he wasn't so excited about his other subjects. Even Professor Kunitsyn complained: "Pushkin expresses himself clearly, intelligently, and wittily, but is extremely lazy." Together with Pushchin and Malinovsky, Pushkin was always getting up to some prank or other, such as brewing illicit hot egg creams laced with rum (for which they were denied meals and made to kneel in prayer for two days) or else leaving school grounds, or chasing girls *(Mon Portrait)*. And "he wrote everywhere, especially in math class." The earliest manuscript of any Pushkin poem is already about love: *To Natalia*, written 1813, was about a young actress in Count Tolstoy's serf theatre. Pushkin wrote over 120 poems during his days in the Lycée, over twenty to Yekaterina Bakunina, a pretty maid in waiting at the palace (*The Bard, To Dorida*). He also began work on his ironic epic *Ruslan and Lyudmila.*

In his last year, Pushkin sometimes cut class to discuss politics and carouse with various hussars stationed near the Palace. One of those hussars was Pyotr Chaadayev, a penetrating critic of serfdom and autocracy, who introduced the poet to the English language, the philosophy of Hume and Locke —and to the freedom-loving, lyrical verse of Byron. In Tsarskoye Selo, he also met famed Russian historian and sentimental novelist Nikolai Karamzin, and also Karamzin's wife Yekaterina, whom some scholars believe was Pushkin's "secret love." On June 9, 1817, Pushkin graduated 26th out of 29 in his class, with top marks only in Russian, French, and fencing. Years later, when Pushkin became famous, one teacher grumbled: "What's all this fuss about Pushkin? He was a scamp — nothing more!" Engelhardt, the Lycée headmaster, took an even stronger dislike to his most famous pupil, and wrote in Pushkin's school report in 1816:

Pushkin's only higher goal is to shine — in poetry, to be precise, though it is doubtful indeed he will ever succeed, because he shuns any serious scholarship, and his mind, utterly lacking in perspicacity or depth, is a completely superficial, frivolous French mind. And that is in fact the best thing that can be said about Pushkin. His heart is cold and empty: there is neither love nor religion in it. It is perhaps as empty as ever any youth's heart has ever been.

Curiously, in Buddhist meditation practice, "emptiness" can be high praise — an achievement of the highest order. Perhaps the very "emptiness"— or openness — of Pushkin's heart made it such a perfect vessel for sublime expressions of love. At any rate, his "emptiness" was to him a treasure, a gift he refused to clutter with mere skills for "the service of the state." Already in the Lycée he had decided:

> Farewell, farewell, cold sciences!
> I'm now from youthful games estranged!
> I am a poet now; I've changed.
> Within my soul both sounds and silence
> Pour into one another, live,
> In measures sweet both take and give.

1817–1820 St. Petersburg

Upon graduation, Pushkin was made a lowly collegiate assessor, or bureaucrat tenth class, in the Russian Foreign Ministry. "Almost at once I got three months' leave to visit my mother's estate in Mikhailovskoye. I was enchanted by the country, the real Russian bathhouse, the abundant strawberries..." He also enjoyed meeting his black great-uncle and downing six shots with him of fiery homemade vodka. Back in St. Petersburg, he lived briefly in the home of Count Apraksin (now 174, Griboyedov Canal) then with his parents in cramped quarters by the Fontanka Canal. The floor above was rented by Pushkin's fellow Lycéen, Baron Modest Korf — whom Pushkin once challenged to a duel for striking the poet's beloved manservant Nikita Kozlov. Korf had been a teacher's pet of Engelhardt's, and sneered at his schoolmate, indeed, at the entire Pushkin family in his memoirs:

> All the Pushkins were oddballs. The father was a rather cheerful conversationalist in the old French school, full of jokes and puns, but was empty, muddleheaded, useless, and a particularly silent slave of his wife. She was not stupid, but was a selfish, ill-

> tempered nag, unbelievably absent-minded and particularly bad at running the home: it was always in some sort of chaos: in one room rich antique furniture, in another bare walls, without even chairs, lots of dishevelled, drunken servants, battered old carriages, tattered nags, gorgeous ladies' gowns and a constant lack of everything, from money on down to the last glass. Whenever two or three people visited them for dinner, they always needed us to lend them crockery!

Korf well may have exaggerated out of spite (as often elsewhere in his memoirs). Yet doubtless after the heady freedom and coziness of the Lycée, life with his parents felt confining, and deprived. He later recalled in a letter to his younger brother Lev: "when I was sick in autumn rains or bitter winter frosts, and hired a coachman to take me home from Anichkov Bridge, Father always scolded me about the 80 kopecks, which doubtless neither you nor I would even begrudge our servants." Paternal stinginess seems to have provoked in his oldest son a certain rebellious, poetic carelessness about money. "One bright summer day," a friend recalled, "he was boating in company together with Sergey Lvovich [Pushkin's father]. It was calm and the water was so clear that you could see the bottom. Pushkin took a few golden coins out from his pocket and one by one deliberately dropped them into the canal, delighted by their clinking, plopping, and marvelling at their bright gleam in the clear water."

He didn't care much for his official duties, but loved the theatre — and wrote keen observations and reviews. And naturally, he also had an eye for pretty actresses, like Elena Sosnitskaya, "into whose net I nearly fell, but I was lucky, and got off with just a poem" *(In Sosnitskaya's Album).* Like most young Russian intellectuals, he was a liberal; unlike most, he was no radical. He joined the freedom-loving "Green Lamp" literary club, and various friends (later known as "Decembrists") were seriously involved in revolutinary societies. But his literary friends at the jovial Arzamas Society of writers nicknamed him "the Cricket" for his habit of singing unseen, and for his approach to life that they felt more resembled the Grasshopper than the Ant.

One evening, at the home of Alexey Olenin, director of the Academy and Public Library, he met the beautiful and coquettish Anna Petrovna Kern, married off against her will at the age of sixteen to a boorish, half-crippled general 35 years her senior. She recollected:

A jovial banter began between us as to who is a sinner and who is not, and who'd go to heaven, and who to hell. Pushkin told my brother: "At least in hell there'd be lots of pretty girls, and we'd all be playing charades! Ask M-me Kern: wouldn't she like to go to hell? I answered seriously and a bit curtly that I would not. "How about you, Pushkin?" asked my brother. "Well, now I've changed my mind," the poet answered, "I don't want to go to hell anymore — even if it does have lots of pretty girls!"

In 1819 he was smitten by Eudoxia Golitsyna, known as "Princesse Nocturne" for her midnight soirées:

> Where is a woman's fairness not like ice,
> But captivating, fiery, and alive?
> Whose conversation's easy and unfrightened,
> With brilliant wit that's happy and enlightened?
> With whom are we not cool, empty, and bland?
> My Fatherland I almost hated, really...
> But then I saw Golitsyna last evening...
> And — now — I'm fine with my dear Fatherland.

That same year he visited the famed German fortune-teller Mme. Alexandra Kirchof (whose advice, supposedly, had helped Tsar Alexander I stand firm in the bleakest hours of the War of 1812). Mme. Kirchof foretold great fame for Pushkin, two terms of exile, and a long happy life, if only at the age of 37 he avoided "trouble over a white horse, white (i.e blond) head, or white man." Pushkin believed without doubt in all her predictions—and in the end they all came true.

Gossip went all over town about this wild young poet-flibbertigibbet, heedless of warnings against wine, women, and song. Engelhardt, Lycée headmaster, complained as usual: "how often have I sighed, if only that good-for-nothing Pushkin would be serious, he'd amount to something special in our literature!" His friend Alexander Turgenev despaired: "An idle laziness, dread slayer of all that's beautiful and talented, looms banefully over Pushkin...Mornings he tells Zhukovsky where he hasn't slept all evening, out with various sluts — or me, or Princess Golitsyna, or playing cards...." The poet Batyushkov wrote back: "We should lock our Cricket up in Göttingen for three years on a diet of milk soup and logic!" But Pushkin was quite happy playing (see *To Turgenev*), and made no apologies:

> I am fond of evening feasts
> Where good cheer rules o'er our revel,
> Where my idol, Freedom, sits,
> Making law for all the table,

> Where the cry is "drink" till dawn,
> Drowning shouts and calls and singing,
> Where the guests crowd wide and far,
> And the bottles crowd in, clinking.

Pushkin would rouse himself at dawn with ice-cold baths, then write for hours, lying in bed. He was finishing *Ruslan and Lyudmila*, an ironic Russian folktale in verse, which created an immediate sensation when it came out in 1820. The Russian public delighted in this new young poet's majestic exuberance and ebullient command of their language:

> You rivals in the art of battle,
> Allow no one of peace to prate,
> Win gloomy glory, prove your mettle,
> Drink jubilantly in your hate!
> The world will watch you numbly, chilly,
> With wonder at your dread display:
> There's no one who your deaths will pity,
> And no one who'll get in your way.
> You rivals of a different station,
> You knights of the Parnassian heights,
> Don't make us laugh throughout our nation
> At your immodest, noisy strife.
> So scold—with caution though; keep stable.
> But you, who rivals are in love,
> Just get along as best you're able!
> My friends, take it from me on trust:
> When Fate unfailing, willy-nilly,
> Decides who fair maid's heart shall win,
> He will be loved though Heaven's reeling,
> So anger's silly — and a sin.

The poet Zhukovsky, a translator of *The Odyssey* into stately Russian hexameter verse, reacted to *Ruslan and Lyudmila* with by sending his portrait to Pushkin, inscribed "to the victorious pupil from his defeated teacher."

As mentioned before, many of Pushkin's closest friends during these three years in St. Petersburg were in secret revolutionary societies. Inconveniently for later Soviet biographers, the "Cricket" was too busy "chirping" to actually join any of these societies himself. Yet Pushkin did more for their cause than they did themselves, with his popular poems and biting epigrams against the government and its ministers (including an *Epigram on Arakcheyev*, the universally loathed man who basically ran Tsar Alexander I's government). And Pushkin set an example in fearless self-expression. Pushchin recalled how Pushkin once, in a crowded theatre, reacted to an announcement that a bear cub had escaped its chains at the Summer Palace and nearly attacked the Tsar— exclaiming loudly, so all could hear: "At last a man's been found in Russia—but he's only a bear!" (The poor bear was executed).

At a party in the Turgenev brothers' apartment (20, Fontanka Canal) overlooking the gloomy Mikhaylovskiy Palace of Tsar Paul I, Pushkin was asked to look out the window and improvise a poem. A few hours later he had penned a draft of his *Ode to Liberty*— banned in Russia until 1906. It and other forbidden works, such as *To Chaadayev*, and *The Country*, spread throughout the land, creating a sensation, inspiring dissidents and secret societies. Tsar Alexander I was particularly incensed by *An Ode to Liberty:* not only did it call for a constitutional monarchy, but it violated the gravest taboo by frankly mentioning the murder, in 1801, of Alexander's father, Paul I, (in which Alexander was complicit). An agent tried to bribe Pushkin's loyal manservant Nikita Kozlov to obtain forbidden manuscripts. Kozlov refused, and warned his master, who burned everything, and "I yearned for Siberia or the [Peter and Paul] Fortress to restore my honor." Instead Mikhail Miloradovich, military governor-general of St. Petersburg, summoned him to interrogation. Pushkin, in an act of true civic courage, wrote out from memory, word for word, his strongest poems against the government — into the now famous "Miloradovich Notebook." Charmed by such bravery and talent, Miloradovich released Pushkin on his own recognizance. But the Tsar was far from amused, and planned to exile Pushkin to Siberia, or the Solovki isles, far above the Artic Circle in the White Sea (later a site of one of the worst Soviet gulags). Luckily, last-minute lobbying by Miloradovich, Zhukovsky, Chaadayev, and Karamzin helped make the place of exile someplace far warmer: Russia's south-west frontier province under the command of General Ivan Nikitich Inzov. On May 6, 1820, Ascension Day, he left St. Petersburg for the South. In the epilogue to *Ruslan and Lyudmila*, Pushkin summed up the past three years of his life:

> I gloried with obedient lyre
> The lore of olden days obscure,
> And sang, and quite forgot offenses
> Both of blind happiness and foes,
> Of my Dorida, flippant, cheating,
> While fools' and gossips' chorus rose.

Borne on the wings of my creation
My spirit flew past earth and sea,
Not seeing nascent storm's formation,
Or gloomy cloud that swelled round me...
Soon I was doomed... Holy Protector
Of my first stormy days of old,
O Friendship, comforter so tender
Of my tormented ailing soul!
You calmed the ocean's gentle seething.
And gave my heart its peace anew,
And you preserved for me my freedom,
The idol of my bubbling youth!

1824–1826 Southern Exile

Tsar Alexander I

After a bone-jarring, dusty, two-week trip on the famously appalling roads of the Russian Empire, Pushkin reported to General Inzov in Yekaterinoslav (now Dnepropetrovsk) — best known for its "Potemkin villages"—facades of non-existent palaces erected to deceive Empress Catherine the Great as she sailed past by riverboat. "After making it to Yekaterinoslav, I got bored, went rowing on the Dnepr river, bathed— and got a fever," he wrote his brother. Lying in bed unattended and delirious, he was met by General Nikolai Rayevsky, a hero of 1812, on his way with his two sons and four daughters to the Caucasus to take the waters. Rayevsky persuaded General Inzov to let Pushkin come along. Two months in the Caucasus mountains, hiking and drinking from healing mineral springs, completely restored his health and creative energies. He later recalled: "most of the springs were in primeval condition, bubbling, steaming, and flowing from the mountains in all directions, leaving red and white traces behind. We would draw up the boiling water with a pitcher, or in the bottom of a broken bottle...Nowadays the Caucasian waters are more comfortable, but I miss the way they were once, completely wild: those steep rocky paths, their bushes, their unguarded precipices, up which I used to clamber." He got inspired to write a new long poem, *The Prisoner of the Caucasus,* about a Russian soldier, taken captive by Chechens, who falls in love with a Chechen girl. (Probably the best film made about the current Chechen conflict is a brilliant adaptation of this poem to modern times; its English title is *Prisoner of the Montains,* starring Sergey Bodrov and Oleg Menshikov). The poem marked Pushkin's continuing growth as a poet, linking romantic passion with distinctive delight in descriptive detail:

It seemed the prisoner so hopeless
Got used to his new dreary life.
Grief of confinement, fire rebellious,
Deep in his heart unseen did hide.
He slouched up gloomy mountainsides
In the first hours of morning chill,
And fixed his ever-curious gaze
Towards distant, giant mountains, still,
Gray, rosy, blue peaks far away:
What views magnificent and sumptuous!
Great thrones eternal of white snows...
To distant eyes it seemed their summits
Were chains of clouds in unmoved rows:
Ringed giant, with twin-peaks dramatic,
Wreathed, sparkling, in a crown of ice,
Elbrus, enormous and majestic,
Whitened above the azure sky.
Then came a muffled roaring, rattling,
A storm-announcing thunderbolt,
Above the village sat the captive,
Not moving from his mountain top!
Clouds at his feet were smoking, writhing,
On plains below dust danced in rising,
And there amidst the cliffs so steep,
The frightened elks did shelter seek,
From precipices eagles flying
Met in the skies, were calling, crying:
The nomads' noises, lowing flocks,
Got drowned by lightning's voices striking...
Hail rained upon the valleys, dropped
From clouds, through thunderbolts came slicing
In rushing waves that steeply carved
And brushed aside the ancient boulders;
The rain in torrents plunged and smoldered,
The captive, from his mountain top,
Alone, beyond the clouds that thundered,
Awaited the bright sun's return,
Untouched by storms beneath him brewing;
He heard the lightning's feeble fury,
And somehow joy within him burned.

Nikolai Gogol (for whom Pushkin was a mentor) considered this youthful trip a watershed in the young poet's life:

The gigantic Caucasus range, with its peaks perpetually snowbound, and its lush, sultry valleys amazed him. You might say it called forth all his soul, and broke the last few chains which had held back the utter freedom of his thoughts. He was captivated by the poetic life of the bold mountain tribes, their battles, their quick, unanswerable raids...From that time his brushstroke acquired that amazing breadth, that quickness and daring, which so amazed and enchanted a Russia only just beginning to learn to read. If he described the skirmish of a Cossack with a Chechen, his words flashed lightning, gleamed like the glint of sabers, flying faster than the battle itself. He alone is the true bard of the Caucasus.

Crossing the Black Sea from the Caucasus to the Crimea aboard the brig *Mingrelia*, "I couldn't sleep all night; there was no moon, and the stars shimmered brightly; the southern mountains beckoned to me in the mist." That night Pushkin composed his lovely, somewhat Byronic elegy "*The day's last gleam is disappearing.*" He reported to his brother:

> Our ship sailed past mountains covered with poplars, vineyards, laurels and cypresses, and little Tatar villages scattered here and there, and stopped in sight of Gurzuf. I spent three weeks there. My friend, the happiest minutes of my life were spent with the family of the admirable Rayevsky...Besides the war hero, the glory of the Russian army, I loved in him the man with a clear mind and simple, open heart, the forgiving, respectful friend...a witness of Catherine's time, a monument of 1812, yet a man without prejudices, forceful, and yet sensitive...All his daughters are enchanting, and the oldest is a remarkable woman. Judge for yourself how happy I was: a free, unworried life in the bosom of a warm family, a life I love and have never before enjoyed: this happy southern sky, this lovely, gorgeous land, this nature made for my imagination: mountains, ocean, gardens!

In a draft of a letter to his friend, the poet Delvig, Pushkin wrote:

> I bathed in the sea, and gorged myself on grapes, and felt at once so at home in this Southern sunshine that I wallowed in it with all the carefree languor of a Neapolitan lazybones. I loved waking at night to the sound of the sea, which I could hear and hear for hours. A young cypress grew near the house; I used to visit it every morning, and by the end I felt we two had developed something resembling friendship..."

General Rayevsky's son Nikolai took him to tour the former palace of the Khans of the Crimean Tatars in Bakhchisarai. He recalled:

> I arrived sick...I had heard of that strange monument of the lovelorn Khan. **** had poetically described it to me, calling it *la fontaine des larmes* (the fountain of tears). When I went in the

palace, I saw a ruined fountain, with water trickling in droplets from its rusted iron pipe. I walked round the whole palace, indignant at the disrepair in which it had been left to decay, at the crude pseudo-European attempts to fix up a few of the rooms. NN practically forced me down a rickety staircase to see the ruins of the harem and the Khan's cemetery. But it wasn't this

> That set my heart back then a-heaving:

I was wracked by fever. Explain to me now why that southern shore and Bakchisarai have for me such inexpressible charm? Why now do I long so violently to go back and visit those places which I left with such indifference? Is memory indeed the strongest force in our souls? And does it charm all it touches?

Pushkin would revisit that rusted "fountain of tears" only in a new romantic meditation, which he called *The Fountain of Bakhchisarai:*

I visited Bakhchisarai,
Its palace now forgot, abandoned.
Amidst its quiet halls medieval
I wandered where that scourge of peoples,
The Tatar fierce, once held his feasts,
And, after raids of dread and horror,
Did laze in splendid languor sweet.
That bliss still breathes and is remembered
In restful garden groves, it seems:
The waters' playing, roses' blushing,
The vineyard grapes so thick and luscious,
And on the walls the gold still gleams.
I saw old wrought-iron tracery:
Cages, behind which, in their spring,
Clasping an amber rosary,
Young silenced wives would sigh, not sing.
I saw the great Khans' burial place,
Great rulers' final residence.
I saw the columns o'er the graves
With marble turbans crowned, but fraying,
It seemed to me the will of Fate
Was speaking loud and clear, and praying.
Where are the Khans and harem now?
Around all's still and drear, hope-killing,
Yes, all has changed. Yet that's not how
I thought back then, with my heart brimming:
...The roses' breath, the fountains' purl
Against my will made me oblivious,
Unwillingly my thoughts did whirl,
Myself not sure why I was nervous;
A shade did flit about the palace,
A maiden flashed before my eyes...
Whose shade, my friends, was it I saw?
Tell me, whose was the form so tender
Who haunted me there for so long,
Unstoppable, with me forever?

Yekaterina Rayevskaya

Was it Yekaterina Rayevskaya? To that "remarkable woman" Pushkin wrote "*The flying wisps of clouds are thinning, scattering far.*" Or was it perhaps her sister? Maria Some scholars call Maria Rayevskaya the anonymous "one love of my soul" to whom Pushkin dedicated the narrative poem *Poltava*. She herself (a faithful "Decembrist wife" who joined her husband, Sergey Volkonsky, willingly in Siberian exile for 30 years) demurred, saying only: "as a poet, Pushkin felt obliged to be in love with every pretty woman and fine young girl...But in truth he adored only his Muse, and poeticized all he saw."

Perhaps all these "secret love" theories merit a digression (Pushkin was quite fond of digressions himself—especially on this very topic).

Let's speak now of the strangenesses of love
(I can't imagine other conversation).

Pushkin was above all a poet of love. No writer in Russia before him or after him ever expressed so much love in so many ways. Love for him was not so much a choice as an unstoppable universal force, of which he was but a blessèd conductor. Love, protean and unpredictable, is in almost everything he wrote. And all he wrote, in the end, is really about love in one way or other. Love at first sight, and at long last, by chance or by arrangement, erotic and platonic, sexual and spiritual, jealous and calm, ironic and accepting, ruefully bitter, or reconciled and uncomplaining, bitter and murderous or soft, faithful and accepting...all kinds of love were his theme, love in which every happiness seemed to lead to grief, yet every grief seemed to lead to happiness. Pushkin captured that mysterious quality of love, which defies definition precisely because it can only be felt. Yet though we cannot define it, love is the mystery that defines us, and "where there is no love, there is no truth."

Certain Soviet and even modern Pushkinists (Freudian Marxists, as it were, or vice-versa) obsess (perhaps enviously?) over every name on Pushkin's jokingly compiled so-called "Don Juan list." (Its very existence is hardly "politically correct"). But hindsight can be uncomprehending, and often misses the wood for the trees. All Pushkin's "experience, sired of errors grievous" blessed us with a transcendent wealth of lyrical love poetry. We should all re-read a letter Pushkin once wrote, rebuking his friend Prince Vyazemsky's interest in gossipy memoirs containing some of the stormier details of Byron's intimate life:

> Leave curiosity to the mob, and be at one with genius. We know all we need to know about Byron. We saw him enthroned in his glory, and in his torments, as a great soul, and then we saw him buried in a Greece reborn. Who needs to see him on his potty? The mob greedily reads confessions and memoirs because, in its baseness, it gloats at the humiliations of the great and the weaknesses of the mighty. At the discovery of any filth, the mob cheers: "he was base, like us; he was filthy, like us!" Lying scoundrels! He was base and filthy, but not like you at all — he was different!

Even Pushkin's earlier, earthier love poems had a unique economy and sense of balance absorbed from the classical masters he had imbibed since childhood. Even his teenaged half-drunken (usually half-joking) odes to easy women were light and graceful, eschewing vulgarity, which, for Pushkin, was one of the ultimate sins. Yet whether it was the Caucasus, as Gogol supposed, that released the last chains on the freedom of his thoughts, or a new inner harmony that sprang forth from communion at dawn with a cypress tree, the Pushkin that emerged from Southern wanderings was — until death — a far more spiritual, meditative, inward-looking, and fundamentally mysterious poet.

Mystery is indeed essential to all great poetry. Pushkin's favorite author, Shakespeare, in his works shrouded himself with such mystery that, as Mark Twain once quipped, "Shakespeare must be the most famous man who never lived." Whoever indeed was the genius of our English language, one senses his fondness for anonymity, his joy in strolling through humanity incognito, like his Henry V on the eve of the battle of Agincourt, or his pensive "fantastical duke of dark corners" in *Measure for Measure*. Even "the Bard's" most personal works, the sonnets, don't reveal much about him: the focus is on the object of his love, on her qualities:

> My mistress' eyes are nothing like the sun;
> Coral is far more red than her lips red;
> If snow be white, why then, her breasts are dun;
> If hair be wires, black wires grow on her head.
> I have seen roses damasked, red and white
> But no such roses see I in her cheeks;
> And in some perfumes there is more delight
> Than in the breath that from my mistress reeks.
> I love to hear her speak, yet well I know
> That music hath a far more pleasing sound;
> I grant I never saw a goddess go;
> My mistress, when she walks, walks on the ground:
> And yet, by heaven I think my love as rare
> As any she belied with false compare. (Sonnet CXXX).

With Pushkin, the mystery is less *her qualities* than *his own feelings*. We learn not how she looks but how she makes him feel: otherwise, we — often deliberately —get no clue whom she might be. (In an age where the bonds of marriage were all too often imposed without love, love all too often arose without the bonds of marriage. Many of Pushkin's loves were unhappily married; their reputations needed guarding). He often struck whole lines and stanzas which he felt might identify who had inspired them (See "*A drizzly day fizzed out, a drizzly night's dull haze*"); many poems were private and not for publication. When "*The flying wisps of clouds are thinning, scattering far*" was published, Pushkin was furious; its last lines' mention of his beloved's astronomical interests, compromised, he feared the star-gazing Yekaterina Raevsky. But in truth secrecy and mysteriousness were not just practical. They were part of the very sadness of love itself:

What is there is my name for you?
It will die out, like sad waves sounding
Their last, on distant shorelines pounding,
As in deaf woods night's sounds ring through.

Within your album it will leave
A deadened trail, like in description
To tracings on a grave's description
In a strange language you can't read.

His poems are more sublime for being utterly independent of whom they're for, or how she looks, or acts, or what she does or says...She just is — and that's enough. Details and reasons would be superfluous (and nothing is superfluous in Pushkin). As the Talmud says, "the love that has a reason lasts only as long as the reason; but the love that has no reason lasts until the end of time." Here Pushkin is like Shakespeare: his words express feeling through sound as well as sense. And if the focus turns from his subjective feelings to the objective qualities of the object of his love, paradoxically, it seems a clue his feelings aren't too serious (e.g. *Confession, To a Kalmyk Girl*, "*Round Izhora I was riding*"). Even in these more jocular poems, he flirts more with less, giving just enough detail to frame the outpouring of his own heart.... His poetry conveys with unparalleled intensity, the feeling, the experience of being in love, of love itself. He takes us ever more deeply into his own revelations, fears, elations — even brings us along with him as he wakes his love, as it seems that with Love itself:

"Our whole room with an amber sparkling
Gleams in the dawn..."

True, Pushkin dedicated certain love poems by name, or wrote others into his beloved's albums. Yet mosly his poems preserve his loves in a kind of blissful Vermeer twilight. To guess (to a greater or lesser degree, perhaps) just whom any given masterpiece is for is to singe that lovely murk with searchlights...why do we search in vain for Pushkin's "secret love" ? Why such need to know whom it was that the poet loved "with such unsated endless passion"?

Alone she'd understand, decipher
My blur of verse, confused, unclear;
Alone within my heart she'd fire
The lamp of love that's pure, austere!
Alas, in vain such aspirations!
My prayers, all my invocations,
My heart's grief – all – she would not heed!
Of cries of earthly joys and passions,
Of the divine, she had no need!

Cherchez la femme! Pushkin's "secret love" may have been the most famous woman who never lived (at least to Russians). And it's sheer folly looking for her in the archives ... She is eternal... She is Woman.

Alas, Pushkin's idyll by Southern seas and mountains was not eternal, but ended abruptly, like the above digression. In September 1820 he was summoned for duty to the desolate flatlands and muddy lanes of Kishinev, Moldavia, whence General Inzov had moved headquarters. There wasn't much to do, and Pushkin found little to like about the place at first, except its dubious honor as the supposed site of exile of the great Roman poet Ovid. In November 1820 Pushkin begged leave to visit Kamenka, the Ukrainian estate of General Rayevsky's relatives, the Davydov family. Granted two weeks, he stayed six months. General Inzov extended his leave and, like a good-natured father, wrote the Davydovs: "I've been so worried about Mr. Pushkin. I feared that in spite of cruel frosts, biting winds, and blizzards he might try to come back, and something bad might happen on those awful roads in the steppes. But after your letter, I am calm and hope your Excellency won't permit him to travel till he regains his health." On December 4, 1820, Pushkin wrote to his publisher and friend Gnedich (the *Iliad's* translator into Russian): "Eight months already, my dear Nikolai Ivanovich, I've been leading the life of a nomad. First the Caucasus, then the Crimea, then Moldavia, and now I'm in Kiev Province, at the estate of the Davydovs', very dear, intelligent brothers of General Rayevsky. My time is spent twixt aristocratic dinners and democratic arguments...a colorful mix of the most original and famous minds in Russia are here. There are few women, but much champagne, much ardent wit, many books, and just a few poems..." Since most of those "original and famous minds" at the estate were in secret revolutionary societies, one of those "few women," the Polish beauty Karolina Sobanskaya (yet another "secret love") was a government spy. Though Pushkin did not join any societies, he tippled much champagne with these future Decembrist revolutionaries to uprisings in Spain and Portugal, the Americas, Naples, and Greece, while continuing work on *The Prisoner of the Mountains* and then *The Fountain of Bakchisarai*.

Not that the elder Davydov brother (another veteran of 1812) needed much excuse for tippling... Pushkin described him thus: "a second Falstaff: lecherous, gluttonous, cowardly, boastful, shrewd, amusing, unscrupulous, whiny, and fat. Yet he had one distinctive feature which gave him still more charm: he was married. Shakespeare never got around to marrying off his bachelor; Falstaff died without learning the joys of becoming a cuckold and a father." Pushkin seems to have had a brief affair with Davydov's wife Aglaia (whose famously easy virtue prompted sharp epigrams from him in Russian and French). He also wrote this sweet little trifle, a song for the Davydovs' twelve year old daughter Adele:

> Play on, Adele,
> And know no sadness.
> The Graces dwell
> With you in gladness.
> Your cradle bells
> They gently rattled.
> Your springtime youth
> Is calm, clear, smooth.
> For sweet sensations
> You're born for sure.
> So catch elation
> On the run!
> Your youth so boisterous
> Give up to love,
> In this world's noises,
> Still love, Adele,
> My pipe's soft swell.

Davydov, "a second Falstaff"

By March 1821 Pushkin was back in Kishinev. General Inzov, angry that the government had not paid the exiled poet's salary, took him into his own house, full of exotic plants and an aviary. Pushkin was fond of "good old Ivan Nikitich," who admired his talent (even for such forbidden songs to freedom as *To a Bird* and *The Captive*) and looked the other way at Pushkin's pranks and eccentricities. Kishinev was a frontier town, peopled by many ethnic groups. Pushkin, who had himself been teased for being "African," was not only free of any prejudice towards other peoples, but fascinated and sympathetic. Sketchpad in hand, he'd stroll round town in a Moldavian cassock, or a fez hat and Turkish robes, or in Hasidic garb... Pushkin had a few Jewish girlfriends; his sympathy for the plight of a poor Jewish family is plain from his fragment *"The lantern in the Jewish hovel."* He thrilled, too, in the Greek struggle for independence and had an affair with a Greek lady rumored to have been Byron's mistress (*To a Greek Woman*). Entranced by a gypsy girl, he ran off to join her troupe for a while. His memories from this adventure set the scene for his tale *The Gypsies*...

> The gypsies in a noisy throng
> Through Bessarabia are wandering.
> This night their tattered tents along
> A riverbank are pitched, meandering.
> Like freedom, happy is their rest,
> Peaceful their sleep beneath the heavens.
> Between the wagon wheels are decked
> The rugs that they hang up like curtains.
> Gathered around a fire's blaze,
> A family cooks; in empty fields
> Beyond their tent their horses graze,
> Their trained bear's sprawled out at his ease.
> All's full of life among the steppes:
> The tranquil cares of roving clans
> Readied to move off in the morning,
> Wives sing, kids shriek; throughout the band
> Their traveling anvil pounds its clonking...
> But soon upon the nomad's troupe
> A sleepy silence shrinks and falls,
> And in the stillness nothing moves:
> A few dogs bark, some horses snort...

A Gypsy in Kishinev

His amorous adventures, biting wit, and keenly felt sense of personal honor involved him in about twenty duels during this period—all bloodless, some even jocular. Yet his friend Colonel Liprandi recalled: "When face to face with death, when a man fully discovers himself, Pushkin was possessed of the highest degree of inner calm, in spite of his emotionality. When the time came to take his paces, he seemed cold as ice." In one duel, while his opponent was aiming and firing at him, Pushkin calmly ate cherries, then cast away his gun. In another duel, fought in a wild snowstorm at sixteen paces, he deliberately missed, then, when his opponent shot and missed, he offered his opponent a chance to hit him from twelve paces. The duel ended with his opponent saying: "you stand up to bullets as well as you write"— and Pushkin embracing him. Periodically, Inzov would try to keep his protégé out of trouble by putting him under house arrest and dragging him off to church. Pushkin, ever a prankster, taught Inzov's parrot vivid blasphemies in several languages — quite startling an Archbishop who had been invited for tea. Pushkin wrote an ironic note in verse to Davydov:

> Now I've grown smart, started pretending,
> And fast, and pray, with faith heart-rending
> That God forgives my acts perverse
> Just as the Tsar forgives my verse.
> As Inzov fasts, my soul he's saving:
> For him I've quit Parnassian ravings,
> My lyre, my sinful gift from Fate,
> For books of hours and midday prayers,
> Dried mushrooms on my Lenten plate.

General Inzov

While in Kishinev, perhaps rebelling against the pieties being imposed on him, Pushkin wrote the *Gabrieliad*, a sparkling "piece of mischief," a spoof of the Annuciation story (never meant for publication, but just as a private prank, a way to kill time). Later this way of killing time almost killed him — on charges of blasphemy and atheism. Yet the charges would be dropped, and indeed, Pushkin's views on faith are hardly easily classified. Would a real "blasphemer" end his "heresy" with a prayer to an angel?

> But fleet the days, and slowly graying time
> With silent silver will anoint my head,
> And solemn marriage with a lovely wife
> Will cause me to an altar to be led.
> O Joseph's dear and beautiful consoler!
> I beg you now, and sink on bended knee:

> Protector and defender of all cuckolds,
> I beg you then cast blessings over me.
> Bequeath me carefree joy and resignation,
> Bequeath me patience, time and time enough,
> And restful sleep, trusting my wife's devotion,
> And peace at home, and for my neighbour love.

These lines read cruelly in light of the poet's final days. Yet at that time he seemed happy as a lark. In May 1823 Pushkin began work on his great novel in verse *Eugene Onegin*. He soon reported to his friend, the poet Delvig: "I'm writing a new long poem, a novel in verse, in which I babble freely on whatever I please, beyond all limits ...Publication is quite unthinkable; the censor would cry if he saw it...Lord only knows when we'll be able to read it together...I write with rapture, and cannot stop." During his southern exile Pushkin wrote several chapters of the novel, concluding with *Tatyana's Letter to Onegin* (used by Tchaikovsky for his most famous operatic aria). In July 1823, Pushkin was transferred to serve under the Governor-General of Southern Russia, Count Mikhail Vorontsov, headquartered in the port of Odessa, which was then "a half-Italian *porto franco*"; all signs were in Italian as well as Russian. Pushkin frolicked at the beach, in the opera, in cafés and restaurants, befriended a former Moorish corsair named Ali, and, pining by the sea, considered fleeing Russia forever.

Yet at leaving General Inzov's tender care, "a new sadness pangs my breast: I miss the chains I've left behind." And, with more distractions, life in Odessa was much more expensive. His salary was paid sporadically, and he had only gotten 500 rubles for his manuscript of the *Prisoner of the Mountains*. (There was no copyright law in Russia until 1828, and even that first weak statute was so weakly enforced that Pushkin was helpless, all his life, to prevent pirates from robbing him of thousands by copying his works without his consent). However, as modern Russia's first professional writer, ("I see a poem as a cobbler would a pair of boots, as a finished good, which I intend to sell as a profit"), he negotiated a great deal for his manuscript of *The Fountain of Bakhchisarai:* three thousand rubles — more than four years pay— soon spent with abandon. Pushkin later poignantly described his memories of life in Odessa in a poetic fragment omitted from *Eugene Onegin* ("*And so, I lived then in Odessa*"). Again and again, Pushkin dreamed of escaping Russia for Italy, immersed himself in Italian culture (having begun to learn "the tongue of golden Italy" in Kishinev).

And he fell in love with Amalia Riznich, an Italian Jewish beauty who had come to Odessa from Trieste with a dullish husband, a Venetian trader. Riznich is thought to have inspired such poems as "*Will you forgive my jealous reverie,*" "*Into your bower, my friend so tender,*" "*Bound for your distant country's shoreline,*" "*Beneath the blue skies of your native land,*" and "*Invocation*" (though the latter is more likely an improvisation on a theme by Barry Cornwall). But Riznich did not stay in Odessa long, and Pushkin was soon (briefly) head over heels in love again with Karolina Sobanskaya, paramour of Witte, head of the secret police in the South (and perhaps the passionate subject of "*Night*").

During Pushkin's last months in Odessa, it is supposed, though unproved, that his love was yet another Polish beauty, Countess Elizaveta Vorontsova. Their relations remain swathed in legends (she is yet another candidate for the role of "Pushkin's secret love"; more than 30 drawings of her are in Pushkin's manuscripts, her husband, though, is in many of those drawings as well). Their strolls by the sea may have been immortalized in *Eugene Onegin's "Pedal Digression,"* Chapter I, xxix-xxxiv, though Nabokov argued that only one of those "sweet feet, sweet feet that I treasured" was Vorontsova's, while the other foot was Maria Rayevskaya's. Some say it is Vorontsova who gave Pushkin the ring with the Hebrew inscription "Simcha" ("Joy"), which he treasured all his life. (He bequeathed it on his deathbed to the poet Zhukovsky, from whom it passed to the novelist Turgenev; in 1917 the ring disappeared). Supposedly that ring was his "*Talisman.*" Pushkin's sister Olga even claimed Vorontsova wrote to Pushkin when he was sent to further exile; some think this is the context for his thrilling *The Burned Letter*. Yet it is hard to believe that the wife of the almighty Governor-General of Bessarabia, Count Vorontsov, would dare risk correspondence with the disgraced poet, knowing all too well his mail was perlustrated. In addition, the French poet André Chenier, whom Pushkin admired greatly, has a work very similar to *The Burned Letter*. Another work written in Odessa, *The Demon*, was, according to Pushkin himself, about the paralyzing effects of doubt, cynicism, and negative emotions. Yet many suppose its subject to be Alexander Rayevsky, General Rayevsky's oldest son, the open, practically official, paramour of Countess Vorontsova, and thus a false friend to the poet.

Pushkin's relations with her husband, Count Vorontsov, were rocky, and complicated by more than jealousy (Vorontsov, notorious for his own philandering, is said to have quite tolerated his wife's dalliances).

Formal and stiff, Vorontsov modeled himself on the English lords with whom he'd been schooled in Cambridge. Yet fine English manners could not conceal ruthless Russian methods for control of the uneasy new provinces of Russia's Southern Empire: spying, intrigue, and repression. Though not above dabbling in trade, and using his official position to profit from his commercial activities, Vorontsov railed against Pushkin's habit of writing poems instead of official memoranda. He tried to force Pushkin to do his bureaucratic duties, and ordered him to write an official report about a plague of locusts attacking the Kherson Peninsula. Pushkin defiantly replied:

> To write a memorandum is completely foreign to my nature. For seven years I've ignored such duties, never wrote a single legal report, never tried to curry favor with any bosses...But I do not consider these years lost. Writing poems is my profession. ...Just because I'm paid 700 rubles a year doesn't mean I am obliged to serve. I accept these 700 rubles a year not as a bureaucrat's salary, but as compensation for involuntary exile... If the Count wishes me to retire, I am ready.

Nonetheless, "the Cricket" was forced to go report about the locusts. But no record exists of his ever having filed the required report. Instead, legend has it that his "memorandum" was this little verse (quite often taught to students of Russian struggling valiantly to master the cruel nuances of Russian perfective and imperfective verbs):

> The locust host was flying, was flying,
> Alighting,
> Sat dining, sat dining — all-smiting,
> Then went back to flying.

Vorontsov's deputy recalled the Count asking: "You seem to like Pushkin. Can't you control him, and get him to do anything useful?" "Excuse me, sir, but people like him can only be great poets. " "Well then — what use are they at all?"

Naturally, Pushkin resented being sneered at. "Vorontsov is a vandal, a Court boor, and petty egotist. All he saw in me was a tenth-class collegiate assessor, and I, I must say, see myself a bit differently." Pushkin wrote several epigrams about Count Vorontsov:

> Half a milord, half merchant, he:
> Half a savant, half ignoramus,
> Just half a knave, but hopes inflame us
> That soon at last he'll be complete!

Vorontsov denounced Pushkin to St. Petersburg as a radical, and urged that the poet be removed. An excuse provided itself when police read this phrase in the poet's letter to his Lycéen friend Wilhelm Küchelbecker: "Do you want to know what I'm up to? Writing romantic poems, and taking lessons in pure atheism from a young Englishman, a deaf philosopher." Atheism was almost as grave a crime under the Tsars as religious belief would one day be under the commissars. By order of Tsar Alexander I, Imperial Chancellor Nesselrode (another butt of biting quips) decreed Pushkin stripped of his official rank and duties, and put under house arrest at the estate of his parents in Pskov Province, "under the supervision of local authorities." His carriage was commanded "to travel exactly following the itinerary given him by the governor of Odessa— straight to the city of Pskov; he may not rest anyplace along the way, but immediately upon arrival in Pskov must report to the Governor." A day before leaving, Pushkin wrote his poetic farewell: *To the Sea*. He set off northwards on July 31, 1824. Yet waiting for fresh post-horses in the town of Mogilev, he was recognized by a cadet with whom he had caroused in the Lycée. Midst bear hugs and tears, he was dragged off to become the occasion for a grand impromptu Russian midnight feast and poetry reading: at four in the morning, the carousers tried to dunk their beloved bard in a champagne bath...He reached his family home on August 9, 1824. The second exile foretold by Madame Kirchof had come to pass.

Countess Vorontsova

"Half a milord, half merchant, he"
Count Vorontsov at billiards with a mask

Exile in Mikhailovskoye 1824–1826

About a week's hard riding from Moscow or St. Petersburg, "in this abandoned hole/ This shrine of desolation, frost, and snowstorms," Mikhailovskoye was a modest manor house, with a few cottages for the surrounding serfs. The whole family was in the living room when he arrived (his father was playing French songs on the guitar). But "being with my family has only added to my griefs and sorrows. The government was brazen enough to request that my father act as its agent in persecuting me...Father was craven enough to accept this 'proposal', which makes him play utterly false with me. As a result every moment I'm not in bed I spend either on horseback or in the fields. Anything that reminds me of the sea grieves me. A fountain's murmur makes me truly ill, and I think a clear blue sky would make me weep with rage, but here, thank God, our sky is grey, and our moon is exactly a turnip." (See "*A drizzly day's fized out*"). Pushkin's father soon gave up, (or refused—versions differ) informing against his own son, and left. The whole family was gone by November 1824, leaving the poet blissfully alone with a few household serfs and Arina Rodionovna, his doting nanny. He had always adored her—and she him. Her constant care, good-natured affection, and singsong speech, full of proverbs and phrases from fairy tales, made her a truly beloved maternal figure. He called her "mama, mamushka," and, after the ruinously expensive oysters and French wines of Odessa's restaurants, revelled in her homegrown buckwheat kasha, baked potatoes, pickled vegetables, hard-boiled eggs and stewed apples, in her home-made berry jams — and moonshine. Pushkin wrote a friend in Odessa:

> I'm stuck in the utter boondocks, bored, with nothing to do. There's no sea here, or southern sky, or Italian opera — though at least there's no locusts, nor Milords Worontsov. My solitude is utter—magnificent idleness! In the evenings I hear fairy tales told by my nanny, the original nanny of my Tatyana. She is my only friend, and with her only am I not bored.

Arina Rodionovna's is one love that was not secret. Her caring and spiritual warmth in bleak times are remembered in *A Winter Evening* and *To my Nanny*, as well as *Eugene Onegin* and "*I went back again.*" Pushkin recorded dozens of songs she taught him, as well as seven fairy tales, three of which (*The Tale of Tsar Saltan*, *Balda's Tale*, and *The Dead Princess*) he transformed into verse while keeping their folktale elements and embellishments of oral tradition. One of those folktale flourishes became the immortal first line of a prologue he added to *Ruslan and Lyudmila*'s second edition. Those who don't know *Ruslan and Lyudmila* may yet recognize the line which sister Masha in Chekhov's *The Three Sisters* repeats as if entranced:

"A green oak grows by a cove curving"...

Other consolations from "magnificent idleness" lived with his neighbours in Trigorsk, the estate of the family of Praskovya Aleksandrovna Osipova-Wulf. Pushkin liked making his entrance leaping into her dining room through her open windows. He made friends with her young son Aleksey Wulf, and courted all of Aleksey's pretty sisters:

> Oh, the hermit's life's a marvel!
> In Trigorsk we play till dusk,
> In Mikhailovskoye till dawn....
> Days to love are given up,
> Nights are ruled by our good tankards,
> And we're either deadly drunkards,
> Or we're smitten dead by love.

In Trigorsk, Pushkin wrote his light-hearted *Confession* for Praskovya's stepdaughter Alexandra ("Alina") Osipova. In the album of Praskovya's daughter Evpraksinya Vulf ("Zizi, the crystal of my soul") he wrote "*If life chances to deceive you.*" In June 1825 , the sisters were visted by their beautiful cousin, Anna Petrovna Kern, whom the poet had met six years ago in St. Petersburg. The night before Kern left for home, Pushkin gave her a manuscript of Chapter II of *Eugene Onegin*. Stuck within its pages was the poem *To ****("*A wondrous moment I remember*")— perhaps the Russian language's most famous love lyric, set to music by Pushkin's friend Glinka, and many other composers.

He rather shocked the sleepy local priest in Trigorsk by requesting a memorial mass for "the Boyar Georgiy" — Lord Byron. Despite his light-hearted skepticism on matters of faith, Pushkin liked frequenting the local Svyatogorsky Monastery, and its chief monk, Father Ioann. He spent much time in the monastic library, reading the old scrolls and chronicles, and also visited the monastery's fairs, wandering among the crowd, hearing the tales of beggars, pilgrims, and "holy fools." It was all grist for his blank verse tragedy, *Boris Godunov*. He would wake before dawn, write by candlelight, and sometimes not leave his little room for days. Verse was pouring out of him. He wrote Nikolai Rayevsky: "My soul has reached full strength: I can create!"

On November 7, 1825, he wrote Prince Vyazemsky: "I have finished my tragedy. I read it aloud to myself, then clapped till my palms hurt, cheering: "Hooray, Pushkin! Hooray! You son-of-a-bitch!" (That was nearly the only applause for this play Pushkin would ever hear. Its public performance was forbidden until 1866). The beautiful, sonorous verse of *Boris Godunov,* and its profound meditation on the nature of power, ethics, and the individual have never really crossed the language barrier; it is known in the West as the plot for the great opera by Mussorgsky. As Pushkin himself wrote: "what is the play about? The fate of a man is the fate of a people." Many consider it the Russian language's finest drama. Russia's most eminent critic, Vissarion Belinsky judged: "Like a giant among pygmies, Pushkin's *Boris Godunov* looms above the host of quasi-Russian tragedies, in splendid sober solitude, in its exalted, unimaginable purity of style, its noble, classical perfection" .

On November 19, 1825 Tsar Alexander I died childless; the news received Pushkin at the end of the month. "As a loyal subject, I ought to be sad at the Tsar's death, but as a poet, I look forward in joyful anticipation..." Alexander's oldest brother Constantine was expected to assume the throne, but Constantine, after a morganatic marriage to a Polish Catholic in 1823, had renounced his claim in favor of his brother Nicholas. Yet few knew this; many soldiers and officers, considering Constantine the true heir, refused to swear allegiance to Nicholas. On December 14, 1825, in what would be called the Decembrist Uprising, officers and soldiers led by nobles from secret revolutionary societies, gathered in Senate Square in St. Petersburg (where the Bronze Horseman stands) demanding: "Constantine and a Constitution." The crowd refused to leave; shooting began: St. Petersburg's governor Miloradovich (who'd been so kind to Pushkin) was killed. Nicholas had the crowd dispersed with grapeshot, and the "snow ran red with blood." Police dumped the wounded into the frozen Neva river with the corpses of those shot dead. Following a six month police inquest, five Decembrists were hanged, and 120 were exiled to Siberia. Pushkin had planned to escape to Petersburg upon hearing of Alexander I's death, and even forged a fake internal travel passport for the purpose. It describes one: "Aleksey Khokhlov, height, two arshins, four vershky [about 5'3"}, dark red hair, blue eyes, clean-shaven, age 29." But scarecely had Pushkin set out for the capital, when a hare crossed his path; then he met an Orthodox priest. At such portents of bad luck, Pushkin, ever superstitious, if not ever religious, turned back for home. Seeking solace in Shakespeare, and perhaps sensing (though unaware of) the bloody events taking place in Petersburg, he pondered the curious quirks of accidents, and the role of individual fate in history:

Rereading *The Rape of Lucrece*, one of Shakespeare's weaker poems, I thought to myself: what if it had just occurred to Lucrece to give Tarquin a good slap in the face? What if, perhaps, that would have cooled his ardor, and he'd have had to retreat in shame? Lucrece would not have stabbed herself, Collatine would not have been enraged, Brutus would not have banished the Kings, and the world and history would be utterly different. And so it seems we owe the Republic, the consuls, the dictators, the censors, and the Caesars all to one overwrought scene of seduction a bit like something that happened the other day to our neighbours in the Novorzhevsky district. The thought of parodying both this story and Shakespeare at once occurred to me, and being unable to withstand such double temptation, I wrote this little tale in two mornings. It is my habit to date my writings... *Count Nulin* was written December 13-14, 1825. There are strange coincidences in life. (*Note on Count Nulin*, 1830).

In *Count Nulin*, Pushkin pokes fun at his "Lucrece," yet sympathizes and identifies with her, merging his feelings with hers as a bell rings:

There by the windowsill she sits,
And Volume Four on her lap flits
Of a most sentimental novel:
The Love of Elise and Armand, or
Letters Twixt Two Families.
A classic tale of morals strong,
Amazingly long, long, long, long,
Most proper, teaching right and wrong,
Without romantic fantasies.
At first Natalia Pavlovna was
Reading, raptured, serious,
But somehow soon she drifted off,
Then out the window came a quarrel
Between a goat and courtyard mongrel:
She was transfixed in watching this.
All round a bunch of boys were laughing.
Beneath her windows, though, there mourned
A gaggle of wild geese, their cackling
Inspired by rain-drenched rooster's dawn.
Three ducks were splashing in a puddle;
Across the yard an old hag went
To hang old linen on the fence;
The weather seemed to presage trouble:
It seemed snow wished to tumble down...
And then a little bell did sound.

Pushkin in a stroll around Mikhaylovskoye

> Whoever's lived in backwoods gloomy,
> My friends, knows, surely all too well,
> How distant tinkling bells can truly
> At times just make our heartbeats swell.
> Is it an old friend out there, lagging,
> A bosom pal of our youth dashing?

As dawn was breaking on January 11, 1825, Pushkin's beloved "Jeannot," Ivan Pushchin, had arrived; Pushkin, hearing the sleigh bells, rushed in his nightshirt barefoot into the snow to hug him. Soon Arina Rodionovna, with no idea who had come, began embracing both of them.[1] Pushchin was in a secret revolutionary society, and could only stay one day. Soon Jeannot would be one of hundreds of Decembrists exiled to Siberia as "criminals against the state." Yet that one embrace with his best friend in a snowy courtyard has lasted longer than his 30 long years of exile; it is remembered in "*My very first and priceless friend.*" After Pushchin's sentence, Pushkin risked a possible new term of exile or worse to send that poem to his friend along with his now-famous (and long forbidden) *Message to Siberia.*

As always, friendship and poetry were linked in his imagination, and "it was Poetry that saved me, Poetry, like a consoling angel, and my soul was reborn." Another close friend, the poet Anton Delvig, risked a visit in the spring of 1825, and helped Pushkin edit his first book of poems. Pushkin thanked his friends in an elegy commemorating the Lycée's anniversary, *October 19th*, a cherished part of every Russian poetry anthology. *October 19th* combines the melancholy splendors of the fall with the warm sensation of the poet's lonely glass of wine to heighten his nostalgia as an exile, his hopes — and pining — for his Lycéen friends.

---

[1] Pushchin's *Notes on Pushkin* brim with the humanitarian warmth and boyish ideals known as "the spirit of the Lycée." However, there are those who ignore all that the good "Jeannot" had to say except two sentences about a little room in Pushkin's home where some serf girls were sewing. "There I saw one figure sharply different from the others...He read my mischievous thought and smiled significantly." The "figure" was Olga Kalashnikova, the winsome daughter of the manager of the Pushkin family estate at Boldino. The Soviet poet Mikhail Dudin called their love, which, though she was his mother's serf, was open and mutual, "the true wonder of 'the wondrous moment''." (Reading To *** ("A Wondrous moment I remember"), Dudin seems quite mistaken— though the national poet's love for a simple peasant girl made for great Soviet propaganda). In 1826, Olga, pregnant by Pushkin, left to give birth at her parents' side in Boldino. Pushkin, exiled and under strict surveillance, could do no more than ensure that his friends looked after their child. But little Pavel died shortly after birth. On receiving title to a portion of Boldino in 1830, Pushkin immediately gave Olga her freedom. She then married a petty nobleman, and became owner of a few serfs herself. Pushkin later stood godfather to her son by her new husband, and assisted her often.

> Blaze up, o hearth, in my bare room, my prison.
> And you, dear wine, friend of the fall's sharp frost,
> Pour joyous tipsiness into my bosom,
> Oblivion brief, make bitter cares seem lost.
>
> For I am sad, and without any friend
> To drink with, healing woes of separation,
> Whose hand I'd clasp in heartfelt admiration
> And wish good cheer for many years on end.

The poet, though unforgiven by the Tsar, nonetheless lightheartedly shows compassion for the human being who had banished him:

> He's but a man, and slave to time's illusions,
> Of rumors, doubts, and passions but a slave,
> So let's forgive his unfair persecution:
> He captured Paris, founded our Lycée!

Shortly after the official coronation in the the Kremlin of Nicholas I, Pushkin was summoned to Moscow to meet with the new Tsar. It is thought that on his way to that fateful meeting, Pushkin composed his magnificent evocation of the poet's role as the conscience of his nation: *The Prophet*. With images from the Book of Isaiah, Chapter VI, it describes what might be called an operation by the Heavenly Surgeon, in which the poet, who once was "babbling, idle, cunning, moody," transforms into an all-seeing, all-hearing vessel of the divine, sensitive and sympathetic to the voice of heaven and earth itself:

> To Heaven's shuddering I hearkened,
> And to the lofty angels' flight,
> To slithering things in deep seas' night,
> And valley grapes grown dull, cold, hardened.

The Prophet is the first of many poems Pushkin would devote to poetry itself, and to the poet's relationship to others (see Chapter 8: *The Poet, The Echo, Autumn*, etc.). *The Prophet* rises above politics and sounds a clarion call for the poet to remember his divine mission in life:

> "Arise, thou prophet, see, and hearken,
> By my will let your soul be stirred,
> And, wandering by lands and waters,
> Burn people's hearts up with my word."

1826–1831 Moscow and St. Petersburg

> And so our maiden was enjoying
> The endless long dull road's delights:
> They rode for seven days and nights.

> But now they're near. Before them glistening
> Already white-stoned Moscow runs,
> Like fire, with golden crosses quivering,
> Its ancient domes gleam in the sun.
> Oh brothers! How my heart was happy
> To see the churches, bell-towers clanging,
> The gardens, courtyards, crescents' sweep
> Before me opened suddenly!
> How often in my exile grieving,
> Throughout my errant odyssey,
> Have I thought, Moscow, but of thee!
> Moscow! How Russian hearts are heaving
> At all that merges in that sound!
> How much in us it makes resound!

Tsar Nicholas I

Pushkin was arrived in Moscow on September 8, 1826, and was immediately brought to the Tsar in the Kremlin's Chudov Palace, without so much as a chance to shave, wash, or dress for the occasion. Rigorous investigation of the condemned Decembrists had found Pushkin's poems in the possession of most of the condemned men. Many, naïve and idealistic, had little in the way of coherent plans or ideology but the sweet hopes Pushkin's verse had stirred. Secret agent A.K. Boshnyak was dispatched to Mikhalovskoye to find out whether Pushkin had been involved in seditious activity. Boshnyak reported that the poet was well liked by the peasants near his home for his good humor and generosity, though he had an odd habit of jotting down all their old wives' tales and folksongs. He seemed oblivious to politics, and instead spent days horseback riding, swimming, and strolling the countryside in a broad straw hat and colorful Russian peasant shirt. Very suspicious indeed! Definitely worth further investigation!

Pushkin spoke with the Tsar for over three hours, and did not deny that many Decembrists were his dearest friends. He added that the harsh sentences meted out against them had not changed his feelings. Asked what he would have done if he had been in St. Petersburg on December 14th, he bravely replied that he would have joined his friends in Senate Square. The Tsar ordered him never again to write against the government, to submit all future writings personally to the Tsar for censorship, then announced that he was free to go, and that his exile was over. Why was Pushkin released from exile? Was the Tsar charmed by him? That evening the Tsar remarked: "Today I spoke with the smartest man in Russia" . Yet in Pushkin's phrase: "The Crown may love, but the master of his hounds loves not." Soon the Third Department, or new imperial secret police ordered Pushkin put under constant personal surveillance. More likely, Pushkin's release was a political gesture of reconciliation towards the liberal intelligentsia of Russia, a half-hearted try by an unloved ruler for popularity. Pushkin was perhaps the most popular man in Russia, the darling of Moscow society. When he gave a public reading of his *Boris Godunov* at the home of a friend in Moscow, it brought down the house:

> He read his verse superbly. Unlike the usual style of declaiming verse in a singsong monotone, he spoke completely naturally, simply, clearly — yet so poetically, and with such animation! We all were beside ourselves: some flushed, some shivered; our hair stood on end, we laughed, we cried...when he was done, a hush fell on us all, then we mobbed him.

But one of those who "mobbed him" had been an informant for the secret police. Pushkin was reprimanded for not submitting his play to the Tsar before reading it aloud. Its performance was soon forbidden. Pushkin's drawings from this time depict gallows and hanged or exiled "friends, brothers, and comrades." Surrounded instead by "spies, whores, and drunkards," he pined again for the simplicity and peace of country life, for his nanny Arina Rodionovna — and she for him (*"To my Nanny"*) . Old and new friends, including the great exiled Polish poet, Adam Mickiewicz, and even the boisterous company of gypsy dancers and singers did not much console the poet. In January 1827 a police proceeding began against him for his ode to *André Chenier*, which contained the following provocative lines:

> No more do ancient thrones cause awe;
> Our chains have fallen, and the Law,
> Propped up by freedom now, proclaims that all are equal.
> We cried out "bliss!" in great throngs cheerful!
> Oh misery! Mad dream gone wrong!
> Where's freedom? Where's the law? Unfettered
> Above us just the axe does reign.
> We've overthrown the Tsar, but killers and cruel henchmen
> Are our new chosen Tsars! Oh horror! Oh, what shame!

Yekaterina Ushakova's cat-loving younger sister
Elizaveta Mikhailovna Ushakova on Don Juan's Angel's Day
(from the Ushakova album)

Yekaterina Ushakova plays the Balcony Scene
(from the Ushakova album)

Pushkin was forced to testify and prove these lines came from a poem submitted to the censor well before December 1825, and thus had nothing to do with the brutal suppression of the Decembrists. Even though it was beyond question that the poem's subject was the poet André Chenier, guillotined in 1794 during Robespierre's Reign of Terror, the matter was only closed in July 1828. (No one could foresee how accurately those lines would describe the Bolshevik Revolution).

For the next four years Pushkin lived several months each year in Moscow and St. Petersburg. The death and exile of his best friends had deepened his loneliness; ever more he longed for a wife, a home, a family. In May 1826 he proposed to Sofia Pushkina, a distant cousin, but nothing came of it. In May 1827, before leaving Moscow to see his parents in St. Petersburg, Pushkin wrote in the album of his new love Yekaterina Ushakova, "*If they send me far from you.*" Ushakova adored Pushkin and his poetry. Yet she was blond, so they never married, for fear her "white head" might cause his death, as prophesied by M-me. Kirchof. They stayed friends; Ushakova's album has many (often whimsical) Pushkin drawings, and his famous so-called "Don Juan list."

In St. Petersburg, ever at work on *Eugene Onegin*, Pushkin renewed relations with Anna Kern, and was inseparable from his Lycée friend Delvig. On the anniversary of the hanging of his Decembrist friends, he wrote the poem *Arion*. He also began a historical novel about his great-grandfather, *The Blackamoor of Peter the Great*, written during a return visit to Mikhailovskoye. It was plotted to be something of a Russian *Othello* in prose. However Pushkin set the novel aside after six chapters. Its crucial scene is sadly revealing of own insecurities and self-doubts in seeking a wife. The Moor Ibrahim converses with Tsar Peter:

> "If I were minded to marry, would the young girl's parents consent? After all, my looks..."
> "Your looks? What nonsense! Why aren't you just fine? A young girl should respect the will of her parents, and let's see what old Gavrila Rzhevsky will say If I myself am your matchmaker!" With these words the Tsar summoned his sleigh and left Ibrahim sunk in profoundest meditation.
> "To marry!" thought the African. "Why not? Am I really doomed to spend my life in loneliness, and never know the highest pleasures and responsibilities of a man simply because I was born beneath the Tropic of Cancer? I can't hope to be loved...So what?! What a childish objection...I won't demand that my wife love me; I'll be content if she is faithful, and will try at least to gain her friendship through constant tenderness, trust, and kindness."

BIOGRAPHY

In October 1827, while changing horses in the country station Zalazy, Pushkin was startled to see police manhandling his schoolfriend, the convicted Decembrist and poet, Wilhelm Küchelbecker. "We threw ourselves in each other's arms, but the guards rudely pulled the two of us apart." Days later, on October 19, 1827 a still-affected Pushkin commemorated the Lycée's anniversary: "*God help you all, my dear, dear friends.*"

Back in St. Petersburg ("*Town so gorgeous, town of beggars*") during 1827–1828 Pushkin unrequitedly courted Annette Olenina ("*Oh, blessed he picked with choice capricious*") as the secret police began yet another formal proceeding against him, this time accusing him of blasphemy for his authorship of the *Gabrieliad*. Annette's father was on the board of the commission. Things looked bleak for Pushkin ("*Foreboding*") and the matter was only dismissed after the poet wrote a personal letter to Tsar Nicholas, which has not survived. In this time of renewed conflict with authority Pushkin wrote *The Poison Tree*. Characteristically, the poem never preaches; it just tells a story. Yet its powerful images, force, and passionate language lead the reader to ponder all the more deeply the problem of evil compounding itself, and the bitter price of blind subservience to unjust authority.

The almost existential grief and loneliness Pushkin experienced in 1828 can be felt in his sleepless meditation: *Remembrance*, as well as a poem – addressed to life itself – on the occasion of his own birthday: "*Gift so futile, gift so random.*" Around this time Pushkin also wrote the lyric "*I loved you once*," a light yet profoundly moving parting gift of love. Again, Pushkin does not singe the twilight of his feelings with glaring and unnecessary details. It does not really matter whom it was he loved; she is Woman, and his deep and abiding love is unrequited. Those who know W.B. Yeats "*When you are old and grey*" may find it evokes a similar mood. Somehow the very act of putting love into the past tense makes it everlasting; the overwhelming wistfulness, warmth, regret, grief, and true generosity of spirit he feels are crowned simultaneously with a bittersweet irony, as what is lost is preserved forever.

Despite his griefs, in 1827–1828, Pushkin kept working on *Eugene Onegin*, completing the work through Chapter VII. In 1828 Pushkin also wrote *Poltava*, a thrilling narrative poem (best known in the West as the basis for Tchaikovsky's opera *Mazeppa*). Maria, the heroine, is asked to choose between her father and the husband she eloped with, his mortal enemy—all against the backdrop of Peter the Great's defeat of the Swedish invasion of Russia in 1709. Pushkin continuously shifts focus to show the points of view of all the characters. On one side is his hero: Tsar Peter the Great, whose eccentric genius and indomitable will created a mighty modern nation, yet not without many innocent victims. On the other side is Peter's bitter foe, the Ukrainian rebel leader Mazeppa, struggling against fate and — at times — his own conscience:

> Hushed the Ukrainian night,
> And clear its sky; the stars are shining.
> The very air, try as it might,
> Can't shake off slumber. Only slightly
> Some poplars quiver silvery leaves.
> But gloomy, weird, unnatural dreams
> Still haunt Mazeppa; constellations,
> Like eyes that fill with accusations,
> Look down at him in mockery.
> Those crowded rows of poplar trees
> All shake their heads now, silently,
> Like judges' whispering secretly,
> The summer night's warm murk is stale
> And stifling, like a great black jail.

Yet "power corrupts," and Pushkin shows:

> That there is nothing he holds cherished,
> That all that's good in him has perished,
> That there is nothing he does love,
> That he would spill our blood like water,
> That of all freedom he is scornful,
> That there's no homeland in his heart.

Mazeppa

Soon after finishing Poltava, Pushkin traveled to Moscow. There, in December 1828, at a friend's house, Pushkin saw a dancing master giving lessons; one of the girls in attendance was sixteen-year-old Natalya Nikolayevna Goncharova. "When I first saw her, her beauty was just barely beginning to be noticed in society; I loved her; she turned my head." Yet turned though his head was, it was still able to revolve in other directions. A few days later he left for St. Petersburg, stopping along the way to visit friends in Malinniki, Tver Province, where he had a fling with Annette Vulf, and wrote his wistful *The Little Flower*. In Petersburg he wrote *"When through the noisy streets I wander"* (one of his most moving meditations).

Pushkin saw Natalya Goncharova again at a ball in Moscow in March 1830. A week later he had proposed. Natalya, or "Tasha" as she was called, was the youngest — and by far the prettiest of three sisters. Her mother, Natalya Ivanovna Zagryazhskaya, had been the mistress of a dashing Guards officer who was also the lover of Empress Elizabeth, Tsar Alexander I's wife). That officer was mysteriously murdered, and Natalya Ivanovna was married off to Nikolai Afanasievich Goncharov, scion of a wealthy paper-making family in Kaluga Province. But Goncharov's father squandered the family wealth on extravagances, and Nikolay, Natalya's father, became a desperate alcoholic, prone to rages, fits, and profound depression. Natalya's mother responded to all these traumas by seeing in them the hand of God, and becoming a religious fanatic (also by having not-very-secret affairs with sundry cooks and coachmen). Though Natalya Ivanovna was, by all accounts, a harsh, domineering, and extraordinarily capricious mother, she made sure at least that her daughters spoke good French and danced perfectly — the only two skills needed in society. And she hoped to improve the dire family finances by marrying off the prettiest of her three daughters, Natalya, in Moscow, "the marketplace of brides."

Natalya Ivanovna was not in the least impressed by the fame and genius of the suitor for her daughter's hand. She disapproved of this "Moor" with scarce means, but ample troubles with the government, whose romantic past was so checkered. Natalya Ivanovna would dictate cutting and haughty letters to Pushkin (which her daughter softened with tender post scripta). Imperiously requiring her daughter to feign cold indifference, in hopes Pushkin would go away, Natalya Ivanovna bluntly told Pushkin she hoped someone more "suitable" would come along. But no one else did, for the Goncharovs could provide their daughter no dowry. So Natalya Ivanovna (playing for time) rejected Pushkin's proposal of marriage as vaguely as possible. On May 1, 1829, the poet wrote back:

> On my knees with tears of gratitude I should write you now...your answer is not a refusal; you leave me hope. Yet if I murmur still, and if sadness and bitterness mix with my feelings of joy, do not tax me with ingratitude; I perceive a mother's prudence and tenderness! But forgive as well a heart that is sick at being deprived of happiness. I am leaving for now, but in the depths of my soul I bear the image of that celestial soul to whom you have brought the light of day.

Pushkin had left for the Caucasus, where his friend Nikolai Rayevsky, the General's son, was fighting in the Russian army's latest war in the Caucasus—this time with Turkey. At one stop to change horses, he was invited by a nomadic Kalmyk family to join them for breakfast:

> A young Kalmyk girl, not at all bad looking, was sewing and smoking tobacco. I sat by her. "What's your name?" " * * * . " "How old are you?" "Ten and eight." "What are you sewing?" "Trousers." "For whom?" "Myself." She gave me her pipe and began breakfast: salted tea with mutton fat. She gave me her ladle. I did not wish to offend by refusal and swallowed, trying not too obviously to take a deep breath. I doubt any national cuisine ever produced anything more revolting. I asked if I could try something else. She gave me a bit of dried mare's meat. Even that was an improvement. But such Kalmyk flirtations alarmed me; I ran from her tent as quickly as possible and fled this Circe of the steppes. (From *A Journey to Arzurum*).

As his carriage rolled south, Pushkin reflected on this encounter in *To a Kalmyk Girl*. He paused by Mount Mashuk to take the mineral waters where he had once found healing and inspiration, then continued south through Chechnya, noting: "the Chechens hate us. We have driven them from their free pastures, ruined their villages, wiped out whole clans. No wonder hour by hour they slip away further into the mountains and from there carry out their raids against us. The friendship of so-called pacified Chechens is doubtful; they are always in the end willing to support their ungovernable compatriots." (Has anyone in the Kremlin pondered these words?). The mountains inspired several new poems, including *The Monastery on Mount Kazbek*. Then he joined the army, and fought when the Turks made a surprise attack on the Cossack vanguard. "He ran from our quarters, leaped on his horse and rode to the front lines. Brave Major Semichev, ordered by General Pashkevich to keep Pushkin safe, had to drag him away by force from the firing line; Pushkin had grabbed a spear from a slain Cossack and charged headlong against the enemy horsemen." This Turkish campaign was Pushkin's only experience of being "abroad": he filled his sketchbooks with drawings of Persian courtiers, minarets, defiant Turkish prisoners. Coming home, and pining for Natalya, he wrote his sublime: "*Upon the Georgian hills there lies the haze of night...*" Once back in Moscow he threw himself at the feet of his beloved — again in vain. As he later wrote his mother in law:

What tortures awaited me on my return. Your silence, cold
manner, and my indifferent and careless reception by M-lle N...
I did not dare express myself. I left for Petersburg with death
in my soul.

Pushkin consoled himself on his way north by staying again with his
friends in Tver' Province, and wrote *"Round Izhora I was riding"* to
Katya Velyasheva, with whom vowed to "till November, fall in love."
Snowbound on the Malinniki estate, he wrote his sardonic yet lyrical
"It's winter. What's to do here in the country?" Its Byronic ennui and
"spleen" are cured by the sudden arrival of sweet, pretty young girls.
They make live worth living again: verses flow and the poet plunges
light-heartedly into the pleasures of flirtation, dances, hints... then
sensuous passion and joy, and "how warm–even in frost–the kiss she
gives is, blazing." For a while, perhaps, he relieved his mind from
obsessing on "Kars" and "Mama Kars" — his nicknames for Natalya and
Natalya Ivanovna (in honor of a Turkish fortress that had
stubbornly withstood a lengthy Russian siege).

Back in Petersburg, he asked the Tsar's permission to travel "Unto
the distant foot of the Great Wall of China,/To Paris bubbling" (*"Let's
leave! I'm ready now*!). As usual, he was refused; Count Benckendorf,
head of the so-called 3rd Department, or secret police, was angry at
Pushkin's trip to the Caucasus without his permission. Henceforth,
until his death (even in transporting his coffin) the poet's every
movement was restricted severely by the 3rd Department.

Foreign travel had long been his fondest dream. Exiled in Kishinev, he
had dreamed of joining Byron in fighting for Greek independence. In
Book I of *Eugene Onegin* he dreamed in verse of fleeing to Italy. And
from Odessa in January 1824, he had written his brother:

> I've twice begged for leave to be allowed at least a foreign vaca-
> tion, and each time received a most august and merciful refusal.
> Only one thing remains: to write straight to So-and-So, address,
> Winter Palace, opposite Peter and Paul Fortress. Or else just
> grab my hat and cane and go check out Constantinople. Holy
> Mother Russia is getting to be quite unbearable!

From Mikhailovskoye Pushkin had begged for leave to go abroad for
medical reasons; his mother wrote the Tsar about this personally.
Again he was refused, and was directed to seek healing only in the
provincial capital, Pskov. He replied:

His Majesty's unexpected kindness greatly touched me, especially as the local governor had already given me leave to visit Pskov, yet I strictly obey our highest authority. Inquiring about getting cured in Pskov, I was referred to a certain Vsevolozhsky, a skilled veterinarian, respected in the scientific community for his book on the treatment of horses."

In May 1826, he had written his friend Prince Vyazemsky:

I, of course, despise my Fatherland from head to toe. How can you, not being tied down like me, stay here in Russia? If the Tsar ever gives me freedom, I won't stay a month. It's a sad age we live in. When I imagine London, and railroads, and steamships, and free English journals, or Parisian theatres — or bordellos, then my desolate Mikhailovskoye just aggrieves and enrages me. In Chapter Four of *Onegin* I've described my life; one day you'll read it and ask with a sweet smile: "Where is my poet? He seemed talented." And you'll hear, my dear, the answer: "He's run off to Paris and will never — ever! — return to his accursed Russia! Hooray! Clever fellow!"

But it was not to be. The closest he ever got to England was the English Club in Moscow. (When someone kidded him that there was no worse contradiction in terms than the Moscow English Club, he replied: "How about the Imperial Humane Society?"). And so, the most completely European of Russian writers was denied even a glimpse of the Europe he so dreamed of. One can only wonder what would have happened had Pushkin been granted his wish to travel. The Russian painter Karl Bryullov recalled:

In the fall [of 1836] Pushkin called one evening and asked me to dinner. I wasn't in the mood, and tried to refuse, but his stubbornness overcame mine, and he dragged me along. His kids were already tucked into bed when he showed them to me, cradling them gently in his arms one by one, and cooing affectionately. But something wasn't right. There was a feeling of sadness, as if he was trying to force upon himself this idyllic picture of family happiness. I couldn't take it anymore and asked him: "why the devil did you ever marry?" He answered: "I really wanted to travel abroad, but they didn't let me. Then I got in such a tizzy that I didn't know what to do. So I got married."

The winter of 1830 was particularly anxious for Pushkin. The Tsarist spy and propagandist Faddey Bulgarin was writing vicious slanders and racial slurs against him and his family in the *Northern Bee*, a paper funded by the secret police. Pushkin shot back with *My Pedigree* and *An*

Epigram on Bulgarin. As his chances to wed Natalya seemed dashed, he met his old flame Karolina Sobanskaya (the secret agent) once more in St. Petersburg. On February 2, 1830, he wrote two notes to her that read like a bit like prose drafts of *Onegin's Letter to Tatyana.* One says: "happiness is so little made for me, that I could not recognize it when it was right in front of me." In the other he wrote:

> Today is the 9th anniversary of the day I saw you for the first time. That day was decisive in my life. The more I think about it, the more I see that my existence is inseparable from yours: I was born to love you and follow you. All other cares on my part are either errors or folly. Apart from you I have nothing but remorse for a happiness I have been unable to attain. Sooner or later I will have to abandon everything and cast myself at your feet.

Pushkin never sent either note. Anna Akhmatova argues they were something of a composition exercise: Sobanskaya was clearly not the marrying kind. However, Sobanskaya did ask Pushkin to write his name in her album. Instead he wrote: "*What is there in my name for you?*" By April 1830 Pushkin was back in Moscow wooing Natalya. Completely despondent, he proposed again to "Mama Kars":

> Only habit and long intimacy can help me win the affection of M-lle your daughter. Eventually I can hope to attach her to me, but I have nothing to please her. If she consents to give me her hand, I will see in this only proof of the tranquil indifference of her heart. Yet will this tranquility of hers last when she is surrounded by admiration, tributes, and seductions? She will be told that just bad luck has prevented her from forming other attachments more fitting, more brilliant, more worthy of her...Maybe these offers will be sincere; doubtless she will think so. Will she not have regrets? Will she not regard me as a fraudulent ravisher? Will she take aversion to me? God is my witness; I am ready to die for her, but to have to die, and leave her a brilliant widow, free to choose a new husband the next day — this idea is hell.

It is hard to imagine a more melancholy proposal, which reads eerily in light of what would follow. Was this self-effacement meant mostly to mollify "Mama Kars"? Or did he genuinely prize himself so little? If so, why did "the most intelligent man in Russia," "the sunshine of Russian poetry," feel "I have nothing to please her"? Why did this poet of romantic love, besieged by pretty admirers, seek to marry someone who regarded him at best with "tranquil indifference"?...Or did she love him after all and merely act aloof to satisfy her mother?

But two seasons had passed and Natalya's mother had received no better offers. Three weeks later Pushkin reflected archly, in a letter to Princess Vyazemskaya: "First love is always a matter of sentiment; the sillier it was, the sweeter its memories. Second love is a matter of voluptuous sensations...I could continue the parallel, but it would take too long. My marriage to Natalie (who is, in parenthesis my 113th love) has been decided." The engagement was announced May 6, 1830.

> My dream's come true. Our Lord Creator
> Sent you down to me, sent you, my own Madonna,
> Of purest grace the purest monument.

But his future mother-in-law was more a nightmare than a dream come true. Ceaselessly she tried to break the engagement, while demanding ever more money from the poet, which he did not have. By August 31, 1830, he was writing his friend and publisher Pletnev:

> I'll tell you what I feel: grief, grief, grief. My future mother in law's finances are a mess, so our wedding gets postponed day by day. All the while my ardor dampens, as I think of the married man's cares and the charms of bachelorhood. To make things worse, all the gossip in Moscow reaches the ears of my fiancée and her mother, causing more tiffs, nasty remarks, uncertain reconciliations — in short, if I'm not unhappy, I'm at least not happy.

In September 1830 Pushkin went to Boldino, in Nizhny Novgord Province, to officially enter into ownership of part of a property his father had given him upon his engagement. (He mortgaged it to pay Natalya's dowry instead of his future in-laws). No sooner had he arrived than cholera broke out in the province. Quarantines and roadblocks were set up, cutting Pushkin off from return to Moscow. Holed up in the simple wooden house in Boldino, he wrote Pletnev: "*Cholera morbus* is all around. Do you know what sort of beast that is? Any moment it may hit Boldino and devour us all...You can't imagine how grand it is to give my fiancée the slip and just get down to writing poems." The famous Boldino Autumn had begun. Three months later: "In Boldino I wrote as I have never written." Indeed, the quality and productivity of what flew from his pen there is astounding. It includes several dramatic scenes or *Little Tragedies* in blank verse: *Mozart and Salieri, The Guest of Stone, The Miserly Knight*, and T*he Feast in a Time of Plague*, and five brilliant short prose tales known as the *Tales of Belkin*, which are a watershed in Russian literature. Tolstoy was to call them the finest prose ever written in Russian, and advise young authors: "read and re-read *The Tales of Belkin*. Every writer ought to study every last word of them." At Boldino he also wrote over thirty poems, including *The Demons, Elegy, The Page, To the Poet, "I can't sleep, fire's out, no light," "Bound for your distant country's shoreline," "When in the grasp of my embrace," Invocation*. There he also finished (except for *Onegin's Letter to Tatyana*) his masterpiece, *Eugene Onegin*, the crown jewel of Russian literature, after seven years, four months and seventeen days' labor of love. Upon finishing, he mused:

> Finally, now the time's come! I have finished my many years' labor.
> Why, strange and secret, does sadness so trouble me now?
> Is it, the deed being done, that I stand like a day-worker, useless,
> Having been given my pay, foreign to all other work?
> Am I sad for the work, for my silent companion at nightimes,
> Friend of my dawns swathed in gold, friend of my home's holy shrine?

Eugene Onegin is best known in the West by the Tchaikovsky opera, which sadly eliminates the novel's main character: the poet-narrator, Pushkin. Those familiar only with the opera should not presume to know the book; while the music captures much of the book's magic and exuberance, it cannot replace the joyous heart that surrounds the unhappy plot of the novel. To many Russian critics *Eugene Onegin* is a tale of a so-called "useless person," a microcosm of the disaffected Russian intellectual. Yet this is only one side of the coin. Balancing its mutual unrequited love and missed opportunities, its friendship gone wrong and misunderstandings that lead to disaster, everywhere is Pushkin himself, joying in life. Even tragedy itself is to him just a metaphor that deepens his abiding love of humanity and nature, his wisdom and acceptance, his poetic happiness. And, by way of a seemingly aimless, but in fact precisely guided, loving, transcendant, poetic ramble, we arrive at "an encyclopedia of Russian life," in Belinsky's famous phrase. But that encyclopedia is truly universal.

He returned to Moscow in December 1830, but quarrels with his future mother-in-law continued to delay the wedding, as did, in January 1831, the grievous news of the death of Pushkin's dearest Lycéen friend, the poet Delvig. His gloom was profound, not at all befitting an eager fiancé. Many noticed the poet's misgivings: one friend wrote: "Soon Pushkin is marrying Miss Goncharova, *entre nous*, a soulless beauty. It seems to me that by now he'd be glad to cancel the engagement." Just a week before his wedding, Pushkin wrote a friend:

> I'm married. Well — almost. I've already pondered all they might tell me in favor of bachelor life and against marriage. I've cold-bloodedly weighed my gains and losses in the estate I am choosing. My youth has passed noisily and fruitlessly. Hitherto I have not lived as most people do, and I was not happy. Happiness lurks only on beaten paths. I'm over thirty. Most people usually marry at 30; I'm acting like most people, and probably won't have grounds to regret. I'm marrying without ecstasy or boyish enchantment; I see the future not all rosily, but in all its naked truth. Griefs will not surprise me; they are part of my domestic calculations. Any joys, though, will be completely unexpected.

Just two days before the wedding, he wrote his publisher: "I can afford to take a wife who has no money, but to plunge into debt just for the sake of her frilly clothes—that I can't afford. Yet I am stubborn and must insist on at least going through with this marriage. Well, there's no remedy. You'll just have to publish my short stories." Pushkin's gloom was not dispelled at his bachelor party; as gypsy maidens danced and sang, he burst into tears. The day of the wedding, February 18, 1831, began even worse: Natalya was ill, and a rude note came from her mother threatening to cancel the marriage unless she got a huge sum of money for a carriage. In spite of everything, Pushkin and Natalya proceeded to marry in the Church of the Grand Ascension in Moscow (opposite where the TASS Building today looms, by the Nikitsky Gates). During the ceremony, the bride dropped the ring meant for the groom, then a sudden draft blew a Bible and cross off the lectern, and snuffed out Pushkin's candle. Princess Dolgorukaya saw Pushkin turn pale and whisper: "*Tous les mauvais augures!*" ("All bad omens!") But he composed himself, and carried on.

> My fate is decided. I am getting married...She whom I have loved for two whole years, whom my eyes ever yearn for first, with whom every meeting has seemed bliss...My God! She's mine...Awaiting the decisive moment was the most painful

feeling in my life. The wait for the last card to be dealt, pangs of conscience, trying to sleep before a duel—all that is nothing in comparison...To marry! Easy enough to say! To most people marriage is about a fancy gown bought on credit, a new carriage, a silk rose nightgown. To others it's about a dowry and settling down. Others marry because everyone else does, because they're thirty...I'm marrying, i.e. giving up my dear freedom, my carefree, whimsical independence, luxurious habits, aimless wanderings, seclusion and inner calm, my inconstancy...to double a life which even now is far from full. I've never sought happiness; I never needed to. Now I seek enough for two. But where will I find it?

M-me & M-lle Kars: Natalya Nikolyavena Goncharova loomed over by her mother, Natalya Ivanovna Goncharova

1831-1837 Married Life   St. Petersburg

Biographers of Pushkin often discount any spiritual component to Pushkin's feelings for Natalya. The great poetess Marina Tsvetayeva opined (a bit jealously, perhaps?) "Natalya had only one good quality: beauty. Just beauty, simply beauty, without intelligence, wit, soul, heart, or talent. Naked beauty — sharp as a sword. And she pierced him through." Vladimir Sollogub (with whom Pushkin almost had a duel for alleged attentions to Natalya) remembered: "I have met many beautiful women, but none whose perfection seemed so complete, classical in both her features and her body...her presence made all other women fade away, even the most charming. Yet she seemed reserved to the point of coldness, and hardly ever spoke." By contrast, the poet Tumansky wrote: "don't imagine she's so extraordinary. She's pale, with pure naïve features, but her eyes are sly and flirty as any grisette's. She is gauche and stiff and reeks of the typical Moscow girl's vulgarity. That she's tasteless is clear by how she dresses, that she's lazy is clear by the mess she makes of her household: soiled napkins, tablecloths, jumbled furniture and crockery."

We do not have Natalya's letters to Pushkin, but 78 letters from Pushkin to Natalya have survived. It is obvious from their tender and deeply intimate tone that the poet, at least, found qualities in his wife beyond mere appearances. His letters evince devoted friendship, kindness, sympathy, caring, and indeed: "I love your soul much more than your face." Pushkin may have truly sympathized with his sweet young damsel in distress, and empathized with her childhood woes.

The newlyweds rented rooms in a charming house on Moscow's Arbat Street. It was there the poet Tumansky visited the new couple and was so singularly unimpressed by Natalya. Pushkin himself, in spite of everything, even bad omens, was truly blissful at the beginning. Just a week after the nerve-wracking ceremony, Pushkin wrote his publisher:

> I'm married — and happy. I have but one wish: for nothing in my life to change. It will never get any better than this. This feeling is so new to me. It seems I am reborn.

Yet Pushkin's mother-in-law did not share his joy. She reproved her son-in-law's anti-clericalism, and commanded her daughter to keep lugubrious vigils, prayers, and fasts. Over and over she complained that her daughter had made a tragic mistake in marrying a good-for-nothing scribbler, a proven trouble-maker, a heretic, a libertine — all the while nagging that same detested new son-in-law for ever greater sums of money. Soon Pushkin could take no more, and left Moscow for good, writing his mother-in law in parting:

> I was forced to leave Moscow to avoid the unpleasantness you caused, which in the end would have robbed me of more than just my peace of mind. You have described me to my wife as an odious man, a greedy, vile bloodsucking usurer; you have told her she just was a fool, that she should not allow her husband even to...etc. You will admit that this is all preaching divorce. I have answered with both patience and mildness. Both, I see now, were quite in vain.

In May 1831, the newlyweds moved to a cozy little home by the park of the Summer Palace in Tsarskoye Selo, not far from Pushkin's beloved Lycée. Each morning he and Natalya would promenade around the lake. His sister Olga was happy that "they seem to adore each other." The poet Zhukovsky wrote: "Pushkin is my neighbor, and we see each other often. His wife seems a quite delightful creature, and he's so happy with her. I am gladder than ever for him that he is married. His soul, life, and poetry all gain from this." While honeymooning in Tsarskoye Selo, Pushkin added *Onegin's Letter to Tatyana* (and a few stanzas before and after) to the completed text of *Eugene Onegin*:

> ...every moment seeing you,
> And following where'er you go,
> Your lips that smile, your eyes that move,
> To catch with eyes in love, aglow.
> To hear and hear you, understand
> With all my soul your sweet perfection,
> In agonies before you stand,
> Turn pale and swoon! What bliss! What blessing!

He expressed his new "tortured joy" in the poem "*No, I do not hold dear that pleasure most rebellious,*" in which Natalya seems cold to his affections "until at last my flame you share unwilling" Some see this poem as "proof" Natalya did not love her husband. Yet to me this poem in fact evokes somehow the intense attraction between his romantic "yang" and her somewhat coy, seductive "yin." It is worth noting that during this very time in Tsarskoye Selo, Pushkin wrote the happiest and most beloved of all his fairy tales, *The Tale of Tsar Saltan*:

> There's a princess, so they say,
> From whom eyes can't look away.
> During day than sun she's brighter,
> Nights she makes the world shine lighter.
> In her locks bright moonbeams are,
> In her forehead gleams a star.
> She herself, majestic, precious,
> Like a peacock stately, paces,
> When she speaks, her sweet speech seems
> Like the murmuring rush of streams.

The poet's wife

In 1831, Pushkin wrote *The Echo*, an allegory of a poet's obligation to sacrifice his own personality, to listen and reflect, to be "empty" as an echo (which lets Truth ring). Still missing his friend Delvig and other Lycée friends, he wrote a melancholy yet philosophical poem on October 19, 1831, the 20th anniversary of the Lycée's founding: "*The more we do commemorate.*"

That same year, while promenading in the park of the Summer Palace, Pushkin and his wife met the Tsar and Tsarina, who were very taken by Natalya. Soon afterwards, Nicholas I restored Pushkin to his rank as a tenth class bureaucrat in the Russian civil service, and gave him access to the State Archives, and later Catherine the Great's celebrated Voltaire Library. Pushkin began work on a projected biography of Peter the Great (never finished) as well as an outstanding history of what might be called the first Russian civil war: the Pugachev Rebellion of 1773-1775. As part of his research, Pushkin received a gift from the Tsar of the *Complete Laws of the Russian Empire*, and studied them intently. Delving in the Archives, Pushkin began to see himself more and more as a historian as well as a poet, and to turn more and more to prose. Uprisings in France, Poland, and peasant revolts in Russia returned his interest to themes of the individual against the state, and the contrasting excesses of power and rebellion, society and mutiny. His next novel, *Dubrovsky*, written in 1832-1833, incorporated many factual and historical materials, including a letter from his dear Arina Rodionovna, and, verbatim, the judgment from a corrupt court case in Murom Province, to create a romantic thriller about a ruined nobleman turned brigand who falls in love with the daughter of the man who ruined him. Yet he cast the work aside at its climax, leaving it, like many other of his works, beautifully unfinished, like a classical Greek torso...Perhaps Pushkin had trouble reconciling within himself the conflict between romantic plot and historical study, between lyric poetry and prose, whose charm (in his view) should be always unadorned, unsentimental, plain, and clear as possible.

Speaking of prose, while in Tsarskoye Selo, Pushkin befriended one of its greatest masters, Nikolai Gogol, just arrived from the provinces, and woefully shy. Pushkin recognized Gogol's talent, encouraged him to write, and helped him get published. Pushkin gave Gogol ideas and plot suggestions for two of his most famous works: the comedy *The Inspector-General*, and the novel *Dead Souls*. He also helped Gogol get a university professorship, edited several of Gogol's *Petersburg Tales*, including *The Nose*, *The Carriage*, and *Nevsky Prospekt*, and urged the Tsar to permit the staging of *The Inspector General*. Gogol was grateful to Pushkin all his life, and revered him as the greatest of poets.

Pushkin's first child Maria was born on May 19, 1832. By most accounts, Pushkin was a doting father. But life in the capital was ruinously expensive, especially in light of Natalya's taste for fancy clothes, carriages, hats, and gloves (though many of her fancy gowns were supplied by her aunt Yekaterina Zagryazhskaya). While Pushkin took some pride in his wife's brilliant success in Petersburg society, he could ill afford it, as he had foreseen before his marriage. As if unconsciously competing with him, she would flirt and provoke his jealousy, and get jealous in turn herself. In the fall of 1832, Pushkin wrote to her from Moscow, where he was being honored:

> I respond to your accusations point by point. 1) A Russian traveler on a road never changes clothes, but once he gets where he was going, piggish as a pig, goes straight to the bath-house, which is to us our second mother. Don't you know this? 2) The post office in Moscow accepts letters only until 12 and I only crossed Tverskaya Gate just after 11, so I put off writing till the next day. Can you see now that you're wrong? Wrong because (1) you've filled your head with all kinds of nonsense (2) out of pique you've sent off Count Benckendorf's (probably important) packet for me off to Lord only knows where and (3) you're flirting with the entire diplomatic corps—and now complaining to boot! ...As for me, I have nothing to write about. Without you I'm so bored, so bored, that I don't know what to do with myself...Goodbye, my angel, I kiss you and Masha.

Although Natalya bore Pushkin four children, and was grateful to him for bringing her into society, she had little interest in his world of ideas and literature, and seems to have had little appreciation or even inkling of her husband's talent. She was bored when he secluded himself to write, or read poetry with his friends. Alexandra Smirnova claimed she heard Natalya say at one reading: "Lord, Pushkin, I'm sick of you and your poems!" Lev Pavlishchev, Pushkin's brother-in-law, recalled being present at another reading and hearing Natalya say: "Go ahead, read, I'm not listening." One night Pushkin woke excited: verses had come to him in a dream. Natalya rebuked him: "nights are for sleeping." As the great Pushkin scholar Valentin Nepomnyashchy notes, soon after marriage, Pushkin stopped writing love lyrics.

There may have been a subconscious competitive aspect to their relationship (in Sollogub's phrase "her dazzling beauty against his magic name"); in response to his literary fame, somehow it seemed imperative to her to triumph in society, to have fancy gowns and hats and carriages, to be the "first beauty" of St. Petersburg. By 1833, Pushkin was writing his friend Nashchokin: "Life here in Petersburg is so-so. Money woes keep me from relaxing. I lack my old freedom, so necessary for writing. I spin about in society, where my wife's a big hit. But that requires money; money comes from work, and my work requires seclusion."

In 1833 *Eugene Onegin* was published for the first time, and Pushkin's second child Alexander was born. Flushed from Onegin's success, Pushkin decided to write a historical novel about the Pugachev Rebellion. On July 30, 1833, he wrote to the acting head of the secret police requesting permission to travel to the provinces in which the rebellion had taken place: "I have devoted the last two years to historical research alone, and have not written one line of pure literature. I need about two months of complete seclusion to relax from my duties and finish research for a book I began long ago, which will bring me the funds I so need." The request was granted; Pushkin made the laborious trip to Kazan, Simbirsk, Orenburg, and the Ural provinces where the rebellion had begun and took copious notes. On his way home he stopped in Boldino to write his impressions, but got scared at the bad omen of seeing a priest while riding onto his estate. From his startled letter home one can guess what kind of "bad luck" was on his mind when he saw that priest:

> This isn't just coincidence. Watch out, dear wife. Soon you may grow spoiled without me, forget me, and flirt too much. All hope lies in God and your Auntie. May they keep you from frivolous temptations. I'm proud to report for my part being pure before you as a newborn babe. All trip long I chased only 70 and 80 year old maids, and as for slutty young 60 year olds—I didn't even spare them a glance. In a village where Pugachev spent 6 months I found a 75 year old Cossack woman who remembers those days just like you and I remember 1830...

Pushkin's second "Boldino Autumn" was again a phenomenal burst of creativity. He wrote his *History of the Pugachev Rebellion*, two verse fairy tales, *The Fisherman and the Little Goldfish* and *The Dead Princess and the Seven Knights*, and over fifteen poems, including *Autumn*, a sublime meditation on nature and its relationship to creativity, and also two long narrative poems. One, *Angelo*, which he later called "my finest work ever" was based on *Measure for Measure*, Pushkin's favorite Shakespeare play (scenes of which Pushkin also translated into Russian). A longer narrative poem, *The Bronze Horseman*, relates how a poor obscure clerk in St. Petersburg loses his home and fiancée in the great flood of November 7, 1824, and comes, bereft and grief-stricken, to confront the statue in Senate Square of "The Bronze Horseman," Peter the Great. Peter has killed his love and ruined his life by building his splendid capital on the banks of the flood-prone Neva, heedless of the cost in human suffering. The clerk threatens the statue: "just you wait!" At that, the Horseman leaves his pedestal to chase the clerk, who flees, and dies a madman, on an outcast island at the mouth of the Neva. *The Bronze Horseman* is both a paean of love for the city of St. Petersburg, and yet a condemnation of the cruelty of Russian state, personified in the poem by the Janus-like figure, ever larger than life, of Tsar Peter the Great. The theme of lost love again stirs profound meditation, subtly ambivalent in its view of the nature of power and its relationship to individual freedom and fate.

Fate and freedom were themes of yet another masterpiece written in that Boldino Autumn of 1833. *The Queen of Spades* was a page-turner, a search for the no-risk risk, a gambling tale (and a ghost story), a romantic intrigue, and a playful, almost satirical examination of the conflicts between the natural versus the supernatural, risk and certainty, free will and personal responsibility, fate, mercy, and madness. Though Pushkin himself loved gambling at cards, in this story he transformed his own unhappy experiences as an inveterate gambler into something at once lighter and more profound. The gambling plot at its core becomes a powerful metaphor for the game of life itself, for the self-destructiveness of ruthless ambition. In Dostoyevsky's words, it is "the height of artistic perfection" (and a major influence on Dostoyevsky's own great works *The Gambler* and *Crime and Punishment*). It has been said that old Princess Golitsyna was Pushkin's model for the tyrannical Countess who possesses the fateful secret of the cards. Others see, in the Countess' caprices, portraits of Natalya's aunt—or mother. Are there clues to Pushkin's sympathy for his wife in his depiction of the heroine Lizaveta Ivanovna, so bitterly oppressed by her relative?

> Countess *** was not, of course, evil-hearted. Yet she was capricious, like a woman spoiled by society and grown mean and stingy, sunk into a cold selfishness, like all old people who have used up what store of love they had in the past and remain alien to the present. She took part in every frivolity of the *beau monde*, dragging herself to balls, where she'd sit in a corner, powdered and rigged up *à l'ancien régime*, a hideous yet indispensable ornament of the ballroom. Arriving guests would bow low to her, in homage to an established rite; then no one bothered with her further. She received the entire town in her own home, where she practiced rigorous etiquette, being unable to recognize anyone at all. Her numerous servants, grown fat and grey in the palace foyer and maid's quarters, did whatever they wanted, constantly robbing their dying old lady every way they could. Lizaveta Ivanovna was the martyr of the house. If she poured tea, she got a scolding for her excessive consumption of sugar. If she read aloud, she was blamed for all the mistakes of the author. In accompanying the Countess on her walks, she was held responsible for the weather and the state of the sidewalk. She had a

salary which was hardly ever paid, and yet it was expected of her that she dress like "everyone," meaning like very few indeed. All knew her, but none saw her. At the balls she only got to dance when a pair could not be found. Ladies grabbed her arm and dragged her off into the toilet anytime they needed to adjust their gowns. She was proud and keenly felt her humiliation, looking around impatiently, awaiting her savior. But young suitors, calculating in their flippant vanity, paid her no heed, even though she was a hundred times dearer than the brazen and cold brides round whom they fluttered. How often had she fled the soporific splendor of the ballroom to weep her eyes out in her shabby little room, with its painted wallpaper screen, commode, small mirror, painted bed, and cheap tallow candle sputtering darkly in its little brass candle-holder!

Alas, by the epilogue of *The Queen of Spades* Lizaveta Ivanovna seems transformed into just the kind of person her Countess was. (Only in Tchaikovsky's opera does she leap into the icy Neva to drown herself: either Tchaikovsky preferred the "*pathétique*" or ambiguous irony is not a grand operatic emotion). And just as Pushkin's creative genius poured forth in Boldino, Natalya, shy and naïve no longer, was writing him, boasting how she had conquered all men's hearts — including the Tsar's. On October 11, 1833 Pushkin wrote back: "Don't scare me, stay healthy, look after the kids, and don't flirt with the Tsar." Three weeks later, he paused from *The Bronze Horseman* to write home:

Yesterday, my friend, I got two letters from you. Thanks, but I want to scold you a bit...You appear to have been flirting way too much...You love it when men run after you like mutts after a bitch, with their tails in the air, sniffing her you-know-where! Is this something to joy in?... It's easy to train bachelor layabouts to chase you; just let them know you're that way inclined. That's the whole idea of flirting. Where there's a trough there are pigs. Why must you allow these men to court you? I kiss you my angel, as though nothing were wrong, and am grateful to you for such honest detailed descriptions of your life of decadence. Well, have fun, dear wife, but not too much, and don't forget me...Tell me how you look at these balls, now that the season, as you write, has started. But please, my angel, do not flirt. I am not jealous, and I know you would never get involved in anything serious. Yet you know how I can't stand anything that smacks of the typical Moscow girl, anything not *comme il faut*, anything *vulgar*...[in English, J.L.] If I find when I come back that your dear, soft, simple, aristocratic manner has changed, I'll divorce you, by Christ, and go be a soldier from grief!

Pushkin came back to St. Petersburg in the wee hours of November 21, 1833; Natalia was out—at a ball. He found her parked carriage, hid in it, and sent a servant to find her, saying only that there was an emergency at home. When she did not come at once (being engaged for the mazurka) Pushkin fumed and fretted. At last, in a sumptuous pink dress, she got into her carriage and "I took her home as a hussar kidnaps a provincial missy from the mayor's wife's birthday party."

His spiritual equanimity, so restored by Boldino, was soon dashed again by two severe blows. First the censors forbade publication of *The Bronze Horseman* (it was only fully printed after 1917). Worse, on the eve of the New Year of 1834, Pushkin was appointed to the post of Imperial Chamber-Page "which is rather indecent to my age" [generally pages were teenagers], "but the Court wanted Natalya to dance at Anichkov Palace" [the Tsar's private residence]. This meant that Pushkin and his wife were now invited to court functions— to his wife's delight, and to his own despair. He loathed his page-boy uniform, and at the balls Natalya's ball-gowns and popularity were ruinous to his pocket and peace of mind alike. He began to gamble again, and run up gaming debts, (having abstained after marriage for three years, though he had once told the English traveler Thomas Raikes "I would rather die than not play cards.") By March 1834 "my *Queen of Spades* is all the rage now; everyone bets on nothing but three, seven, and ace!"

Yet cards were hardly consolation for his wife's being queen of all ballrooms while he sulked in a corner in his flunkey's costume. He hated the costume so much that he once attended a court ceremony in simple evening dress, for which he got an official scolding. The humiliation was galling. In his diary he fumed: "I am willing to be a subject, even a slave, but I will not be a flunkey or a fool even before the Tsar of Heaven!...These balls and amusements will cost the state half a million. What of all our poor people dying of hunger? Whatever will they think?... Our sovereign has in him a great deal of second lieutenant, and only just a wee bit of Peter the Great..."

Tsar Nicholas I   Pushkin as an Eastern flunkey

By 1834 Natalya was dancing in the Anichkov Palace twice a day, at noon and again at eight in the evening. Gogol fretted for his friend and mentor: "one only ever sees Pushkin at balls anymore. His whole life will be wasted this way, unless by good luck he can return to the country." But he could not leave his work and researches in the Archives. Nonetheless, frightened by rumors that Natalya was having an affair with the Tsar, he sent her and the children to summer in the country, at the Goncharov family estate near Moscow[2]. The anguish he was feeling in the year 1834 and the desire to escape this "piggish Petersburg" can be clearly felt in the poem "*It's time, my friend, it's time! For peace the heart is calling.*" The relief he felt at extracting his wife to the country may be part of "*In mournful storms I have become a man,*" also written at this time.

The usual surveillance and perlustration of his letters intensified. One of his letters to his wife was opened and passed along to the Tsar to read. In it, the poet had written: "I've seen three Tsars. The first [Paul I] commanded me to remove my baby cap, and scolded my nanny about it. The second [Alexander I] didn't like me at all. The third at least made me a pageboy in my old age, but I've no wish to see a fourth. Leave well enough alone."

This letter provoked an official warning against *lèse-majesté* (disdain or disrespect for the Sovereign). As he wrote in his diary: "What a profound lack of any conscience or morals underpins our entire government! Police open a husband's private letters to his wife and bring them to the Tsar. And the Tsar (a well-brought up and honest man) has no shame in admitting it!"

But Pushkin was not intimidated. Clearly understanding that his letters would be read, he wrote frankly to his wife about what he thought of his tormentors. And, in spite of everything, again, as in *October 19th,* the unforgiven poet forgave the unforgiving Tsar:

---

2. Did Natalya had an affair with the Tsar at this time? This is hotly disputed. Noted Pushkin scholar Mikhail Tsyavlovsky belives she did, though most biographers conclude she didn't. In her memoirs, A.P. Arapova, Natalya's daughter by her second marriage, hinted unsubtly that she was born of a liaison between her mother and the Tsar long after Pushkin's death. But was this just "social climbing" on Arapova's part? Scholars do not take Arapova seriously. Who knows—or cares? What matters to us is that Pushkin's fears about the Tsar's intentions were not at all unjustified, for Nicholas I was indeed a notorious womanizer (Chapter XV of Tolstoy's *Khadji-Murat* depicts the Tsar trying to seduce a lady in a little ante-chamber of the Winter Palace kept just for this purpose).

It's been so very long now you haven't written me, that, even though I don't like to worry myself about trifles, I worry...Are the kids in good health? And you? I've not written either: I was furious. Not at you, but at *the others*. One of my letters ended up in the police and so on...No one should know what goes on between us; no one should be allowed into our bedroom. Without privacy there is no family life...but swinishness in anyone has long since ceased to surprise me. Yet that swinishness has quite chilled my pen in writing you. The thought that we are being snooped on enrages me. I can live without political freedom, but without the inviolability of the family it is impossible. To be a convict laborer is far preferable. All that's not written for you. For you: how are the mineral baths? Helping? Does Masha have new teeth?

...Be healthy, clever, charming, don't ride any more wild horses, look after the kids, and make sure their nanny does too, and write me more often...my *Peter the Great* is coming along; by winter, Volume I may be done. As for *him*, [the Tsar] I have stopped being angry, because, upon reflection, *he* is not really to blame for all the filth surrounding him. If you live in an outhouse, you get used to the shit, whether you like it or not; after a while it doesn't even stink anymore, never mind if you're a gentleman. Ah, but if only I could escape to the fresh air!

In the summer of 1834 Pushkin formally requested that the Tsar relieve him of any official duties and allowed to retire to the country. But it was all in vain; Natalya was adamant against his plan, and the Tsar threatened to revoke his access to the State Archives, with his history of Peter the Great still in progress. He was obliged to retract his request and surveillance on him increased even more. About this time Pushkin wrote "*May God forbid I go insane.*"

Granted leave to visit Boldino briefly, he went again hoping for another miraculous autumn. But sadness so consumed him that he could not write. On September 25, 1834, he wrote Natalya: "I've been in the country for more than two weeks now, and there's still no letter from you. I'm bored, my angel. And poems no longer come into my head, and I can't re-write my novel. So I re-read Walter Scott and the Bible, and pine all the time for you. I don't think I'll stay long in Boldino this fall." The "novel" he was writing was *The Captain's Daughter*, which would take him until October 1836 to finish. In this last stay in Boldino, Pushkin wrote just the charming verse fairy tale *The Golden Cockerel*, based on *The Legend of the Arabian Astrologer* from

Washington Irving's Tales of the Alhambra. *The Golden Cockerel* is an almost existential portrayal of the corrupting effects of power, greed, and lust, and yet its tale of a magic gift, which Man turns into a curse, is executed so light-heartedly that even the Tsar permitted publication, censoring as "*lèse-majésté*" only the Cockerel's refrain:

"Kiri-ku-ku," the Cockerel cried,
"Rule, while lying on your side!"

The Golden Cockerel

Emelyan Pugachev, leader of the so-called Pugachev Rebellion

Finances continued to worsen when he got back to Petersburg. Natalya, over Pushkin's objections, decided to bring her two older sisters, Yekaterina and Alexandra, to come and live with her and be brought out in society. This forced Pushkin to move into a bigger, more expensive apartment. And now to that interminable round of balls, receptions, and parties which made up their lives in St. Petersburg, Pushkin found himself escorting not just one woman — but three. Pushkin remarked mournfully: "I thought my expenses would triple because of this — and what do you know? They increased tenfold."

He had placed great hopes to recoup his finances on his *History of the Pugachev Rebellion*, which came out in December 1834. Unfortunately, the very politicized Russian readership was not ready for Pushkin's neutral historical perspective. Liberal reviewers panned its frank recounting of the vicious, arbitrary lawlessness of the rebellion, and its unromantic portraits of the rebel leader Pugachev as an arbitrary bloodthirsty, power-mad brigand, not some idealistic hero struggling against Tsarist oppression. But conservatives, led by Sergey Uvarov, Minister of Education, were even more outraged. To them the book bordered on subversion in its honest evaluation of the cruelty and inefficiency on the part of the government which had not only led to the rebellion in the first place, but made it very hard to suppress. (On the basis of this history, Pushkin wrote his prose masterpiece, the novel *The Captain's Daughter*). Pushkin's diary contains this note on Uvarov's meteoric career: "Began as pimp, rose to babysitter for the Finance Minister's kids...now suddenly he's President of the Academy of Sciences." But Pushkin's poems and quips on Uvarov's notorious corruption created a powerful new enemy: suddenly his travelogue *A Journey to Arzurum* was delayed in censorship, as was a second edition of the *Tales of Belkin*. Meanwhile, he had lost any peace in his home, now consumed by the social whirl of his wife and two sisters. In January 1835 Pushkin's ailing mother remarked sadly:

> Natalie's out dancing every single day. Yesterday we had a family reunion here with all the kids. She and her sisters talk but of feasts, balls, and spectacles. Little Masha is so used to seeing only luxuriously dressed people that when she saw me, she began to cry. We asked her why she didn't want to kiss Grandma, and she said: "her hat's old, and her dress is shabby."

In May 1835, a son, Grigory was born: the family kept growing. "But I earn my income from the 33 letters of the Russian alphabet, nothing else." And the increasingly arduous process of censorship was making it impossible for him to work. Frustrated by the length of time it took other journals to get his works through the four separate layers of censorship required for publishing his works, he asked permission to start his own literary review; the request was denied. Four years of married life in the capital had plunged him over 60,000 rubles in debt. Desperately, he renewed his request to be allowed to move to the country for a few years, writing Count Benckendorf on June 1, 1835:

> I have no fortune; neither I nor my wife received any legacies. Till now I have lived through my works. My only constant income is the salary the Emperor has deigned to grant me. There's nothing humiliating to me about working for my daily bread. Yet, used as I am to independence, I am completely unable to write something just for money. The mere thought of this completely shuts me down. Life here in St. Petersburg is frightfully expensive. I am faced now by the need to do away with the expenses it entails, which drag me into debt and set up further worries and troubles—and perhaps poverty and despair. Yet three or four years of seclusion in the country would give me a chance to recover, and then return to Petersburg to resume the duties for which I am indebted to His Majesty.

But the Tsar enjoyed having Natalya at his balls, and Count Benckendorf wanted Pushkin under close surveillance. Knowing how Pushkin valued his historical research, they stipulated that if he moved, he would not just lose his salary, but all access for good to the State Archives. At last the Tsar consented to give Pushkin a loan of 30,000 rubles, to be paid for by suspension of his salary for the next six years. But that loan was still not enough; it vanished at once on urgent old debts, and—even more urgent— new debts. (Each of Natalya's new hats cost about 250 rubles apiece). In the fall of 1835, the Tsar gave him leave to go back briefly to Mikhailovskoye to finish *The Captain's Daughter*. From there he wrote Natalya:

> You can't imagine how lively the imagination becomes here, sitting all alone, or walking in the woods, where no one stops you from thinking, thinking—thinking till one's head spins. But what am I thinking of? Here's what: how are we going to live? Father won't give me this estate, besides, he's squandered near half of it away already. Your family property is a hair's breadth from total ruin. The Tsar won't let me move to the country or be a journalist. To sell out and write what I'm told just for money —as God is my witness—I cannot do that. We haven't a penny of stable income left, with stable expenses of at least 30,000...What will come of all this, Lord only knows. For now, it's sad. But just kiss me, and maybe the grief will pass...If possible, could you please send me Montaigne's *Essays*? The four blue volumes on the long bookcase. Please find them...The weather is very cloudy...I walk a lot, and ride a lot as well, on some old nags who are very happy about this, because they get oats afterwards, which they weren't treated to before...I kiss you, my own dear soul, and all the kids, and bless you with all my heart.

Yet all that "thinking, thinking, thinking" was beginning to weigh on him, and a few days later he wrote home again:

> I've found everything in Mikhailovskoye the same as always, except my nanny is here no more. And in my absence, next to my old friends, the ancient pines, a new family of young evergreens has sprung up, which sight saddens me — just as I'm sad to see dashing young guardsmen at all those balls where I no longer dance.

These observations form part of his haunting elegy "*I came back again*" written that day, walking around Mikhailovskoye:

>   ...I came back again
> To that small plot of land, where once I spent
> Two years living in exile and unnoticed.
> By now ten years have passed since then, and many
> Have been the changes coming to my life.
> I too, to universal law submissive,
> Have changed myself, but, once more here,
> All of my past embraces me with vigor,
> And so it seems but yesterday I walked
> In these groves, wand'ring.
>   ...Here the forlorn cottage,
> Where with my poor old nanny I did live.
> The dear old lady's gone—beyond the wall now
> I cannot hear her footsteps heavy trooping,
> Nor her devoted, always-caring snooping.
> And here's the wooded hillock, on which often
> I used to sit, not moving, and look down
> Into the lake, remembering with sadness
> The look of other waves, of other shorelines....

In this elegy (whose blank-versed freedom marked a watershed in Russian poetry), Pushkin transcended his sadness and rose above thoughts of his own death, hailing, albeit wistfully, nature's eternal promise and life itself renewed through future generations:

> But now a new young grove is growing up,
> A family of green, its bushes thickening,
> Sheltering beneath like children. Further off,
> Their brooding gloomy friend is still there, standing
> Like some old bachelor, and all around
> Him still all is deserted...

> Greetings, youngsters!
> So young, and so unknown to me. I won't
> Be blessed to see your greening growth in fullness,
> When you outgrow and pass my old companions
> And hide their ancient heads with your new boughs
> From sight to passersby. But one day may
> My grandson hear your greetings whispered soft
> When riding back from chatting at a friend's house,
> Filled in his heart with happy, pleasant musings,
> And, passing by your shade in gloom of nighttime,
> Then think of me, remembering.

New griefs mounted back in St. Petersburg. One of those "dashing young guardsmen at balls, where I no longer dance" was a tall, blond, handsome Frenchman named Georges D'Anthès. A partisan of Charles X who fled France after the July Revolution of 1830, D'Anthès had been inducted in the Russian Imperial Horse Guards (earning, in his brief service to the Tsar, 44 separate reprimands for conduct unbecoming). D'Anthès was the live-in "toyboy" of Baron Heckeren, the Dutch ambassador to Russia. Heckeren adopted" D'Anthès as his "son" when the "boy" turned 24 (although the adoption had not been recognized by the Dutch government). There are many indications of a secret homosexual relationship between D'Anthès and Heeckeren, including a passionate correspondence between them. Yet D'Anthès was also a renowned lady-killer, a flashy hussar playboy, a dandy fond of dancing, a foppish rake, a fashionable roué. His breezy charm, good looks, and the inestimable *cachet* of being a French nobleman in a society of Gallomanes, made him all the rage at court balls — in a way Pushkin could never hope to be. And besides being popular, D'Anthès was rolling in his "father's" money. In short, he was the antithesis of Pushkin, and the ideal suitor "Madame Kars" (Natalya's mother, Natalya Ivanovna Goncharova) would have wanted for her daughter. Little wonder, then, that he quite turned Natalya's head (and the heads of her two sisters as well).

By late 1835 D'Anthès lusted for the ultimate society triumph: to seduce and conquer the first beauty in St. Petersburg: "Natalie" Pushkina. That she was the wife of the "sunshine of Russian poetry" concerned him not at all. He knew (and needed) no Russian — save a few simple drill commands (and curses). Even his French was mediocre: he had read nothing, and the Muses were Greek to him. Yet D'Anthès later claimed that he had taken his Natalie's heart by siege, by constantly declaring her his soulmate...And perhaps she was. At any rate, she believed him, or at least was flattered to see D'Anthès woo her, almost, one might say, with the passion of Onegin wooing Tatyana at the end of *Eugene Onegin*. As Juliet frets to Romeo (Act II, sc. ii, 92-93) : "At lover's perjuries they say Jove laughs"... By January 20, 1836, D'Anthès wrote Baron Heckeren to say that he loved Natalya, and "she loves me too, but we cannot see each other, for the husband is revoltingly jealous." Did Natalya in fact become D'Anthès' mistress? Many years later in Paris, this question was put to D'Anthès by Pushkin's friend Sobolevsky. D'Anthès replied: "Of course, it goes without saying." Was this mere hussar boasting? Whatever the true extent of their relationship, what matters to our story is that Natalya did not trouble to conceal from her husband her delight in openly flirting with her handsome Guardsman.

She did this even as Pushkin's mother, Nadyezhda Osipovna Pushkina, was dying. Pushkin's old friend from Mikhalovskoye, Zizi remembered: "Pushkin was always extraordinarily attached to and fond of his mother, even though she plainly preferred her younger son to him. But in the last year of her life, Alexander Sergeyevich looked after her with such tender care and affection that she at last recognized her former unfairness to him, and begged his forgiveness, confessing sadly that she had never been capable of appreciating him." Anna Kern (who remained a faithful friend of the family) remembered in her memoirs:

> I saw him one last time with his wife at his mother's house, not long before her death; she was too weak to get out of bed anymore, and was just lying on a cot moved to the middle of the room, facing the windows. They sat by her on a little couch, and Nadyezhda Osipovna just looked at them tenderly with love. Alexander Sergeyevich returned her gaze while holding in one hand the soft end of his wife's elegant fur boa, with which he gently stroked his mother, as if expressing, in that one gesture, all his love and tenderness at once for both his mother and his wife. All the while he could not speak a word. Natalya Nikolayevna's hair was in curlers. She was getting herself ready for a ball.

Pushkin's mother died on March 29, 1836. Riding all by himself through 250 miles of roads turned into quagmires by the spring thaw, he drove her coffin to the Gannibal family burial plot, by Mikhailovskoye, in Svyatogorsky Monastery. After burying her, he paid the monastery in advance for his own grave — right by hers. To Zizi he "lamented with exceptional distress how cruel Fate had been to him once again, giving him so little time to feel maternal tenderness which he had never in his life known before. And when he got back to St. Petersburg, the gossips were spreading malicious stories that he had laughed all through his mother's funeral."

Meanwhile, the Tsar had finally given Pushkin permission to publish his own quarterly journal, *The Contemporary* (under tough censorship). In April 1836 the first issue came out featuring *A Journey to Arzurum* and several Pushkin poems, as well as the first publication of Gogol's *The Nose*. Unfortunately, circulation was poor, and reviews (by enemies, chiefly Bulgarin and Uvarov) were vicious. The entire year of 1836 was financially disastrous for Pushkin. *The Contemporary* was struggling to survive and gain circulation. Virtually no income remained to support four children (a daughter was born May 27, 1836) his wife and her two sisters (in attendance at three balls per week), and his own younger brother. He was forced to fawn to pawnbrokers and visit moneylenders; to borrow from Peter to pay Paul... Though handsome new publishing contracts for future years promised relief, in 1836 things got so bad that he very nearly had to give up buying books!

But perhaps biographers care more about the poet's bleak finances than he did himself. We should remember that it was a fairly normal, even stylish, habit of the Russian aristocracy to live for years on debt, as described in *Eugene Onegin* I, iii: "By serving honestly and nobly/His father lived, from debt to debt." And even though Pushkin could be quite unsentimental about money (he once quipped "I write for the same reason that the singer sings, the baker bakes, and the quack kills — for money"), there was always a part of him that had remained as carefree about finances as the youth who cast a gold coin in a canal just to admire its gleam underwater. He knew that what he wrote might well not get past the four separate layers of censorship to which his work was subjected, and thus end up forbidden. Yet to him beauty and artistic integrity were far, far more important than profit. He could always find happiness in himself as long as he was "filled with the silent Muse" (*"By lands where sovereignty of golden Venice rules"*).

What made 1836 the bitterest year of his life was unquestionably loneliness. In his grief at the death of his mother, at his increasing loss of freedom, he missed more than ever his true Lycéen friends, like Pushchin or Küchelbecker, exiled to Siberia — or Delvig. ("No one was closer to me than Delvig: with him I could speak of what wracks the soul and pangs the heart"). By the end of 1836, he was forbidden to read his work aloud to friends even in the privacy of his own home. His letters kept being opened, and his every movement watched. He complained: "spies to us are like our letter "ъ" [a silent letter at the end of any word ending in a consonant until post-Revolutionary spelling reforms]. They are soundless, useless—and ubiquitous."

While Pushkin was finding no one with whom to assuage the grief and jealousy gnawing at his heart, D'Anthès was finding "Natalie" in every ballroom in town. Natalya seems not to have noticed that, in the finest hussar traditions, D'Anthès was wooing her, her own sister Yekaterina, Princess Baratinskaya— and not neglecting his "Daddy" either!

In the summer of 1836, after a post-natal illness, Natalya rented an expensive summer house — or *dacha*, as the Russians call it– for the family in Kamenniy Ostrov, a fashionable suburb of St. Petersburg (D'Anthès' regiment had been posted nearby). Every day "Natalie" and D'Anthès (and sister "Catherine") went out horseback riding together. Pushkin stayed in the *dacha*, writing brooding poems on death, the soul, and his own poetic legacy, including "*In vain I seek to flee to Zion's heights*," "*Our hermit fathers and our nuns blessed and blameless,*" "*When past the city gates with wistful thoughts I roam,*" *From Pindemonti*, and *Exegi Monumentum*. This so-called "Kamenniy Ostrov Cycle" reaches, perhaps, the very summit of the great Russian poetic legacy. In the *dacha*, Pushkin also finished *The Captain's Daughter*, printed in the December 1836 issue of *The Contemporary*. Many Russian critics consider it the finest novel ever written in their language. Its gripping plot and themes of coming of age and love amidst rebellion, civil war, imprisonment, treachery, death, and yet compassion combined to make it an instant classic, selling out that issue of *The Contemporary* almost at once. In the novel, Pushkin warned prophetically: "God forbid an uprising in Russia. It will be pointless — and pitiless." The critic Belinsky called the novel "a miracle of artistic perfection," and no less a genius than Gogol wrote: "compared to *The Captain's Daughter* all our other novels and short stories are like watery gruel. Its purity and poetic restraint attain such heights that reality itself seems an artificial caricature by comparison."

Yet his woes blocked him from finishing yet another extraordinary work, which he had begun the previous year in Mikhaylovskoye. *Egyptian Nights* is an enchantingly intricate fabric of poetry and prose, mixing cynical Russian reality and Italian Renaissance ideals, and treating clearly autobiographical themes of a poet's struggle to keep his freedom amidst the emnity of authority and high society. The novel's poetic improvisations (*"The poet walks...his eyes are open"*) link poetry with the nature of love itself, its utter self-sacrifice, its predatory, voluptuous sexuality, its inexplicable magic and power personfied by the cruel yet sublime, life-consuming and yet majestic figure of Egypt's fabled harlot queen, Cleopatra:

> In passion's auction who'll start vying?
> I sell my love, so speak, be free!
> Which one of you dares to be buying—
> Paid with your life — one night with me?

October 19, 1836, was the 25th anniversary of the founding of the Lycée. Pushkin, who saw himself as a a chronicler of the Lycée had that morning begun a poem for the occasion, promising to read it at the traditional festive dinner party. He began to read:

> There was a time our youthful holiday
> Just shined, made noise, when roses crowned our hymning,
> When goblets' clinking merged into our singing,
> We sat together tight in warm affray.
> Back then we all were carefree as a novice,
> We all lived much more lightly, boldly, then,
> We all did drink to hope, did lift our chalice
> To youth itself, and all youth comprehends.
> That's over now: we're tamed when we carouse.
> With passing time, our feast no more is furious.
> We've compromised, grown still, become more serious,
> More hollow now our clinking healths do sound.
> Our speech is much less playful now and daring:
> With more space midst us, sadder now we sit,
> Amidst our singing, laughter now is rarer;
> We sigh more often, hushed in gloomy fit.

As he was reading, Pavel Annenkov relates, "tears welled up in his eyes and he began to sob. He put down his paper and withdrew quietly to a couch in the corner of the room. A friend picked up the paper and read the next six stanzas for him." Earlier that same day, he had just finished *The Captain's Daughter* and dated it "October 19, 1836." That very day, Pushkin had also drafted a letter to his old friend, Pyotr Chaadayev, responding to Chaadayev's "indictment of Russia," or *Philosophical Letter,* which attacked Russia's autocracy, serfdom, corrupt servility before brute power, and lack of any civil society; Chaadayev blamed these ills on Russia's Orthodox faith and Byzantine heritage. The very idea of writing Chaadayev (who was promptly declared insane, and placed under strict house arrest) was frightfully risky. Yet true discourse with his friend was more important:

> Thanks for the pamphlet you sent me. I read it with great pleasure, though I am amazed to see it translated and printed. I am far from agreeing with you entirely. Certainly the Schism of the Church separated us from the rest of Europe and we were left out of many of the grand events that followed. Yet we have had our own mission. It was Russia with its endless spaces that swallowed up the Mongol invaders; they were not able to pass our Western borders, leaving us dangerously in their rear. And so they withdrew to their desolate steppes; Western civilization was saved…We have been forced to develop a separate existence, which, even while we remained Christians, nonetheless made us strangers to the rest of Christendom. Still it was by our sufferings that Catholic Europe was able to develop energetically. You say that the source of our Christianity is impure, that Byzantium was contemptible. Excuse me, my friend! Who cares? Was not Jesus Christ himself a Jew? Is not Jerusalem the cradle of us all? The Russian clergy is indeed backward. Yet it has never stooped to some of the infamies of the Papist Inquisition, or provoked great wars of "reformation," exactly when mankind needed unity and brotherhood above all else. I flatly cannot agree with you that we have no history, and that our civilization is a nullity. Our history is a sad but magnificent painting…[From Kievan Rus through the Time of Troubles] is that not all history? And is Peter the Great not a universal history all by himself? What of Catherine II, who put us on the doorstep of Europe? And Tsar Alexander, who took you along with him to Paris? And put your hand on your heart: can you truly see nothing in the story of today's Russia which will one day be memorable to future historians? Although personally I am loyal in my heart to the Tsar, I am far from admiring all that I see around me. As a man of letters, I am harassed, embittered; as a man of principle, I am appalled. And yet I swear to you on my honor that I would not

switch my country for any other, nor switch our history, even that of our forefathers, even that which God has given us...Yet, having just contradicted you, I must say, much of what you write in your Epistle is profoundly true. It cannot be denied that the state of our civil society is simply woeful. Our absence of free public opinion, our indifference to all concepts of honor and justice and truth, our cynical contempt for ideas, for the dignity of man, for all that is not mere personal necessity — this indeed is something truly sorrowful.

From this sorrow Pushkin still longed to escape, to move to the country. But he was trapped in a gilded cage. On October 20, 1836, he wrote his father: "I had wanted to go to Mikhailovskoye, but was not able to. This will set me back by another year at least. In the country I would have gotten a lot of work done. Here I do nothing but brood." Uvarov and Bulgarin in his *Northen Bee*, which had panned even *Eugene Onegin,* renewed their onslaughts on the poet, and Zhukovsky noted: "our journalistic liars wrote that Pushkin was all washed up."

No matter where I go, there I hear slander's buzz,
And lying nonsense passing judgment,
Hear envy's whisper, vanity and fuss
Rebuking cheerfully with intent bloody.

The flirtation between Natalya and D'Anthès grew to a fever pitch, as did the mockery it aroused, and the many rumors. Allegedly, on November 2, 1836, D'Anthès lured Natalya to an assignation and threatened to kill himself unless she at once consented to become (or resume being) his mistress. There (unless she already was his mistress) she supposedly answered "you have my heart; why do you need my body?" (A sort of tawdry imitation of Tatyana's rebuff to Onegin...What in fact took place at this tryst—if there was one— we will never know for sure. But society gloated pitilessly over the wild rumors).

On November 4, 1836, Pushkin and his friends received anonymous "diplomas" in French, "certifying" Pushkin as "coadjutor to the Grand Master of the Order of Cuckolds and Historiographer of the Order." The "diplomas" implied that Pushkin had been cuckolded not by D'Anthès, but by the Tsar. Pushkin subjected them to careful forensic analysis. "From the type of paper used, the vocabulary, and the style, I immediately verified for myself that the letter is from a foreigner, a member of high society, and a diplomat"— in other words, from Baron Heckeren. Anna Akhmatova argues Pushkin was right, and that he even proved his case to Count Benckendorf and the Tsar. Baron Heckeren genuinely hated Pushkin on behalf of his "son"; yet perhaps he was no less jealous than Pushkin of a relationship that was taking his "son" away from him. Akhmatova argues forcefully that the letters were Heckeren's "blind." Unable to challenge the Tsar to a duel, Pushkin would have to move away with his family, or at least send his wife away, thereby ending Natalya's relationship to D'Anthès, who would be left to be consoled by his "father." Other scholars believe that the "diplomas" were not from Heckeren, who could not, they argue, risk a scandal. (Others rejoin that this is precisely why the letters were anonymous). Still others say the letters were just a prank. Yet whoever wrote them had for taken a grave risk, impeaching the honor not just of Russia's national poet, but of two Sovereigns (the "diplomas" referred to Prince Naryshkin, who had been cuckolded by Alexander I, again clearly implying that it was Nicholas I who had cuckolded Pushkin). Such risks could only be run either by someone with an extremely high rank in the government or with diplomatic immunity. Different "diplomas" were in different handwritings, so it may well have been a conspiracy. Many years later, in a private dinner at the Winter Palace, Tsar Alexander II said that the diplomas were authored by the man who had once written the order for Pushkin's exile to Mikhalovskoye twelve years back, Count Nesselrode, Russia's Foreign Minister—and also Baron Heckeren's best friend in St. Petersburg.

That same evening, November 4, 1836, Pushkin showed his "diploma" to Natalya, which, it seems, prompted her to tell her husband her rather doubtful version of the supposed tryst of November 2nd, according to which she had behaved with exemplary modesty, while D'Anthès was little more than a stalker. Yet Pushkin found that she had various love notes and letters from D'Anthès...and as he read them, he realized she had accepted them, and kept them...

Enraged, the poet immediately challenged D'Anthès to a duel. The next morning, November 5th, Baron Heckeren promptly visited Pushkin, accepted the challenge on behalf of his "son," but requested a two- week extension to inquire as to the circumstances. During the interim, a duel was avoided. To the utter amazement of everyone in St. Petersburg society, D'Anthès' announced his engagement to Yekaterina Goncharova, Natalya's sister (it seems Pushkin learned Yekaterina was pregnant by D'Anthès, which has recently been proven by unearthed–and very earthy– correspondence between D'Anthès and Yekaterina). Under these circumstances,

Pushkin reluctantly withdrew his challenge, on condition, however, that D'Anthès stay completely away from his home and from Natalya, and never expect either of them to socialize with the newlyweds. In vain: "my wife and her sisters do nothing but fuss over the dowry; it keeps them busy and completely engulfs them, but they enrage me, as they have turned my home into a fashionable dress shop." On January 10, 1837, D'Anthès and Yekaterina were married. Brooding, Pushkin yet managed to quip that he was curious what nationality his sister-in-law should by rights now claim: French, Dutch, or Russian!

Yet D'Anthès carried on with Natalya as always, finding her at every ball in town, ostentatiously casting "longing looks" at her, as she in turned blushed, and cast her eyes down coyly...Even in Pushkin's presence, they danced together. Worse, in Pushkin's hearing, D'Anthès dropped sexual innuendoes about Natalya for all to hear. Malicious rumors spread throughout St. Petersburg that D'Anthès had married Yekaterina solely in order to save Natalya's honor, while, in fact, D'Anthès was doing everything he could to compromise it further. Pushkin could bear no more. On January 25, 1837, he wrote Baron Heckeren a letter which he knew would be certain to provoke a challenge:

> I have long known the conduct of your son and could not remain indifferent to it. I was content to play observer, ready to intervene when I judged it meet. An incident, which in all other cases would have been very disagreeable, happily rescued me from the affair. I received the anonymous letters. I saw that the time was right and I took advantage of it. You know the rest: I made your son play such a pitiable role that my wife, shocked by such cowardice and banality, could not help laughing, and the emotion that she had perhaps felt for this grand and sublime passion evaporated into the calmest contempt and most deserved disgust. I am obliged to admit, Baron, that your role has hardly been seemly. You, the representative of a sovereign crown, have been the paternal pimp for your own son. It seems his (by the way, quite inept) conduct has all been directed by you. It is you who probably dictated to him the sorry phrases and blather he tried to write. Like an obscene old woman, you've lain in wait for my wife to speak of the love of your bastard or self-styled "son" for her. While he in fact was laid up in your home with the clap, you'd tell her he was dying of love for her; you murmured: "Give me back my son!"

> You must grasp, Baron, that after all this I cannot permit my family to have the least relationship with yours. It was exactly on this condition that I consented not to follow through with this dirty affair, and not to dishonor you in the eyes of our court and yours, as I have the power and the intention to do. But I do not care for my wife to have to hear any more of your paternal exhortations. I cannot permit your "son," after his base behavior, to dare address a word to my wife, and still less will I let him subject her to barrack-room puns, and his overacted role of devoted, grand, unhappy passion when he is in fact no more than a coward and a scoundrelly roué. I am therefore obliged to ask that you put an end to all this scheming, if you wish to avoid a new scandal, from which I will certainly not retreat.

There was no getting round such words. D'Anthès's challenge came on January 26, 1837; the duel took place on the afternoon of the next day, January 27, 1837. Getting dressed to go to the duel, Pushkin did not put on his lucky talisman against violent death, a present from his close friend and patron Nashchokin. Having left his home, he stopped, turned around, and went back to get his warm bearskin coat. As the ever-superstitious poet surely knew, in Russian tradition "to turn back is bad luck" ...and yet...On his way to the duel, Pushkin's sleigh rode right past his wife's carriage (on her way back from an afternoon spent sledding). But she was near-sighted and he happened to be looking the other way, and so they missed each other — potent symbolism, perhaps, of all the problems in their relationship that had led to such a fatal calamity.

The duel between Pushkin and D'Anthès on the snowy banks of the Black River near St. Petersburg bears an eerie resemblance to the duel between the poet Lensky and Onegin in *Eugene Onegin*. Both took place on nearly the same day of the year, both duels were provoked by an affront to the poet's honor by a rake; like Tatyana and Olga, Natalya and Yekaterina were sisters. Pushkin used Lepage pistols, as in *Eugene Onegin*, VI, xxv... (D'Anthès used a German Ulbrich model: three years later the French ambassador's son would duel with another great Russian poet, Mikhail Lermontov, using the very same fateful pistol once used by the Dutch ambassador's "son" against Pushkin). One wonders what thoughts raced through the poet's mind on that fateful day. Had he not taken Mme. Kirchof's prophecy so seriously that he had stopped courting Yekaterina Ushakova — just because she was blond?

Why — precisely in his 37th year — was he getting into a duel with a blond man? According to his old friend Zizi, who saw him days before his duel, Pushkin had confided in her his desire to seek death, and his confidence that the Tsar would care for his wife and children. (He had certainly not shared these longings with the Tsar. In fact, after the first challenge in November, the Tsar had requested that Pushkin promise not to fight a duel). Zizi's account may be belied–or maybe not?–by these lines he had also written, not long before:

> Oh no, I am not tired of living,
> I love to live, I want to live!
> Not all within my soul's gone chilly,
> Although from me my youth has slipped.

One senses an internal dialogue: was the cry "Oh no" responding perhaps, to some voice inside—saying "yes"?

On the morning of his duel Pushkin seemed much happier than in a long time. All morning he was singing. Then he wrote a short letter connected to the upcoming issue of *The Contemporary*. He did not at all seem like a man planning to die (few of his friends even guessed what was going on). Yet at Pushkin's insistence the duel was fought at ten paces, nearly point-blank range ("the bloodier the better"), and he did not put on (forgot?) his turquoise ring, a "lucky talisman against violent death." D'Anthès fired first; his bullet landed where a button was missing on Pushkin's waistcoat, bursting through the abdominal cavity and shattering the sacrum. The wound was fatal. Bleeding in the snow, and unable to rise, in great pain, Pushkin nevertheless insisted on taking his shot. It glanced D'Anthès' right arm, and bounced off a button on D'Anthès' chest, knocking D'Anthès down, but no more. Thinking D'Anthès was dead, Pushkin remarked: "Strange; I thought I'd be pleased if I killed him, but now I feel I'm not."

The wounded poet was brought home and eight doctors were summoned, including Dr. Arendt, the Tsar's personal physician. All told him there was nothing they could do to save him. Pushkin thanked them, then summoned a priest, as Zhukovsky remembered, and "confessed himself and heards rites of extreme unction with great passion." Then he summoned his second, Konstantin Danzas, and dictated a list of all his debts, including those not evidenced by any writing, and signed it. Dr. Arendt returned with a note from the Tsar, urging Pushkin to "die as a Christian. Don't worry about your wife and children. I will look after them. " Pushkin asked Arendt to thank the Tsar and pass along his request for clemency for his second, his schoolmate Danzas (dueling, though quite common, was technically a serious crime in Russia). In spite of agonizing pain, and great loss of blood, he lived on for forty-six hours after the duel. In his memoirs, Dr. Arendt wrote: "I've been in thirty battles, and have seen many people 's deaths, but never saw anyone die with so much courage in the face of so much pain." Pushkin blessed his children, then Natalya, and then told her, in French: "Move to the country and mourn me for two years. Then, if you like, remarry — but not to a good-for-nothing." Waving to his bookshelf, he whispered: "Farewell, my friends!" By his side were the poet Zhukovsky, and the dictionary compiler Dal, with whom the poet joked that for the the first — and unfortunately the last — time in his life, he was permitting himself the liberty of addressing the learned doctor intimately, with *ty*, the informal second person singular pronoun, instead of the formal *Vy*.) Yet even as his apartment thronged with well-wishers, he was lonely, missing above all his old friends from the Lycée: "What a pity neither Pushchin no Malinovsky are here! It would have been easier to die." In his final moments, he asked for cloudberries; Natalya spoon-fed him cloudberry jam...

He died January 29, 1837 at 2: 45 in the afternoon. (Even the time of his death gives pause: the malevolent spirit of Countess in *The Queen of Spades* had fatefully appeared at 2:45 in the dead of night. Pushkin's benevolent spirit departed his body at 2:45 in the waning of the northern wintry afternoon).

Natalya began sobbing convulsively, hysterically crying out: "I killed my husband! I'm the reason he died!" Anna Akhmatova, with 100 years of hindsight behind her indignation, agreed: "She always did what she wanted and never cared about his feelings. She bankrupted him, denied him all peace of mind, didn't even let his dying mother into their home, yet brought her two sisters in, rented the most expensive villas and apartments, forgot his address whenever he traveled, ceaselessly related to him all her amatory victories, yet complained to D'Anthès about his jealousy. Then she made her own husband her confidant in the whole situation — which precipitated the tragedy."

Yet Pushkin himself expressed no recrimination. On the contrary, he was tender and affectionate with his wife till his final breath. He told his friends "my wife is blameless in this affair," and also refused to let them challenge Baron Heckeren and D'Anthès: "do not avenge me; I have forgiven everything." Had he simply resigned himself calmly to the fate once foretold to him? Or had death raised his consciousness to a higher level of sublime serenity? After stopping the clock, when everyone else left the room, the poet Zhukovsky stayed a while by his friend's side. He wrote Pushkin's father later:

> I sat down by him just looking at his face for a long time all alone. I never saw anything quite like his face in that first instant of death. His head was sunken slightly and his hands folded, as if resting after hard labors. Yet there was an odd expression on his face that I simply can't put into words, so new, yet so familiar; relaxed, yet neither sleeping nor resting. Not the usual wit and intelligence that always sparkled in him, nor some poetic pose. No! It was a sense of profound surprise, yet contemplation, of contentment, of some sort of all-encompassing divine, profound wisdom and light. As I kept looking at him, I wanted to ask: "What are you seeing, my friend?" What would he have said, could he only have been resurrected for an instant? I assure you that I never before saw in him such profound contentment, such majestic and triumphant joy. Of course joy had always danced before him and about him, but never was it revealed in such utter purity as in that moment when the hand of death lifted from him all earthly cares. That was the end of our Pushkin.

Pushkin's friend,
the poet Zhukovsky

Profound shock gripped the capital at the news of Pushkin's death. Thousand gathered to mourn, thousands more bought his works, in a matter of days earning his estate many times more than what it owed in debts. There was widespread outrage that a foreign favorite of the Court had murdered the national poet; many felt that the authorities who had so harassed the poet in life were responsible in some way for his death. Young Mikhail Lermontov expressed the public's fury in his *Death of a Poet* (which earned its author immediate exile):

> ...You crowd that throng our throne with greed relentless —
> Of freedom, genius, glory —killers true!
> You hide yourselves behind the law's protection,
> You hush the truth, and silence justice too.
> But there's a higher court, accomplices of evil!
> A dreaded court that waits —
> Whose judgment is quite deaf to clinking silver,
> And knows your thoughts and deeds every which way.
> Then you in vain will grasp at gossip's libel,
> No help to you from lies will come;
> Your black blood will not wash, for all your trying,
> The righteous noble poet's blood!

Gogol, more gently, wrote: "All my joy and pleasure in life vanished with him. I never again wrote a single line without seeing him in my mind standing before me, and asking myself: what would he say of this? Would he like it? Would it make him laugh?"

Another friend, the writer Nikolai Gogol

Thousands of people gathered by the poet's apartment on the Moika Canal (now Moika, 12), not far from the Winter Palace, quite alarming the Tsar and Count Benckendorf, ever vigilant against another Decembrist uprising. They reacted as always: repressively. Obituaries in the press were strictly forbidden. Only one journal, *The Literary Supplement*, dared print a headline on January 30, 1837 which read: "The sunshine of our poetry has darkened! Pushkin is dead!" Its editor was at once summoned and reprimanded personally by Benckendorf: "How dare you run a banner headline to announce the death of a civil servant of absolutely no consequence? 'Sunshine of our poetry?' Ha! What kind of position is that? Why does he deserve any honor?"

Natalya sent invitations for a funeral to be held in St. Isaac's Cathedral (then in the Admiralty, not on what is now St. Isaac's Square). But the service was cancelled, as Metropolitan Serafim, head of the Orthodox Church in St. Petersburg, refused to conduct a memorial mass (on the grounds that duelers, like suicides, were unworthy of Christian burial). The poet's body was already decaying as the Tsar intervened, granting personal permission for the use of a small imperial church right by the Winter Palace, the Konyushennaya Church, "about which," Zhukovsky recalled, "we had no right even to dream." (In Soviet times the church would be turned into a taxi garage). By holding Pushkin's funeral in an imperial church, Tsar Nicholas had effectively made paying last respects to Pushkin into an act of state. Major bureaucrats, the General Staff, and members of the diplomatic corps were invited to attend as well as all those whom Natalya had invited. Thus, the blame heaped by most historians on Tsar Nicholas I for moving the site of the funeral to a smaller church is unfair. In any case, no church in the capital could possibly have fit all the mourners who wished to pay their last respects to their beloved poet.

Still, the traditional bearing of the coffin into church was cancelled; instead, it was brought into the crypt from the poet's apartment in the wee hours of February 1, 1837, as troops blocked the streets. Prince Vyazemsky noted, "there were more gendarmes than mourners." The funeral took place on the morning of February 1, 1837. Admission was by tickets only. All teachers and students in the capital were forbidden to miss classes to attend the ceremony. Still, the police had trouble holding back the silent throngs surrounding the church in the bitter cold.

To avoid any further demonstration of popular feeling, authorities had the poet's coffin removed from the church crypt in the dead of night on February 3, 1837 and placed on a fast police sleigh to be sent for burial in Svyatogorsky Monastery, by Mikhailovskoye. All demonstrations of grief or even respect for the national poet were strictly forbidden. As the sleigh's horses were changed in a small station not far from Petersburg, the wife of the censor Nikitenko asked a peasant about the sled. "Yeah… some guy named Pushkin got killed, and, dear Lord, they're shipping his body out like a dog's, in burlap and straw!" Only two persons were allowed to accompany the coffin on the long trip: the gendarme Rakeyev, and Pushkin's old friend Alexander Turgenev, by command of the Tsar. Yet Nikita Kozlov, the poet's devoted servant from cradle to grave, stayed by the coffin ceaselessly, and "neither ate nor drank for three days from grief." The "sunshine of Russian poetry" was buried at dawn on February 6, 1837. Just two of the Osipova-Vulf sisters and a few serfs joined Turgenev and Kozlov in mourning him.

Natalya came with her children to visit her husband's grave only twice: first in 1841, when an obelisk was placed on his tomb, then finally in 1842. In 1844 she remarried General Pyotr Lanskoy. She later spent time together with D'Anthès again in the Slovakian landed estate of her older sister, Alexandra Nikolayevna Goncharova, who married the Austrian diplomat Baron Gustav Friesonhof. Natalya died on November 26, 1863 in St. Petersburg.

Russia's first monument to Pushkin (indeed, to any poet at all) was only erected in 1880, in Moscow, in an occasion for famous speeches about Russia's national bard by Dostoyevsky, Turgenev, and others. Today that monument stands in Moscow's Pushkin Square.

If you chance to be there about seven o'clock in the evening, it may seem to you that all the fretting lovers in the city are waiting by the poet's statue. Perhaps for an instant, before their dates begin, they are taking in a bit of his loving energy, his warmth, wit, passion, and intensity. Of course, there is a more prosaic explanation (his statue is directly over the hub connecting Moscow's three busiest subway lines). Yet it feels right that lovers bearing flowers should stand right by where Pushkin stands, by those central arteries, in the very heart of Moscow, the heart of Russia, the city where the poet was born and married. When his statue was moved after construction, it ended up on a little mound, his back turned (more or less) to the nearby Kremlin. It seems he pays no heed to that great seat of power; instead, he gazes with majestic melancholy at the constant stream of everyday humanity spilling in and out of perhaps the busiest single branch of McDonald's in the entire world.

As a poet (if only an American poet), I am sentimentally attached to Pushkin Square; it has given me much personal joy — and grief. Yet few places on Earth are quite as soulful and serene as the graveyard in the Svyatogorsky Monastery where Pushkin rests by his mother, where:

> Above the solid graves an oak stands, broad boughs spanning
> With quivering, rustling leaves.

Such peacefulness and love seem to abide in that place, such simple grace, such dignity! A graveyard is ever a place of quiet mourning and wordless contemplation. Yet I have stood by Pushkin's grave, and felt an odd lightness in the heart, a mysterious warmth and inner comfort which no logic could explain...As if this great soul — this "soul in sacred lyre" —has there received at last — at least from Mother Nature — that one true maternal, ever-caring, ever-feminine love he was always seeking.

> And though the body without feeling
> Will wither anywhere and keep,
> Yet closer to a place endearing
> Is where I feel I'd rather sleep.
>
> I'd like, if by my graveyard's entrance,
> A sweet young life would bloom and play,
> And nature, shining with indifference,
> Forever beauty would display.

Слыхали ль вы за рощей глас ночной
Певца любви, певца своей печали?

Have you not heard his voice through groves at night —
The bard of love, the bard of his own sorrow?

ПЕВЕЦ

Слыхали ль вы за рощей глас ночной
Певца любви, певца своей печали?
Когда поля в час утренний молчали,
Свирели звук унылый и простой
        Слыхали ль вы?

Встречали ль вы в пустынной тьме лесной
Певца любви, певца своей печали?
Следы ли слез, улыбку ль замечали,
Иль тихий взор, исполненный тоской,
        Встречали вы?

Вздохнули ль вы, внимая тихий глас
Певца любви, певца своей печали?
Когда в лесах вы юношу видали,
Встречая взор его потухших глаз,
        Вздохнули ль вы?

THE BARD

Have you not heard his voice through groves at night —
The bard of love, the bard of his own sorrow?
When silent fields did wake upon the morrow,
That sound so sad and simple of his pipe —
      Have you not heard?

Have you not met in bare dark forest bleak
The bard of love, the bard of his own sorrow?
Did you his hints of tears, his smiles not follow,
Or quiet looks whose eyes are filled with grief —
      Have you not met?

Have you not sighed, hearing his quiet voice,
The bard of love, the bard of his own sorrow?
When you looked at that youth in wooded hollow,
And met the gaze of his despondent eyes
      Have you not sighed?

The Minstrel's Pipes

Наперсница волшебной старины,
Друг вымыслов игривых и печальных,
Тебя я знал во дни моей весны,
Во дни утех и снов первоначальных.
Я ждал тебя; в вечерней тишине
Являлась ты веселою старушкой
И надо мной сидела в шушуне,
В больших очках и с резвою гремушкой.
Ты, детскую качая колыбель,
Мой юный слух напевами пленила
И меж пелен оставила свирель,
Которую сама заворожила.
Младенчество прошло, как легкий сон.
Ты отрока беспечного любила,
Средь важных муз тебя лишь помнил он,
И ты его тихонько посетила;
Но тот ли был твой образ, твой убор?
Как мило ты, как быстро изменилась!
Каким огнем улыбка оживилась!
Каким огнем блеснул приветный взор!
Покров, клубясь волною непослушной,
Чуть осенял твой стан полувоздушный;
Вся в локонах, обвитая венком,
Прелестницы глава благоухала;
Грудь белая под желтым жемчугом
Румянилась и тихо трепетала...

MY CONFIDANTE OF MAGICAL OLD TIMES

My confidante of magical old times,
Friend of my fancies playful, melancholy,
I knew you in the spring of my young life,
In my first dreams and frolics jolly.
I'd wait for you; in quiet evening rest
You would appear, a laughing, merry granny,
And sit by me, wrapped in your peasant dress,
Wearing huge glasses, playful rattle clanging.
And as you rocked my cradle to sweet sleep
You captivated my young ear with song,
And in my cradle you a pipe did leave,
Which you yourself entranced with magic charm.
As childhood passed by, light as a light dream,
You loved then a young man, a carefree spirit,
Of all great Muses you alone did he
Remember later, when you'd sneak a visit.
But was it really you, your dress, your form?
How sweetly now, how quickly you transformed!
What fire lit up your smile as — through my door —
What fire in looks of welcome blazed! What storm!
Your cape that swirled in stirred-up waves contrary
So slightly veiled your lithe frame, almost airy,
Sweet locks that flowed, wreathed once more in a curl,
Your face of an enchantress, fragrant sweetly,
Your bosom whitened 'neath a yellow pearl,
Blushed red and glowed, and quietly was heaving...

MON PORTRAIT

Vous me demandez mon portrait,
Mais peint d'après nature;
Mon cher, il sera bientôt fait,
Quoique en miniature.

Je suis un jeune polisson,
Encore dans les classes;
Point sot, je le dis sans façon,
Et sans fades grimaces.

Onc il ne fut de babillard,
Ni docteur en Sorbonne —
Plus ennuyeux et plus braillard,
Que moi-même, en personne.

Ma taille à celles des plus longs
Ne peut être égalée;
J'ai le teint frais, les cheveux blonds,
Et la tête bouclée.

J'aime le monde et son fracas,
Je haïs la solitude;
J'abhorre et noises, et débats,
Et tant, soit peu, l'étude.

Spectacles, bals me plaisent fort,
Et d'après ma pensée,
Je dirais ce que j'aime encore...
Si je n'étais au Lycée.

Après cela, mon cher ami,
L'on peut me reconnaître.
Oui! tel que le bon Dieu me fit,
Je veux toujours paraître.

Vrai démon pour l'espièglerie,
Vrai singe par sa mine,
Beaucoup--et trop--d'étourderie!
Ma foi! Voilà Pouchkine!

MY PORTRAIT

My portrait you demand –
But painted true to life.
My dear, it's coming, on command,
Though in miniature size.

A young flibbertigibbet I,
Who still must sit in class,
Not dumb, though, I say, nor shy,
Nor fond of posed grimace.

There never was a babbler worse
Or Doctor of the Sorbonne
Who caused more trouble and more fuss
Than moi-même, en personne.

My height cannot much be compared
To much, much larger churls;
I have fresh skin, light reddish hair,
And my head in curls.

I love the world, all its events,
And I hate solitude.
I abhor quarrels and arguments,
And sometimes, slightly, school.

I'm fond of balls and dancing–– much,
Of going to a play,
I'd say what else is it I love...
Were I not still in Lycée.

By all of this, mon cher ami,
You'll recognize my portrait.
Yes! Just as our good Lord fashioned me
I'd like to still look always.

True demon in delinquency,
True monkey in his mien,
A lot–– way too much –– flippancy!
My word! Voilà Pouchkine!

Mon Portrait

ПАЖ, ИЛИ ПЯТНАДЦАТЫЙ ГОД

C'est l'âge de Chérubin...

Пятнадцать лет мне скоро минет;
Дождусь ли радостного дня?
Как он вперед меня подвинет!
Но и теперь никто не кинет
С презреньем взгляда на меня.

Уж я не мальчик — уж над губой
Могу свой ус я защипнуть;
Я важен, как старик беззубый;
Вы слышите мой голос грубый,
Попробуй кто меня толкнуть.

Я нравлюсь дамам, ибо скромен,
И между ими есть одна...
И гордый взор ее так томен,
И цвет ланит ее так тёмен,
Что жизни мне милей она.

Она строга, властолюбива,
Я сам дивлюсь ее уму —
И ужас как она ревнива;
Зато со всеми горделива
И мне доступна одному.

Вечор она мне величаво
Клялась, что если буду вновь
Глядеть налево и направо,
То даст она мне яду; право —
Вот какова ее любовь!

Она готова хоть в пустыню
Бежать со мной, презрев молву...
Хотите знать мою богиню,
Мою севильскую графиню?..
Нет! ни за что не назову!

THE PAGE, OR MY FIFTEENTH YEAR
    It's Cherubino's age…

My fifteenth year I'll soon be reaching;
Will I last till that joyous day?
Oh! How it sets my head a-reeling!
No one again will dare be needling
Me, or look with scorn my way.

I'm not a boy now. No! Already
A moustache bristles o'er my lips.
Like toothless old men, haughty, heady,
I walk; my voice is rough and ready,
If you push me, it's you who trips!

The ladies like me, shy and modest,
And one of them I too revere…
Her proud gaze is so tempting, luscious,
Her dark cheeks blushing give me rushes,
More than my life I prize her dear.

She's strict, loves power, is ambitious,
I'm just astonished by her mind.
But it's just awful how she's jealous,
Yet fends the world off with pride zealous,
Yet just to me alone is kind.

Just yesterday to me she grandly
Did vow: if I again act dumb
And give my eyes free rein in scattering –
She'll give me poison: so, exactly,
Is just how madly she does love!

She'd fly with me to deserts lawless
And feel contempt for gossip's whirl.
You want to know who is my goddess,
My Sevillana, peerless countess?
No! I won't name her for the world!

ЕВГЕНИЙ ОНЕГИН, ГЛ. VIII
(Из неопубликованной версии)

I. В те дни, когда в садах Лицея
Я безмятежно расцветал,
Читал охотно Елисея,
А Цицерона проклинал,
В те дни, как я поэме редкий
Не предпочел бы мячик меткой,
Считал схоластику за вздор
И прыгал в сад через забор,
Когда порой бывал прилежен,
Порой ленив, порой упрям,
Порой лукав, порою прям,
Порой смирен, порой мятежен,
Порой печален, молчалив,
Порой сердечно говорлив,

II. Когда в забвенье перед классом
Порой терял я взор и слух,
И говорить старался басом,
И стриг над губой первый пух,
В те дни... в те дни, когда впервые
Заметил я черты живые
Прелестной девы и любовь
Младую взволновала кровь,
И я, тоскуя безнадежно,
Томясь обманом пылких снов,
Везде искал ее следов,
Об ней задумывался нежно,
Весь день минутной встречи ждал
И счастье тайных мук узнал.

EUGENE ONEGIN, CHAPTER 8
(From the Unpublished Verses)

I. Back then, when in the Lycée's garden
   I unrebelliously bloomed,
   Read keenly *Elisey's Tale* charming,
   Thought Cicero an old buffoon,
   Back then, when even a rare poem
   Meant less to me than balls well thrown,
   And I thought schoolwork was a bore,
   Into the park the fence leaped o'er,
   When I at times could be quite zealous,
   Lazy at times, other times tough,
   Sometimes quite cunning, sometimes gruff,
   Subdued at times, at times rebellious,
   Sometimes be sad, in silence pent,
   Sometimes heartfeltly eloquent,

II. When I would daydream before lessons,
    Sometimes my sight, my hearing dimmed,
    I tried with bass voice asking questions,
    And shaved the first down off my lip,
    Back then...back then, when I first noted
    The traits and ways, with eyes devoted,
    Of maids enchanting, and when love
    Was always stirring my young blood,
    And I, just sighing for love vainly,
    Thrashed in the wake of passion's dreams,
    I sought love everywhere, it seems,
    And daydreamed just of love so gently,
    All day for one fleet meeting yearned,
    The joys of secret suffering learned.

III. В те дни — во мгле дубравных сводов,
Близ вод, текущих в тишине,
В углах лицейских переходов
Являться муза стала мне.
Моя студенческая келья,
Доселе чуждая веселья,
Вдруг озарилась! Муза в ней
Открыла пир своих затей;
Простите, хладные науки!
Простите, игры первых лет!
Я изменился, я поэт,
В душе моей едины звуки
Переливаются, живут,
В размеры сладкие бегут.

IV. И, первой нежностью томима,
Мне муза пела, пела вновь
(Amorem canat aetas prima)
Все про любовь да про любовь.
Я вторил ей — младые други
В освобожденные досуги
Любили слушать голос мой.
Они, пристрастною душой
Ревнуя к братскому союзу,
Мне первый поднесли венец,
Чтоб им украсил их певец
Свою застенчивую музу.
О торжество невинных дней!
Твой сладок сон душе моей.

III. Back then, 'neath oak-groves' arching sadness,
By waters flowing quietly,
In my Lyceum's corner pathways
The Muse began to come to me.
My little student cell monastic,
Which, until now, had not known gladness,
At once was gleaming, and the Muse
Laid there a feast of songs to choose.
Farewell, farewell, cold sciences!
I'm now from youthful games estranged!
I am a poet now; I've changed.
Within my soul both sounds and silence
Pour into one another, live,
In measures sweet both take and give.

IV. Still of first tenderness a dreamer,
My Muse could never sing enough
(Amorem canat aetas prima)*
All about love, and love, and love.
I echoed Her, and my friends youthful
In leisured hours at ease, unrueful,
Would love to listen to my voice.
How passionately their souls rejoiced
With zealous brotherly enthusing:
They first of all did laurels bring
To me, that for them I might sing
The fruits of my still timid musing.
Oh, joy of innocence of old!
How sweet your dream is to my soul!

---

*"Let youth's song be of love." From Sextus Propertius, *Elegies*, Book II, x, line 7.

The Lycée

Pushkin and Voltaire

ДРУЗЬЯМ

Богами вам еще даны
Златые дни, златые ночи,
И томных дев устремлены
На вас внимательные очи.
Играйте, пойте, о друзья!
Утратьте вечер скоротечный;
И вашей радости беспечной
Сквозь слезы улыбнуся я.

Schoolfriends

TO MY FRIENDS

For you the gods but briefly will
Give golden days and golden nights,
With languor lovely maidens still
Will cast upon you watchful eyes.
So sing and gambol, friends, the while!
Spend every hour of fleet eve's racing,
And at your carefree merrymaking
I'll look through my bright tears and smile!

Pushkin's friend Pyotr Chaadayev

В АЛЬБОМ СОСНИЦКОЙ

Вы съединить могли с холодностью сердечной
 Чудесный жар пленительных очей.
 Кто любит вас, тот очень глуп, конечно;
Но кто не любит вас, тот во сто раз глупей.

A St.Petersburg Actress

IN THE ALBUM OF [the Actress] SOSNITSKAYA

You managed to combine a coldness very heartfelt
    With wondrous warmth of captivating eyes.
    Whoever loves you's certainly a dumbbell;
But he who loves you not's dumber a hundred times.

Another St. Petersburg Actress

ДОРИДЕ

Я верю: я любим; для сердца нужно верить.
Нет, милая моя не может лицемерить;
Все непритворно в ней: желаний томный жар,
Стыдливость робкая, харит бесценный дар,
Нарядов и речей приятная небрежность
И ласковых имен младенческая нежность.

Demons ablaze with love

TO DORIDA

She loves me! I believe! The heart must keep believing.
No, never would my darling be deceiving!
There's no pretense in her dear languid passion swift,
Shy sense of modesty, the Graces' priceless gift,
Her costume and her speech, charming in carefree manner,
The youthful way she calls me soft pet names so tender.

The temptation of St. Anthony

ЭПИГРАММА «На Аракчеева»

Всей России притеснитель,
Губернаторов мучитель
И Совета он учитель,
А царю он — друг и брат.
Полон злобы, полон мести,
Без ума, без чувств, без чести,
Кто ж он? *Преданный без лести*,
Б...и грошевой солдат.

EPIGRAM About Arakcheyev*

Persecuting all of Russia,
Even governors he'll torture,
And the State Council will lecture:
He's the Tsar's brother and friend.
Full of malice, full of vengeance,
Without wit, heart, honor, conscience,
Who's he? "*Unflattering in reverence*,"
And whore's toy solider, in the end.

Count Arakcheyev

---

*Count Aleksey Arakcheyev was Deputy President of the Council of Ministers, and effectively headed Tsar Alexander I's government from 1815–1825. An extreme reactionary and martinet who founded brutal military colonies, he chose "Unflattering in reverence" as the device for his coat-of-arms. His mistress, a former prostitute named Anastasia Minkina, was so ill-tempered that it was said she was the only man Count Arakcheyev feared. She was murdered in 1825, it is believed, by her serfs.

Краев чужих неопытный любитель
И своего всегдашний обвинитель,
Я говорил: в отечестве моем
Где верный ум, где гений мы найдем?
Где гражданин с душою благородной,
Возвышенной и пламенно свободной?
Где женщина — не с хладной красотой,
Но с пламенной, пленительной, живой?
Где разговор найду непринужденный,
Блистательный, веселый, просвещенный?
С кем можно быть не хладным, не пустым?
Отечество почти я ненавидел —
Но я вчера Голицыну увидел
И примирен с Отечеством моим.

Of foreign lands an inexperienced lover,
'Gainst my own land, though, constantly a mutterer,
I'd say out loud: in this country of mine
Where would one honest wit or genius find?
Where is a man who's civil, noble-hearted?
Who's fiery, free, outspoken and exalted?
Where is a woman's fairness not like ice,
But captivating, fiery, and alive?
Whose conversation's easy and unfrightened,
With brilliant wit that's happy and enlightened?
With whom are we not cool, empty, and bland?
My Fatherland I almost hated, really...
But then I saw Golitsyna last evening...
And — now — I'm fine with my dear Fatherland.

ВОЛЬНОСТЬ. ОДА

Беги, сокройся от очей,
Цитеры слабая царица!
Где ты, где ты, гроза царей,
Свободы гордая певица?
Приди, сорви с меня венок,
Разбей изнеженную лиру...
Хочу воспеть свободу миру
На тронах поразить порок!

Открой мне благородный след
Того возвышенного галла,
Кому сама средь славных бед
Ты гимны смелые внушала.
Питомцы ветреной Судьбы,
Тираны мира! трепещите!
А вы, мужайтесь и внемлите,
Восстаньте, падшие рабы!

Увы! куда ни брошу взор —
Везде бичи, везде железы,
Законов гибельный позор,
Неволи немощные слезы;
Везде неправедная власть
В сгущенной мгле предрассуждений
Воссела — рабства грозный гений
И славы роковая страсть.

Лишь там над царскою главой
Народов не легло страданье,
Где крепко с вольностью святой
Законов мощных сочетанье;
Где всем простерт их твердый щит,
Где сжатый верными руками
Граждан над равными главами
Их меч без выбора скользит

AN ODE TO LIBERTY

Begone, and vanish from my sight,
You Cytherean queen so feeble.
But where are you, of Tsars the blight,
You songstress proud of heady freedom?
Tear off my laurel, cast it down
And smash my over-precious lyre!
With freedom set the world on fire
And smash the vice upon its thrones!

And show me now the noble road
You made for that inspired Gaul*
Into whose heart, 'midst glorious woe,
You hymns courageous did install,
You foster-sons of flighty Fate,
World's tyrants, tremble and take heed,
Whilst you— take courage, hear indeed —
Arise, arise, you downcast slaves!

Alas! Where'er I cast my gaze
Always the scourge, the rod appears
Of laws' oppressive deadly shame
And impotent caged peoples' tears.
And unjust power everywhere
In hazy prejudice does dwell
Enslaves us through a genius fell
That but for deadly glory cares.

O'er all crowned monarchs' majesty,
Alone those lands don't groan and cower
Where wed to holy liberty,
With ties that bind, are just laws' power,
Whose broad shield firm defends us all,
Where, held in faithful hands unquiv'ring,
The sword of Justice, never slipping,
Impartial, fair, holds all in thrall.

*Refers to the poet French André Chénier, guillotined in 1794.

И преступленье свысока
Сражает правильным размахом;
Где не подкупна их рука
Ни алчной скупостью, ни страхом.
Владыки! вам венец и трон
Дает Закон — а не природа;
Стоите выше вы народа,
Но вечный выше вас Закон.

И горе, горе племенам,
Где дремлет он неосторожно,
Где иль народу, иль царям
Законом властвовать возможно!

...
Самовластительный злодей!
Тебя, твой трон я ненавижу,
Твою погибель, смерть детей
С жестокой радостию вижу.
Читают на твоем челе
Печать проклятия народы,
Ты ужас мира, стыд природы,
Упрек ты Богу на земле.

Когда на мрачную Неву
Звезда полуночи сверкает
И беззаботную главу
Спокойный сон отягощает,
Глядит задумчивый певец
На грозно спящий средь тумана
Пустынный памятник тирана,
Забвенью брошенный дворец –

И слышит Клии страшный глас
За сими страшными стенами,
Калигулы последний час
Он видит живо пред очами,

FROM AN ODE TO LIBERTY

Even the mighty's crimes are stayed
When that sword firm and fair appears,
Where hands that wield that sword aren't swayed
By selfish greed or yet by fears.
Rulers! Your crowns and laurels do
Not come from God, but from Law's hand.
Above the people you do stand,
But Law Eternal's over you.

And woe to those unhappy lands
Where heedlessly that sword is slumb'ring,
Where either mob or crownèd king
Do take the law in their own hands.

...
You tyrant rogue, 'gainst whom none dares!
You and your throne I hate with passion!
Your doom, the death of all your heirs,
With cruel joy I can imagine.
Upon your brow all read displayed
The stamp of countless people's curses.
You're nature's shame, world's blight outrageous!
That you exist is God's disgrace!

When on Neva's dark gloomy flow
The star of midnight sparkles, prances,
To pillows carefree heads sink slow,
As calm sleep burdens them in trances,
The poet only stares till morn,
At dreaded outline, in mist skirted,
At tyrant's monument deserted,
A palace now forgot, forlorn.

The bard hears History's voice dread, cowers:
Beyond where that wall dreaded lies,
Our Tsar Caligula's last hours
He sees before his very eyes,

Он видит — в лентах и звездах,
Вином и злобой упоенны,
Идут убийцы потаенны,
На лицах дерзость, в сердце страх.

Молчит неверный часовой,
Опущен молча мост подъемный,
Врата отверсты в тьме ночной
Рукой предательства наемной...
О стыд! о ужас наших дней!
Как звери, вторглись янычары!..
Падут бесславные удары...
Погиб увенчанный злодей.

И днесь учитесь, о цари:
Ни наказанья, ни награды,
Ни кров темниц, ни алтари
Не верные для вас ограды.
Склонитесь первые главой
Под сень надежную Закона,
И станут вечной стражей трона
Народов вольность и покой.

Tsar Alexander I

Sees how, with stars and ribbons strewed,
With wine and malice drunk, approaching,
The secret killers come, with loathing,
Fear in the hearts, their faces rude.

The faithless sentry silent stands,
The drawbridge lowering stealthily,
The gates to Treason's hired hands
In darkness ope relentlessly...
Oh shame and horror of our times!
Those janissaries, beasts, invaded,
Their blows rained down, inglorious traitors!
A crownèd villain murdered lies.

And hence, take heed, great heads of states!
Nor executions, nor promotions,
Nor altars, nor barred dungeons' gates
Defend you against heaven's motions.
But bow your heads first, willingly
Beneath the Law's unerring portal,
Then o'er your throne stand guard, immortal,
The people's peace and liberty.

Marianne, Spirit of Liberty

ТУРГЕНЕВУ

Тургенев, верный покровитель
Попов, евреев и скопцов,
Но слишком счастливый гонитель
И езуитов, и глупцов,
И лености моей бесплодной,
Всегда беспечной и свободной,
Подруги благотворных снов!
К чему смеяться надо мною,
Когда я слабою рукою
По лире с трепетом брожу
И лишь изнеженные звуки
Любви, сей милой сердцу муки,
В струнах незвонких нахожу?
Душой предавшись наслажденью,
Я сладко, сладко задремал.
Один лишь ты с глубокой ленью
К трудам охоту сочетал;
Один лишь ты, любовник страстный
И Соломирской, и креста,
То ночью прыгаешь с прекрасной,
То проповедуешь Христа.
...Нося мучительное бремя
Пустых иль тяжких должностей,
Один лишь ты находишь время
Смеяться лености моей.

Не вызывай меня ты боле
К навек оставленным трудам,
Ни к поэтической неволе,
Ни к обработанным стихам.
Что нужды, если и с ошибкой
И слабо иногда пою?
Пускай Нинета лишь улыбкой
Любовь беспечную мою
Воспламенит и успокоит!
А труд и холоден и пуст;
Поэма никогда не стоит
Улыбки сладострастных уст.

TO TURGENEV*

Turgenev, the protector faithful
Of holy priests, skoptsý**, and Jews,
Yet over-zealous scourge most baneful
Of Jesuits — as well as fools,
And of my wastrel life so idle,
My heedless freedom so delightful
Whose gifts are dreams and sleep that soothes!
Why do you mock me feverishly
Whenever my hand, quivering feebly,
Lost on my lyre, only refined
And tender chords of dearest rapture
Of love, the heart's exquisite torture,
In its still untuned strings can find?
Yes, being given up to pleasure,
Most sweetly do I sweetly sleep —
Just you— an idler beyond measure—
For zealous work still ardor keep;
Just you alone, wild lover truly
Of Madame S. and of the Cross
Leap up at nightime from your beauty
And preach the love of Christ to us.
...Bearing your crushing duties' burden
Of empty, serious, heavy chores,
Alone you find the time for sermons
To mock my idleness and mores.

But summon me no more, I'm pleading,
To Work, forever dropped, despised,
Nor to poetic lack of freedom,
Nor yet to verses I've revised!
What is the point? Is it worthwhile
To weakly sing of how I pine?
Yet let Ninette but with a smile
Arouse this carefree love of mine,
While calming, setting it on fire!
But Work is cold and flat — not missed:
No epic poem could ever rival
A smile from sweet and passionate lips!

*Alexander Ivanovich Turgenev was the poet's close friend (it was he who in the end escorted Pushkin's coffin for burial in Svyatogorsky Monastery). Though a fellow member of the jovial Arzamas literary society, Turgenev was Director of the Department of Religious Affairs in the government. By contrast, his brother Nikolay was a Decembrist firebrand who escaped execution only by fleeing to England. Pushkin wrote his *Ode to Liberty* at a party at the Turgenev brothers' home (20, Fontanka Canal, overlooking Tsar Paul I's Mikhatlovskiy Palace in St. Petersburg).
**Skoptsy—a religious sect whose members castrated themselves.

ДЕРЕВНЯ

Приветствую тебя, пустынный уголок,
Приют спокойствия, трудов и вдохновенья,
Где льется дней моих невидимый поток
    На лоне счастья и забвенья!
Я твой: я променял порочный двор цирцей,
Роскошные пиры, забавы, заблужденья
На мирный шум дубров, на тишину полей,
На праздность вольную, подругу размышленья.
    Я твой — люблю сей темный сад
    С его прохладой и цветами,
Сей луг, уставленный душистыми скирдами,
Где светлые ручьи в кустарниках шумят.
Везде передо мной подвижные картины:
Здесь вижу двух озер лазурные равнины,
Где парус рыбаря белеет иногда,
За ними ряд холмов и нивы полосаты,
    Вдали рассыпанные хаты,
На влажных берегах бродящие стада,
Овины дымные и мельницы крылаты;
    Везде следы довольства и труда.

Я здесь, от суетных оков освобожденный,
Учуся в истине блаженство находить,
Свободною душой закон боготворить,
Роптанью не внимать толпы непросвещенной,
Участьем отвечать застенчивой мольбе
    И не завидовать судьбе
Злодея иль глупца — в величии неправом.

Оракулы веков, здесь вопрошаю вас!
    В уединенье величавом
    Слышнее ваш отрадный глас;
Он гонит лени сон угрюмый,
К трудам рождает жар во мне,
И ваши творческие думы
В душевной зреют глубине.

THE COUNTRY

I'm glad to see you, lonely barren nook,
Of calm and work my haven, full of inspiration,
Where my life's days stream by, flow in an unseen brook,
   Of sheer oblivion and elation!
I'm yours! I've fled our Circes' sinful reels,
Balls, sumptuous feasts, amusements, false temptations,
For rustling oak trees' peace, and silence in the fields,
For freedom's idleness, true friend of cogitation.

   I'm yours: I love this garden dark.
   I love its coolness and its flowers,
This meadow, where sweet hayricks make their bowers,
The light streams gurgling, banked by hedges gnarled.
Whichever way I look are paintings, always moving,
Before me two lakes' plains, agleam in their vast bluing;
Sometimes a fisherman hoists up his sail's white span
Beyond, a row of hills, and golden harvest growing.
   Far off the wandering herds are lowing,
Above the lakes' moist banks, where scattered huts do stand,
Are wingèd windmills, byres, and barns for drying, smoky:
   Signs everywhere of peaceful works of man.

Here I, from chains of fuss, in vain find freedom,
I'm learning how, in truth, true blessings can be found,
In reverence for law my soul's freedom finds ground,
No mutterings of mob's benighted malice heeding,
With sympathy I hear each shy prayer that's made,
 Yet have no envy for the fate
Of wicked men or fools who strut their grand injustice.

Oh oracles of time, now I call unto you!
   In this seclusion so majestic,
     Your joyous voice rings clearly through,
Casts torpor off from tired grieving:
For work a fever takes its stead,
Creative thoughts from you and feelings
Mature within my soul's own depths.

Но мысль ужасная здесь душу омрачает:
    Среди цветущих нив и гор
Друг человечества печально замечает
Везде невежества убийственный позор.
    Не видя слез, не внемля стона,
На пагубу людей избранное судьбой,
Здесь барство дикое, без чувства, без закона,
Присвоило себе насильственной лозой
И труд, и собственность, и время земледельца.
Склонясь на чуждый плуг, покорствуя бичам,
Здесь рабство тощее влачится по браздам
    Неумолимого владельца.
Здесь тягостный ярем до гроба все влекут,
Надежд и склонностей в душе питать не смея,
 Здесь девы юные цветут
    Для прихоти бесчувственной злодея.
Опора милая стареющих отцов,
Младые сыновья, товарищи трудов,
Из хижины родной идут собой умножить
Дворовые толпы измученных рабов.
О, если б голос мой умел сердца тревожить!
Почто в груди моей горит бесплодный жар?
И не дан мне судьбой витийства грозный дар?
Увижу ль, о друзья! народ неугнетенный
И рабство, падшее по манию царя,
И над отечеством свободы просвещенной
Взойдет ли наконец прекрасная заря?

THE COUNTRY

Yet here a horrid thought the heart forever darkens:
    For, midst the hilltops and the wheat field's golden mane,
A friend of mankind looks around and sadly hearkens
To inhumanity, to murderous, bloody shame.
    For, blind to tears and deaf to groaning,
As if chosen by Fate for people's doom and harm,
Here serfdom savage, neither heart nor true law knowing,
Has stolen for itself — by Violence's rod —
The work and property and time of peasants grieving.
Bent over others' ploughs, and sullen, tamed by whips,
Here scrawny slavery must drag through furrows rich —
    Just for the landowner unyielding.
Here everyone must bear harsh yokes until the grave;
To heed one's hopes and souls' own voice no one here's daring,
 Here every blossoming fair maid
    Gets forced to be a toy for villains cold, uncaring.
And here the dear support of fathers as they age
Their younger sons, their friends in toil, in labor brave,
March off to multiply, teeming from poor huts dirty,
In courtyards shambling, a crowd of tortured slaves.
Oh, if my voice but knew how others' hearts to worry!
Oh why within my breast does useless fever sit?
And why has fate denied me rhetoric's great gift?
Friends! Will I live to see my people no more blightened
And slavery cast down upon the Tsar's command?
Above my fatherland by freedom's grace enlightened
 — At last — is a dawn beautiful at hand?

К ЧААДАЕВУ

Любви, надежды, тихой славы
Недолго нежил нас обман,
Исчезли юные забавы,
Как сон, как утренний туман;
Но в нас горит еще желанье,
Под гнетом власти роковой
Нетерпеливою душой
Отчизны внемлем призыванье.
Мы ждем с томленьем упованья
Минуты вольности святой,
Как ждет любовник молодой
Минуты верного свиданья.
Пока свободою горим,
Пока сердца для чести живы,
Мой друг, отчизне посвятим
Души прекрасные порывы!
Товарищ, верь: взойдет она,
Звезда пленительного счастья,
Россия вспрянет ото сна,
И на обломках самовластья
Напишут наши имена!

TO CHAADAYEV

Of love, and hope, and quiet glory
Deceptions dear did not long last.
Our youthful games have vanished wholly,
Like dreams, like drifting morning fog.
But in us still desire's burning,
Oppressed by power's deadly yoke,
Impatiently our souls are yearning:
We hear the calling of our folk.
We wait each minute, yearning, longing,
For Freedom's sacred fleeting bliss,
The way young lovers fret while counting
The minutes to a secret tryst.
For while of freedom we all dream,
While in our hearts there still lives honor,
For our land's aid, my friend, let's turn
All beauteous flights of fancy soaring!
Believe, my friend, she'll climb high, steep,
That star of captivating rapture,
For Russia will arise from sleep,
And on the shards of slavery fractured
Our names will be writ large, and keep!

Pyotr Chaadayev

Я вижу берег отдаленный,
Земли полуденной волшебные края;

The Caucasus

II. SOUTHERN IDYLLS

I see the shoreline in the distance,
The magic South, land of the noonday sun;

A Scene in Chechnya

Погасло дне́вное светило;
На море синее вечерний пал туман.
    Шуми, шуми, послушное ветрило,
Волнуйся подо мной, угрюмый океан.
    Я вижу берег отдаленный,
Земли полуденной волшебные края;
С волненьем и тоской туда стремлюся я,
    Воспоминаньем упоенный...
И чувствую: в очах родились слезы вновь;
    Душа кипит и замирает;
Мечта знакомая вокруг меня летает;
Я вспомнил прежних лет безумную любовь,
И всё, чем я страдал, и всё, что сердцу мило,
Желаний и надежд томительный обман...
    Шуми, шуми, послушное ветрило,
Волнуйся подо мной, угрюмый океан.
Лети, корабль, неси меня к пределам дальным
По грозной прихоти обманчивых морей,
    Но только не к брегам печальным
    Туманной родины моей,
    Страны, где пламенем страстей
    Впервые чувства разгорались,
Где музы нежные мне тайно улыбались,
    Где рано в бурях отцвела
    Моя потерянная младость,
Где легкокрылая мне изменила радость
И сердце хладное страданью предала.
    Искатель новых впечатлений,
    Я вас бежал, отечески края;
    Я вас бежал, питомцы наслаждений,
Минутной младости минутные друзья;
И вы, наперсницы порочных заблуждений,

The day's last gleam fades out, is disappearing,
In evening mist the ocean blue is sheathed.
      Make sound, make sound, you little breeze obedient!
Wave, worry under me, you gloomy, giant sea.
      I see the shoreline in the distance,
The magic South, land of the noonday sun;
With turmoil and with grief my soul must thither run,
      Aglow with recollections wistful!
My eyes again give birth to tears from God above;
      My soul's aboil, and shudders, sighing,
My dream of old, familiar, round me flickers, flying,
Remembered from years past it comes back: Crazy love!
And all I suffered from, all my heart finds endearing,
All hopes, and all desires that languorously deceive...
      Make sound, make sound, you little breeze obedient!
Wave, worry under me, you gloomy, giant sea.
Fly on, my vessel, bear me off to distant shorelines,
By dreaded whimsy of the treacherous great seas,
      Don't bring me back to bleak coasts pining,
      To my own country's misty leas!
      That land where passion's fire first seized
      My heart, and feelings warmed my spirit,
Where tender Muses first did smile on me in secret,
      Where in first storms the bloom did pall,
      Of youth that now is lost forever,
Where joy betrayed, and fled with wings light-feathered,
Abandoned my cold heart to suffering and gall.
      I, restless, searched for new sensations,
      And fled from you, coasts where my homeland ends!
      I fled from you, you fount of brief elations,
Of youth's brief moment momentary friends!
And you, you temptresses of sinful aberrations,

Которым без любви я жертвовал собой,
Покоем, славою, свободой и душой,
И вы забыты мной, изменницы младые,
Подруги тайные моей весны златые,
И вы забыты мной... Но прежних сердца ран,
Глубоких ран любви, ничто не излечило...
    Шуми, шуми, послушное вертило,
Волнуйся подо мной, угрюмый океан...

For whom I gave myself up, loveless, whole,
Gave up my rest, my glory, freedom, and my soul,
Yes, you're forgotten too, fair-weather girlfriends fleeting,
So young, of my gold springtime my best friends in secret,
Yes, you're forgotten too! Though still they live in me,
Old heart wounds, wounds of love, that never healed, still bleeding...
      Make sound, make sound, you little wind obedient,
Wave, worry under me, you gloomy, giant sea.

Увы! зачем она блистает
Минутной, нежной красотой?
Она приметно увядает
Во цвете юности живой...
Увянет! Жизнью молодою
Не долго наслаждаться ей;
Не долго радовать собою
Счастливый круг семьи своей,
Беспечной, милой остротою
Беседы наши оживлять
И тихой, ясною душою
Страдальца душу услаждать.
Спешу в волненье дум тяжелых,
Сокрыв уныние мое,
Наслушаться речей веселых
И наглядеться на нее.
Смотрю на все ее движенья,
Внимаю каждый звук речей,
И миг единый разлученья
Ужасен для души моей.

Alas! Say, why is she so shining
With tender beauty brief, which soon
So noticeably fades, declining
In youth, just as it most does bloom?
T'will fade! The life her youth possesses
Will not be hers long to enjoy.
Not long will she be raining blessings,
Her family circle's greatest joy,
With carefree wittiness, endearing,
Our chats be sweetly brightening,
And with her soul so calm, all healing,
Assuage my soul that's suffering.
My melancholy woe concealing
With nervous thoughts, I, burdened, rush
To hear and hear her phrases cheering
And cannot look at her enough!
I watch each movement that she's started,
Each sound she utters take in whole:
The slightest moment being parted
Is sheerest torment to my soul.

Редеет облаков летучая гряда.
Звезда печальная, вечерняя звезда!
Твой луч осеребрил увядшие равнины,
И дремлющий залив, и черных скал вершины.
Люблю твой слабый свет в небесной вышине;
Он думы разбудил, уснувшие во мне:
Я помню твой восход, знакомое светило,
Над мирною страной, где все для сердца мило,
Где стройны тополи в долинах вознеслись,
Где дремлет нежный мирт и темный кипарис,
И сладостно шумят полуденные волны.
Там некогда в горах, сердечной думы полный,
Над морем я влачил задумчивую лень,
Когда на хижины сходила ночи тень —
И дева юная во мгле тебя искала
И именем своим подругам называла.

The flying wisps of clouds are thinning, scattering far.
O star of melancholy, oh bright evening star!
Your ray silvers the plains, the vast steppe slowly fading,
The bay that dozes hushed, black cliff-peaks silver painting,
I love your feeble light in Heaven's height a-glimmering,
It wakens thoughts in me that long since had been slumbering,
Your rising clings to me, familiar shining sphere,
Above that peaceful land, where all to my heart's dear,
Where graceful poplars spring up tall in valleys steep,
Where tender myrtles and dark cypresses do sleep,
And sweetly soft the surf of southern waves is sounding,
There in those mountains I, wrapped up in my heart's pounding,
Did take my pensive ease, and loomed above the sea,
Watched night's soft shade lull huts to sleep there wistfully,
And through the mists, o star, for you, searching the ether,
With her own name a girl named you to girlfriends eager.

БУРЯ

Ты видел деву на скале
В одежде белой над волнами,
Когда, бушуя в бурной мгле,
Играло море с берегами,
Когда луч молний озарял
Ее всечасно блеском алым
И ветер бился и летал
С ее летучим покрывалом?
Прекрасно море в бурной мгле
И небо в блесках без лазури;
Но верь мне: дева на скале
Прекрасней волн, небес и бури.

THE STORM

Have you seen, perched upon a cliff,
A maid in white, above the whitecaps?
In stormy mist the raging swish
Of waves that raced ashore in rising,
When rays from lightning bolts did shine
Upon her with a scarlet gilting,
And furious wind did beat and fly
From her in evanescent quilting?
The sea is fair in stormy mist
And fair the sky gleams in foul weather.
That maid, though, trust me, on that cliff,
Than waves or sky or storm is fairer.

ВИНОГРАД

Не стану я жалеть о розах,
Увядших с легкою весной;
Мне мил и виноград на лозах,
В кистях созревший под горой,
Краса моей долины злачной,
Отрада осени златой,
Продолговатый и прозрачный,
Как персты девы молодой.

Pushkin self-portrait

GRAPES

No, I'm not going to mourn the roses
That faded with the slight fleet spring;
I'm fond of grapes before they're chosen,
On hillside vineyards ripening.
They make my fertile valley splendid,
Bring joy to autumn's golden whirl,
Caressing, thin, long, sweet, and tender,
Like fingers of a little girl.

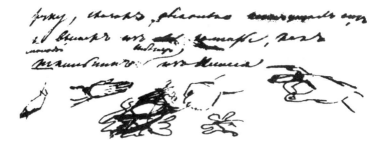

ГРЕЧАНКЕ

Ты рождена воспламенять
Воображение поэтов,
Его тревожить и пленять
Любезной живостью приветов,
Восточной странностью речей,
Блистаньем зеркальных очей
И этой ножкою нескромной...
Ты рождена для неги томной,
Для упоения страстей.
Скажи: когда певец Леилы
В мечтах небесных рисовал
Свой неизменный идеал,
Уж не тебя ль изображал
Поэт мучительный и милый?
Быть может, в дальпой стороне,
Под небом Греции священной,
Тебя страдалец вдохновенный
Узнал иль видел, как во сне,
И скрылся образ незабвенный
В его сердечной глубине?
Быть может, лирою счастливой
Тебя волшебник искушал;
Невольный трепет возникал
В твоей груди самолюбивой,
И ты, склонясь к его плечу...
Нет, нет, мой друг, мечты ревнивой
Питать я пламя не хочу;
Мне долго счастье чуждо было,
Мне ново наслаждаться им,
И, тайной грустию томим,
Боюсь: неверно все, что мило.

Calypso Polychroni, mistress of both Byron and Pushkin

TO A GREEK GIRL

You have been born to set afire
Imagination in us poets,
To captivate it, to inspire
With lively greetings, charming habits,
With your exotic Eastern speech,
Your eyes, that like a mirror gleam,
Your tiny little foot so tempting...
Yes, you were born for blissful splendor,
For passion, living fervently.
But tell me, when the bard of Leila[1]
Was singing his celestial dream
Of his ineffable ideal,
Was it not you he made appear,
That bard of heartache so delightful?
Did, very far away, perhaps,
Beneath the skies of sacred Hellas,
That skald of griefs inspired, zealous,
Perceive you in a dream perchance?
And was your memorable visage
Concealed within his heartfelt depths?
What if, to his glad harp you, listening,
Let that magician's tempting skill
Make murmurs rise against your will
Within your breast so proud, yet quivering,
Which you, slight, on his shoulder, laid?...
No, no, my friend! Of jealous whispering
I do not wish to feed the flame;
For ages, no joy could I feel,
T'is new to me, this pleasure brief,
And sunk in a mysterious grief,
I fear what's lovely can't be real.

1 – "The Bard of Leila"...i.e. Byron

В еврейской хижине лампада
В одном углу бледна горит,
Перед лампадою старик
Читает Библию. Седые
На книгу падают власы.
Над колыбелию пустой
Еврейка плачет молодая.
Сидит в другом углу, главой
Поникнув, молодой еврей,
Глубоко в думу погруженный.
В печальной хижине старушка
Готовит позднюю трапезу.
Старик, закрыв святую книгу,
Застежки медные сомкнул.
Старушка ставит бедный ужин
На стол и всю семью зовет.
Никто нейдет, забыв о пище.
Текут в безмолвии часы.
Уснуло всё под сенью ночи.
Еврейской хижины одной
Не посетил отрадный сон.
На колокольне городской
Бьет полночь. — Вдруг рукой тяжелой
Стучатся к ним. Семья вздрогнула,
Младой еврей встает и дверь
С недоуменьем отворяет —
И входит незнакомый странник.
В его руке дорожный посох
....
....

A LANTERN IN A JEWISH HOVEL (FRAGMENT)

A lantern in a Jewish hovel
In just one corner flickers, pales,
Beneath that lantern an old man
Re-reads the Bible. His grey hairs
In curled locks fall upon his book,
While a young Jewish woman weeps
Above a cradle lying empty.
Across the hut, in his thoughts steeped,
Head downcast, her young husband sits,
And ponders something very deeply.
And in that sad hut an old woman
Prepares the meager evening meal.
Closing his Holy Book, the old man
Now folds it shut with clasps of brass.
His old wife sets down their poor supper
And calls the family to eat.
But no one comes, heedless of food.
The silent hours slip away.
All slumbers 'neath night's vaulting murky.
The Jewish hovel, all alone,
Withstands sleep's happy visitation.
The bell-tower of their small town
Strikes midnight. Suddenly a knocking,
Dread, pounding, startles them. They shudder,
The young Jew gets up, quite unnerved,
Opens the door with shock and horror,
And in lumbers an unknown wanderer,
Holding a heavy walking staff

....
....

Я пережил свои желанья,
Я разлюбил свои мечты;
Остались мне одни страданья,
Плоды сердечной пустоты.

Под бурями судьбы жестокой
Увял цветущий мой венец;
Живу печальный, одинокий,
И жду: придет ли мой конец?

Так, поздним хладом пораженный,
Как бури слышен зимний свист,
Один на ветке обнаженной
Трепещет запоздалый лист...

I HAVE OUTGROWN MY ASPIRATIONS

I have outgrown my aspirations,
No longer do I love my dreams.
I'm left with suffering in patience
My heart's own emptiness, it seems.

In Fate's cruel storms and pointless roamings,
My flowering laurel wreathe did fade.
And so I live in sadness, lonely,
And wait: Is my end on its way?

Just so, by fall's last chills defeated,
When first cold winter snowstorms shriek,
Alone, on the bare branch depleted,
Trembles the long–delayed last leaf...

Умолкну скоро я. Но если в день печали
Задумчивой игрой мне струны отвечали;
Но если юноши, внимая молча мне,
Дивились долгому любви моей мученью;
Но если ты сама, предавшись умиленью,
Печальные стихи твердила в тишине
И сердца моего язык любила страстный;
Но если я любим: позволь, о милый друг,
Позволь одушевить прощальный лиры звук
Заветным именем любовницы прекрасной.
Когда меня навек обымет смертный сон,
Над урною моей промолви с умиленьем:
Он мною был любим, он мне был одолжен
И песен и любви последним вдохновеньем.

I will fall silent soon. But if, on days of sadness,
With pensive play my heart's harp-strings once answered,
If ever once bright youths my voice in silence heard,
And if they ever once admired my long love's torture,
If ever you yourself indulged in loving rapture,
And murmured mournful verse alone when no one stirred,
And loved the passion of my heart's own language...
If, if I still am loved, allow me, friend so dear,
To with my lyre give life and bring to ear
The name my beautiful and cherished love once carried.
But when the sleep of death takes me for evermore,
Utter above my urn, with tender resignation:
Oh, he was loved by me, for me his heart did pour
Forth songs and love with his last inspiration.

A Noble Youth

Мой друг, забыты мной следы минувших лет
И младости моей мятежное теченье.
Не спрашивай меня о том, чего уж нет,
Что было мне дано в печаль и в наслажденье,
    Что я любил, что изменило мне.
Пускай я радости вкушаю не вполне;
Но ты, невинная, ты рождена для счастья.
Беспечно верь ему, летучий миг лови:
Душа твоя жива для дружбы, для любви,
    Для поцелуев сладострастья;
Душа твоя чиста: унынье чуждо ей;
Светла, как ясный день, младенческая совесть.
К чему тебе внимать безумства и страстей
    Незанимательную повесть?
Она твой тихий ум невольно возмутит;
Ты слезы будешь лить, ты сердцем содрогнешься;
Доверчивой души беспечность улетит,
И ты моей любви, быть может, ужаснешься.
Быть может, навсегда... Нет, милая моя,
Лишиться я боюсь последних наслаждений.
Не требуй от меня опасных откровений:
Сегодня я люблю, сегодня счастлив я.

My friend, I have forgot all trace of passing years,
And all the torrents wild of being young, rebellious,
Don't ask me to tell more of what's no longer here,
Of what was given me in sadness and in pleasure,
    What I did love, by what I was betrayed,
Though not entirely of joy perhaps I taste
Still you are innocent, and born to just be happy.
Believe in happiness, seize each fleet moment, trust:
Your soul's alive for friendship and for love,
    For kisses lingering with sweet passion.
Your soul is clean and pure, and never has known grief,
For light as a clear day's the adolescent conscience.
Why should you hear from me how crazy passions sear
    The unsurprising story artless?
That tale, against your will, will stir your quiet mind.
Tears out of you will pour, your heart in pangs will tighten,
In carefree trusting soul, the carefree trust will blighten,
And then my love for you, perhaps, will only frighten,
Scare you, perhaps for good. Darling! No, let's just dally…
I am afraid to lose my last sensations pleasant.
Demand from me no more such dangerous confessions.
Today, today, I love; today, today, I'm happy.

ПТИЧКА

В чужбине свято наблюдаю
Родной обычай старины:
На волю птичку выпускаю
При светлом празднике весны.

Я стал доступен утешенью;
За что на Бога мне роптать,
Когда хоть одному творенью
Я мог свободу даровать!

A LITTLE BIRD

Though exiled, I observe, still heeding,
A custom old from upbringing:
I give a little bird its freedom
To mark the holy rites of spring.

I'm worthy now of consolations.
Why should I grumble to my God?
Since even one of his creations
Through me goes free, I have enough!

Отрывок из Путешествий Онегина

Я жил тогда в Одессе пыльной...
Там долго ясны небеса,
Там хлопотливо торг обильной
Свои подъемлет паруса;
Там все Европой дышит, веет,
Все блещет югом и пестреет
Разнообразностью живой.
Язык Италии златой
Звучит по улице веселой
Где ходит гордый славянин,
Француз, испанец, армянин,
И грек, и молдаван тяжелый,
И сын египетской земли,
Корсар в отставке, Морали.

Одессу звучными стихами
Наш друг Туманский описал,
Но он пристрастными глазами
В то время на нее взирал.
Приехав, он прямым поэтом
Пошел бродить с своим лорнетом
Один над морем — и потом
Очаровательным пером
Сады одесские прославил.
Все хорошо, но дело в том,
Что степь нагая там кругом;
Кой-где недавний труд заставил
Младые ветви в знойный день
Давать насильственную тень.

Fragment from Onegin's Journeys

I lived then in Odessa dusty,
The skies are clear and free down there,
And busy trade abounds, is fussy
Erecting broad sails in the air,
Of Europe all there hints and hearkens,
Breathes, has a southern shine, and sparkles,
Flaunts lively, vast variety:
The golden tongue of Italy
Resounds along its happy streets
Where proud Slavs strut, and Frenchmen preen,
Where Spaniard greets Armenian,
Where Greek, Moldavian fat with sweets,
Or Egypt's son walks by that sea,
Retired corsair, Moor Ali.

Odessa in melodious verses
Our friend Tumansky has described.
But he with passionate prejudices
Too much within his gaze imbibed.
He came, marched straight off, like a poet,
Lone o'er the sea to gaze with lorgnette,
And then wrote paeans with charming pen
Of green Odessa's garden glen,
All in a panegyric *thème*.
And that's all fine; there's just one thing:
Bare steppes around that point are ringed.
His work, like magic, forces, then,
On hot days, bare shrubs on the hill,
To spread broad shade against their will!

А где, бишь, мой рассказ несвязный?
В Одессе пыльной, я сказал.
Я б мог сказать: в Одессе грязной —
И тут бы, право, не солгал.
В году недель пять-шесть Одесса
По воле бурного Зевеса,
Потоплена, запружена,
В густой грязи погружена.
Все домы на аршин загрязнут,
Лишь на ходулях пешеход
По улице дерзает вброд;
Кареты, люди тонут, вязнут,
И в дрожках вол, рога склоня,
Сменяет хилого коня.

Но уж дробит каменья молот,
И скоро звонкой мостовой
Покроется спасенный город,
Как будто кованой броней.
Однако в сей Одессе влажной
Еще есть недостаток важный;
Чего б вы думали? — воды!
Потребны тяжкие труды...
Что ж? это небольшое горе,
Особенно, когда вино
Без пошлины привезено.
Но солнце южное, но море...
Чего ж вам более, друзья?
Благословенные края!

But where's my tale now run off, silly?
"Odessa dusty," I had said:
I could have said "Odessa swilly,"
And not lied, either, 't must be plead.
For five-six weeks a year's the norm,
By will of Zeus, Lord of the Storm,
The place gets drowned, drenched, mushed, and mashed,
Into thick mud sinking at last.
All homes with yards of mud get flayed.
Only on stilts foolhardy walkers
Vainly attempt to ford streets swollen;
Coaches and people sink, dismayed:
Hitched oxen, their broad horns bent down,
Take feeble stallions' places now.

But soon the masons' hammers sound,
Set, soon, a stone pavement resounding,
Real stone covers the new, saved town,
Like smithies' horseshoes' bronzes pounding.
Although, in this Odessa humid,
There's one more problem, don't you know it?
Of all the things they lack! it's water!
It's going to be a frightful bother!
Although, it's no great cause to pine—
Especially when so much wine
Gets brought in free, evading customs.
But southern sunshine? But the ocean?
What could one ask for more, my friends?
A land the gods themselves have blessed!

Бывало, пушка зоревая
Лишь только грянет с корабля,
С крутого берега сбегая,
Уж к морю отправляюсь я.
Потом за трубкой раскаленной,
Волной соленой оживленный,
Как мусульман в своем раю,
С восточной гущей кофе пью.
Иду гулять. Уж благосклонный
Открыт Casino; чашек звон
Там раздается; на балкон
Маркёр выходит полусонный
С метлой в руках, и у крыльца
Уже сошлися два купца.

Глядишь — и площадь запестрела.
Все оживилось; здесь и там
Бегут за делом и без дела,
Однако больше по делам.
Дитя расчета и отваги,
Идет купец взглянуть на флаги,
Проведать, шлют ли небеса
Ему знакомы паруса.
Какие новые товары
Вступили нынче в карантин?
Пришли ли бочки жданных вин?
И что чума? и где пожары?
И нет ли голода, войны
Или подобной новизны?

FRAGMENT FROM ONEGIN'S JOURNEYS

When the dawn cannon shot got fired,
Called to the hills forth from its ship,
Straight down the dunes I'd race inspired,
At first light to the sea I'd slip.
And then, ah! through a hot pipe stave,
Enlivened by the salty wave,
Like Muslim gone to heaven and back,
I'd sip thick Eastern coffee, black.
Then off to stroll...By now, appealing,
The Casino starts, cups clinking.
Can be heard, the croupier yawning
Comes to the balcony, half sleeping,
A broom in hand, and by the gate
Two merchants have already met.

And look! The whole square bursts with colors!
All's come alive: and to and fro
On business, or for fun, streets flutter –
Though more, it seems, on business go.
Scanning the flags of every nation,
The merchant, child of calculation
And risk, inquires if the skies
Send welcome sails home as his prize.
And what new goods now are required
To be declared in quarantine?
Perhaps it's come at last, their wine
In barrels? Where's there plague or fire
Or famine, perhaps, or a war?
Or something new like that in store?

Но мы, ребята без печали,
Среди заботливых купцов,
Мы только устриц ожидали
От цареградских берегов.
Что устрицы? Пришли? О радость!
Летит обжорливая младость
Глотать из раковин морских
Затворниц жирных и живых,
Слегка обрызнутых лимоном.
Шум, споры — легкое вино
Из погребов принесено
На стол услужливым Отоном;
Часы летят, а грозный счет
Меж тем невидимо растет.

Но уж темнеет вечер синий,
Пора нам в оперу скорей:
Там упоительный Россини,
Европы баловень — Орфей.
Не внемля критике суровой,
Он вечно тот же, вечно новый,
Он звуки льет — они кипят,
Они текут, они горят,
Как поцелуи молодые,
Все в неге, в пламени любви,
Как зашипевшего Аи
Струя и брызги золотые...
Но господа, позволено ль
С вином равнять do-re-mi-sol?

FRAGMENT FROM ONEGIN'S JOURNEYS

But we, like kids who know no sadness,
Ignored the worried traders' woes.
We only wanted oysters' brought us
From far Constantinople's coasts.
Now they have come, our oysters! Wondrous!
Our happy ranks of youthful gluttons
Fly to devour, from ocean shells
Their captives lush, fat, and alive,
With just a bit of lemon sprinkled.
Noise, argument, and light white wine
Gets brought from cellars to be tippled
By Automne's* waiters, seeming kind,
(As time flies by, their bill of woe.
Invisibly the while does grow).

But dusky blue the sky is darkening,
The Opera awaits, we race,
There Europe's darling, ever–charming,
Rossini now our Orpheus plays!
He pays no heed to direst critics;
Always the same, yet new, and witty,
He pours forth sounds: and how they boil!
And how they flow and burn and hiss!
Passion'd as young lovers who kiss
In bliss, in happiness of love,
Like champagne, ever bubbling, rolling,
In streams and sprays of droplets golden
But folks, is it perhaps a crime,
With do--re--mi comparing wine?

---

* César Automne – The fanciest French restaurant in Odessa at that time.

А только ль там очарований?
А разыскательный лорнет?
А закулисные свиданья?
A prima donna? а балет?
А ложа, где, красой блистая,
Негоциантка молодая,
Самолюбива и томна,
Толпой рабов окружена?
Она и внемлет и не внемлет
И каватине, и мольбам,
И шутке с лестью пополам...
А муж — в углу за нею дремлет,
Впросонках фора закричит,
Зевнет — и снова захрапит.

Финал гремит; пустеет зала;
Шумя, торопится разъезд;
Толпа на площадь побежала
При блеске фонарей и звезд,
Сыны Авзонии счастливой
Слегка поют мотив игривый,
Его невольно затвердив,
А мы ревем речитатив.
Но поздно. Тихо спит Одесса;
И бездыханна и тепла
Немая ночь. Луна взошла,
Прозрачно-легкая завеса
Объемлет небо. Все молчит;
Лишь море Черное шумит...

Итак, я жил тогда в Одессе...

Does naught else makes the evening charming?
Aren't opera-glasses fond of play?
Can't trysts be had in darkened corners?
And prima donnas? And ballet?
Can't we watch beauty in the loge,
Where trader's daughter flaunts and shows
Her youth and grace, her languor proud—
Around her willing slaves all crowd?
She hears and yet she doesn't hear
The cavatina, or the prayers,
The jokes and flattery mixed in layers...
Her husband slumbers, by her near,
Half-sleeping, he calls out "encores"
Then yawns, and once again he snores.

Finale played, the hall grows bare,
And bustling, rushing off, crushed, spars
The crowd, running about the square
Amid the gleam of lamps and stars.
And blessed Italy's bright sons
With their light touch croon playful runs
By heart, half automatically,
While we sob the recitative.
But now it's late. Odessa sleeps,
Soft is its warm and breathless night,
Numbed. The moon arises calm and bright,
Diaphanous its curtained light meets
And embraces heaven. All is still
But the Black Sea's murmuring rill...

And so, I lived then in Odessa...

НОЧЬ

Мой голос для тебя и ласковый и томной
Тревожит позднее молчанье ночи темной.
Близ ложа моего печальная свеча
Горит; мои стихи, сливаясь и журча,
Текут, ручьи любви, текут, полны тобою.
Во тьме твои глаза блистают предо мною,
Мне улыбаются, и звуки слышу я:
Мой друг, мой нежный друг.... люблю... твоя... твоя!

NIGHT

My voice, when meant for you, affectionate and yearning,
The darkened silent lull of late night wakes, disturbing.
A candle by my bed with sadness lonely burns.
My verse begins to spring, pours bubbling out and churns,
And flows, a brook of love, it flows, full of you, brimming,
Your eyes before me shine, in darkness gleam, a–shimmering,
And when they smile at me, I hear you say, my love,
My friend, my tender friend...I love!... I'm yours... I'm yours!

Nude underneath a tree

В твою светлицу, друг мой нежный,
Я прихожу в последний раз.
Любви, отрады безмятежной
Делю с тобой последний час.
Вперед одна в надежде томной
Не жди меня средь ночи темной,
До первых утренних лучей
      Не жги свечей.

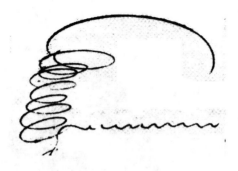

FOR ONE LAST TIME, MY FRIEND SO TENDER

For one last time, my friend so tender,
I come again to your sweet bower.
To love and happiness surrender,
In peace with you share one last hour.
Henceforth no more with hopeful longing
Pass dark night just to me belonging,
No more, until the sun's first rays,
      Let candles blaze.

Amalia Riznich

Ночной зефир
   Струит эфир.
     Шумит,
  Бежит
Гвадалквивир.

Вот взошла луна златая,
Тише... чу... гитары звон...
Вот испанка молодая
Оперлася на балкон.

 Ночной зефир
    Струит эфир.
      Шумит,
   Бежит
Гвадалквивир.

Скинь мантилью, ангел милый,
И явись как яркий день!
Сквозь чугунные перилы
Ножку дивную продень!

 Ночной зефир
    Струит эфир.
      Шумит,
   Бежит
Гвадалквивир.

Night's soft breeze
   Streams easeful; clear
      And foaming
   Flows
Guadalquivir.

Mark the golden moon appearing,
Hush! As a guitar sings free...
As a youthful señorita
Leans against her balcony.

Night's soft breeze
   Streams easeful; clear
      And foaming
   Flows
Guadalquivir.

Cast your shawl off, darling angel,
Show yourself, as bright as day!
Through grilled bars of wrought-iron tracery
Slip your sweet foot through, and play!

Night's soft breeze
   Streams easeful; clear
      And foaming
   Flows
Guadalquivir.

Пред испанкой благородной
Двое рыцарей стоят,
Оба смело и свободно
В очи прямо ей глядят.
Блещут оба красотою,
Оба сердцем горячи,
Оба мощною рукою
Оперлися на мечи.

Жизни им она дороже
И, как слава, им мила;
Но один ей мил — кого же
Дева сердцем избрала?
«Кто, реши, любим тобою?» —
Оба деве говорят
И с надеждой молодою
В очи прямо ей глядят.

BY A NOBLE SEÑORITA

By a noble señorita,
Spanish beauty, stand two knights,
Both are daring, both are freely
Looking straight into her eyes.
Both with handsomeness are gleaming,
Bright of mind, of fiery hearts,
Both of them alertly leaning
With strong hands upon their swords.

Dearer than their lives they prize her,
Bright as glory shines her star,
But just one her heart replies to:
Who has won this maiden's heart?
"Who, decide, is your beloved?"
To the maiden say both knights,
Standing both with hopes so young and
Looking straight into her eyes.

Под небом голубым страны своей родной
     Она томилась, увядала...
Увяла наконец, и верно надо мной
     Младая тень уже летала;
Но недоступная черта меж нами есть.
     Напрасно чувство возбуждал я:
Из равнодушных уст я слышал смерти весть,
     И равнодушно ей внимал я.
Так вот кого любил я пламенной душой
     С таким тяжелым напряженьем,
С такою нежною, томительной тоской,
     С таким безумством и мученьем!
Где муки, где любовь? Увы, в душе моей
     Для бедной, легковерной тени,
Для сладкой памяти невозвратимых дней
     Не нахожу ни слез, ни пени.

Beneath the light blue skies of her own native land,
        In languor languishing and pining,
She faded out at last, till faithfully she spanned
        Her shadow young above me flying.
Yet twixt us looms a bound beyond our ken:
        In vain I sought for feelings searing.
I heard from lips indifferent of her death,
        The news indifferently hearing.
But is this whom I loved with all my fiery soul
        In constant, burdened consternation?
For whom my tenderness and grief did endless flow,
        With so much craziness and torment and elation?
And now? Where's woe, where's love? Alas! My soul can find
        For that poor shadow trusting, hoping,
For memories sweet of days forever left behind,
        No hint of tears or self-reproaching.

Для берегов отчизны дальной
Ты покидала край чужой;
В час незабвенный, в час печальный
Я долго плакал пред тобой.
Мои хладеющие руки
Тебя старались удержать;
Томленья страшного разлуки
Мой стон молил не прерывать.

Но ты от горького лобзанья
Свои уста оторвала;
Из края мрачного изгнанья
Ты в край иной меня звала.
Ты говорила: «В день свиданья
Под небом вечно голубым
В тени олив, любви лобзанья
Мы вновь, мой друг, соединим».

Но там, увы, где неба своды
Сияют в блеске голубом,
Где тень олив легла на воды,
Заснула ты последним сном.
Твоя краса, твои страданья
Исчезли в урне гробовой —
А с ними поцелуй свиданья...
Но жду его; он за тобой...

BOUND FOR YOUR DISTANT HOMELAND'S SHORELINE

Bound for your homeland's distant shoreline,
Our distant foreign land you left.
That hour of memory, hour mournful
Long time in front of you I wept.
My arms, as they were growing number,
Tried, tried to hold you tightly tucked,
And separation's frightful suffering
My moans prayed you'd not interrupt.

But you from our caressing bitter
Pulled back your lips and tore them free.
And from this land of exile wistful
To a new land were calling me.
You said: "that day reunion graces,
Beneath a sky that's always blue,
Where olive trees give shade, love's kisses,
We'll once again, my friend, renew.

But there, alas, where heaven's vaulting
Is sparkling light cerulean blue,
Where olives' shades lie on the waters,
Your final sleep has come to you.
Your suffering, your beauty fleeting,
Into the grave's urn vanished then,
With them the kisses of our meeting...
But I still wait; you owe me them.

ЗАКЛИНАНИЕ

О, если правда, что в ночи,
Когда покоятся живые,
И с неба лунные лучи
Скользят на камни гробовые,
О, если правда, что тогда
Пустеют тихие могилы —
Я тень зову, я жду Леилы:
Ко мне, мой друг, сюда, сюда!

Явись, возлюбленная тень,
Как ты была перед разлукой,
Бледна, хладна, как зимний день,
Искажена последней мукой.
Приди, как дальняя звезда,
Как легкий звук иль дуновенье,
Иль как ужасное виденье,
Мне все равно: сюда, сюда!..

Зову тебя не для того,
Чтоб укорять людей, чья злоба
Убила друга моего,
Иль чтоб изведать тайны гроба,
Не для того, что иногда
Сомненьем мучусь... Но, тоскуя,
Хочу сказать, что всё люблю я,
Что всё я твой: сюда, сюда!

INVOCATION

Oh, if it's true that in the night,
When sleep embraces all the living,
And, down from heaven, moonbeams bright,
Play on the tombstones, tripping, slipping,
Oh, if it's true that then, indeed,
The silent graves are oped, and empty,
I call Leila's shade, I'm waiting:
To me, my friend, come here, come here!

Appear, oh shade that I have loved,
The way you were before we parted,
Like winter's day, cold, pale and dulled,
By final agonies distorted.
Shine like a distant star, appear
Like a light sound or wind's soft swishing,
Or like a dreaded apparition:
I do not care, come here, come here!

I do not call you to reproach
The guilty ones, whose malice needless
Did kill the dearest friend I know,
Or to discover the grave's secrets,
Nor yet because my heart's still seared
With doubts and griefs, sometimes... No! Mourning,
I want to say, I still, still love you,
I'm still all yours, come here, come here!

УЗНИК

Сижу за решеткой в темнице сырой.
Вскормленный в неволе орел молодой,
Мой грустный товарищ, махая крылом,
Кровавую пищу клюет под окном,

Клюет, и бросает, и смотрит в окно,
Как будто со мною задумал одно;
Зовет меня взглядом и криком своим
И вымолвить хочет: «Давай улетим!

Мы вольные птицы; пора, брат, пора!
Туда, где за тучей белеет гора,
Туда, где синеют морские края,
Туда, где гуляем лишь ветер... да я!...»

THE CAPTIVE

Imprisoned, I'm caged in a dungeon that's dank,
A young eaglet, fed but on slavish grains rank,
Then aggrieved, my companion flies nigh, flaps his wings,
And food, fresh, still bloody, to my window brings.

He pecks, casts it through my caged bars with his beak,
Then stares at me, as if his heart heard me speak,
With looks that are calling, with calls that would say,
If shrieks could find words, "Come! Let's fly, fly away!

We're free spirits, brother, let's go, the time's right!
Let's rise through the clouds to the peak ever white!
Let's soar to the borders of blue sea and sky,
And stroll on the wind where just wind strolls – and I!"

The Eaglet

ДЕМОН

В те дни, когда мне были новы
Все впечатленья бытия —
И взоры дев, и шум дубровы,
И ночью пенье соловья, —
Когда возвышенные чувства,
Свобода, слава и любовь
И вдохновенные искусства
Так сильно волновали кровь,
Часы надежд и наслаждений
Тоской внезапной осеня,
Тогда какой-то злобный гений
Стал тайно навещать меня.
Печальны были наши встречи:
Его улыбка, чудный взгляд,
Его язвительные речи
Вливали в душу хладный яд.
Неистощимой клеветою
Он провиденье искушал;
Он звал прекрасное мечтою;
Он вдохновенье презирал;
Не верил он любви, свободе;
На жизнь насмешливо глядел —
И ничего во всей природе
Благословить он не хотел.

Alexander Rayevsky — The Demon

THE DEMON

Back when, to me, all things shone newly,
All the impressions of this life.
The looks of girls, the wind in oak trees,
The nightingale that sings at night,
When all the loftiest of feelings
Of freedom, glory and of love,
Of arts inspired, just set me reeling,
And powerfully stirred my blood.
Those days of hopes and pleasures easy,
And shocks revealed by sudden grief,
Were when a certain evil genius
In secret came to visit me.
And melancholy were our meetings,
Because his smile, his look so bold
And charming, his sarcastic speeches
Poured chilling poison in my soul.
With slander that was ever–biting,
He taunted, tempted Providence.
He called the beautiful a pipe–dream,
For inspiration had contempt,
And he did not believe in freedom.
He doubted love, held life in scorn.
He could not see the slightest reason
To bless one thing this world had born.

К МОРЮ

Прощай, свободная стихия!
В последний раз передо мной
Ты катишь волны голубые
И блещешь гордою красой.

Как друга ропот заунывный,
Как зов его в прощальный час,
Твой грустный шум, твой шум призывный
Услышал я в последний раз.

Моей души предел желанный!
Как часто по брегам твоим
Бродил я тихий и туманный,
Заветным умыслом томим!

Как я любил твои отзывы,
Глухие звуки, бездны глас
И тишину в вечерний час,
И своенравные порывы!

Смиренный парус рыбарей,
Твоею прихотью хранимый,
Скользит отважно средь зыбей:
Но ты взыграл, неодолимый,
И стая тонет кораблей.

Не удалось навек оставить
Мне скучный, неподвижный брег,
Тебя восторгами поздравить
И по хребтам твоим направить
Мой поэтический побег.

TO THE SEA

Farewell, farewell, free force of nature!
This is the last time I will see
You cast and hurl your breakers azure,
Your beauty proud, your sparkling sheen!

Like friends when parting, moaning, whimpering,
When time has come to say goodbye,
Your sound's so sad, your sound sighs, whispering,
For the last time I hear you cry.

Oh bound of all my soul's desire!
How often by your shores I've roved,
With silent misty dreams afire,
With languor, full of cherished hopes!

And how I loved your echoes precious,
Your voice of the abyss, dull pounds,
Your calm, when evening stills all sounds,
Your moods, your roaring gusts capricious!

A fisherman's meek sail is cowed,
And so protected by your whimsy,
And slips through towering waves, stays proud,
But then you play, with untamed frenzy,
And fleets of mighty ships are drowned.

Alas, I could not leave forever
My boring, dull, unmoving shores
To celebrate your joys, and quiver,
Tossed by your wave–crests, hither–thither,
Escape, poetic, my locked doors.

Ты ждал, ты звал... Я был окован;
Вотще рвалась душа моя:
Могучей страстью очарован,
У берегов остался я.

О чем жалеть? Куда бы ныне
Я путь беспечный устремил?
Один предмет в твоей пустыне
Мою бы душу поразил.

Одна скала, гробница славы...
Там погружались в хладный сон
Воспоминанья величавы:
Там угасал Наполеон.

Там он почил среди мучений.
И вслед за ним, как бури шум,
Другой от нас умчался гений,
Другой властитель наших дум.

Исчез, оплаканный свободой,
Оставя миру свой венец.
Шуми, взволнуйся непогодой:
Он был, о море, твой певец.

Твой образ был на нем означен,
Он духом создан был твоим:
Как ты, могущ, глубок и мрачен,
Как ты, ничем не укротим.

TO THE SEA

You called, you waited, but imprisoned,
I tore my soul in two, and moaned.
Your utter power charmed, impassioned
Me, left by your shores, alone.

Why such regret? And now say whither
Would I now set my careless course?
There's still one object in your desert
That strikes within my soul a chord.

One distant cliff, the grave of glory...
There into cold oblivion
Great memories did sink, deeds storied,
For there did fade Napoleon.

He passed away in suffering, grieving.
Soon after, sudden as a squall,
Another genius disappeared then,
Another ruler of our thoughts.

He vanished, mourned by tears of Freedom,
But left this world his laurelled art.
So rise up, howl, you storm-winds shrieking!
For he, oh Ocean, was your bard.

Your image all his work was moving:
His soul was fitted to your frame.
Like you, he too was strong, deep, brooding,
And he, like you, could not be tamed.

Мир опустел... Теперь куда же
Меня б ты вынес, океан?
Судьба земли повсюду та же:
Где капля блага, там на страже
Уж просвещенье иль тиран.

Прощай же, море! Не забуду
Твоей торжественной красы
И долго, долго слышать буду
Твой гул в вечерние часы.

В леса, в пустыни молчаливы
Перенесу, тобою полн,
Твои скалы, твои заливы,
И блеск, и тень, и говор волн.

Napoleon

TO THE SEA

The world's gone bare. So where now, ocean,
Where would you wildly carry me?
For Fate's the same the whole world over:
Where some good's left, it's guarded ever
By Progress or by Tyranny.

Farewell, my Ocean! I'll remember
Your beauty, your triumphant grace!
I'll hear and hear and hear forever
Your roar when evening lights do blaze.

To forests, wildernesses silent,
I take with me, my spirit raves
But of your cliffs and gulfs, your tides and
Your sheen, and shades, and speaking waves!

Lord Byron

Я был рожден для жизни мирной,
Для деревенской тишины;

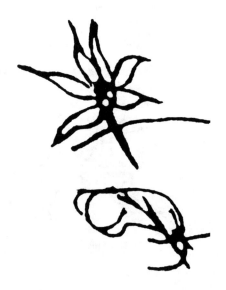

III. RUSTIC EXILE: MIKHAYLOVSKOYE

I was just born for this life peaceful,
For stillness pastoral, it seems...

Ненастный день потух; ненастной ночи мгла
По небу стелется одеждою свинцовой;
Как приведение, за рощею сосновой
    Луна туманная взошла...
Всё мрачную тоску на душу мне наводит.
Далёко, там, луна в сиянии восходит;
Там воздух напоен вечерней теплотой;
Там море движется роскошной пеленой
    Под голубыми небесами...
Вот время: по горе теперь идет она
К брегам, потопленным шумящими волнами;
    Там, под заветными скалами,
Теперь она сидит печальна и одна...
Одна... никто пред ней не плачет, не тоскует;
Никто ее колен в забвенье не целует;
Одна... ничьим устам она не предает
Ни плеч, ни влажных уст, ни персей белоснежных.
. . . .
. . . .
. . . .
Никто ее любви небесной не достоин.
Не правда ль: ты одна... ты плачешь... я спокоен;
. . . .
Но если . . . .

A drizzly day's fizzed out; a drizzly night's dull haze
Across the heavens spreads like leaden clothing;
Like a dread ghost, beyond the pine grove roaming,
        The misty moon disperses rays...
As always, gloomy grief upon my soul it's casting...
Way far off, there, the moonrise glitters, glancing,
Down there the air gets drunk, and fills with gloaming warmth,
Down there the sea heaves sheathes of sumptuous foam in swarms
        Beneath the light blue heavens swelling...
Right now's when down the mountainside she likes to roam
To shores completely drowned by waves' roaring and yelling,
        There, underneath the black cliffs blessèd,
In melancholy now, she's sitting there, alone...
Alone! And near her no one's crying, no one's grieving,
No one kisses her knees in bliss, bereavement;
Alone! To no one's lips does she give up
Her shoulders, soft lips moist, her snowy-white soft bosom.
. . . .
. . . .
. . . .
Of her love heavenly no one on earth is worthy.
You are alone, aren't you? You're crying...I won't worry.
. . . .
But if, though. . . . .

ТАЛИСМАН

Там, где море вечно плещет
На пустынные скалы,
Где луна теплее блещет
В сладкий час вечерней мглы,
Где, в гаремах наслаждаясь,
Дни проводит мусульман,
Там волшебница, ласкаясь,
Мне вручила талисман.

И, ласкаясь, говорила:
«Сохрани мой талисман:
В нем таинственная сила!
Он тебе любовью дан.
От недуга, от могилы,
В бурю, в грозный ураган,
Головы твоей, мой милый,
Не спасет мой талисман.

И богатствами Востока
Он тебя не одарит,
И поклонников пророка
Он тебе не покорит;
И тебя на лоно друга,
От печальных чуждых стран,
В край родной на север с юга
Не умчит мой талисман...

Но когда коварны очи
Очаруют вдруг тебя,
Иль уста во мраке ночи
Поцелуют не любя —
Милый друг! от преступленья,
От сердечных новых ран,
От измены, от забвенья
Сохранит мой талисман!»

Yelizaveta Vorontsova

THE TALISMAN

Where the ocean comes careening
Against desolate, bare cliffs,
Where the moon is warmly gleaming
On the evening hour's sweet mists,
Where, in harems, at his pleasure,
Days find the Mohammedan,
There a sorceress gave me treasure,
Kissed me, gave a talisman.

She caressed me in our bower,
Said: "My talisman you'll keep.
It is full of hidden power
And t'is given with love deep.
From disease, the grave, storm's rages,
From the hurricane's dread wave,
Your sweet head, my own, my angel,
This, my talisman, won't save.

Of the Orient the riches,
None my talisman can bring.
Where the Prophet's faithful preaches,
This, my gift, won't make you King.
Longing for your dear friend's bosom,
Forth out of a sad, strange land,
Homewards, northwards, o! my true one!
No speed gives my talisman...

But should cunning eyes behold you,
Suddenly bewitch your mind,
Some dark night, if lips too bold should
Kiss unloving and unkind —
My sweet friend! From sin heart-rending,
From new wounds the heart can't stand,
From betrayal, from forgetting,
Saves you then my talisman!"

СОЖЖЕННОЕ ПИСЬМО

Прощай, письмо любви, прощай! Она велела...
Как долго медлил я! Как долго не хотела
Рука предать огню все радости мои!...
Но полно, час настал: гори, письмо любви.
Готов я; ничему душа моя не внемлет.
Уж пламя жадное листы твои приемлет...
Минуту!... вспыхнули!... пылают... легкий дым,
Виясь, теряется с молением моим.
Уж перстня верного утратя впечатленье,
Растопленный сургуч кипит... О провиденье!
Свершилось! Темные свернулися листы;
На легком пепле их заветные черты
Белеют...грудь моя стеснилась. Пепел милый,
Отрада бедная в судьбе моей унылой,
Останься век со мной на горестной груди...

THE BURNT LETTER

Farewell, letter of love, farewell. It was her order...
How long I have delayed! How long my poor hand dawdled
Refused to drag my joys to flame...Enough!
The time has come: burn up, letter of love.
I'm ready; not a thing now is my soul perceiving.
The greedy flame will soon your pages be receiving...
One minute! Sparks fly up, it's blazing, light smoke flares
And winds itself around, gets lost with all my prayers.
Of faithful seal the former evidence,
The melted wax, boils up...Oh, Providence!
The deed is done! The darkened pages curl,
In ashes light, now twirling their last traces blest,
They whiten. How my breast is tightened! Dearest ashes,
Poor joy and comfort of my fate's bleak, hopeless passions,
Remain forever with me on my grieving breast.

Vorontsova in profile

ЖЕЛАНИЕ СЛАВЫ

Когда, любовию и негой упоенный,
Безмолвно пред тобой коленопреклоненный,
Я на тебя глядел и думал: ты моя, —
Ты знаешь, милая, желал ли славы я;
Ты знаешь: удален от ветреного света,
Скучая суетным прозванием поэта,
Устав от долгих бурь, я вовсе не внимал
Жужжанью дальному упреков и похвал.
Могли ль меня молвы тревожить приговоры,
Когда, склонив ко мне томительные взоры
И руку на главу мне тихо наложив,
Шептала ты: скажи, ты любишь, ты счастлив?
Другую, как меня, скажи, любить не будешь?
Ты никогда, мой друг, меня не позабудешь?
А я стесненное молчание хранил,
Я наслаждением весь полон был, я мнил,
Что нет грядущего, что грозный день разлуки
Не придет никогда...И что же? Слезы, муки,
Измены, клевета, все на главу мою
Обрушилося вдруг...Что я, где я? Стою,
Как путник, молнией постигнутый в пустыне,
И все передо мной затмилося! И ныне
Я новым для меня желанием томим:
Желаю славы я, чтоб именем моим
Твой слух был поражен всечасно, чтоб ты мною
Окружена была, чтоб громкою молвою
Все, все вокруг тебя звучало обо мне,
Чтоб, гласу верному внимая в тишине,
Ты помнила мои последние моленья
В саду, во тьме ночной, в минуту разлученья.

WISH FOR GLORY

When full of love and bliss I felt complete elation,
And on my knees, at you in silent supplication
I looked and looked, just thinking: "You are mine!" —
You know, my dear, was glory on my mind?
You know how I just fled society's fuss showy,
Bored with my gossipy vain title as a poet,
Tired out by endless storms, I paid no heed at all
To distant buzzing praise, or to catcalls.
How could I even care for ignorant crowds' answers,
When leaning close to me, so languorously glancing,
You, slightly, on my head, laying your hand, your glove,
Would whispering, ask me, "Are you happy? Do you love?
Will you love someone else the way you loved me?
Tell me, my friend, will you one day forget me?"
But I an awkward silence then preserved,
And being filled with pleasure totally, inferred
That what would come won't come, that the dread day, us sundering,
Would not—ever! arrive. Instead: what? Tears and sufferings,
Betrayal, slander, all on my head now land
All of a sudden... Who am I and where? I stand,
Like a wanderer struck by lightning in the desert.
And all's grown dark before me now; all's altered.
A new desire cooks me in its flame:
I wish for glory now, I wish that with my name
Each hour would e'er confound your hearing, so by me
You'd be surrounded e'er, so that with plaintive crying
All, everything around you sounded with my noise,
So, in the silence, hearkening to my faithful voice,
You'd not forget my last words to you, broken-hearted,
That night in garden's shade, when we were being parted.

СЦЕНА ИЗ ФАУСТА
БЕРЕГ МОРЯ. ФАУСТ И МЕФИСТОФЕЛЬ.

Фауст
Мне скучно, бес.

Мефистофель
Что делать, Фауст?
Таков вам положен предел,
Его ж никто не преступает.
Вся тварь разумная скучает:
Иной от лени, тот от дел;
Кто верит, кто утратил веру;
Тот насладиться не успел,
Тот насладился через меру,
И всяк зевает да живет –
И всех вас гроб, зевая, ждет.
Зевай и ты.

Фауст
Сухая шутка!
Найди мне способ как-нибудь
Рассеяться.

Мефистофель
Доволен будь
Ты доказательством рассудка.
В своем альбоме запиши:
Fastidium est quies — скука
Отдохновение души.
Я психолог... о вот наука!..
Скажи, когда ты не скучал?
Подумай, поищи. Тогда ли,
Как над Виргилием дремал,
А розги ум твой возбуждали?
Тогда ль, как розами венчал
Ты благосклонных дев веселья
И в буйстве шумном посвящал
Им пыл вечернего похмелья?
Тогда ль, как погрузился ты
В великодушные мечты,
В пучину темную науки?
Но, помнится, тогда со скуки,
Как арлекина, из огня
Ты вызвал наконец меня.
Я мелким бесом извивался,
Развеселить тебя старался,
Возил и к ведьмам и к духам,
И что же? всё по пустякам.
Желал ты славы — и добился,
Хотел влюбиться — и влюбился.
Ты с жизни взял возможну дань,
А был ли счастлив?

Tempt me not, demon (Self-portrait)

SCENE FROM FAUST
FAUST AND MEPHISTOPHELES BY THE SEASHORE.

Faust
Demon, I'm bored.

Mephistopheles
What of it, Faust?
Such is the bound you're bound to bear.
And there is none who oversteps it.
All clever creatures end up fretting:
Some boredom bores — and some affairs,
One's faithful, one has lost all faith.
One never got of lust his share,
One's shares of pleasures was too great.
Yet all are yawning, all live on,
And for them all the grave does yawn.
So you yawn too.

Faust
How dry that joke is!
Find me some manner nonetheless
To keep amused.

Mephistopheles
Just be content
At this, the proof of your own reason.
Write in your album, if you please,
Fastidium est quies. Tedium
In truth is but the soul's release.
I'm a psychologist: It's science, really!
Just say: when was it you weren't bored?
Think well. Search in your memory. Own up!
Remember how o'er Virgil you once snored
And only caning woke your wit up?
Or how once roses from you poured
Forth, all thoughts to eager girls gave over,
Carousing loud, for them songs roared
With lust from last night's hangover?
Or when you'd disappeared, it seemed,
To the great dreams your great soul dreamed
Into the darkest depths of science?
Yet weren't you bored then? Do confide it!
Like Harlequin forth from the flame
You summoned me at last by name.
I fluttered in, a petty demon,
Endeavoring to make you cheery,
Brought you to witches' dens, to ghosts,
For what? For trifles, nonsense gross!
You wanted glory? And-- you got it!
Would fall in love? You did! What of it?
You took from life all life puts out
But were you happy?

Фауст
Перестань,
Не растравляй мне язвы тайной.
В глубоком знанье жизни нет —
Я проклял знаний ложный свет,
А слава... луч ее случайный
Неуловим. Мирская честь
Бессмысленна, как сон... Но есть
Прямое благо: сочетанье
Двух душ...

Мефистофель
И первое свиданье,
Не правда ль? Но нельзя ль узнать,
Кого изволишь поминать,
Не Гретхен ли?

Фауст
О сон чудесный!
О пламя чистое любви!
Там, там — где тень, где шум древесный,
Где сладко-звонкие струи —
Там, на груди ее прелестной
Покоя томную главу,
Я счастлив был...

Мефистофель
Творец небесный!
Ты бредишь, Фауст, наяву!
Услужливым воспоминаньем
Себя обманываешь ты.
Не я ль тебе своим стараньем
Доставил чудо красоты?
И в час полуночи глубокой
С тобою свел ее? Тогда
Плодами своего труда
Я забавлялся одинокий,
Как вы вдвоем — все помню я.
Когда красавица твоя
Была в восторге, в упоенье,
Ты беспокойною душой
Уж погружался в размышленье
(А доказали мы с тобой,
Что размышленье — скуки семя).
И знаешь ли, философ мой,
Что́ думал ты в такое время,
Когда не думает никто?
Сказать ли?

Фауст
Говори. Ну, что?

Faust
Cut it out.
Poison me not with hidden ulcer.
In deepest knowledge there's no life.
I've cursed the sciences' false light,
And glory...Its rays random, glancing,
Are meaningless as sleep. But there's
Still one good thing left: the joining
Of two souls.
Mephistopheles
And the first tryst's enjoyment,
No? But if inquiry won't offend,
Just whom were you remembering then?
Not Gretchen, now?
Faust
Oh dream so wondrous!
Oh pure and perfect flame of love!
There, where the shady grove soft flutters,
Where sweetly purling streams do rush,
Upon her breast so marvelous
When I my raptured head did lay
I was happy...
Mephistopheles
Oh Father, save us!
You're raving, Faust, by light of day!
Your memory is too convenient
And you deceive yourself, it seems,
Was it not I whose striving eager
Got you your wondrous, beauteous queen,
And in the depths of midnight murky
Brought her to you? And then
I was amused alone to spend
That time, finding my labors worthy.
As you two were ensconced, enthralled,
And as that fine beauty of yours,
Ecstatic, shuddered in elation,
Your soul stayed in a worried state,
Had sunk by now to contemplation
(And you and I did demonstrate
 That contemplation's boredom's seed)
So, my dear Sophist, need I state
What you were thinking at that time
When no one thinks?
Should I say?
Faust
Say it! Tell me. Well?

Мефистофель
Ты думал: агнец мой послушный!
Как жадно я тебя желал!
Как хитро в деве простодушной
Я грезы сердца возмущал!
Любви невольной, бескорыстной
Невинно предалась она...
Что ж грудь моя теперь полна
Тоской и скукой ненавистной?..
На жертву прихоти моей
Гляжу, упившись наслажденьем,
С неодолимым отвращеньем:
Так безрасчетный дуралей,
Вотще решась на злое дело,
Зарезав нищего в лесу,
Бранит ободранное тело;
Так на продажную красу,
Насытясь ею торопливо,
Разврат косится боязливо...
Потом из этого всего
Одно ты вывел заключенье...

Фауст
Сокройся, адское творенье!
Беги от взора моего!

Мефистофель
Изволь. Задай лишь мне задачу:
Без дела, знаешь, от тебя
Не смею отлучаться я —
Я даром времени не трачу.

Фауст
Что там белеет? Говори.

Мефистофель
Корабль испанский трехмачтовый,
Пристать в Голландию готовый:
На нем мерзавцев сотки три,
Две обезьяны, бочки злата,
Да груз богатый шоколата,
Да модная болезнь: она
Недавно вам подарена.

Фауст
Всё утопить.
Мефистофель
Сейчас. *(Исчезает)*

Mephistopheles
You thought then: my meek lamb obedient!
How hungrily I longed for you!
How slyly in a simple maiden
I caused dreams of the heart to stew!
To selfless, helpless love repining,
She gave herself with blameless will.
So why's my own breast now so full
Of grief and boredom so despisèd?
I see the victim of my whim
And look on, sated with my pleasure,
And my contempt now knows no measure,
Just so, a heedless fool might grin
In vain determined on some evil,
Knifing a beggar in the wood
And curse the cut–up corpse with fever:
So at some venal tart one would
Sating one's lust on upon her, hurried,
From lechery look askance, now worried.
And you, from all of this delight,
Could only draw one cruel conclusion...

Faust
Begone, hell–hound and dark illusion!
Begone, and vanish from my sight!

Mephistopheles
Gladly—just give me an assignment.
Without one, as you know, I can't
Just separate from you like that—
My time is never frittered idly.

Faust
Say! What's that gleams white from afar?

Mephistopheles
A Spanish galleon, with three masts,
That's reaching Holland now, at last:
Aboard three hundred villains are,
Two monkeys, and gold bullion also,
Of chocolate, too, quite a rich cargo,
Plus one disease...It's stylish, though,
You got its gift not long ago.

Faust
Drown everything.

Mephistopheles
At once.

(Disappears)

ЗИМНИЙ ВЕЧЕР

Буря мглою небо кроет,
Вихри снежные крутя:
То, как зверь, она завоет,
То заплачет, как дитя,
То по кровле обветшалой
Вдруг соломой зашумит,
То, как путник запоздалый,
К нам в окошко застучит.

Наша ветхая лачужка
И печальна и темна.
Что же ты, моя старушка,
Приумолкла у окна?
Или бури завываньем
Ты, мой друг, утомлена,
Или дремлешь под жужжаньем
Своего веретена?

Выпьем, добрая подружка
Бедной юности моей,
Выпьем с горя; где же кружка?
Сердцу будет веселей.
Спой мне песню, как синица
Тихо за морем жила;
Спой мне песню, как девица
За водой поутру шла.

Буря мглою небо кроет,
Вихри снежные крутя;
То, как зверь, она завоет,
То заплачет, как дитя.
Выпьем, добрая подружка
Бедной юности моей,
Выпьем с горя; где же кружка?
Сердцу будет веселей.

A WINTER EVENING

Snowstorm, gloom-filled, heavens drowning,
Wild the snowy whirlwind flies:
Sometimes, like a beast, it's howling,
Sometimes, like a child, it cries,
Sometimes, on our roof's frayed border
With a gust the straw resounds;
Sometimes, like a lost late wanderer,
On our little window pounds.

Our ramshackle hut, half-ruined,
Feels so dark, by sadness crushed,
Why do you, my dear old woman,
By the window sit so hushed?
Say, my friend, has the storm's muttering
Worn you out, brought you to heel?
Or are you just somewhat slumbering,
As you click your spinning wheel?

Let's just drink, my dear old friend (from even
When I was a poor, small boy);
Where's your mug now? Drink from grieving,
And the heart will feel more joy.
Sing for me your song, how bluebird
Lived in peace beyond the sea.
Sing how one morning a girl heard,
As to fetch water went she.

Snowstorm, gloom-filled, heavens drowning,
Wild the snowy whirlwind flies:
Sometimes, like a beast, it's howling,
Sometimes, like a child, it cries.
Let's just drink, my dear old friend (from even
When I was a poor, small boy);
Where's your mug now? Drink from grieving,
And the heart will feel more joy.

Сват Иван, как пить мы станем,
Непременно уж помянем
Трех Матрен, Луку с Петром,
Да Пахомовну потом.
Мы живали с ними дружно,
Уж как хочешь — будь что будь —
Этих надо помянуть,
Помянуть нам этих нужно.
Поминать так поминать,
Начинать так начинать,
Лить так лить, разлив разливом.
Начинай-ка, сват, пора.
Трех Матрен, Луку, Петра
В первый раз помянем пивом,
А Пахомовну потом
Пирогами да вином,
Да еще ее помянем:
Сказки сказывать мы станем —
Мастерица ведь была
И откуда что брала.
А куды разумны шутки,
Приговорки, прибаутки,
Небылицы, былины
Православной старины!..
Слушать, так душе отрадно.
И не пил бы и не ел,
Всё бы слушал да сидел.
Кто придумал их так ладно?
Стариков когда-нибудь
(Жаль, теперь нам не досужно)
Надо будет помянуть —
Помянуть и этих нужно...
Слушай, сват, начну первой,
Сказка будет за тобой.

Iván, dear coz'*, if we start drinking,
Surely we must toast, I'm thinking,
The three Matryonas, Peter, Luke,
And Pakhomovna to boot!
Long we've lived with them and, truly,
All such friends, no matter what,
Must be toasted, ne'er forgot!
Must be toasted, absolutely!
If we're drinking, then let's drink!
Glasses clinking, then let's clink!
Pouring pour, with froth brims brimming,
Let's begin, my dear, in truth!
The three Matryonas, Peter, Luke,
First with beer we'll toast, head swimming,
Then Pakhomovna as well,
After pies, with wine — and tell —
Just to show how much we love her —
Fairy tales of that fair mother —
Oh, how sweet and bright her tongue!
Where did all her tales come from?
Where'd she get her plots so witty?
All her proverbs, songs, and ditties,
Wonders, wives' tales, gifts galore
From our ancient faith's true lore!
How the soul rejoiced in hearing!
I'd not eat or drink a week;
I'd just sit and hear her speak!
Who spun such grand tales endearing?
Don't forget those elders true!
(That they're gone's a pity, truly)
Yet they must be toasted too,
Must be toasted absolutely!
Listen, I'll begin, my dear:
Next, your fairy tale I'll hear.

*The word сват literally refers to a relative, the father of the son-in-law or daughter-in-law. It also means "matchmaker". Ah, well... all relationships blur a bit "if we start drinking"...

РУСЛАН И ЛЮДМИЛА: ВСТУПЛЕНИЕ

У лукоморья дуб зеленый;
Златая цепь на дубе том:
И днем и ночью кот ученый
Все ходит по цепи кругом;
Идет направо — песнь заводит,
Налево — сказку говорит.

Там чудеса: там леший бродит,
Русалка на ветвях сидит;
Там на неведомых дорожках
Следы невиданных зверей;
Избушка там на курьих ножках
Стоит без окон, без дверей;
Там лес и дол видений полны;
Там о заре прихлынут волны
На брег песчаный и пустой,
И тридцать витязей прекрасных
Чредой из вод выходят ясных,
И с ними дядька их морской;
Там королевич мимоходом
Пленяет грозного царя;
Там в облаках перед народом
Через леса, через моря
Колдун несет богатыря;
В темнице там царевна тужит,
А бурый волк ей верно служит;
Там ступа с Бабою-Ягой
Идет, бредет сама собой;
Там царь Кащей над златом чахнет;
Там русский дух... там Русью пахнет!
И там я был, и мед я пил;
У моря видел дуб зеленый;
Под ним сидел, и кот ученый
Свои мне сказки говорил.
Одну я помню: сказку эту
Поведаю теперь я свету...

RUSLAN AND LYUDMILA: THE PROLOGUE

A green oak tree's by a cove curving;
A gold chain on that oak is found,
And night and day a cat most learnèd
Walks by that chain, around, around,
When he walks right, sweet songs intoning,
When leftwards, tells a fairy tale.

Wonders are there, wood-sprites are roaming,
Mermaids from branches hang their tail,
On paths of which no one has knowledge
Of unseen beasts there lurk the spoors,
On chicken legs, a little cottage
Stands without windows, without doors.
With visions wood and dale are yawning,
There waves come crashing at light's dawning
Upon the sandy, empty beach,
And thirty knights, in armor gorgeous,
The clear sea one by one disgorges
With their sea–sword–coach, them to teach.
And there a king's son, that way chancing,
Does a dread monarch captive seize,
There past the people, past clouds passing,
Right through the woods, right through the seas,
A wizard bears a knight with ease.
A princess there's in prison pining,
A brown wolf faithful by her lying,
There Baba–Yaga's mortar dread
Itself, with her inside, does tread.
There Tsar Kashey on his gold moulders,
There Russian scents of Rus' give odors!
And there I've passed, and honey quaffed,
And seen the oak by that cove curving,
Sat under it, and the cat learnèd
His fairy tales to me repassed.
I've one remembered, and this story
Through me now comes to light, world, glory.

В крови горит огонь желанья,
Душа тобой уязвлена,
Лобзай меня: твои лобзанья
Мне слаще мирра и вина.
Склонись ко мне главою нежной,
И да почию безмятежный,
Пока дохнет веселый день
И двигнется ночная тень.

MY BLOOD IS BLAZING WITH DESIRE

My blood is blazing with desire.
My stricken soul for you does pine.
Oh, kiss me now! Your kisses' fire
Is sweeter far than myrrh and wine.
Incline your head to me but softly,
And tamed, I'll linger with you calmly,
Until the cheerful light of day
Chases the gloom of night away.

ЗИМНЕЕ УТРО

Мороз и солнце; день чудесный!
Еще ты дремлешь, друг прелестный —
Пора, красавица, проснись:
Открой сомкнуты негой взоры
Навстречу северной Авроры
Звездою севера явись!

Вечор, ты помнишь, вьюга злилась,
На мутном небе мгла носилась;
Луна, как бледное пятно,
Сквозь тучи мрачные желтела,
И ты печальная сидела —
А нынче... погляди в окно:

Под голубыми небесами
Великолепными коврами,
Блестя на солнце, снег лежит;
Прозрачный лес один чернеет,
И ель сквозь иней зеленеет,
И речка подо льдом блестит.

Вся комната янтарным блеском
Озарена. Веселым треском
Трещит затопленная печь.
Приятно думать у лежанки.
Но знаешь: не велеть ли в санки
Кобылку бурую запречь?

Скользя по утреннему снегу,
Друг милый, предадимся бегу
Нетерпеливого коня
И навестим поля пустые,
Леса, недавно столь густые,
И берег, милый для меня.

A WINTER MORNING

It's frost and sunshine – wondrous morning! –
My lovely friend, and you're still snoring.
It's time, my beauty, open eyes!
Ope wide your bliss enveloped gazing,
And to the North's Aurora blazing,
As the North Star come forth, arise!

Last night, remember snowstorm's raging?
In murky skies that gloom rampaging?
The moon was but a faint, pale stain.
Through gloomy clouds it yellowed, flitting.
And, oh, how sadly you were sitting!
And now – look out our windowpane!

'Neath blue cerrulean heavens' gleaming,
In wondrous carpets, softly keening,
In sunlight sparkling, the snow lies.
Transparent woods are all that darkens.
The fir greens o'er the frost and harkens,
The river shines beneath the ice.

And our whole room, with amber sparkling,
Gleams in the dawn. With merry gargling
The hearth-stove crackles, wood piled high.
It's pleasant lying in bed thinking.
But say, though, shouldn't we be ringing
To yoke the brown mare to the sleigh?

As we on morning snow go sliding,
My darling, feeling the full riding,
As our horse runs impatiently,
We'll see the fields, their barren bleakness,
The woods, which recently were leafy,
The lakeshore, that's so dear to me.

К ***

Я помню чудное мгновенье:
Передо мной явилась ты,
Как мимолетное виденье,
Как гений чистой красоты.

В томленьях грусти безнадежной,
В тревогах шумной суеты,
Звучал мне долго голос нежный
И снились милые черты.

Шли годы. Бурь порыв мятежный
Рассеял прежние мечты,
И я забыл твой голос нежный,
Твои небесные черты.

В глуши, во мраке заточенья
Тянулись тихо дни мои
Без божества, без вдохновенья,
Без слез, без жизни, без любви.

Душе настало пробужденье:
И вот опять явилась ты,
Как мимолетное виденье,
Как гений чистой красоты.

И сердце бьется в упоенье,
И для него воскресли вновь
И божество, и вдохновенье,
И жизнь, и слезы, и любовь.

TO ***

A wondrous moment I remember:
Before me once you did appear;
A fleeting vision you resembled
Of beauty's genius pure and clear.

By grief and languor hopeless rendered,
Beset by noisy vanity,
Long time in me your voice rang tender,
Of your dear features were my dreams.

Years passed. Rebellious storm winds sundered
And scattered hopes that used to be,
And I forgot your voice so tender,
Your features dear and heavenly.

In gloom of backwoods' isolation,
My days dragged by, a silent drudge.
Without God's spark or inspiration,
Or tears, or any life, or love.

My soul awoke in precognition:
And once again you did appear,
Resembling a fleeting vision
Of beauty's genius pure and clear.

And how the heart beats in elation!
And once again in it rise up
The spark of God, and inspiration,
And life, and tears at last, and love.

Anna Petrovna Kern

Self-Portrait

ПРИЗНАНИЕ (К Александре Ивановне Осиповой)

Я вас люблю — хоть я бешусь,
Хоть это труд и стыд напрасный,
И в этой глупости несчастной
У ваших ног я признаюсь!
Мне не к лицу и не по летам...
Пора, пора мне быть умней!
Но узнаю по всем приметам
Болезнь любви в душе моей:
Без вас мне скучно, — я зеваю;
При вас мне грустно, — я терплю;
И, мочи нет, сказать желаю,
Мой ангел, как я вас люблю!
Когда я слышу из гостиной
Ваш легкий шаг, иль платья шум,
Иль голос девственный, невинный,
Я вдруг теряю весь свой ум.
Вы улыбнетесь — мне отрада;
Вы отвернетесь — мне тоска;
За день мучения — награда
Мне ваша бледная рука.
Когда за пяльцами прилежно
Сидите вы, склонясь небрежно,
Глаза и кудри опустя, —
Я в умиленье, молча, нежно
Любуюсь вами, как дитя!..
Сказать ли вам мое несчастье,
Мою ревнивую печаль,
Когда гулять, порой, в ненастье,
Вы собираетеся вдаль?
И ваши слезы в одиночку,
И речи в уголку вдвоем,
И путешествия в Опочку,
И фортепьяно вечерком?..
Алина! сжальтесь надо мною.
Не смею требовать любви:
Быть может, за грехи мои,
Мой ангел, я любви не стою!
Но притворитесь! Этот взгляд
Все может выразить так чудно!
Ах, обмануть меня не трудно!..
Я сам обманываться рад!

«Alina! Pity me my suffering!

CONFESSION (To Alexandra Ivanovna Osipova)

I love you so — though it's distress,
And work in vain and shame most fruitless,
And in this silly suffering foolish
Cast at your feet I must confess.
It doesn't fit me; I'm too old now,
It's time that I got smarter, please!
Yet all the signs have clearly told now
That in my soul is love's disease.
I yawn with boredom when without you.
I'm sad when with you, wait with woe,
And I've no strength, I want to tell you,
My angel, how I love you so!
When from your hall I hear emerging
Your rustling dress, your steps so fine,
Or voice so innocent and virgin,
I suddenly quite lose my mind.
You smile at me — joy, heaven's praises!
You turn away — and I'm in grief.
For all day suffering my pay is
Your little hand so pale and brief.
When to embroidering you render
For hours and hours yourself, and bend your
Eyes and curls down, a bit wild,
I'm so endeared, in silence tender,
Admiring you just like a child!
And should I tell you of my misery,
And of the jealous grief I feel
When you sometimes, in weather drizzly,
Decide to wander far afield?
Your solitary tears' immersions?
Your little corner têtes-à-têtes?
And to Opochka your excursions,
Your piano, when the evening frets?
Alina, pity me my suffering!
I do not dare to seek your love.
It may be I have sinned so much,
My angel, I am not worth loving.
But just pretend it! Your look sweet
Sublimely says all things demurcly!
Oh dear! It isn't hard to fool me!
I'm glad myself to be deceived!

19 ОКТЯБРЯ

Роняет лес багряный свой убор,
Сребрит мороз увянувшее поле,
Проглянет день как будто поневоле
И скроется за край окружных гор.
Пылай, камин, в моей пустынной келье;
А ты, вино, осенней стужи друг,
Пролей мне в грудь отрадное похмелье,
Минутное забвенье горьких мук.

Печален я: со мною друга нет,
С кем долгую запил бы я разлуку,
Кому бы мог пожать от сердца руку
И пожелать веселых много лет.
Я пью один: вотще воображенье
Вокруг меня товарищей зовет;
Знакомое не слышно приближенье,
И милого душа моя не ждет.

Я пью один, и на брегах Невы
Меня друзья сегодня именуют...
Но многие ль и там из вас пируют?
Еще кого не досчитались вы?
Кто изменил пленительной привычке?
Кого от вас увлек холодный свет?
Чей глас умолк на братской перекличке?
Кто не пришел? Кого меж вами нет?

Он не пришел, кудрявый наш певец,
С огнем в очах, с гитарой сладкогласной:
Под миртами Италии прекрасной
Он тихо спит, и дружеский резец
Не начертал над русскою могилой
Слов несколько на языке родном,
Чтоб некогда нашел привет унылый
Сын севера, бродя в краю чужом.

OCTOBER 19TH

The forest casts its scarlet garments off,
The frost bedecks the withered fields in silver,
The light of day peeps out, as if unwilling,
And hides in the surrounding mountaintops.
Blaze up, o hearth, in my bare room, my prison.
And you, dear wine, friend of the fall's sharp frost,
Pour joyous tipsiness into my bosom,
Oblivion brief, make bitter cares seem lost.

For I am sad, and without any friend
To drink with, healing woes of separation,
Whose hand I'd clasp in heartfelt admiration
And wish good cheer for many years on end.
I drink alone. Imagination lonely
In vain calls out for comrades who aren't here.
No steps familiar can I hear approaching.
My soul gives up on waiting for friends dear.

I drink alone, and on the Neva's banks
Today my gathered friends my name are naming.
But --even there--aren't many of you failing?
Who isn't feasting now in your glad ranks?
Who's not kept faith with our tradition charming?
Whom has the cold *beau monde* stolen away?
Whose voice is stilled midst brotherly catcalling?
Who didn't come? Who's not there, couldn't stay?

Our frizzy-haired free singer hasn't come.
His eyes afire, with his guitar sweet-sounding.
In some Italian myrtle grove abounding
He sleeps in peace.[1] No friendly local son
Carved out with care upon a Russian gravestone
A few brief words in his own native tongue
To give a gloomy greeting and sad haven
To northern sons lost, wandering far from home.

---

[1] This refers to Nikolai Korsakov, 1800–1820, a Lycée classmate and bard, who died while traveling in Italy.

Сидишь ли ты в кругу своих друзей,
Чужих небес любовник беспокойный?
Иль снова ты проходишь тропик знойный
И вечный лед полунощных морей?
Счастливый путь!... С лицейского порога
Ты на корабль перешагнул шутя,
И с той поры в морях твоя дорога,
О волн и бурь любимое дитя!

Ты сохранил в блуждающей судьбе
Прекрасных лет первоначальны нравы:
Лицейский шум, лицейские забавы
Средь бурных волн мечталися тебе;
Ты простирал из-за моря нам руку,
Ты нас одних в младой душе носил
И повторял: «На долгую разлуку
Нас тайный рок, быть может, осудил!»

Друзья мои, прекрасен наш союз!
Он, как душа, неразделим и вечен —
Неколебим, свободен и беспечен,
Срастался он под сенью дружных муз.
Куда бы нас ни бросила судьбина
И счастие куда б ни повело,
Всё те же мы: нам целый мир чужбина;
Отечество нам Царское Село.

Are you now sitting 'midst your group of friends
You restless lover of strange skies and lees? [2]
Or still crossing Earth's steamy tropic ends,
And endless ice on midnight Arctic seas?
Godspeed to you! From our Lycée's gates striding,
You, full of jokes, boarded a ship, set forth,
And since that time, the ocean is your highway,
Beloved child of seething waves and storms!

Wherever Fate did cast you on the seas,
You kept those morals taught in first, fair years.
Lycéen fun, pranks' clamor, yearning, tears
In stormy waves came back to you in dreams,
And o'er the seas your hand to us extending,
In your young soul our memories are kept,
And you'd repeat: "to parting never-ending
By secret destiny we are, perhaps, condemned."

My friends, how beautiful our union is!
Eternal like the soul, it can't be broken.
It withstands all, free, careless, and outspoken,
Our links were formed by friendship and the Muse.
Where'er we're cast by Fate, whate'er it's storing,
Wherever happiness might let us roam,
We're still the same: the whole world's strange and foreign,
And Tsarskoye Selo is our true home.

---

[2] Fyodor Matyushkin, 1799–1872, another classmate, circumnavigated the globe and became Admiral of the Imperial Russian Navy.

Из края в край преследуем грозой,
Запутанный в сетях судьбы суровой,
Я с трепетом на лоно дружбы новой,
Устав, приник ласкающей главой...
С мольбой моей печальной и мятежной,
С доверчивой надеждой первых лет,
Друзьям иным душой предался нежной;
Но горек был небратский их привет.

И ныне здесь, в забытой сей глуши,
В обители пустынных вьюг и хлада,
Мне сладкая готовилась отрада:
Троих из вас, друзей моей души,
Здесь обнял я. Поэта дом опальный,
О Пущин мой, ты первый посетил;
Ты усладил изгнанья день печальный,
Ты в день его Лицея превратил.

Ты, Горчаков, счастливец с первых дней,
Хвала тебе — фортуны блеск холодный
Не изменил души твоей свободной:
Всё тот же ты для чести и друзей.
Нам разный путь судьбой назначен строгой;
Ступая в жизнь, мы быстро разошлись:
Но невзначай проселочной дорогой
Мы встретились и братски обнялись.

Когда постиг меня судьбины гнев,
Для всех чужой, как сирота бездомный,
Под бурею главой поник я томной
И ждал тебя, вещун пермесских дев,
И ты пришел, сын лени вдохновенный,
О Дельвиг мой: твой голос пробудил
Сердечный жар, так долго усыпленный,
И бодро я судьбу благословил.

From place to place, though chased by lightning dread,
In nets of cruel fate caught, uncomprehending,
I'd quaver in the bosom of new friendship,
And sink caressingly my weary head...
Midst upstart angry prayers melancholy,
And trusting hopes of my first eagerness,
My tender soul, which other friends sought really,
Unbrotherly made greetings' bitterness.

And now, stuck here, in this abandoned hole,
This shrine of desolation, frost and snowstorms,
A sweet reward was given me, rejoicing:
With three of you, three dear friends of my soul,
I have embraced. My outcast place of pining,
Pushchin, my dear, you were the first to grace!
You sweetened one more day in exile writhing,
Transformed it to a day of the Lycée.

You, Gorchakov -- born lucky to the end,
Praise be to you! For Fortune's chilly gleaming
Have not traduced within your soul your freedom;
You're still the same for honor and your friend!
Completely different paths strict Fate assigned us*;
We parted soon, once we set forth in life.
And yet by chance upon a country crossroads,
We met, and like two brothers clasped arms tight.

When I was chased by wrathful Fate so cruel,
Estranged to all, an orphan with no home,
I'd sink my dreamy head down all alone,
Awaiting you, the Muses' herald true,
And then you came, inspired dawdling's offspring,
Delvig, my dear, your voice did then awake
My heart's own warmth, so long stilled in me, slumbering,
And cheerfully I then did bless my Fate.

*Gorchakov became Foreign Minister, then Chancellor of the Russian Empire.

С младенчества дух песен в нас горел,
И дивное волненье мы познали;
С младенчества две музы к нам летали,
И сладок был их лаской наш удел:
Но я любил уже рукоплесканья,
Ты, гордый, пел для муз и для души;
Свой дар, как жизнь, я тратил без вниманья,
Ты гений свой воспитывал в тиши.

Служенье муз не терпит суеты;
Прекрасное должно быть величаво:
Но юность нам советует лукаво,
И шумные нас радуют мечты...
Опомнимся, но поздно! И уныло
Глядим назад, следов не видя там.
Скажи, Вильгельм, не то ль и с нами было,
Мой брат родной по музе, по судьбам?

Пора, пора! душевных наших мук
Не стоит мир; оставим заблужденья!
Сокроем жизнь под сень уединенья!
Я жду тебя, мой запоздалый друг --
Приди; огнем волшебного рассказа
Сердечные преданья оживи;
Поговорим о бурных днях Кавказа,
О Шиллере, о славе, о любви.

Пора и мне... пируйте, о друзья!
Предчувствую отрадное свиданье;
Запомните ж поэта предсказанье:
Промчится год, и с вами снова я,
Исполнится завет моих мечтаний;
Промчится год, и я явлюся к вам!
О, сколько слез и сколько восклицаний,
И сколько чаш, подъятых к небесам!

OCTOBER 19TH

Since youth, in us Song's spirit ever burned,
With a divine disquiet us inspiring;
Since youth towards us two Muses fleet came flying,
Sweet was our lot caressing them in turn.
But I already loved applause, shouts feverish.
You proudly sang just for your Muse, your heart.
My gift, like life, I frittered away heedless,
While you in silence honed your perfect art.

The Muses' service brooks no vanity.
The beautiful must always be majestic.
Deceitful guidance gain we from youth frantic.
In noisy daydreams we rejoice, are free.
Then we awake – too late though! And now grievous
We gaze back whence we came, yet cannot see.
Say, Wilhelm**, isn't that how life did treat us,
My brother in the Muse, in Fate's decree?

It's time, it's time! Our heartaches unallayed
Aren't worth this world; let's leave behind illusions!
Let's hide our life away in shade's seclusion!
I wait for you, my friend so long delayed...
Approach, and with the fire of magic Story,
Revive the heart's true teaching deep in us.
We'll speak of snowy Caucasus peaks stormy,
Of Schiller, and of glory, and of love!

For me too, now, it's time. My friends, feast on!
Within I feel a joyful premonition:
Remember my poetical prediction!
When one year's passed, we'll meet again anon!
Then will come true my dearest aspirations,
When one year's passed and I come back to you!
How many tears, how many declamations!
How many cups raised high towards Heaven's blue!

**Refers to Wilhelm Küchelbecker, a poet and Decembrist.

И первую полней, друзья, полней!
И всю до дна в честь нашего союза!
Благослови, ликующая муза,
Благослови: да здравствует Лицей!
Наставникам, хранившим юность нашу,
Всем честию, и мертвым и живым,
К устам подъяв признательную чашу,
Не помня зла, за благо воздадим.

Полней, полней! И сердцем возгоря,
Опять до дна, до капли выпивайте!
Но за кого? о други, угадайте!...
Ура, наш царь! так! выпьем за царя.
Он человек! Им властвует мгновенье.
Он раб молвы, сомнений и страстей,
Простим ему неправое гоненье:
Он взял Париж, он основал Лицей.

Пируйте же, пока еще мы тут!
Увы, наш круг час от часу редеет;
Кто в гробе спит, кто, дальный, сиротеет;
Судьба глядит, мы вянем; дни бегут;
Невидимо склоняясь и хладея,
Мы близимся к началу своему...
Кому из нас под старость в день Лицея
Торжествовать придется одному?

Несчастный друг! Средь новых поколений
Докучный гость и лишний, и чужой,
Он вспомнит нас и дни соединений,
Закрыв глаза дрожащею рукой...
Пускай же он с отрадой хоть печальной
Тогда сей день за чашей проведет,
Как ныне я, затворник ваш опальный,
Его провел без горя и забот.

OCTOBER 19TH

Refill your cups, friends, fill them up, I say!
Drink each last drop in honor of our union!
Now bless us with your jubilation, Muses!
Now bless us all, and long live our Lycée!
To all our tutors, our youth's noble keepers,
All honors to the living and the dead!
As we with gratitude lift up our beakers,
All ills forgot, give thanks for blessings yet.

Refill, refill with passion, all your heart,
Again now, bottoms up, drink each drop blessèd!
And yet for whom? O friends, I'll let you guess it!
Hurrah! Our Tsar! Yes, let's drink to the Tsar!
He's but a man, and slave to time's illusion,
Of rumors, doubts, and passions but a slave,
So let's forgive his unfair persecution:
He captured Paris, founded our Lycée!

Feast on, feast on, while we are all still here!
Alas, our circle hour by hour is thinning.
Who sleeps in coffin now, who's orphaned, distant?
Fate sees us fade as our days disappear.
We bend invisibly, and chill, are fading,
Drawn back to our beginnings, to our home...
Which one of us in old age on Lycée Day
Will be obliged to celebrate alone?

Unhappy friend! Amidst new generations,
Unwanted stranger, guest who just won't leave,
He'll think of us united in libations,
With shaky hand he'll close his eyes, and grieve...
Yet may he still be joyous in his sadness,
And pass that day but with his goblet old,
As I today, disgraced, locked in my fastness,
Have passed it without worry, without woe.

СЦЕНА XIII ИЗ «БОРИСА ГОДУНОВА»

НОЧЬ. САД. ФОНТАН

Самозванец
(*входит*)
Вот и фонтан; она сюда придет.
Я, кажется, рожден не боязливым;
Перед собой вблизи видал я смерть,
Пред смертию душа не содрогалась.
Мне вечная неволя угрожала,
За мной гнались — я духом не смутился
И дерзостью неволи избежал.
Но что ж теперь теснит мое дыханье?
Что значит сей неодолимый трепет?
Иль это дрожь желаний напряженных?
Нет, это страх. День целый ожидал
Я тайного свидания с Мариной,
Обдумывал все то, что ей скажу,
Как обольщу ее надменный ум,
Как назову московскою царицей, —
Но час настал — и ничего не помню.
Не нахожу затверженных речей;
Любовь мутит мое воображенье...
Но что-то вдруг мелькнуло... шорох... тише...
Нет, это свет обманчивой луны,
И прошумел здесь ветерок.

Марина
(*входит*)
Царевич!

Самозванец
Она!.. Вся кровь во мне остановилась.

SCENE XIII FROM BORIS GODUNOV

NIGHT. A GARDEN. A FOUNTAIN

The Pretender
(enters)
The fountain's here. And here is where she'll come.
It seems to me I wasn't born a coward;
Flashing before me close I have seen death.
And before death my soul has never quivered.
By slavery forever I've been threatened,
I've been chased down; my spirit was unfailing,
With daring I escaped unfreedom's bonds.
So now what is it so stops up my breathing?
What is this tremor I can't overpower?
Is it desire suppressed that in me trembles?
No – it is fear. The whole day I did wait
For this brief secret tryst now with Marina,
And weighed within my mind all I would say,
How I'd seduce her proud and haughty mind,
And christen her the Empress of great Moscow,
But now's the time, and I remember nothing.
I've quite forgot those speeches I made up,
And love casts murk on my imagination.
But something just flashed by! It's swishing!...Quiet!
No, it's the light of the deceitful moon,
A little breeze blew lightly by...

Marina
(enters)
Tsarevich!

Pretender
It's her! Now all the blood's stopped up inside me!

Марина
Димитрий! Вы?

Самозванец
Волшебный, сладкий голос!
(*Идет к ней.*)
Ты ль наконец? Тебя ли вижу я,
Одну со мной, под сенью тихой ночи?
Как медленно катился скучный день!
Как медленно заря вечерня гасла!
Как долго ждал во мраке я ночном!

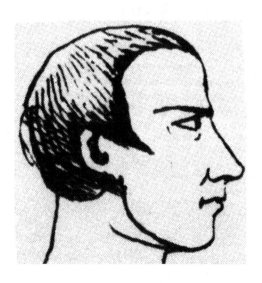

The Pretender Dmitry

SCENE XIII FROM BORIS GODUNOV

Marina
'S that you, Dmitry?

Pretender
Oh voice, so sweet, so magic!
(walks towards her)
Oh is it you at last! Is that you whom I see,
Alone with me in nighttime's silent stillness?
How slow the wheel of boring day did turn!
How slow the gleam of twilight was in fading!
How long I waited in the gloom of night!

Yekaterina Rayevskaya ("My Marina Mniszek is a real Yekaterina Rayevskaya!")

Марина
Часы бегут, и дорого мне время —
Я здесь тебе назначила свиданье
Не для того, чтоб слушать нежны речи
Любовника. Слова не нужны. Верю,
Что любишь ты; но слушай: я решилась
С твоей судьбой и бурной и неверной
Соединить судьбу мою; то вправе
Я требовать, Димитрий, одного:
Я требую, чтоб ты души своей
Мне тайные открыл теперь надежды,
Намеренья и даже опасенья;
Чтоб об руку с тобой могла я смело
Пуститься в жизнь — не с детской слепотой,
Не как раба желаний легких мужа,
Наложница безмолвная твоя,
Но как тебя достойная супруга,
Помощница московского царя.

Самозванец
О, дай забыть хоть на единый час
Моей судьбы заботы и тревоги!
Забудь сама, что видишь пред собой
Царевича. Марина! зри во мне
Любовника, избранного тобою,
Счастливого твоим единым взором.
О, выслушай моления любви!
Дай высказать все то, чем сердце полно!

SCENE XIII FROM BORIS GODUNOV

Marina
The hours race, and every minute's precious.
And I instructed you that we should meet here
Not so I'd have to hear the tender speeches
A lover makes! I don't need words. I'm certain
That you do love. But listen: I've decided
That to your fate both stormy and uncertain
I'll link my own. And so I have the right,
Dmitry, to demand of you one thing:
And I demand that you open your soul,
Tell me your secret hopes and aspirations,
Reveal your plans and even apprehensions,
So hand in hand with you I could with valor
Set forth in life – but not blind as a child,
Or merely slave to slight whims of my husband,
Nor yet to be your silent concubine,
No, but as wife to you, who's fully worthy,
A helpmeet to the Tsar of Muscovy.

Pretender
Oh let me for a single hour forget
My destiny's unending cares and worries!
Please, just forget that you are looking at
The Tsar's own son. Marina! See in me
A lover, and a man whom you have chosen,
See someone whom your slightest glance makes happy.
Oh hear me out! Oh hear my prayer of love!
Let me express what in my heart is brimming!

Марина

Не время, князь. Ты медлишь — и меж тем
Приверженность твоих клевретов стынет,
Час от часу опасность и труды
Становятся опасней и труднее,
Уж носятся сомнительные слухи,
Уж новизна сменяет новизну;
А Годунов свои приемлет меры...

Самозванец

Что Годунов? во власти ли Бориса
Твоя любовь, одно мое блаженство?
Нет, нет. Теперь гляжу я равнодушно
На трон его, на царственную власть.
Твоя любовь... что без нее мне жизнь,
И славы блеск, и русская держава?
В глухой степи, в землянке бедной — ты,
Ты заменишь мне царскую корону,
Твоя любовь...

Марина

Стыдись; не забывай
Высокого, святого назначенья:
Тебе твой сан дороже должен быть
Всех радостей, всех обольщений жизни,
Его ни с чем не можешь ты равнять.
Не юноше кипящему, безумно
Плененному моею красотой,
Знай: отдаю торжественно я руку
Наследнику московского престола,
Царевичу, спасенному судьбой.

SCENE XIII FROM BORIS GODUNOV

Marina

But not now, prince. You dawdle — all the while
The ardor of your followers is cooling,
And hour by hour the dangers and the toils
Become ever more dangerous and hard.
And doubtful rumors already are spreading.
The latest news supplants the latest news,
And Godunov is also taking measures.

Pretender

Who's Godunov? Does Boris have the power
To rule your love, my only bliss and blessing?
No, no! In truth I look with pure indifference
Upon his throne and his imperial might.
Your love alone! What is my life without it?
Or glory's gleam, or all the power of Russia?
In barren steppe, in bare mud hut with you
You would replace my regal crown, much dearer--
Your love alone!

Marina

For shame! Do not forget
Your lofty errand or your sacred mission!
To you your rank must ever dearer be
Than all the blandishments and joys of living.
With power there is naught that can compare.
I'll have no seething youth who bubbles madly,
Kept by my looks in plaintive captive state,
Know: I have pledged my hand in troth most solemn
But to the one true heir to Moscow's throne,
The Tsar's own son, preserved and kept by Fate.

Самозванец
Не мучь меня, прелестная Марина,
Не говори, что сан, а не меня
Избрала ты. Марина! ты не знаешь,
Как больно тем ты сердце мне язвишь —
Как! ежели... о страшное сомненье! —
Скажи: когда б не царское рожденье
Назначила слепая мне судьба,
Когда б я был не Иоаннов сын,
Не сей давно забытый миром отрок, —
Тогда б... тогда б любила ль ты меня?..

Марина
Димитрий ты и быть иным не можешь;
Другого мне любить нельзя.

Самозванец
Нет! полно:
Я не хочу делиться с мертвецом
Любовницей, ему принадлежащей.
Нет, полно мне притворствовать! Скажу
Всю истину; так знай же: твой Димитрий
Давно погиб, зарыт — и не воскреснет;
А хочешь ли ты знать, кто я таков?
Изволь, скажу: я бедный черноризец;
Монашеской неволею скучая,
Под клобуком, свой замысел отважный
Обдумал я, готовил миру чудо —
И наконец из келии бежал
К украинцам, в их буйные курени;
Владеть конем и саблей научился;
Явился к вам; Димитрием назвался
И поляков безмозглых обманул.
Что скажешь ты, надменная Марина?
Довольна ль ты признанием моим?
Что ж ты молчишь?

SCENE XIII FROM BORIS GODUNOV

Pretender
Don't torture me, dear ravishing Marina!
Don't say that it's my rank instead of me
That you did choose. Marina! You've no inkling
How painfully you sear my heart with that.
How – for what if? Oh! What a frightful doubt I feel!
Do say: had I not chanced to be born royal,
Had blinded Fate not so appointed me,
If I were not the son of dread Iván,
His outcast child, by this world long forgotten,
Say then…then would you love me still? Or not?

Marina
Dmitry's who you are. You're not some other.
Some other I could never love.

Pretender
No! No more!
I've heard enough! I'll not share with a corpse
A lover who belongs to him entirely.
No, that's enough imposturing: I'll tell
The whole truth now! So listen: Your Dmitry
Is long since dead and buried, gone forever.
But would you like to know just who I am?
In truth, I'm but a poor black-robed monk-novice
On whom monastic discipline grew boring.
Beneath my cowl I plotted my grand project:
I planned how I'd present the world a wonder.
And finally I fled from my dark cell
To the Ukraine, where dwell the rowdy Cossacks.
I learned to ride a horse and wield a sabre,
Then I came here and called myself Dmitri,
Ans so deceived your silly Polish courtiers,
What do you say now, arrogant Marina?
Are you not pleased with what I've just confessed?
Why won't you speak?

Марина
О стыд! о горе мне! *(Молчание.)*

Самозванец
(*тихо*)
Куда завлек меня порыв досады!
С таким трудом устроенное счастье
Я, может быть, навеки погубил.
Что сделал я, безумец? — (*Вслух.*) Вижу, вижу:
Стыдишься ты не княжеской любви.
Так вымолви ж мне роковое слово;
В твоих руках теперь моя судьба,
Реши: я жду (*бросается на колени*)

Марина
Встань, бедный самозванец.
Не мнишь ли ты коленопреклоненьем,
Как девочки доверчивой и слабой
Тщеславное мне сердце умилить?
Ошибся, друг: у ног своих видала
Я рыцарей и графов благородных;
Но их мольбы я хладно отвергала
Не для того, чтоб беглого монаха...

Самозванец
(*встает*)
Не презирай младого самозванца;
В нем доблести таятся, может быть,
Достойные московского престола,
Достойные руки твоей бесценной...

Марина
Достойные позорной петли, дерзкий!

SCENE XIII FROM BORIS GODUNOV

Marina
Oh shame! Oh woe is me! *(Pause)*

Pretender
(quietly)
Where has this vexing outburst lured me?
The happiness I'd built up with such labor
I have perhaps forever cast away.
What did I do? Oh madman! *(out loud)* I see! I see!
You are ashamed of love that isn't princely..
So go ahead, pronounce your final verdict.
For now my fate lies only on your hands.
Decide! I'll wait! *(falls on his knees)*

Marina
Rise, miserable pretender!
Do you imagine just because you're kneeling
As if before a trusting girl, a weakling,
That you could win my proud, ambitious heart?
You're wrong, my friend! For, at my feet prostrated,
I've seen my share of counts and knights and nobles,
And coldly I rejected all their prayers
But not so that some runaway ex-monk should--

Pretender
(gets up)
Do not despise or scorn the young pretender;
For it may be that valor hides within him
That's worthy of the mighty throne of Moscow,
That's worthy of that hand of yours so priceless...

Marina
That's worthy of a shameful noose, man shameless!

Самозванец

Виновен я: гордыней обуянный,
Обманывал я Бога и царей,
Я миру лгал; но не тебе, Марина,
Меня казнить; я прав перед тобою.
Нет, я не мог обманывать тебя.
Ты мне была единственной святыней,
Пред ней же я притворствовать не смел.
Любовь, любовь ревнивая, слепая,
Одна любовь принудила меня
Все высказать.

Марина

Чем хвалится, безумец!
Кто требовал признанья твоего?
Уж если ты, бродяга безымянный,
Мог ослепить чудесно два народа,
Так должен уж по крайней мере ты
Достоин быть успеха своего
И свой обман отважный обеспечить
Упорною, глубокой, вечной тайной.
Могу ль, скажи, предаться я тебе,
Могу ль, забыв свой род и стыд девичий,
Соединить судьбу мою с твоею,
Когда ты сам с такою простотой,
Так ветрено позор свой обличаешь?
Он из любви со мною проболтался!
Дивлюся: как перед моим отцом
Из дружбы ты доселе не открылся,
От радости пред нашим королем
Или еще пред паном Вишневецким
Из верного усердия слуги.

SCENE XIII FROM BORIS GODUNOV

Pretender

It's my fault that ambition overweening
Made me deceive both God and courts of kings.
To all the world I lied, and yet you can't, Marina,
Dare punish me; to you I've acted fairly,
For you are someone I would not deceive.
The thought of you for me is all that's sacred,
I'd never dare dissimulate with you.
For love, oh love! A jealous love, a blind love!
T'was love alone that ever could impel me
To tell you all.

Marina

You're boasting of this, madman?
Who asked for such confessions out of you?
If you're indeed a nameless, wandering beggar,
Who managed to keep blinded two great peoples,
Then at the very least you always must
Stay worthy of your fraudulent success,
And must secure your own deceit audacious
By keeping it a deep, eternal secret.
How could I ever give myself to you,
Forget my birth, my shame that keeps me virgin,
And merge my destiny with that of yours,
When you yourself, as simply as just now,
So flippantly your scandal go revealing?
Because of love he bubbled out his secret!
I am amazed that in my father's court
You haven't yet revealed yourself through friendship,
Or out of joy when brought before our King,
Or spilled your tale to Father Wisnowiecky
Out of the faithful zeal with which you serve!

Самозванец
Клянусь тебе, что сердца моего
Ты вымучить одна могла признанье.
Клянусь тебе, что никогда, нигде,
Ни в пиршестве за чашею безумства,
Ни в дружеском, заветном разговоре,
Ни под ножом, ни в муках истязаний
Сих тяжких тайн не выдаст мой язык.

Марина
Клянешься ты! итак, должна я верить —
О, верю я! — но чем, нельзя ль узнать,
Клянешься ты? не именем ли Бога,
Как набожный приемыш езуитов?
Иль честию, как витязь благородный,
Иль, может быть, единым царским словом,
Как царский сын? не так ли? говори.

Д и м и т р и й
(гордо)
Тень Грозного меня усыновила,
Димитрием из гроба нарекла,
Вокруг меня народы возмутила
И в жертву мне Бориса обрекла —
Царевич я. Довольно, стыдно мне
Пред гордою полячкой унижаться. —
Прощай навек. Игра войны кровавой,
Судьбы моей обширные заботы
Тоску любви, надеюсь, заглушат.
О как тебя я стану ненавидеть,
Когда пройдет постыдной страсти жар!
Теперь иду — погибель иль венец
Мою главу в России ожидает,
Найду ли смерть, как воин в битве честной,
Иль как злодей на плахе площадной,
Не будешь ты подругою моею,
Моей судьбы не разделишь со мною;
Но — может быть, ты будешь сожалеть
Об участи, отвергнутой тобою.

SCENE XIII FROM BORIS GODUNOV

Pretender
I swear to you that you alone could force
And torture my wracked heart to its confession.
I swear to you, at no time, and in no place,
Not at great feasts, while quaffing folly's goblets,
Nor yet with friends while preciously discoursing,
Threatened by knives, spread on the rack, tormented,
My tongue won't give these secrets dread away.

Marina
Oh? So you swear? That means I should believe you?
Oh, I believe! But first, might I inquire,
By what you swear? Not by our Lord's name holy,
Devoutly as a Jesuit-schooled foundling?
Or on your honor, like some knight gone questing?
Or do you merely pledge your royal honor,
As the Tsar's heir? Is that it? Won't you speak?

Dmitry
(proudly)
The shade of dread Iván himself did choose me,
And christened me Dmitry from his grave.
That shade did stir our peoples up, unruly,
Judged doom on Boris, whom I will replace.
I'm the Tsar's heir! Enough! For it is galling
To stoop so to a haughty Polish maiden!
Farewell for good! The game of war most bloody,
And vast concerns of Destiny all-touching
Will dim, I hope, love's grief within my heart.
Oh! How I will begin to hate you truly
When passion's shameful fever shall have passed!
Now I shall go–– though whether Russia crowns
With doom or laurel-wreathes my expectations––
If I find death in battle like a warrior,
Or like a villain on the scaffold block,
You nevermore shall be my faithful helpmeet.
No more shall you of my fate be partaking.
And yet, perhaps, one day you may regret
That destiny you with such scorn rejected.

Марина
А если я твой дерзостный обман
Заранее пред всеми обнаружу?

Самозванец
Не мнишь ли ты, что я тебя боюсь?
Что более поверят польской деве,
Чем русскому царевичу? Но знай,
Что ни король, ни Папа, ни вельможи
Не думают о правде слов моих.
Димитрий я иль нет — что им за дело?
Но я предлог раздоров и войны.
Им это лишь и нужно, и тебя,
Мятежница! поверь, молчать заставят.
Прощай.

Марина
Постой, царевич. Наконец
Я слышу речь не мальчика, но мужа.
С тобою, князь, она меня мирит.
Безумный твой порыв я забываю
И вижу вновь Димитрия. Но слушай:
Пора, пора! проснись, не медли боле;
Веди полки скорее на Москву —
Очисти Кремль, садись на трон московский,
Тогда за мной шли брачного посла;
Но — слышит Бог — пока твоя нога
Не оперлась на тронные ступени,
Пока тобой не свержен Годунов,
Любви речей не буду слушать я.
(*Уходит.*)

SCENE XIII FROM BORIS GODUNOV

Marina

But what if I reveal your shameless hoax
And warn the world about you ere you go?

Pretender

How could you fancy I'm afraid of you?
Whom will the world believe? Some Polish schoolgirl?
Or the Tsar's son of Muscovy? Yet know
That nor your King nor Pope nor nobles
Could slightly care whether I speak the truth.
Am I Dmitri? That's not their concern!
I'm but a pretext for their feuding war,
Just the excuse they looked for. As for you,
Rebellious wench! Be sure, they'll curb your tongue!
Farewell!

Marina

No, wait! Tsarevich! Now at last
I hear the speech of husbands, not of schoolboys.
It reconciles me to you, my dear prince.
Yes, I forget your outburst of sheer folly
And see Dmitri once again. But — listen:
It's time! It's time! Stir up! And no more dawdling!
To Moscow march and lead your armies on,
Clean out the Kremlin, take the throne of Moscow.
Then send your nuptial envoys back to me.
But—God's my witness! Until those feet of yours
Have not ascended up the throne-room staircase,
Until at last you've cast out Godunov,
I'll listen to no speeches about love.
(Exits)

Самозванец
Нет — легче мне сражаться с Годуновым
Или хитрить с придворным езуитом,
Чем с женщиной! Черт с ними; мочи нет.
И путает, и вьется, и ползет,
Скользит из рук, шипит, грозит и жалит.
Змея! змея! — Недаром я дрожал.
Она меня чуть-чуть не погубила.
Но решено: заутра двину рать.

Pretender

No! With Godunov it's easier to battle,
It's easier testing cunning with court Jesuits
Than -- with a woman! Damn them! I've no strength!
Confusing me, she weaves and winds, and crawls,
Slips from my hand, and hisses, threatens, stinging!
A snake! A snake! No wonder I did shake!
She very nearly brought about my ruin!
But now I'm firm. Our armies march at dawn.

Цветы последние милей
Роскошных первенцев полей.
Они унылые мечтанья
Живее пробуждают в нас.
Так иногда разлуки час
Живее сладкого свиданья.

THE LAST LATE FLOWERS ARE MORE DEAR

The last late flowers are more dear
Than gorgeous first queens of the field.
They daydreams melancholy, wistful,
Do stir more strongly in our heart.
Just so, the hour when we must part
Evokes more than the sweetest trysting.

Если жизнь тебя обманет;
Не печалься, не сердись!
В день уныния смирись:
День веселья, верь, настанет.

Сердце в будущем живет;
Настоящее уныло:
Всё мгновенно, всё пройдет;
Что пройдет, то будет мило.

Self-portrait with new sideburns

IF, PERHAPS, LIFE SHOULD DECEIVE YOU

If, perhaps, life should deceive you,
Be not gloomy, be not riled!
To sad days be reconciled;
Days of gladness, trust, are near you.

In the future the heart lives,
And the present is not cheering:
All's but a moment, passing swift;
What has passed will be endearing.

Yevpraksia Nikolaievna Vulf — "Zizi"

Лишь я, таинственный певец,
На берег выброшен грозою

Decembrists Pushchin, Ryleyev, Pestel, Küchelbecker
with Prince and Princess Vyazemsky

IV. THE STORMS OF FATE

And only I, mysterious bard,
Was cast ashore by storm and lightning

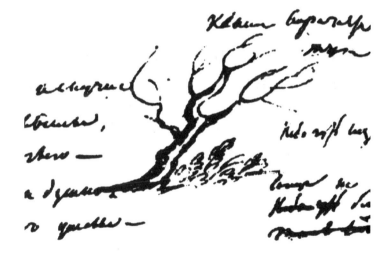

Анчар (The The Poison Tree)

АРИОН

Нас было много на челне;
Иные парус напрягали,
Другие дружно упирали
В глубь мощны веслы. В тишине
На руль склонясь, наш кормщик умный
В молчанье правил грузный челн;
А я — беспечной веры полн, —
Пловцам я пел... Вдруг лоно волн
Измял с налету вихорь шумный...
Погиб и кормщик и пловец! —
Лишь я, таинственный певец,
На берег выброшен грозою,
Я гимны прежние пою
И ризу влажную мою
Сушу на солнце под скалою.

ARION*

A lot of us were on that skiff.
While some of us broad sails were spanning,
The rest were amiably manning
Great oars beneath. And still and stiff,
Hunched o'er our tiller, our sage captain
Our crowded skiff in silence steered.
But I, by carefree faith e'er cheered,
Sang to my mates. Then great waves sheered
Up, swept, smashed, whirlwinds blasted, crashing,
Our captain and his mates were lost!
And only I, mysterious bard,
Was cast ashore by storm and lightning.
I sing the hymns I sang before,
And my drenched raiment on that shore
In sunshine under cliffs am drying.

---

*In Greek mythology, the shipwrecked poet Arion sang to the storm-waves, and was rescued and brought ashore by a dolphin.

И. И. ПУЩИНУ

Мой первый друг, мой друг бесценный!
И я судьбу благословил,
Когда мой двор уединенный,
Печальным снегом занесенный,
Твой колокольчик огласил.

Молю святое провиденье:
Да голос мой душе твоей
Дарует то же утешенье,
Да озарит он заточенье
Лучом лицейских ясных дней!

TO IVAN IVANOVICH PUSHCHIN

My very first, my priceless friend,
I too gave blessings to strange Fate,
When through bleak snowstorms she did send
Your sleighbell-heralded advent
To my secluded courtyard gate...

To blessèd fate I make oration:
Let my voice too, in future days,
Return your gift of consolation,
Shine light through your incarceration
From our Lycée's clear loving rays.

"Jeannot" — Ivan Pushchin

ПОСЛАНИЕ В СИБИРЬ

Во глубине сибирских руд
Храните гордое терпенье,
Не пропадет ваш скорбный труд
И дум высокое стремленье.

Несчастью верная сестра,
Надежда в мрачном подземелье
Разбудит бодрость и веселье,
Придет желанная пора:

Любовь и дружество до вас
Дойдут сквозь мрачные затворы,
Как в ваши каторжные норы
Доходит мой свободный глас.

Оковы тяжкие падут,
Темницы рухнут — и свобода
Вас примет радостно у входа,
И братья меч вам отдадут.

A MESSAGE TO SIBERIA

Deep in your dark Siberian mine
Preserve with pride your stubborn patience.
Your toil of grief is not in vain,
Nor are your lofty aspirations.

Misfortune's loyal sister, Hope,
Will find your underground so gloomy,
Both cheer and joyousness renewing;
The time you've longed for shall approach:

Of love and friendship true, the joys
Break through all locks, cross all dark spaces,
As through your hard-barred convict cages
You hear my free, resounding voice.

Your heavy handcuffs down will fall,
Your jails will crumble. Liberty
Will greet you as you step forth free
Your brothers will return your sword.

Изыде сеятель сеяти семена своя.

Свободы сеятель пустынный,
Я вышел рано, до звезды;
Рукою чистой и безвинной
В порабощенные бразды
Бросал живительное семя —
Но потерял я только время,
Благие мысли и труды...

Паситесь, мирные народы!
Вас не разбудит чести клич.
К чему стадам дары свободы?
Их должно резать или стричь.
Наследство их из рода в роды
Ярмо с гремушками да бич.

IN LONESOME WASTELAND FREEDOM SOWING

> Behold, a sower went forth to sow. *

In lonesome wasteland freedom sowing,**
Ere morning star I walked, ere sun.
With hands still clean, pure and unknowing,
In earth where slave-drawn furrows run,
I cast the freeing seed of life--
But I was only wasting time,
Good aspirations, deeds--for none.

So graze on, graze, you peaceful peoples!
You will not wake to honor's call.
What need have herds for gifts of freedom?
They're used to shears and butcher's stall,
For ages to their heirs bequeathing
Just yokes with ringlets, whips that gall.

---

*ced *Matthew*: 13, 3

**Some consider this Pushkin's meditation on the Greek and Rumanian struggles for freedom from the Ottoman Empire (the poet's drawings in this period show pictures of Greeks rebels, as at left). Yet it is also about Russian political apathy in the face of serdom and autocracy — or perhaps just about apathy in general.

АНЧАР

В пустыне чахлой и скупой,
На почве, зноем раскаленной,
Анчар, как грозный часовой,
Стоит, один во всей вселенной.

Природа жаждущих степей
Его в день гнева породила,
И зелень мертвую ветвей
И корни ядом напоила.

Яд каплет сквозь его кору,
К полудню растопясь от зною,
И застывает ввечеру
Густой прозрачною смолою.

К нему и птица не летит,
И тигр нейдет: лишь вихорь черный
На древо смерти набежит --
И мчится прочь, уже тлетворный.

И если туча оросит,
Блуждая, лист его дремучий,
С его ветвей, уж ядовит,
Стекает дождь в песок горючий.

Но человека человек
Послал к анчару властным взглядом,
И тот послушно в путь потек
И к утру возвратился с ядом.

THE POISON TREE*

In fearsome desert, barren, dead,
On sands that from the heat are blazing,
The poison tree, like sentry dread,
Stands, lone in all the world remaining.

For Nature of these thirsting steppes
One day of wrath caused its conception,
And made its greening leaves all dead,
And filled its roots with purest poison.

The poison seeps right through its bark,
By noonday's heat is boiling, melting,
And by the evening chill grows hard
Into a thickened tar transparent.

And to this tree the bird flies not;
The tiger flees it. Just a whirlwind
That's black to this death-tree runs up—
And races past, but now accursed.

And if a cloud by chance bedews,
Lost on its wanderings, those thick branches,
Down from its leaves a poisoned juice,
Like rain, falls which the hot sand catches.

But once, one man sent out a man,
Off to the death tree with glance awesome,
Who trudged, obedient, through the sand,
And next morning brought back the poison.

Принес он смертную смолу
Да ветвь с увядшими листами,
И пот по бледному челу
Струился хладными ручьями;

Принес — и ослабел и лег
Под сводом шалаша на лыки,
И умер бедный раб у ног
Непобедимого владыки.

А князь тем ядом напитал
Свои послушливые стрелы
И с ними гибель разослал
К соседам в чуждые пределы.

"Who trudged, obedient through the sand"
(the slave in *The Poison Tree*)

He had brought back the tar of death,
The branches with their leaves all withered,
And on his forehead pale the sweat
Dripped down in rivulets, but chilly.

Brought them — and then lay down, grown weak,
On rough rush mats 'neath those vaults tented.
The poor slave died then at the feet
Of his invincible potentate.

The prince then with that poison fed
His arrows sharp and to him slavish,
And then with them sent doom and death
In distant lands to all his neighbors.

---

*The literal and correct translation of the Russian word "анчар" is actually "upas." In turn, as the Oxford English Dictionary relates, the word "upas" means "poison" in Malaysian. In 1785, the British seafarer Erasmus Darwin described the "dread Upas": a "fell tree of fate on a blasted heath," around which nothing lived for fifteen miles around in any direction—allegedly somewhere near Batavia (now Djakarta) on the isle of Java, Dutch East Indies (now Indonesia). Byron, in *Childe Harolde* IV, cxxvi, referred figuratively to: "This uneradicable taint of sin, This boundless Upas, this all-blasting tree." I would normally never hesitate to use Byron's words for rendering Pushkin, especially as the Oxford Russian-English dictionary gives no other entry for "анчар." Yet I fear that such scholarly and literal correctness might puzzle those of our readers whose reading knowledge of Malaysian is as rusty as mine. Besides, "The Poison Tree" just sounds better!

19 ОКТЯБРЯ 1827

Бог помочь вам, друзья мои,
В заботах жизни, царской службы,
И на пирах разгульной дружбы,
И в сладких таинствах любви!

Бог помочь вам, друзья мои,
И в бурях, и в житейском горе,
В краю чужом, в пустынном море,
И в мрачных пропастях земли!

Decembrist Friends, Küchelbecker and Ryleyev

OCTOBER 19, 1827

God help you all, my dear, dear friends,
In all life's cares, in Tsarist service,
In friendship's wild carousing reckless,
In all sweet Love's mysterious beds!

God help you all, my dear, dear friends,
Through storms or everyday griefs blowing,
In foreign lands, in desert ocean,
Or in Earth's dark, abysmal ends!

The Decembrist Yakubovich

ЕК. Н. УШАКОВОЙ

В отдалении от вас
С вами буду неразлучен,
Томных уст и томных глаз
Буду памятью размучен;
Изнывая в тишине,
Не хочу я быть утешен, —
Вы ж вздохнете ль обо мне,
Если буду я повешен?

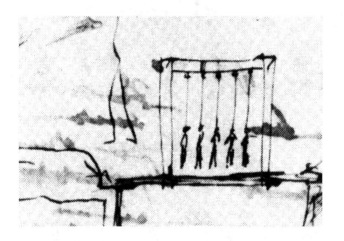

TO YEKATERINA USHAKOVA

If they send me far from you,
Still I'll never, ever, leave you.
Luscious lips and deep eyes true
In my memory will be keeping.
Bored and pining silently,
I'll not wish to find new gladness.
Say though, will you sigh for me,
If, one day, they ever hang me?

Yekaterina Nikolayevna Ushakova

ЭПИГРАММА НА Ф. БУЛГАРИНА

Не то беда, что ты поляк:
Костюшко лях, Мицкевич лях!
Пожалуй, будь себе татарин,—
И тут не вижу я стыда;
Будь жид — и это не беда;
Беда, что ты Видок Фиглярин.

Secret agent Faddey Bulgarin (wearing thick glasses, lower left corner) eavesdropping on the rumormongers

EPIGRAM ON FADDEY BULGARIN*

There's nothing wrong with being Polish:
Kosciuszko is, and so's Mickiewicz.
Were you a Tatar, that's no crime;
In this, again, I see no shame.
Be Jewish? That's no cause for blame.
What's wrong, Boulevardin,** is your spying.

Pushkin's friend, the great Polish poet Adam
Mickiewicz, as Catullus

*Faddey Bulgarin, originally from Poland, was editor of the *Northern Bee*, a newspaper funded entirely by the Tsarist 3rd Section (secret police). Bulgarin made vicious racist attacks on Pushkin, mocking his African origins, and wrote copious denunciations against Pushkin, greatly complicating both his secret police file and his ability to get published.

**Фигляр in Russian means a poseur. Видок refers to Vidocque, the head of the French secret police.

ТРИ КЛЮЧА

В степи мирской, печальной и безбрежной,
Таинственно пробились три ключа:
Ключ юности, ключ быстрый и мятежный,
Кипит, бежит, сверкая и журча.
Кастальский ключ волною вдохновенья
В степи мирской изгнанников поит.
Последний ключ — холодный ключ забвенья,
Он слаще всех жар сердца утолит.

THREE SPRINGS

In this world's plain, that stretches sad and endless,
Mysteriously three springs have risen up.
The spring of youth, a spring quick and rebellious,
Does bubble, race, and sparkling flow and run.
Next, the Castalian* spring gives wondrous vision;
From it the exile in that plain partakes.
The final spring's the cold spring of oblivion:
Sweetest of all the heart's hot thirst it slakes.

---

*The Castalian brook flows down Mount Parnassus to Delphi. Its hot springs' vapors caused the Pythian oracle to see prophetic visions.

ВАКХИЧЕСКАЯ ПЕСНЯ

Что смолкнул веселия глас?
Раздайтесь, вакхальны припевы!
Да здравствуют нежные девы
И юные жены, любившие нас!
Полнее стакан наливайте!
На звонкое дно
В густое вино
Заветные кольца бросайте!
Подымем стаканы, содвинем их разом!
Да здравствуют музы, да здравствует разум!
Ты, солнце святое, гори!
Как эта лампада бледнеет
Пред ясным восходом зари,
Так ложная мудрость мерцает и тлеет
Пред солнцем бессмертным ума.
Да здравствует солнце, да скроется тьма!

BACCHANALIAN SONG

    How is it that Joy lost its voice?
    Ring out, Bacchanalian singing!
    And long live the maidens appealing,
The lovely young wives who're so loving of us!
    So fill up your goblets, now, higher!
        With bright, clinging chime
        Into the thick wine
    Let's drop rings of heartfelt desire!
Let's raise up the glass, with one gulp, relieve it!
And long live the Muses, and long live sweet Reason!
    May you, holy sun, long burn on!
    As this little lamp pales and flickers
    Before the clear rising of Dawn,
So every false wisdom but glances and withers
    Before your immortal mind's spark!
And long live your sunshine that vanquishes dark!

Каков я прежде был, таков и ныне я:
Беспечный, влюбчивый

V. MEDITATIONS

The way I used to be, that way I still am now:
In love with love, carefree...

Self-portraits before and after growing sideburns

Tel j'étais autrefois et tel je suis encore...

Каков я прежде был, таков и ныне я:
Беспечный, влюбчивый. Вы знаете, друзья,
Могу ль на красоту взирать без умиленья,
Без робкой нежности и тайного волненья.
Уж мало ли любовь играла в жизни мной?
Уж мало ль бился я, как ястреб молодой,
В обманчивых сетях, раскинутых Кипридой:
А не исправленный стократною обидой,
Я новым идолам несу мои мольбы...

THE WAY I USED TO BE

Tel j'étais autrefois et tel je suis encore...

The way I used to be, that way I still am now:
In love with love, carefree...My friends, don't you know how
At beauty I can't look without feeling affection?
Without shy tenderness and secret pangs of tension?
Has love not played enough in life with me, untaught?
Have I not thrashed enough like a young hawk that's caught
In nets of treachery that Venus has been casting?
But having nothing learned from hundred wounds in passing,
Unto new idols I still bring and bring my prayers.

Self-portrait as a horse; see
the letter on top of p. 68

НЯНЕ

Подруга дней моих суровых,
Голубка дряхлая моя!
Одна в глуши лесов сосновых
Давно, давно ты ждешь меня.
Ты под окном своей светлицы
Горюешь, будто на часах,
И медлят поминутно спицы
В твоих наморщенных руках.
Глядишь в забытые вороты
На черный отдаленный путь;
Тоска, предчувствия, заботы
Теснят твою всечасно грудь.
То чудится тебе. . . . .

Nanny Arina Rodionovna imagined in her youth

TO NANNY

My friend through my travails, woes hardest,
My dear bedraggled little dove!
Alone you pine, in deep pine forests,
And wait for me, so long, so long!
There, by the window of your bower,
You grieve and wait as if entranced,
Your knitting needles, by the hour,
Are slowing in your wrinkled hands.
You stare out past the gates forgotten,
Look towards a long black path outstretched,
And grief, foreboding, cares, do tighten
And tug each hour in your breast.
And visions come to you. . . . .

Nanny Arina Rodionovna in her old age

Весна, весна, пора любви,
Как тяжко мне твое явленье,
Какое томное волненье
В моей душе, в моей крови...
Как чуждо сердцу наслажденье...
Все, что ликует и блестит,
Наводит скуку и томленье.

Отдайте мне метель и вьюгу
И зимний долгий мрак ночей!
...

OH SPRING, OH SPRING, OH TIME OF LOVE

Oh spring, oh spring, oh time of love,
How cruel and heavy is your coming!
What lang'rous worry and what longing
Are in my soul, are in my blood!
My heart's estranged to pleasure wholly.
All that exults and, sparkling, shines,
Leaves me but cold and melancholy...

Give back my blizzards, snowstorms bleak,
And long dark gloom of winter nights!
...

ВСТУПЛЕНИЕ К ПОЭМЕ «МЕДНЫЙ ВСАДНИК»

На берегу пустынных волн
Стоял он, дум великих полн,
И вдаль глядел. Пред ним широко
Река неслася; бедный чёлн
По ней стремился одиноко.
По мшистым, топким берегам
Чернели избы здесь и там,
Приют убогого чухонца;
И лес, неведомый лучам
В тумане спрятанного солнца,
Кругом шумел.
                    И думал он:
Отсель грозить мы будем шведу,
Здесь будет город заложен
На зло надменному соседу.
Природой здесь нам суждено
В Европу прорубить окно,
Ногою твердой стать при море.
Сюда по новым им волнам
Все флаги в гости будут к нам,
И запируем на просторе.

Прошло сто лет, и юный град,
Полнощных стран краса и диво,
Из тьмы лесов, из топи блат
Вознесся пышно, горделиво;
Где прежде финский рыболов,
Печальный пасынок природы,
Один у низких берегов
Бросал в неведомые воды
Свой ветхий невод, ныне там
По оживленным берегам
Громады стройные теснятся
Дворцов и башен; корабли
Толпой со всех концов земли
К богатым пристаням стремятся;
В гранит оделася Нева;
Мосты повисли над водами;
Темно-зелеными садами
Ее покрылись острова,
И перед младшею столицей
Померкла старая Москва,
Как перед новою царицей
Порфироносная вдова.

THE PROLOGUE TO *THE BRONZE HORSEMAN*

By coasts where desolate crash the waves
Stood he, filled full of grand thoughts brave,
And looked afar. Before him only
The broad flood flowed, bare river — save
One poor skiff on its whitecaps lonely.
By such thick mossy, swampy clay
Just god-forsaken mad Finns stay
But here and there their black huts dotting.
The woods, kept secret from all rays
Of sunshine that the fog was swathing,
Stirred, rustling round.
                      And then he thought:
From here the mighty Swede we'll menace;
Here we will build a city up
To spite our haughty neighbour jealous.
Here Nature has decreed that we
To Europe force a window free,
With mighty step bestride the ocean.
And o'er these waves which no one knew
The whole world's flags will stream hereto;
We'll feast on this vast space in motion.

        A century's past, and this young town
Is now the midnight-sun-lands' wonder.
From deep dark woods, swamps' soggy ground
A sumptuous beauty rose in grandeur.
Where once some Finnish fisherman,
Bleak nature's melancholy stepson,
Alone stood in the shallow sand,
Casting his tattered net unresting
In murky waters, now look round!
All bustles by the river's bounds;
Great gleaming giants crowd in, graceful,
Of towers and palaces! And boats
From every one of this world's coasts
Throng to our wealthy dockyards, racing.
In granite our Nevá is clad,
And bridges drape over our waters;
With rich dark-green grand lawns and gardens
Have claimed the river's islands back.
Next to our new capital splendid
Our ancient Moscow dimmed, did fade,
Stands, by a beautiful young Empress,
A dowdy dowager old maid.

Люблю тебя, Петра творенье,
Люблю твой строгий, стройный вид,
Невы державное теченье,
Береговой ее гранит,
Твоих оград узор чугунный,
Твоих задумчивых ночей
Прозрачный сумрак, блеск безлунный,
Когда я в комнате моей
Пишу, читаю без лампады,
И ясны спящие громады
Пустынных улиц, и светла
Адмиралтейская игла.
И, не пуская тьму ночную
На золотые небеса,
Одна заря сменить другую
Спешит, дав ночи полчаса.
Люблю зимы твоей жестокой
Недвижный воздух и мороз,
Бег санок вдоль Невы широкой,
Девичьи лица ярче роз,
И блеск, и шум, и говор балов,
А в час пирушки холостой
Шипенье пенистых бокалов
И пунша пламень голубой.
Люблю воинственную живость
Потешных Марсовых полей,
Пехотных ратей и коней
Однообразную красивость,
В их стройно зыблемом строю
Лоскутья сих знамен победных,
Сиянье шапок этих медных,
Насквозь простреленных в бою,

I love you, place of Peter's making,
I love your stern and stylish face,
The Nevá's mighty current breaking
On her embankments' granite grace,
The wrought-iron patterns of your fences,
Your twilight's clear and thoughtful gloom
On summer evenings, shining moonless,
When I sit sleepless in my room,
And write and read and need no lanterns:
How gleam the buildings, sleeping monsters,
On streets deserted! And I see
The Needle of the Admiralty.
And not allowing murk nocturnal
Into the heavens' golden bower,
Each dawn relieves each dawn eternal:
That race leaves night but half an hour.
I love your winter's cruel broadsides,
Unyielding air and frosts that bite,
Across the broad Nevá the sleigh rides,
The girlish faces rosy bright,
At balls: the gleam, the hum, the chatter,
At feasts, where bachelors make their fame,
The foaming champagne-glasses' clatter,
The punch-bowl's light blue tongue of flame.
I love the warlike animation
Upon the Fields of Mars displayed,
The troops of horse and foot arrayed,
Their beauty lacking variation,
The rows that sway and then grow tight,
Victorious banners' tattered remnants,
The glittering bronze of soldiers' helmets
Shot through by bullets in the fight,

Люблю, военная столица,
Твоей твердыни дым и гром,
Когда полнощная царица
Дарует сына в царский дом,
Или победу над врагом
Россия снова торжествует,
Или, взломав свой синий лед,
Нева к морям его несет
И, чуя вешни дни, ликует.

Красуйся, град Петров, и стой
Неколебимо, как Россия,
Да умирится же с тобой
И побежденная стихия;
Вражду и плен старинный свой
Пусть волны финские забудут
И тщетной злобою не будут
Тревожить вечный сон Петра!

The Bronze Horseman without the Horseman

I love, war-capital, your fortress,
Your smoke, your shooting with a boom,
To mark when midnight-sun-land's Empress
Brings forth a son to the Tsar's home,
Also when victory o'er the foe
Is hailed with Russia's celebration,
Or, from its blue ice breaking free,
Neva flows, bears it to the sea,
Feels spring days coming with elation.

Be gorgeous, Peter's town, steadfast!
Remain unconquerable, like Russia!
And may the elements at last,
With being tamed, make peace, be hushed.
And may the Finnish waves not keep
Their grudge 'gainst being tamed forever,
And may their futile malice never
Rouse Peter from eternal sleep!

Город пышный, город бедный,
Дух неволи, стройный вид,
Свод небес зелено-бледный,
Скука, холод и гранит —
Все же мне вас жаль немножко,
Потому что здесь порой
Ходит маленькая ножка,
Вьется локон золотой.

Town so gorgeous, town of beggars,
Air of slavery, splendid face,
Pale green archway of your heaven,
Boredom, cold, and granite grace.
Yet I'm sad for you too, truly
Because, sometimes, here, a girl
Walks with sweet small foot alluring,
Waving, soft, a golden curl.

Tsar Nicholas I

Счастлив, кто избран своенравно
Твоей тоскливою мечтой,
При ком любовью млеешь явно,
Чьи взоры властвуют тобой;
Но жалок тот, кто молчаливо,
Сгорая пламенем любви,
Потупя голову ревниво,
Признанья слушает твои.

"Afire with the flame of love…"

Oh, blessed, he picked with choice capricious,
By all your dreams so full of rue,
Whose love your obvious sighing wishes,
Whose looks have power over you.
But woeful he, whose silence zealous,
Afire with the flame of love,
His head down dipping slightly, jealous,
Hears what you can't confess enough.

Annette Olenina

Я вас любил: любовь еще, быть может,
В душе моей угасла не совсем;
Но пусть она вас больше не тревожит;
Я не хочу печалить вас ничем.
Я вас любил безмолвно, безнадежно,
То робостью, то ревностью томим;
Я вас любил так искренно, так нежно,
Как дай вам Бог любимой быть другим.

Annette Olenina turns her back on Pushkin

I LOVED YOU ONCE, AND STILL, PERHAPS, LOVE'S YEARNING

I loved you once, and still, perhaps, love's yearning
Within my soul has not quite burned away.
Yett may that nevermore you be concerning;
I would not wish you sad in any way.
My love for you was wordless, hopeless cruelly,
Drowned now in shyness, now in jealousy,
And I loved you so tenderly, so truly,
As God grant by another you may be.

СТИХИ, СОЧИНЕННЫЕ НОЧЬЮ ВО ВРЕМЯ БЕССОННИЦЫ

Мне не спится, нет огня;
Всюду мрак и сон докучный.
Ход часов лишь однозвучный
Раздается близ меня,
Парки бабье лепетанье,
Спящей ночи трепетанье,
Жизни мышья беготня...
Что тревожишь ты меня?
Что ты значишь, скучный шепот?
Укоризна, или ропот
Мной утраченного дня?
От меня чего ты хочешь?
Ты зовешь или пророчишь?
Я понять тебя хочу,
Смысла я в тебе ищу...

WRITTEN ON A SLEEPLESS NIGHT

I can't sleep, fire's out, no light.
All is bleak, rests restless, tiresome.
Just the clock near me sounds lonesome,
Ticks on with no end in sight,
Ticks the Fates' cruel chitter-chatter,
Drowsy night's dull pitter-patter,
Mouse-life's darting busily...
What's your point in bothering me?
What's your meaning, droning ticker?
Are you of reproach a flicker
Of the way I waste my day?
What is it from me you're needing?
Are you calling or foreseeing?
Oh, to glimpse your truth, to peek!
Sense in you is what I seek...

ЦВЕТОК

Цветок засохший, безуханный,
Забытый в книге вижу я;
И вот уже мечтою странной
Душа наполнилась моя:

Где цвел? когда? какой весною?
И долго ль цвел? и сорван кем,
Чужой, знакомой ли рукою?
И положен сюда зачем?

На память нежного ль свиданья,
Или разлуки роковой,
Иль одинокого гулянья
В тиши полей, в тени лесной?

И жив ли тот, и та жива ли?
И нынче где их уголок?
Или уже они увяли,
Как сей неведомый цветок?

THE FLOWER

A dried-out flower, without fragrance,
Forgotten in a book I see;
My soul's somehow already racing,
And fills with a strange reverie.

Where did it bloom? In which spring? When?
Did it bloom long? Who picked it then?
Was it a stranger or a friend?
Who put it here and to what end?

In memory of tender trysting?
Or else of fateful parting day?
Or else perhaps of lone walk wistful
In silent fields and wooded shade?

Do he and she still live, I wonder?
And where now is their little nook?
Or have they faded, lost their luster,
Like this small flower in this book?

26 МАЯ 1828

Дар напрасный, дар случайный,
Жизнь, зачем ты мне дана?
Иль зачем судьбою тайной
Ты на казнь осуждена?

Кто меня враждебной властью
Из ничтожества воззвал,
Душу мне наполнил страстью,
Ум сомненьем взволновал?..

Цели нет передо мною:
Сердце пусто, празден ум,
И томит меня тоскою
Однозвучный жизни шум.

MAY 26, 1828*

Gift so futile, gift so random,
Life, why were you given me?
Or else why has Fate unfathomed
Doomed you to Death's penalty?

Whose malevolent attraction
From the void has called me out,
Filled my soul with so much passion,
Racked my mind with raging doubt?

No goals beckon now before me,
Empty-hearted, idle-brained,
Always a dull grief torments me,
Sounds monotonous life's strains.

---

*On the occasion of his 29th birthday according to the Julian calendar. May 26, 1828 would have been June 7, 1828, by our Gregorian Calendar.

ВОСПОМИНАНИЕ

Когда для смертного умолкнет шумный день
    И на немые стогны града
Полупрозрачная наляжет ночи тень
    И сон, дневных трудов награда,
В то время для меня влачатся в тишине
    Часы томительного бденья:
В бездействии ночном живей горят во мне
    Змеи сердечной угрызенья;
Мечты кипят; в уме, подавленном тоской,
    Теснится тяжких дум избыток;
Воспоминание безмолвно предо мной
    Свой длинный развивает свиток:
И с отвращением читая жизнь мою,
    Я трепещу и проклинаю,
И горько жалуюсь, и горько слезы лью,
    Но строк печальных не смываю.

REMEMBRANCE*

When to most mortals sounds of noisy day do fade,
    And on the mutened city's hayricks,
The half-transparent night casts down its shade,
    And sleep's rewarding the day's labors,
I, in that time, in silence toss and turn,
    Those wakeful hours that so try the patience.
Through night's inaction stronger in me burn
    Of heartfelt self-reproach the serpents.
With dreams aboil, my mind, oppressed, beset with grief,
    Into a crowd drives thoughts appalling...
And silent recollections pass before my eyes,
    The scroll in which they're writ unfolding:
And, with repulsion, as I'm reading there my life,
    I tremble, cursing with rue awful,
Complaining bitterly, with bitter tears I cry,
    Yet don't wash off the lines so mournful.

*This was Leo Tolstoy's favorite poem; he would declaim it to himself loudly, at the end substituting the word "shameful" for the word "mournful."

ВОЗРОЖДЕНИЕ

Художник-варвар кистью сонной
Картину гения чернит
И свой рисунок беззаконный
Над ней бессмысленно чертит.

Но краски чуждые, с летами,
Спадают ветхой чешуей;
Созданье гения пред нами
Выходит с прежней красотой.

Так исчезают заблужденья
С измученной души моей,
И возникают в ней виденья
Первоначальных, чистых дней.

REBIRTH

A savage artist, brushstrokes drooping,
The painting of a genius mars,
With sacrilegious scrawl unruly
A senseless mess on it he tars.

But as the years pass, colors foreign
Fall off, like snakeskin's ancient flakes,
What genius wrought once gets reborn
Again, and former beauty takes.

Just so, my erring ways do vanish,
And in my wracked soul leave no trace,
Then visions rise up, with abandon,
From pure and innocent first days.

Когда порой воспоминанье
Грызет мне сердце в тишине,
И отдаленное страданье
Как тень опять бежит ко мне;
Когда, людей повсюду видя,
В пустыню скрыться я хочу,
Их слабый глас возненавидя, —
Тогда, забывшись, я лечу
Не в светлый край, где небо блещет
Неизъяснимой синевой,
Где море теплою волной
На пожелтелый мрамор плещет,
И лавр и темный кипарис
На воле пышно разрослись,
Где пел Торквато величавый,
Где и теперь во мгле ночной
Далече звонкою скалой
Повторены пловца октавы.

Стремлюсь привычною мечтою
К студеным северным волнам.
Меж белоглавой их толпою
Открытый остров вижу там.
Печальный остров — берег дикий
Усеян зимнею брусникой,
Увядшей тундрою покрыт
И хладной пеною подмыт.
Сюда порою приплывает
Отважный северный рыбак,
Здесь невод мокрый расстилает
И свой разводит он очаг.
Сюда погода волновая
Заносит утлый мой челнок...
....

Sometimes when moody reminiscence
Gnaws at my heart with silent grief,
And suffering comes back from a distance,
And like a spectre chases me,
When everywhere I look are people,
And in a desert I would hide,
Feeling I hate their voices feeble–
Then I forget myself and fly–
Not to that blessed land, whose heaven
So sparkles deep, mysterious blue,
Whose ocean waves splash warmly through
Embankments marble, faded, yellowed,
Whose laurel, and whose cypress dark,
Grow up in freedom, splendor, art,
Where once Torquato sang majestic,
Where, even now, in gloom of night,
'Neath cliffs that echo in the bight
His octaves boatmen aren't forgetting.

Instead, it seems I'm always yearning
For grey and chilly northern waves,
Amidst their crowded whitecaps churning
I see a barren island's capes,
A saddened island's savage coastline,
Where scattered whortleberries grow,
'Midst faded tundra, melting snow,
And washed at times by chilly foam.
At certain times you'll see arriving
A northern fisherman, tough breed:
He stretches out his nets for drying,
And stokes a campfire by the sea.
It's always there the whitecapped weather
Casts up my frail and flimsy boat...
....

Ямщик лихой, седое время,
Везет, не слезет с облучка.

View of the Turkish city of Arzurum

VI. ON THE ROAD

Grey time, wild coachman ever steady,
Drives on, won't leave his driver's seat.

A Funeral Procession

Поедем, я готов; куда бы вы, друзья,
Куда б ни вздумали, готов за вами я
Повсюду следовать, надменной убегая:
К подножию ль стены далекого Китая,
В кипящий ли Париж, туда ли наконец,
Где Тасса не поет уже ночной гребец,
Где древних городов под пеплом дремлют мощи,
Где кипарисные благоухают рощи,
Повсюду я готов. Поедем... но, друзья,
Скажите: в странствиях умрет ли страсть моя?
Забуду ль гордую, мучительную деву,
Или к ее ногам, ее младому гневу,
Как дань привычную, любовь я принесу?

LET'S LEAVE, I'M READY NOW!

Let's leave, I'm ready now! Wherever you, my friends,
Have whims you'd like to go, even to the earth's ends,
I'll gladly follow, from haughty maiden flying:
Unto the distant foot of the Great Wall of China,
To Paris bubbling, or-- at last! to that land yet
Where Tasso's quatrains gondoliers at night forget,
Where ancient cities' ruins beneath the ash are slumb'ring,
Where cypress groves' sweet scents set all the senses humming:
Wherever! Let's go now! But friends, say, by and by,
In all these pilgrimages will my passions die?
Will I that maiden, proud tormentress, be forgetting,
Or, at her feet cast down, her youthful rage begetting,
Will I, as if paying a common debt, bring love?

ЗИМНЯЯ ДОРОГА

Сквозь волнистые туманы
Пробирается луна,
На печальные поляны
Льет печально свет она.

По дороге зимней, скучной
Тройка борзая бежит,
Колокольчик однозвучный
Утомительно гремит.

Что-то слышится родное
В долгих песнях ямщика:
То разгулье удалое,
То сердечная тоска...

Ни огня, ни черной хаты,
Глушь и снег... Навстречу мне
Только версты полосаты
Попадаются одне.

Скучно, грустно... Завтра, Нина,
Завтра, к милой возвратясь,
Я забудусь у камина,
Загляжусь не наглядясь.

Звучно стрелка часовая
Мерный круг свой совершит,
И, докучных удаляя,
Полночь нас не разлучит.

Грустно, Нина: путь мой скучен,
Дремля смолкнул мой ямщик,
Колокольчик однозвучен,
Отуманен лунный лик.

A WINTER ROAD

Through a mist that's waving, rolling,
Breaking through, the moon does pass;
On the meadows melancholy
Melancholy light does cast.

On a winter road so dreary,
Fleet my little troika runs;
Of its little bell I'm weary
Clinking with but one note dull.

Something strikes a chord within me,
In the coachman's endless song:
Sometimes fiery, daring, cheery,
Sometimes grieving in my heart.

Not one light, no black hut looming,
Barren snow round barren path,
Just the milestones striped and gloomy
Are the only things I pass.

Dreary, sad…Tomorrow, Nina,
I'll be back by your dear fire,
Lose myself and clutch you nearer,
Look and look, and never tire.

When the sonorous clock-hand arrows
Keep their measured rounds so hard,
Fleeing all things dull and shallowá
Midnight won't keep us apart.

I'm sad, Nina: my path's dreary,
Hushed, my coachman nods, apace,
From his little bell I'm weary,
Wrapped in mist is the moon's face.

ТЕЛЕГА ЖИЗНИ

Хоть тяжело подчас в ней бремя,
Телега на ходу легка;
Ямщик лихой, седое время,
Везет, не слезет с облучка.

С утра садимся мы в телегу;
Мы рады голову сломать
И, презирая лень и негу,
Кричим: «пошел, ...!»

Но в полдень нет уж той отваги;
Порастрясло нас; нам страшней
И косогоры и овраги;
Кричим: полегче, дуралей!

Катит по-прежнему телега,
Под вечер мы привыкли к ней
И дремля едем до ночлега,
А время гонит лошадей.

THE CART OF LIFE

Although at times the burden's heavy,
The cart rides with a rhythm fleet.
Grey time, wild coachman ever steady,
Drives on, won't leave his driver's seat.

We mount the cart when morn's arising,
We'd gladly break our head in two,
Our haste, comfort and ease despising,
Leads us to yell.. "let's go! **** ***."

But when it's noon, we've lost that valor
And fear more, having rattled through
The little rolling hills and valleys,
We yell: "Ease up there, silly fool!"

But still the cart keeps rolling, rolling,
By evening we're quite used to it.
As towards our shelter we ride dozing:
Time drives the horses with a whip.

ПРИМЕТЫ

Я ехал к вам: живые сны
За мной вились толпой игривой,
И месяц с правой стороны
Сопровождал мой бег ретивый.

Я ехал прочь: иные сны...
Душе влюбленной грустно было,
И месяц с левой стороны
Сопровождал меня уныло.

Мечтанью вечному в тиши
Так предаемся мы, поэты;
Так суеверные приметы
Согласны с чувствами души.

SUPERSTITIONS

I rode towards you, and waking dreams
Did wind in playful thought around me.
The moon, on my right side, cast beams
On our race ardent, hoofbeats pounding.

I rode away, and other dreams
Made my soul lovelorn, melancholy.
The moon, now on my left, cast beams
With gloomy gleams, on me, despondent.

Removed in quiet reverie,
We poets ever are capricious;
And thus traditions superstitious
Live with our hearts in harmony.

Подъезжая под Ижоры,
Я взглянул на небеса
И воспомнил ваши взоры,
Ваши синие глаза.

Хоть я грустно очарован
Вашей девственной красой,
Хоть вампиром именован
Я в губернии Тверской,

Но колен моих пред вами
Преклонить я не посмел
И влюбленными мольбами
Вас тревожить не хотел.

Упиваясь неприятно
Хмелем светской суеты,
Позабуду, вероятно,
Ваши милые черты,

Легкий стан, движений стройность,
Осторожный разговор,
Эту скромную спокойность,
Хитрый смех и хитрый взор.

Если ж нет... по прежню следу
В ваши мирные края
Через год опять заеду
И влюблюсь до ноября.

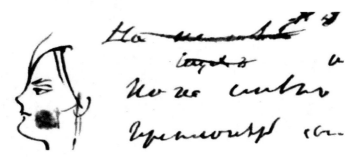

"And–till November–fall in love" (Katya Velyasheva)

ROUND IZHORA I WAS RIDING

Round Izhora I was riding,
When I looked up at the skies.
For your glances I was pining,
For the dark blue of your eyes.
Though most sadly I am smitten
By your beauty chaste, austere,
Though it's "vampire" I am christened
In the province known as Tver',
Still on bended knee before you
To offend I would not dare,
Or with lovelorn pleas implore you.
I've no wish to cause you care.
So I'll revel, pointless, clueless,
In society's vain fuss.
Soon, it's likely, I'll be heedless
Just how sweet your face once was,
Lithe your build, graceful your movements,
Prudent speech, quite by the book.
Your mild calm, so unassuming,
Cunning laugh and cunning look
I'll forget...If not, be certain,
I'll ride back quite soon enough
In a year to your sweet province
And — till November — fall in love.

Another profile of Katya Velyasheva

(2 ноября)

Зима. Что делать нам в деревне? Я встречаю
Слугу, несущего мне утром чашку чаю,
Вопросами: тепло ль? утихла ли метель?
Пороша есть иль нет? и можно ли постель
Покинуть для седла, иль лучше до обеда
Возиться с старыми журналами соседа?
Пороша. Мы встаем, и тотчас на коня,
И рысью по полю при первом свете дня;
Арапники в руках, собаки вслед за нами;
Глядим на бледный снег прилежными глазами,
Кружимся, рыскаем и поздней уж порой,
Двух зайцев протравив, являемся домой.
Куда как весело! Вот вечер: вьюга воет;
Свеча темно горит; стесняясь, сердце ноет;
По капле, медленно глотаю скуки яд.
Читать хочу; глаза над буквами скользят,
А мысли далеко...Я книгу закрываю;
Беру перо, сижу; насильно вырываю
У музы дремлющей несвязные слова.
Ко звуку звук нейдет... Теряю все права
Над рифмой, над моей прислужницею странной:
Стих вяло тянется, холодный и туманный.
Усталый, с лирою я прекращаю спор,
Иду в гостиную; там слышу разговор
О близких выборах, о сахарном заводе;
Хозяйка хмурится в подобие погоде,
Стальными спицами проворно шевеля,
Иль про червонного гадает короля.
Тоска! Так день за днем идет в уединенье!
Но если под вечер в печальное селенье,
Когда за шашками сижу я в уголке,
Приедет издали в кибитке иль возке

A COUNTRY WINTER

(November 2nd)*

A country winter. What's to do here? I am greeting
My servant, as he brings my morning teacup
With questions: Is it warmer? Has the storm died down?
Is there powder or not? Should I go riding now,
Abandoning my bed, or till dinner's at table
Should I just fuss with the old journals of my neighbor?
It's powder. We get up, and on the horse we ride
And gallop through the fields just at the day's first light,
And carry hunting whips, the dogs behind us racing,
Our eyes with fervor scan pale snow, keep gazing,
We circle, trot around, and it has gotten late
When, having missed two hares, we ride back to our gate.
Oh what a joy that was! It's evening. Snowstorm's crying...
A candle darkly burns, my heart is gnawing shyly.
Of boredom, drop by drop, I slowly poison sip
I want to read; my eyes over the letters slip;
My thoughts are far away...I close the book, despairing,
I take my pen, I sit, with violence am tearing
Disjointed words out of my grudging, slumbering Muse,
But sound does not match sound, and soon all rights I lose
To Rhyme, to old maid muse gone somewhat balmy,
My poem weakly drags, is getting cold and foggy.
I'm tired; and with my lyre my quarrel I stop,
Go to the living room, and there I hear the talk:
Elections on their way, some sugar factory's founding,
And very weather-like, the house mistress is frowning,
As she her steel needles for knitting nimbly darts,
As she tells fortunes for a certain king of hearts...
How dull! Thus day by day goes by in solitary,
But if, one evening time, upon our village dreary,
When, in my corner, I'm half-sleeping over checkers,
When, from far off, a covered sled or carriage enters,

*I.e. November 14th, by our Gregorian Calendar.

Нежданная семья: старушка, две девицы
(Две белокурые, две стройные сестрицы), —
Как оживляется глухая сторона!
Как жизнь, о Боже мой, становится полна!
Сначала косвенно-внимательные взоры,
Потом слов несколько, потом и разговоры,
А там и дружный смех, и песни вечерком,
И вальсы резвые, и шепот за столом,
И взоры томные, и ветреные речи,
На узкой лестнице замедленные встречи;
И дева в сумерки выходит на крыльцо:
Открыты шея, грудь, и вьюга ей в лицо!
Но бури севера не вредны русской розе.
Как жарко поцелуй пылает на морозе!
Как дева русская свежа в пыли снегов!

A family by surprise: two maidens with one spinster
(Two curly charming blondes, two slender, graceful sisters)
How lively, suddenly, these boondocks get!
How life, my God, fills up, seems hopeful yet!
First passing glances, looks full of attention,
Then a few words, and then the conversations,
Then friendly laughs, songs in the evening reel,
With waltzes rollicking, and whispers at the meal
Then looks all languorous, light-hearted, airy speeches,
And lingering, on narrow stairways, meetings:
One girl at twilight on the porch does pace:
Her neck and breast are bare — the snowstorm's in her face!
But northern storms are to our Russian rose not fazing!
How warm— even in frost — the kiss she gives is, blazing!
How fresh the Russian maid when snowflakes fly!

"A family by surprise: two maidens with one spinster"
(with little demons dancing attendance on them)

КАЛМЫЧКЕ

Прощай, любезная калмычка!
Чуть-чуть, на зло моих затей,
Меня похвальная привычка
Не увлекла среди степей
Вслед за кибиткою твоей.
Твои глаза, конечно, узки,
И плосок нос, и лоб широк,
Ты не лепечешь по-французски,
Ты шелком не сжимаешь ног,
По-английски пред самоваром
Узором хлеба не крошишь,
Не восхищаешься Сен-Маром,
Слегка Шекспира не ценишь,
Не погружаешься в мечтанье,
Когда нет мысли в голове,
Не распеваешь: *Ma dov'è*,
Галоп не прыгаешь в собранье...
Что нужды? Ровно полчаса,
Пока коней мне запрягали,
Мне ум и сердце занимали
Твой взор и дикая краса.
Друзья! Не все ль одно и то же:
Забыться праздною душой
В блестящей зале, в модной ложе
Или в кибитке кочевой?

TO A KALMYK GIRL*

Farewell, dear, pleasant Kalmyk maiden!
For, nearly spoiling all my plans,
My good old habit almost played me,
Seduced me in this broad expanse
Of steppes, where your broad tent did span.
Your eyes, of course, are rather narrow.
Your nose is flat, your forehead's broad,
Your grasp of French is rather shallow,
In silk your legs you don't swathe taut.
You don't, o'er samovar, o'er campfire,
Make English patterns of your bread,
By CinqMar's feats** you're not inspired,
In Shakespeare you're a bit unread.
You do not lose yourself daydreaming
When there are no thoughts in your head,
You don't sing arias: *Ma dov'è*,***
Or dance galopes in gatherings teeming.
Who needs that? But for half an hour,
While they were hitching up my team,
My heart and spirit were o'erpowered
By your wild grace and look so keen.
My friends! What does it really matter
Just where our idle heart gets rent?
In ballrooms bright, smart box-seat chatter,
Or in a nomad's wicker tent?****

*For Natalie Melikyan, who loves this poem.

***The Plot of CinqMars against Louis XIII*, a popular historical novel by the French Romantic poet Alfred de Vigny, was published in 1826.

*** "But where is" (Italian)

****See page 66 for more details about this "half an hour."

МОНАСТЫРЬ НА КАЗБЕКЕ

Высоко над семьею гор,
Казбек, твой царственный шатер
Сияет вечными лучами.
Твой монастырь за облаками,
Как в небе реющий ковчег,
Парит, чуть видный, над горами.

Далекий вожделенный брег!
Туда б, сказав прости ущелью,
Подняться к вольной вышине!
Туда б, в заоблачную келью,
В соседство Бога скрыться мне!..

THE MONASTERY OF MOUNT KAZBEK

High o'er mountain family,
Kazbek, your vault majestically
Shines rays eternal, blessed and airy.
Beyond the clouds, your monastery,
An ark in heaven fluttering,
Steams o'er the peaks, is seen but barely.

Goal strived-for long in wandering!
To climb, leave in ravines all crowds,
To rise to freedom, high, aloft!
To you, my cell beyond the clouds!
To hide, and neighbors be with God!

The Caucasus

Не пой, красавица, при мне
Ты песен Грузии печальной:
Напоминают мне оне
Другую жизнь и берег дальный.

Увы, напоминают мне
Твои жестокие напевы
И степь, и ночь, и при луне
Черты далекой, бедной девы!..

Я призрак милый, роковой,
Тебя увидев, забываю;
Но ты поешь — и предо мной
Его я вновь воображаю.

Не пой, красавица, при мне
Ты песен Грузии печальной:
Напоминают мне оне
Другую жизнь и берег дальный.

Oh beauty, do not sing* to me
More songs of melancholy Georgia.
For they bring up, evoke in me
Another life, a distant shoreline.

Alas! You call forth in your tune,
In your cruel melody's refraining,
The steppe, the night, and 'neath the moon
The face of a poor, distant maiden.

That darling fateful spectre—when
I see you—I'm forgetting.
But then you sing, and, once again,
Before my eyes it is engendered.

Oh beauty, do not sing to me
More songs of melancholy Georgia.
For they bring up, evoke, in me
Another life, a distant shoreline.

A Georgian Beauty

*There are countless romances and songs set to Pushkin poems. This poem is actually a rare case of the reverse. It was written by special request as the lyrical accompaniment to a Georgian melody improvised by Pushkin's friend Alexander Griboyedov, the poet, playwright, diplomat and composer, during a musical evening with the composer Mikhail Glinka. In turn, this poem was set again to hauntingly beautiful music by Rachmaninoff.

Зорю бьют... из рук моих
Ветхий Данте выпадает,
На устах начатый стих
Недочитанный затих —
Дух далече улетает.
Звук привычный, звук живой,
Сколь ты часто раздавался
Там, где тихо развивался
Я давнишнею порой.

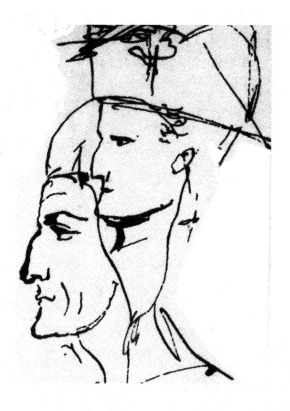

Napoleon looming over Dante

DAWN DRUMS SOUND

Dawn drums sound...From my hand tips
Dante's poem, now in tatters,
And a verse, sprung to my lips,
Unsaid, into stillness slips —
Farther still my spirit scatters.
Beat familiar, beat alive,
Say, how often were you booming
Back in days of quiet blooming,*
Once upon a distant time?

* Refers to the reveille drum of the Lycée.

ДЕЛИБАШ

Перестрелка за холмами;
Смотрит лагерь их и наш;
На холме пред казаками
Вьется красный делибаш.

Делибаш! Не суйся к лаве,
Пожалей свое житье;
Вмиг аминь лихой забаве:
Попадешься на копье.

Эй, казак! не рвися к бою:
Делибаш на всем скаку
Срежет саблею кривою
С плеч удалую башку.

Мчатся, сшиблись в общем крике...
Посмотрите! каковы?
Делибаш уже на пике,
А казак без головы.

Pushkin as a Cossack

DELIBASH (The Turkish Captain)

Shots ring out beyond the hillocks:
Their camp looks down; so does ours.
On a hill before the Cossacks
A red Turkish standard glowers.

Hey there, Turk! Don't charge our horse charge;
Have some pity for your life.
Poor amusement deaths in war are:
You will end up on a pike.

Cossack, hey! Race not to battle:
For the Turk, with gallop dread,
Curving scimitar a-rattle,
Will cut off your daring head.

Charging, both sides screaming, crashes...
Look! You see what's happened yet?
Speared straight through their Delibash is,
— And our Cossack's lost his head.

A Cossack and his horse

ТУЧА

Последняя туча рассеянной бури!
Одна ты несешься по ясной лазури,
Одна ты наводишь унылую тень,
Одна ты печалишь ликующий день.

Ты небо недавно кругом облегала,
И молния грозно тебя обвивала;
И ты издавала таинственный гром,
И алчную землю поила дождем.

Довольно, сокройся! Пора миновалась,
Земля освежилась, и буря промчалась,
И ветер, лаская листочки древес,
Тебя с успокоенных гонит небес.

THE CLOUD

O very last cloud of the storm that has scattered!
Alone, you are borne off along the clear azure,
Alone, you are casting a bleak shadow grey,
Alone, you bring sadness to joy felt by day.

Just recently you had all heaven surrounded,
And lightning and thunder all round you resounded.
Mysterious rumbling from your billows came,
And then the parched earth you did slake with your rain.

Enough, though, be hidden! That storm now is chastened,
The earth has been freshened, the squall has passed, racing,
The wind, now caressing the tips of the trees,
From skies that are calm now does chase you with ease.

ПРЕДЧУВСТВИЕ

Снова тучи надо мною
Собралися в тишине;
Рок завистливой бедою
Угрожает снова мне...
Сохраню ль к судьбе презренье?
Понесу ль навстречу ей
Непреклонность и терпенье
Гордой юности моей?

Бурной жизнью утомленный,
Равнодушно бури жду:
Может быть, еще спасенный,
Снова пристань я найду...
Но, предчувствуя разлуку,
Неизбежный, грозный час,
Сжать твою, мой ангел, руку,
Я спешу в последний раз.

Ангел кроткий, безмятежный,
Тихо молви мне: *прости*,
Опечалься: взор свой нежный
Подыми иль опусти;
И твое воспоминанье
Заменит душе моей
Силу, гордость, упованье
И отвагу юных дней.

FOREBODING

Once again the black clouds gather
In the silence overhead,
Ever-envious Fate unhappy
Once more sends me a new threat...
Shall I scorn predestination,
In its face look, keep aloof,
Patient, with determination
From the proud days of my youth?

I, of stormy life so tired,
Wait indifferent for the storm:
Yes, perhaps, it may transpire,
Safe again, I'll find the shore.
But foreseeing separation,
That dread hour I can't escape,
Just to press your hand, my angel,
Just for one last time I race.

Angel mild and unrebellious,
Gently murmur then: "Farewell!"
Let, with sadness, your look tendrest
Be downcast, or rising, swell.
And of you those memories' fires
In my soul will then replace
All my strength, pride, hopes, desires,
And brave heart of younger days.

Чем чаще празднует Лицей
Свою святую годовщину,
Тем робче старый круг друзей
В семью стесняется едину,
Тем реже он; тем праздник наш
В своем веселии мрачнее;
Тем глуше звон заздравных чаш
И наши песни тем грустнее.

Так дуновенья бурь земных
И нас нечаянно касались,
И мы средь пиршеств молодых
Душою часто омрачались;
Мы возмужали; рок судил
И нам житейски испытанья,
И смерти дух средь нас ходил
И назначал свои закланья.

Шесть мест упраздненных стоят,
Шести друзей не узрим боле,
Они разбросанные спят —
Кто здесь, кто там на ратном поле,
Кто дома, кто в земле чужой,
Кого недуг, кого печали
Свели во мрак земли сырой,
И надо всеми мы рыдали.

И мнится, очередь за мной,
Зовет меня мой Дельвиг милый,
Товарищ юности живой,
Товарищ юности унылой,
Товарищ песен молодых,
Пиров и чистых помышлений,
Туда, в толпу теней родных
Навек от нас утекший гений.

THE MORE WE DO COMMEMORATE

The more we do commemorate
Our Lycée's sacred founding day,
The shyer our group of old friends great,
Does press into one family fray,
The more it thins, the more it does
In merrymaking make us gloomy,
The hollower our feasting cups;
Sadder the old songs we are crooning.

So has the breath of earthly storm
With freak winds buffeted us, starkly,
That we, twixt youthful feasts till morn,
Have turned, within our own souls, darkly.
We've come of age, and Fate has willed
That we encounter all she offers.
And Death has strolled through us and killed,
And made appointments for more slaughters.

Six places are no longer here,
Six friends we had — and see no longer,
And scattered here and there they sleep:
Some on the battlefield now slumber,
Some home, and some abroad are dead,
Some by disease, and some by keening
Sadness to moist earth were led…
And over each we have been weeping.

And now it seems, it is my turn.
I hear my dear friend Delvig calling,
My friend from youth, when I did yearn,
My friend from youth, when I was lonely,
My friend of all my youthful songs,
Of feasts and purest thoughts imagined,
He calls our crowding shades beloved,
That genius lost for good, impassioned.

Тесней, о милые друзья,
Тесней наш верный круг составим,
Почившим песнь окончил я,
Живых надеждою поздравим,
Надеждой некогда опять
В пиру лицейском очутиться,
Всех остальных еще обнять
И новых жертв уж не страшиться.

Hanged Decembrists

Close in, come closer, my dear friends!
Tighten our group of old friends great,
My song of those who've perished ends:
Survivors we congratulate
With hope that soon again we'll face
A feast of our Lycée's good cheer,
That all still here will still embrace
And learn new losses not to fear.

The poet Delvig

БЕСЫ

Мчатся тучи, вьются тучи;
Невидимкою луна
Освещает снег летучий;
Мутно небо, ночь мутна.
Еду, еду в чистом поле;
Колокольчик дин-дин-дин...
Страшно, страшно поневоле
Средь неведомых равнин!

«Эй, пошел, ямщик!...» — «Нет мочи:
Коням, барин, тяжело;
Вьюга мне слипает очи;
Все дороги занесло;
Хоть убей, следа не видно;
Сбились мы. Что делать нам!
В поле бес нас водит, видно,
Да кружит по сторонам.

Посмотри: вон, вон играет,
Дует, плюет на меня;
Вон — теперь в овраг толкает
Одичалого коня;
Там верстою небывалой,
Он торчал передо мной;
Там сверкнул он искрой малой
И пропал во тьме пустой».

Мчатся тучи, вьются тучи ;
Невидимкою луна
Освещает снег летучий;
Мутно небо, ночь мутна .
Сил нам нет кружиться доле;
Колокольчик вдруг умолк;
Кони стали... «Что там в поле?» —
«Кто их знает? пень или волк?»

DEMONS

Clouds are racing, clouds are writhing,
And, invisibly, the moon
Lights the snow up as it's flying;
Gloom's in heaven, night's in gloom.
In a bare field I am riding.
Din-din-din! the bell complains,
I can't help but being frightened,
'Midst these strange and unknown plains.

"Coachman! Hey! Let's go!" ... "I can't, sir,
See the horses walk so slow.
Snowstorm's done clear blown my eyes in,
All the roads are drowned in snow.
Kill me, but I see no traces,
We're quite lost. What shall we do?
For it seems a demon leads us
Round these fields and whirls us through.

Look right there, right there he's teasing,
Blowing, spitting at me, coarse.
There, towards a ravine he's leading,
With a push, our lonely horse.
There, like a fantastic milestone,
He before my eyes did lurk.
There he flashed with a spark tiny,
Vanished in the empty murk."

Clouds are racing, clouds are writhing,
And, invisibly, the moon
Lights the snow up as it's flying,
Gloom's in heaven, night's in gloom.
We've no strength to circle longer.
Suddenly the horses froze,
Bell fell silent. "What's that yonder?
Tree-stump or a wolf? Who knows?"

Вьюга злится, вьюга плачет;
Кони чуткие храпят;
Вот уж он далече скачет;
Лишь глаза во мгле горят;
Кони снова понеслися;
Колокольчик дин-дин-дин...
Вижу: духи собралися
Средь белеющих равнин.

Бесконечны, безобразны,
В мутной месяца игре
Закружились бесы разны,
Будто листья в ноябре...
Сколько их! куда их гонят?
Что так жалобно поют?
Домового ли хоронят,
Ведьму ль замуж выдают?

Мчатся тучи, вьются тучи;
Невидимкою луна
Освещает снег летучий;
Мутно небо, ночь мутна.
Мчатся бесы рой за роем
В беспредельной вышине,
Визгом жалобным и воем
Надрывая сердце мне...

THE DEMONS

Snowstorm rages, snowstorm weeping,
Snorting horses ill-at-ease,
There! There! — off he darts now, sweeping,
But his eyes in this gloom blaze.
Horses start off in a lather,
Din-din-din! the bell complains...
Now I see the spirits gathered
In the ever-whitening plains!

Never-ending, ugly, formless,
In the gloom that this moon weaves
Demons whirl around me, various,
Like November's falling leaves.
Hosts! What hounds them! Where to their flight?
Why this singing, plaintive screech?
Are they burying a house sprite?
Are they marrying off a witch?

Clouds are racing, clouds are writhing,
And, invisibly, the moon
Lights the snow up as it's flying;
Gloom's in heaven, night's in gloom.
Demons racing, boundless, mounting,
Row on row, high, long, and far...
With their mournful, plaintive howling,
They are tearing up my heart...

Есть в мире сердце, где живу я.

Karolina Sobanskaya

VII. FROM THE HEART

There is a heart where I'm still living.

Natalya Nikolayevna Goncharova, Pushkin's wife

МАДОННА (Сонет)

Не множеством картин старинных мастеров
Украсить я всегда желал свою обитель,
Чтоб суеверно им дивился посетитель,
Внимая важному сужденью знатоков.

В простом углу моем, средь медленных трудов,
Одной картины я желал быть вечно зритель,
Одной: чтоб на меня с холста, как с облаков,
Пречистая и наш божественный Спаситель —

Она с величием, Он с разумом в очах —
Взирали, кроткие, во славе и в лучах,
Одни, без ангелов, под пальмою Сиона.

Исполнились мои желания. Творец
Тебя мне ниспослал, тебя, моя Мадонна,
Чистейшей прелести чистейший образец.

Natalya, his wife, walking away from him

MADONNA (A Sonnet)

Of all the great old masters' paintings, few, indeed,
I'd decorate my home with— if at all,
To cause my visitors sheer superstitious awe,
Impressing those who to grand critics pay blind heed,

O'er my meek little nook, which slothful labor crowds,
There's just one picture I'd hope ever would keep near,
Just one, from canvas glancing down, as from the clouds,
Our purest Maid, with Heaven's Son, our Savior,

So She'd with majesty, and He'd with reason gaze,
With looks of meekness, soft, yet with bright glory's rays,
No angels near, alone, 'neath Zion's green palm fronded...

My dream's come true. Our Lord Creator sent
You down to me, sent you, my own Madonna,
Of purest grace the purest monument.

Что в имени тебе моем?
Оно умрет, как шум печальный
Волны, плеснувшей в берег дальный,
Как звук ночной в лесу глухом.

Оно на памятном листке
Оставит мертвый след, подобный
Узору надписи надгробной
На непонятном языке.

Что в нем? Забытое давно
В волненьях новых и мятежных,
Твоей душе не даст оно
Воспоминаний чистых, нежных.

Но в день печали, в тишине,
Произнеси его тоскуя;
Скажи: есть память обо мне,
Есть в мире сердце, где живу я.

Pushkin surrounded by images of Karolina Sobanskaya

What is there is my name for you?
It will die out, like sad waves sounding
Their last, on distant shorelines pounding,
As in deaf woods night's sounds ring through.

Within your album it will leave
A deadened trail, like in description
To tracings on a grave's inscription
In a strange language you can't read.

What's in't? Forgotten long ago,
By new rebellious passions rendered,
It will not give your soul a glow
Of recollections pure and tender.

But in still sadness, undisturbed,
Pronounce aloud my name while grieving;
Say: I'm remembered in this world;
There is a heart where I'm still living.

На холмах Грузии лежит ночная мгла;
Шумит Арагва предо мною.
Мне грустно и легко; печаль моя светла;
Печаль моя полна тобою,
Тобой, одной тобой... Унынья моего
Ничто не мучит, не тревожит,
И сердце вновь горит и любит — оттого,
Что не любить оно не может.

Profile of his fiancée, Natalya Nikolayevna Goncharova

Upon the Georgian hills there lies the haze of night.
Aragva's river foams beside me.
I feel sad and at ease; my melancholy's bright;
My melancholy's full entirely
Of you and just of you... This gloominess of mine
Nothing's tormenting, nothing's moving.
My heart again burns up with loving, because – why?
It simply cannot not be loving.

"Upon the Georgian hills..." (manuscript)

Когда в объятия мои
Твой стройный стан я заключаю
И речи нежные любви
Тебе с восторгом расточаю,
Безмолвна, от стесненных рук
Освобождая стан свой гибкий,
Ты отвечаешь, милый друг,
Мне недоверчивой улыбкой;
Прилежно в памяти храня
Измен печальные преданья,
Ты без участья и вниманья
Уныло слушаешь меня...
Кляну коварные старанья
Преступной юности моей
И встреч условных ожиданья
В садах, в безмолвии ночей.
Кляну речей любовный шепот,
Стихов таинственный напев,
И ласки легковерных дев,
И слезы их, и поздний ропот.

Again his fiancée, Natalya Nikolayeva Goncharova

When in the Grasp of My Embrace

When in the grasp of my embrace,
I wrap your slender waist, enfold you,
With tender words of love and grace,
With raptured words and arms I hold you,
You're silent, from my arms extend
Your own, freeing your body supple,
Then answer me, my dearest friend,
But with a smile that's slight, untrustful...
So diligent, your memory
Collects sad tales of treachery,
So uninvolved and listlessly
You listen gloomily to me.
I rue then my past cleverness,
My reckless, sinful, youthful days,
The wakeful waiting for the trysts
On silent nights in garden glades,
I rue then words that lovers whisper,
How poems mysterious in me sing,
How carefree maids caress and cling,
And how they cry, and later whimper.

«ИЗ СКАЗКИ О ЦАРЕ САЛТАНЕ»

...Князь у синя моря ходит,
С синя моря глаз не сводит;
Глядь — поверх текучих вод
Лебедь белая плывет.
«Здравствуй, князь ты мой прекрасный!
Что ж ты тих, как день ненастный?
Опечалился чему?» —
Говорит она ему.
Князь Гвидон ей отвечает:
«Грусть-тоска меня съедает —
Люди женятся; гляжу,
Не женат лишь я хожу».
«А кого же на примете
Ты имеешь?» — «Да на свете,
Говорят, царевна есть,
Что не можно глаз отвесть.
Днем свет Божий затмевает,
Ночью землю освещает –
Месяц под косой блестит,
А во лбу звезда горит.
А сама-то величава,
Выступает, будто пава,
Сладку речь-то говорит,
Будто реченька журчит.
Только, полно, правда ль это?"
Князь со страхом ждет ответа.
Лебедь белая молчит
И, подумав, говорит:
«Да! Такая есть девица.
Но жена не рукавица:
С белой ручки не стряхнешь
Да за пояс не заткнешь.

FROM THE TALE OF TSAR SALTAN

...By the blue sea our prince, moving,
From blue sea eyes not removing,
Looks — and where its waters flow,
A white swan appears, swims slow.
"How are you, my lovely princeling?"
Why so still, like a day drizzly?
What is it that makes you sad?
Says the swan to him at last.
Prince Guidon to her makes answer:
"Grief eats up my heart with sadness.
All get married, yet I see,
Still unmarried only me."
"But just whom is it you're seeking?"
"On this earth somewhere lives, breathing,
A Tsar's daughter, so they say,
From whom eyes can't look away.
In the day than sun she's brighter,
In dark night makes world shine lighter.
In her locks bright moonbeams are,
In her forehead gleams a star.
And herself, majestic, precious,
Like a peacock stately, paces,
When she speaks, her sweet speech seems
Like the murmuring rush of streams.
But enough, could this be true?"
Asks the prince, and waits in fright.
For a long time the white swan
Hushes, thinks, and then goes on:
"Yes, indeed, there's such a maiden,
But a wife's no mitten braided,
Can't be shook from your white wrist,
Pinned upon your belt, then missed.

Услужу тебе советом —
Слушай: обо всем об этом
Пораздумай ты путем,
Не раскаяться б потом.»
Князь пред нею стал божиться,
Что пора ему жениться,
Что об этом обо всем
Передумал он путем;
Что готов душою страстной
За царевною прекрасной
Он пешком идти отсель
Хоть за тридевять земель.
Лебедь тут, вздохнув глубоко,
Молвила: «Зачем далёко?
Знай, близка судьба твоя,
Ведь царевна эта — я».
Тут она, взмахнув крылами,
Полетела над волнами
И на берег с высоты
Опустилася в кусты,
Встрепенулась, отряхнулась
И царевной обернулась:
Месяц под косой блестит,
А во лбу звезда горит;
А сама-то величава,
Выступает, будто пава;
А как речь-то говорит,
Словно реченька журчит.
Князь царевну обнимает,
К белой груди прижимает
И ведет её скорей
К милой матушке своей.

A Swan

Let me give you some good counsel,
Listen, think before you answer,
Think again, and think it through,
Lest you'll later rashness rue."
Then the prince got down before her,
Swore his readiness, implored her,
Said he'd marry and be true,
Said he'd thought the whole thing through,
For his princess lovely he
Was prepared most passionately
To march miles no measure spans
Forth beyond the thrice-nine lands...
Deeply the swan started sighing:
"Why so far?" she asked, replying,
"Know: your fate is close nearby,
For that princess true – am I."
Then she flapped her wings in motion,
Flew up high above the ocean,
Back to shore did, diving, rush,
Landed in some underbrush.
Shook her wings off, scraped, made great fuss,
Then she turns into a princess:
In her locks bright moonbeams are,
In her forehead gleams a star.
And herself, majestic, gracious,
Like a peacock stately, paces,
When she speaks, her sweet speech seems
Like the murmuring rush of streams.
Prince then princess hugs, caresses,
To his bosom pale close presses,
Then in great haste takes her home,
To his mother dear, his own.

Князь ей в ноги, умоляя:
«Государыня-родная!
Выбрал я жену себе,
Дочь послушную тебе.
Просим оба разрешенья,
Твоего благословенья:
Ты детей благослови
Жить в совете и любви».
Над главою их покорной
Мать с иконой чудотворной
Слезы льёт и говорит:
«Бог вас, дети, наградит».
Князь не долго собирался,
На царевне обвенчался;
Стали жить да поживать,
Да приплода поджидать.

Maria Aleksandrovna Pushkina, the poet's daughter

At her feet he fell, imploring:
"Mother, our land's queen, who bore me,
I have found myself a wife,
Your new daughter true, for life.
Your permission we're requesting
To be granted your full blessing.
Bless us, may we live like doves,
In true harmony and love."
As their heads bent in orison,
'Neath her magic-working icon
Mother poured forth tears and cried:
"God, my children, be your guide".
Not for long did our prince tarry,
Till his princess he did marry,
And they settled, loving, mild,
And expected soon a child...

Нет, я не дорожу мятежным наслажденьем,
Восторгом чувственным, безумством, исступленьем,
Стенаньем, криками вакханки молодой,
Когда, виясь в моих объятиях змией,
Порывом пылких ласк и язвою лобзаний
Она торопит миг последних содроганий!

О, как милее ты, смиренница моя!
О, как мучительно тобою счастлив я,
Когда, склоняяся на долгие моленья,
Ты предаешься мне нежна без упоенья,
Стыдливо-холодна, восторгу моему
Едва ответствуешь, не внемлешь ничему
И оживляешься потом все боле, боле —
И делишь наконец мой пламень поневоле!

Natalya and Pushkin's shade

No, I do not hold dear that pleasure so rebellious,
That joy all sensual, insane, frenzied, delirious,
The groans, the crying out a young drunk nymph may make
When winding round in my embraces like a snake,
With gusts of kisses, wild, caressing, feverish, smoth'ring,
She hurries up the flash, last moment's final shuddering!

How much more dear are you, meek, sweet subduer mine!
Oh, with what tortured joy for you alone I pine,
When you, at last yielding to lengthy supplication,
Give yourself tenderly to me without elation,
Feeling ashamed and cold, my joyousness within
But scarcely answering, and not feeling a thing.
Till livening with time, you too start thrilling —
Till more and more at last my flame you share unwilling!

КРАСАВИЦА

(в альбом Г ***)

Всё в ней гармония, всё диво,
Всё выше мира и страстей;
Она покоится стыдливо
В красе торжественной своей;
Она кругом себя взирает:
Ей нет соперниц, нет подруг;
Красавиц наших бледный круг
В ее сиянье исчезает.

Куда бы ты ни поспешал,
Хоть на любовное свиданье,
Какое б в сердце ни питал
Ты сокровенное мечтанье, --
Но, встретясь с ней, смущенный, ты
Вдруг остановишься невольно,
Благоговея богомольно
Перед святыней красоты.

BEAUTY

(in the album of ***)

She is all harmony, all marvel,
All far above mere worldly lust,
With girlish modesty she dawdles,
In her majestic grace untouched.
And when she gazes all around her,
She has no rivals, has no friends.
Our beauties' meager circle ends
And flees the first gleams of her splendor.

No matter where you might have raced,
Even to tryst and meet your lover,
Whatever myth your heart still graced,
What sacred daydream in you hovered,
Yet meeting her, you'll blush and pine;
Unwittingly you'll stop and stay there,
With reverence and pious prayer
Before her sacred beauty's shrine.

Я думал, сердце позабыло
Способность легкую страдать,
Я говорил: тому, что было,
Уж не бывать! уж не бывать!
Прошли восторги, и печали,
И легковерные мечты...
Но вот опять затрепетали
Пред мощной властью красоты.

Self portrait with feminine profile

I thought my heart had long forgotten
Its ease in suffering of yore.
I told myself: all that has happened
Can come no more! Can come no more!
The joys are gone, with sadness racing,
And trusting dreams so fanciful,
But once again they quiver facing
The power of the beautiful.

К***

Нет, нет, не должен я, не смею, не могу
Волнениям любви безумно предаваться;
Спокойствие мое я строго берегу
И сердцу не даю пылать и забываться;
Нет, полно мне любить; но почему ж порой
Не погружуся я в минутное мечтанье,
Когда нечаянно пройдет передо мной
Младое, чистое, небесное созданье,
Пройдет и скроется?.. Ужель не можно мне,
Любуясь девою в печальном сладострастье,
Глазами следовать за ней и в тишине
Благословлять ее на радость и на счастье,
И сердцем ей желать все блага жизни сей,
Веселый мир души, беспечные досуги,
Всё — даже счастие того, кто избран ей,
Кто милой деве даст название супруги.

"...why not, betimes
Just daydream, sunk in minute's contemplation"

TO ***

No, no, it isn't right, I cannot, I don't dare
Give myself madly up to love's worry and anguish;
My peace of mind I strictly guard with care,
And don't permit my heart to blaze with searing passion.
No, no more love for me! ...Although, why not, betimes,
Just daydream, for a minute's contemplation,
When just by chance, before my very eyes,
A young and pure and heavenly creation
Passes and disappears? Am I really forbid,
Charmed by a maid, with passionate sweet sadness,
To follow, watch her with my eyes, and when all's still,
To bless her, wish her joy, just wish her gladness?
Wish her, with all my heart, all blessings in this life:
Happiness in her soul, carefree leisures abundant,
All! – Even joy to him she chose, who'll call her wife,
Who'll give that maiden fair a brand new name – as husband.

Пора, мой друг, пора! покоя сердце просит —
Летят за днями дни, и каждый час уносит
Частичку бытия, а мы с тобой вдвоем
Предполагаем жить...И глядь — как раз — умрем.

На свете счастья нет, но есть покой и воля.
Давно завидная мечтается мне доля --
Давно, усталый раб, замыслил я побег
В обитель дальную трудов и чистых нег.

IT'S TIME, MY FRIEND, IT'S TIME!

It's time, my friend, it's time! For peace the heart is calling.
Day flies by after day, and every hour is tolling
 A bit of being away: together you and I
Suppose that we will live – but see! Just then – we die.

There is no joy on earth, but there is peace and freedom:
Long time of enviable fate I have been dreaming,
Long time, I, tired slave, have dreamed of secret flight
Unto a distant shrine of toil and pure delight.

Natalya squinting at him slightly

Я возмужал среди печальных бурь,
И дней моих поток, так долго мутный,
Теперь утих дремотою минутной
И отразил небесную лазурь.

Надолго ли?.. а кажется, прошли
Дни мрачных бурь, дни горьких искушений...

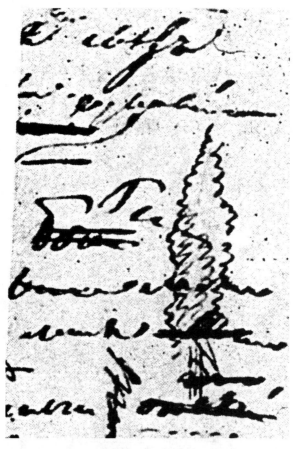

A Poplar growing in the manuscript

In mournful storms I have become a man.
The stream of all my days, for so long murky,
Has stilled now with a moment's slumber quirky,
And now reflect the heavens' azure span.

Is it for long? Somehow it seems they've gone,
Those bleak storm days, days bitter in temptations...

Когда б не смутное влеченье
Чего-то жаждущей души,
Я здесь остался б — наслажденье
Вкушать в неведомой тиши:
Забыл бы всех желаний трепет,
Мечтою б целый мир назвал —
И всё бы слушал этот лепет,
Всё б эти ножки целовал...

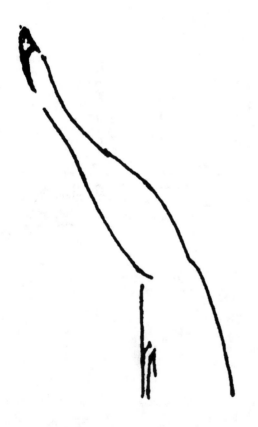

IF NOT FOR SOMETHING MURKY GNAWING

If not for something murky gnawing
Within my something-seeking soul,
I'd gladly stay, sheer pleasure drawing
In this mysterious silence whole.
Forgetting deep desires' murmuring,
I'd call the whole wide world a dream,
Just hear your babble sweet, not stirring,
And kiss and kiss your darling feet...

Простишь ли мне ревнивые мечты,
Моей любви безумное волненье?
Ты мне верна: зачем же любишь ты
Всегда пугать мое воображенье?
Окружена поклонников толпой,
Зачем для всех казаться хочешь милой,
И всех дарит надеждою пустой
Твой чудный взор, то нежный, то унылый?
Мной овладев, мне разум омрачив,
Уверена в любви моей несчастной,
Не видишь ты, когда, в толпе их страстной,
Беседы чужд, один и молчалив,
Терзаюсь я досадой одинокой;
Ни слова мне, ни взгляда... друг жестокий!
Хочу ль бежать, — с боязнью и мольбой
Твои глаза не следуют за мной.
Заводит ли красавица другая
Двусмысленный со мною разговор, —
Спокойна ты; веселый твой укор
Меня мертвит, любви не выражая.
Скажи еще: соперник вечный мой,
Наедине застав меня с тобой,
Зачем тебя приветствует лукаво?..
Что ж он тебе? Скажи, какое право
Имеет он бледнеть и ревновать?..
В нескромный час меж вечера и света,
Без матери, одна, полуодета,
Зачем его должна ты принимать?..
Но я любим...Наедине со мною
Ты так нежна! Лобзания твои
Так пламенны! Слова твоей любви
Так искренно полны твоей душою!
Тебе смешны мучения мои;
Но я любим, тебя я понимаю.
Мой милый друг, не мучь меня, молю:
Не знаешь ты, как сильно я люблю,
Не знаешь ты, как тяжко я страдаю.

WILL YOU FORGIVE MY JEALOUS REVERIE

Will you forgive my jealous reverie,
My love's tormented crazy agitation?
Why be so fond–if you're faithful to me –
Of always frightening my imagination?
Surrounded by admirers in a crowd,
Why must you always try to be everyone's "cutie"?
Why are all others' empty hopes always allowed
Your wondrous looks, now tender, and now gloomy?
You've dimmed my mind; I'm taken, all your own!
You're certain of my constant love unhappy...
Can't you see how, midst throngs round you impassioned,
Shunning all chatting, silent and alone,
I writhe in lonesome agony distressing?
From you no word, nor glance! Cruel friend, tormenting!
If I would flee – with worry or with plea
Your eyes never attempt to follow me.
And if some other beauty towards me coming
Starts chatting, fills her speech with playful hints,
You are so calm, your gay reproachful squints
Kill, stop me cold, without expressing loving.
As for my constant rival, also, tell me true,
Whenever he sees me alone with you,
Why does he greet you far too casually and slyly?
Who's he to you? Explain it! By what right's he
Allowed to pale, and have a jealous fit?
Between nightfall and dawn, at hours and times immodest,
Mother not watching by, alone, and only half-dressed
How is it you receive him, let him sit?
But I'm your love. When we are by ourselves
You are so sweet, your kiss, caressing, rough
So fiery! The words that speak your love
Are so sincere and soulful and heartfelt!
Yet at my sufferings you laugh and mock;
But I'm your love, we understand each other.
My darling, don't torment me, please, enough!
You do not know how powerfully I love;
You do not know how bitterly I suffer.

Self-portrait in Eastern garb

...И, тихой музы полн,
Умеет услаждать свой путь над бездной волн.

VIII. ...AND I FORGET THE WORLD 401

...Filled by the silent Muse,
Above the waves' abyss with bliss his wake he hews:

Близ мест, где царствует Венеция златая,
Один, ночной гребец, гондолой управляя,
При свете Веспера по взморию плывет,
Ринальда, Годфреда, Эрминию поет.
Он любит песнь свою, поет он для забавы,
Без дальных умыслов; не ведает ни славы,
Ни страха, ни надежд, и, тихой музы полн,
Умеет услаждать свой путь над бездной волн.
На море жизненном, где бури так жестоко
Преследуют во мгле мой парус одинокий,
Как он, без отзыва утешно я пою
И тайные стихи обдумывать люблю.

Near lands where sovereignty of golden Venice rules,
A lone nocturnal gondolier his way plies through the pools.
By evenstar's soft light, he – singing – turns his oars
– Of Reynald, Godfred, and Erminia – by their shores.
He loves singing his song, for pleasure sings his story,
Lacking all further plans, he sings heedless of glory,
Of fears heedless, of hopes...Filled by the silent Muse,
Above the waves' abyss with bliss his wake he hews:
So, in this sea of life, where cruelly the tempest
In darkening gloom to my lone sail grants no rest,
Not minding what men say, I sing and I rejoice,
Dreaming up secret poems with my secret voice.

Не дай мне Бог сойти с ума.
Нет, легче посох и сума;
Нет, легче труд и глад.
Не то, чтоб разумом моим
Я дорожил; не то, чтоб с ним
Расстаться был не рад:

Когда б оставили меня
На воле, как бы резво я
Пустился в темный лес!
Я пел бы в пламенном бреду.
Я забывался бы в чаду
Нестройных, чудных грез.

И я б заслушивался волн,
И я глядел бы, счастья полн,
В пустые небеса;
И силен, волен был бы я,
Как вихорь, роющий поля,
Ломающий леса.

Да вот беда: сойди с ума,
И страшен будешь как чума,
Как раз тебя запрут,
Посадят на цепь дурака
И сквозь решетку как зверка
Дразнить тебя придут.

А ночью слышать буду я
Не голос яркий соловья,
Не шум глухой дубров —
А крик товарищей моих,
Да брань смотрителей ночных,
Да визг, да звон оков.

MAY GOD FORBID I GO INSANE

May God forbid I go insane.
No, better beggar's pouch and cane!
No, better work and starve.
Not that my faculties of mind
Are dear to me, for I'm inclined
With them to gladly part.

If only I were left alone
With what a lively gait I'd roam
'Neath darkest forest's trees!
I'd sing, deliriously ablaze,
And lose myself all in a daze
Of blurred and wondrous dreams.

And I would hear and hear the waves,
And full of gladness I would gaze
At Heaven's empty crown:
And strong and wilful would I reel,
A whirlwind, stirring up the fields
And casting forests down...

Alas, though, if you go insane,
Then like the plague you'll be a bane,
Indeed, they'll lock you up.
And to a fool's chain you'll be leashed,
And when you're caged up like a beast,
They'll come to tease and mock.

And I won't hear at night in jail
The clear voice of the nightingale,
The oak grove's muffled strains.
Instead I'll hear my cell-mates' shrieks,
The night-watch cursing as it peeks,
And rattling, clanking chains.

ПОЭТ

Пока не требует поэта
К священной жертве Аполлон,
В заботах суетного света
Он малодушно погружен;

Молчит его святая лира;
Душа вкушает хладный сон,
И меж детей ничтожных мира,
Быть может, всех ничтожней он.

Но лишь божественный глагол
До слуха чуткого коснется,
Душа поэта встрепенется,
Как пробудившийся орел.

Тоскует он в забавах мира,
Людской чуждается молвы,
К ногам народного кумира
Не клонит гордой головы;

Бежит он, дикий и суровый,
И звуков и смятенья полн,
На берега пустынных волн,
В широкошумные дубровы...

THE POET

Until the poet by Apollo
To sacred sacrifice is called,
In this world's cares, so vain and hollow,
He is faint-heartedly enthralled.

Stilled is his holy lyre, unlistened to;
Cold sleep his soul tastes bitterly,
And 'midst this world's unhappy children,
Unhappiest, perhaps, is he.

But once, divine, the word, the prize,
So slightly nuzzles his keen ears,
The poet's soul stirs up and rears,
Like an awakened eagle, cries.

He grieves at this world's pastimes idle,
He flees the rumor of the crowd.
Before the feet of all men's idol
He does not bend his head so proud.

But stern, but wild, away he roves,
And full of sounds and aches he raves
By coasts where desolate crash the waves,
By spreading, rustling oak-leaved groves...

"By coasts where desolate crash the waves"

ЭХО

Ревет ли зверь в лесу глухом,
Трубит ли рог, гремит ли гром,
Поет ли дева за холмом —
　На всякий звук
Свой отклик в воздухе пустом
　Родишь ты вдруг.

Ты внемлешь грохоту громов,
И гласу бури и валов,
И крику сельских пастухов —
　И шлешь ответ;
Тебе ж нет отзыва... Таков
　И ты, поэт!

THE ECHO

If in thick woods a wild beast roars,
A horn gets blown, or lightning storms,
If fair maid sings o'er green hill's bourn,
    To any sound
Your answer in the air forlorn,
    Cries newborn round.

You heed the thunder pealing loud,
The voice of storms, the billows' howl,
    And rural shepherds crying out,
 And send answer true.
Like you, to whom reply's not found,
    Is the poet too.

"You heed the thunder pealing loud,
    The voice of storms, the billows' howl..."

ПРОРОК

Духовной жаждою томим,
В пустыне мрачной я влачился,
И шестикрылый Серафим
На перепутье мне явился.
Перстами легкими, как сон
Моих зениц коснулся он:
Отверзлись вещие зеницы,
Как у испуганной орлицы.
Моих ушей коснулся он,
И их наполнил шум и звон:
И внял я неба содроганье,
И горний ангелов полет,
И гад морских подводный ход,
И дольней лозы прозябанье.
И он к устам моим приник,
И вырвал грешный мой язык,
И празднословный и лукавый,
И жало мудрыя змеи
В уста замершие мои
Вложил десницею кровавой.
И он мне грудь рассек мечом,
И сердце трепетное вынул,
И угль, пылающий огнем,
Во грудь отверстую водвинул.
Как труп в пустыне я лежал,
И Бога глас ко мне воззвал:
«Восстань, пророк, и виждь, и внемли,
Исполнись волею моей,
И, обходя моря и земли,
Глаголом жги сердца людей».

THE PROPHET

With thirsting soul wracked, worn and thin,
I marched through bleakest desert onwards,
And a six-wingèd Seraphim
Appeared to me upon a crossroads.
With fingers light as sleep then he
But grazed my eyes most gracefully,
And my foreseeing eyelids started,
Like a young frightened eaglet, startled.
And to my ears then he reached out,
And filled them with a ringing shout:
To Heaven's shuddering I hearkened,
And to the lofty angels' flight,
To slithering things in deep seas' night,
To valley grapes grown dull, cold, hardened.
And then upon my lips he clung,
And then tore out my sinner's tongue,
That babbles, idle, cunning, moody.
In my mouth, numb now to all things,
He placed the sharp wise serpent's sting,
He placed it with his right hand bloody,
Took sword, in my breast cut a hole,
Took out my feeble heart a-quaking,
Then, while it blazed, put in a coal,
The gap in gaping breast replacing.
In desert sand I corpse-like lay.
To me then God's voice called, to say:
"Arise, thou Prophet, see and hearken,
By my will let your soul be stirred,
And, wandering by lands and waters,
Burn people's hearts up with my word."

ПОЭТУ.
(Сонет)

Поэт! не дорожи любовию народной.
Восторженных похвал пройдет минутный шум;
Услышишь суд глупца и смех толпы холодной:
Но ты останься тверд, спокоен и угрюм.

Ты царь: живи один. Дорогою свободной
Иди, куда влечет тебя свободный ум,
Усовершенствуя плоды любимых дум,
Не требуя наград за подвиг благородный.

Они в самом тебе. Ты сам свой высший суд;
Всех строже оценить умеешь ты свой труд.
Ты им доволен ли, взыскательный художник?

Доволен? Так пускай толпа его бранит
И плюет на алтарь, где твой огонь горит
И в детской резвости колеблет твой треножник.

The poet Hafiz

TO THE POET
(A Sonnet)

Poet! Care not for love through fame, now or hereafter.
Elated cheers will pass after a minute's din,
You'll hear judgments of fools, and hear the crowd's cold laughter:
But you must just stay firm, and ever calm and grim.

You're king: so live alone. Walk freely on your pathway:
Wherever your free spirit leads you, go,
Perfect the fruits of favorite thoughts until they glow.
For no rewards for noble deeds be asking.

For they're inside of you. You're your own highest judge.
Strictest of all praise for your work you'll grudge.
Does it content you, artist true, demanding?

It does? Then let the crowd scoff, spurn,
And spit upon the altar where your flame does burn.
Let them in childish rage your easel-stand be rattling!

Goethe

ОСЕНЬ (отрывок)

Чего в мой дремлющий тогда не входит ум?

Державин.

I.

Октябрь уж наступил — уж роща отряхает
Последние листы с нагих своих ветвей;
Дохнул осенний хлад — дорога промерзает.
Журча еще бежит за мельницу ручей,
Но пруд уже застыл; сосед мой поспешает
В отъезжие поля с охотою своей,
И страждут озими от бешеной забавы,
И будит лай собак уснувшие дубравы.

II.

Теперь моя пора: я не люблю весны;
Скучна мне оттепель; вонь, грязь — весной я болен;
Кровь бродит; чувства, ум тоскою стеснены.
Суровою зимой я более доволен,
Люблю ее снега; в присутствии луны
Как легкий бег саней с подругой быстр и волен,
Когда под соболем, согрета и свежа,
Она вам руку жмет, пылая и дрожа!

III.

Как весело, обув железом острым ноги,
Скользить по зеркалу стоячих, ровных рек!
А зимних праздников блестящие тревоги?..
Но надо знать и честь; полгода снег да снег,
Ведь это наконец и жителю берлоги,
Медведю надоест. Нельзя же целый век
Кататься нам в санях с Армидами младыми
Иль киснуть у печей за стеклами двойными.

AUTUMN (A Fragment)

"What thought won't at that time walk in my slumbering mind?"

Derzhavin*

I.

October has arrived. The grove's already shaking
From branches stripped all bare the very last few leaves.
Fall's cold breath blows. With frost the road's now flaking.
The brook behind the mill still runs and, bubbling, breathes,
But ice quiets the pond. Meanwhile, my neighbor's taking
Out to the hunting fields his pack of dogs which seethes.
The winter wheat gets trampled in that furious larking;
The sleeping woods wake up to the sound of hounds barking.

II.

Now is my time of year. I do not love the spring:
The thaw's a bore to me: smells, dirt...spring gives me ailment,
Blood stirring, feelings, mind restrained in longing's sling.
From winter's bitter blasts I find much more contentment;
I love her fallen snows, the moonlit sleighbell's ring!
So quick and free the sleigh runs with your girlfriend,
When, wrapped in sable furs so warm and fresh, you race;
She gives your arm a squeeze, shivering and ablaze!

III.

What fun it is, with skates of sharpened steel strapped on me,
To glide on mirrorlike stilled rivers' even glow!
And winter holidays so glittering, alarming?
But honestly, enough: half the year snow and snow —
Why even, in his lair, the hibernating bruin
Gets sick of it at last! You can't just always go
Out sleigh-riding, entranced by Armida the maiden,
Or sour by the stove by double windows hidden!

---

* From *To Eugene: Courtly Life* by Gavrila Derzhavin, 1743–1816, famous Russian poet who hailed Pushkin's *Memories in Tsarkoye Selo* (1815), which Pushkin declaimed before Derzhavin at a public examination at his Lyceum; this incident was immortalized by the painter Repin, and is referred to in *Eugene Onegin*, Book VIII, ii. See Biography at page 31.

IV.

Ох, лето красное! любил бы я тебя,
Когда б не зной, да пыль, да комары, да мухи.
Ты, все душевные способности губя,
Нас мучишь; как поля, мы страждем от засухи;
Лишь как бы напоить, да освежить себя —
Иной в нас мысли нет, и жаль зимы старухи,
И, проводив ее блинами и вином,
Поминки ей творим мороженым и льдом.

V.

Дни поздней осени бранят обыкновенно,
Но мне она мила, читатель дорогой,
Красою тихою, блистающей смиренно.
Так нелюбимое дитя в семье родной
К себе меня влечет. Сказать вам откровенно,
Из годовых времен я рад лишь ей одной,
В ней много доброго; любовник не тщеславный,
Я нечто в ней нашел мечтою своенравной.

VI.

Как это объяснить? Мне нравится она,
Как, вероятно, вам чахоточная дева
Порою нравится. На смерть осуждена,
Бедняжка клонится без ропота, без гнева.
Улыбка на устах увянувших видна;
Могильной пропасти она не слышит зева;
Играет на лице еще багровый цвет.
Она жива еще сегодня, завтра нет.

IV.
Oh, summer beautiful! I'd be in love with you--
But for the heat, the dust, and the mosquitoes, horseflies,
You, leaving all our spirit's faculties sapped through,
Torment us: like the fields, with suffering our mind dries:
Save how to freshen up, and drink and drink anew,
We have no other thoughts. And old hag Winter's now prized:
With pancakes and with wine our leave of her we take,
With ice-cream and with ice we celebrate her wake.

V.
The days of autumn's end most scorn when they're upon us,
But she is dear to me, and makes my heart her own
With beauty still and mild, so brilliantly modest,
Just so a child unloved in her own home
Draws me near her. And, to be truly honest,
Of all the times of year I joy in her alone.
There's so much good in her! I, lover, not much preening,
Found something in her out with my capricious dreaming.

VI.
How can it be explained? I'm fond of her, at length,
As, somehow, maybe, a consumptive girl's weak waning
Sometimes appeals to you. She is condemned to death:
The poor thing bows her head, not angered, uncomplaining:
Her smile's still visible on lips all out of breath,
The yawn of grave's abyss she can't hear, through her straining:
Yet on her face, still playing, velvet light's still caught,
Today her spirit's still alive, tomorrow -- not.

VII.

Унылая пора! очей очарованье,

Приятна мне твоя прощальная краса —

Люблю я пышное природы увяданье,

В багрец и в золото одетые леса,

В их сенях ветра шум и свежее дыханье,

И мглой волнистою покрыты небеса,

И редкий солнца луч, и первые морозы,

И отдаленные седой зимы угрозы.

VIII.

И с каждой осенью я расцветаю вновь;

Здоровью моему полезен русский холод;

К привычкам бытия вновь чувствую любовь:

Чредой слетает сон, чредой находит голод;

Легко и радостно играет в сердце кровь,

Желания кипят — я снова счастлив, молод,

Я снова жизни полн — таков мой организм

(Извольте мне простить ненужный прозаизм).

IX.

Ведут ко мне коня; в раздолии открытом,

Махая гривою, он всадника несет,

И звонко под его блистающим копытом

Звенит промерзлый дол и трескается лед.

Но гаснет краткий день, и в камельке забытом

Огонь опять горит — то яркий свет лиет,

То тлеет медленно — а я пред ним читаю

Иль думы долгие в душе моей питаю.

VII.
Oh, gloomy season mine! My eyes' delight, enchanting!
How pleasant to me is your beauteous farewell grace!
I love the sumptuousness of nature softly passing,
In raiments crimson now and gold the forests dress:
Their treetops sound— so light, with wind's fresh breath but glancing—
And waves of misty fog beshroud the skies like lace,
The sun's rays, so rare now, and the first frost upon us,
And seeming far off now, dread winter's greyhaired menace.

VIII.
And with each autumn chill my heart blossoms anew.
The bitter Russian cold upon my health works wonder,
For everyday, plain life my old love I renew.
I sleep at the right time, at dinner I feel hunger.
How light and joyous in the heart is my blood's stew
Of boiling desires! And I feel happy, younger,
And full of life again! Such is my organism!
(I hope that you'll forgive this needless prosaism).

IX.
They bring a horse to me: through open fields, he, shaking
His mane, and riding off, far off his rider bears,
The echo of his hooves, so brilliantly quaking,
Sounds through the frozen vale; ice under hoofbeats tears.
But short day fades away, and in the hearth forsaken
A fire burns again: now brilliant light it flares,
Now sputters, ebbing slowly. I sit before it reading--
Or lingering thoughts within my soul I'm feeding.

X.

И забываю мир — и в сладкой тишине
Я сладко усыплен моим воображеньем,
И пробуждается поэзия во мне:
Душа стесняется лирическим волненьем,
Трепещет и звучит, и ищет, как во сне,
Излиться наконец свободным проявленьем —
И тут ко мне идет незримый рой гостей,
Знакомцы давние, плоды мечты моей.

XI.

И мысли в голове волнуются в отваге,
И рифмы легкие навстречу им бегут,
И пальцы просятся к перу, перо к бумаге,
Минута — и стихи свободно потекут.
Так дремлет недвижим корабль в недвижной влаге,
Но чу! — матросы вдруг кидаются, ползут
Вверх, вниз — и паруса надулись, ветра полны;
Громада двинулась и рассекает волны.

XII.

Плывет. Куда ж нам плыть?. . . . .
. . . .
. . . .

"Now is my time of year"

AUTUMN

X.

And I forget the world, and in a silence sweet,
I sweetly lull myself by my imagination,
And deep inside of me awakens poetry.
My soul is shy of its own lyrical elation,
And trembling it resounds, and dreamlike, tries to meet
With words, pour forth at last, expressed in free creation:
A throng of guests, invisible, then at me streams,
Old friends of mine, the fruits of all my dreams.

XI.

And thoughts within my head rise up and boldly quaver,
And rhymes so easily to meet them lightly go!
My fingers seem to seek my pen, my pen seeks paper...
One minute! — and how free the verses flow!
Just so a docked ship sleeps in harbor's waters tapered –
But ho! The sailors up and down the ship run, throw
Themselves, and then the sails fill up, in the wind heaving,
The monster leaves its berth and moves, the waters cleaving...

XII.

And sails...Where shall we sail? ....
....
....
....

"Where shall we sail?"

...Вновь я посетил
Тот уголок земли, где я провел
Изгнанником два года незаметных.
Уж десять лет ушло с тех пор -- и много
Переменилось в жизни для меня,
И сам, покорный общему закону,
Переменился я -- но здесь опять
Минувшее меня объемлет живо,
И, кажется, вечор еще бродил
Я в этих рощах.
                Вот опальный домик,
Где жил я с бедной нянею моей.
Уже старушки нет -- уж за стеною
Не слышу я шагов ее тяжелых,
Ни кропотливого ее дозора.
Вот холм лесистый, над которым часто
Я сиживал недвижим -- и глядел
На озеро, воспоминая с грустью
Иные берега, иные волны...
Меж нив златых и пажитей зеленых
Оно синея стелется широко;
Через его неведомые воды
Плывет рыбак и тянет за собою
Убогий невод. По брегам отлогим
Рассеяны деревни — там за ними
Скривилась мельница, насилу крылья
Ворочая при ветре...

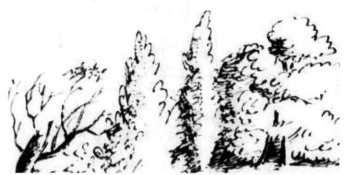

...I came back again
To that small plot of land, where once I spent
Two years living in exile and unnoticed.
By now ten years have passed since then, and many
Have been the changes coming to my life.
I too, to universal law submissive,
Have changed myself, but, once more here,
All of my past embraces me with vigor,
And so it seems but yesterday I walked
Through these groves, wand'ring.
      Here's the forlorn cottage
Where with my poor old nanny I did live.
The old lady has gone–beyond the wall now
I cannot hear her footsteps heavy tramping,
Nor her devoted, always-caring snooping.
And here's the wooded hillock, on which often
I used to sit, not moving, and look down
Into the lake, remembering with sadness
The look of other waves, of other shorelines....
By crops of gold, and pastures gently greening,
Dark blue, and sparkling broadly, the lake's gleaming,
And through its waters deep, unknown, mysterious,
A fisherman sails by and, dragging, pulls behind him
His net in tatters. On the shorelines sloping
Some villages are scattered; there, behind them,
The mill is crooked now; its wings with effort
Are flutt'ring when the wind blows...

...На границе
Владений дедовских, на месте том,
Где в гору подымается дорога,
Изрытая дождями, три сосны
Стоят — одна поодаль, две другие
Друг к дружке близко, — здесь, когда их мимо
Я проезжал верхом при свете лунном,
Знакомым шумом шорох их вершин
Меня приветствовал. По той дороге
Теперь поехал я и пред собою
Увидел их опять. Они все те же,
Все тот же их, знакомый уху шорох —
Но около корней их устарелых
(Где некогда все было пусто, голо)
Теперь младая роща разрослась,
Зеленая семья; кусты теснятся
Под сенью их как дети. А вдали
Стоит один угрюмый их товарищ,
Как старый холостяк, и вкруг него
По-прежнему все пусто.
          Здравствуй, племя
Младое, незнакомое! Не я
Увижу твой могучий поздний возраст,
Когда перерастешь моих знакомцев
И старую главу их заслонишь
От глаз прохожего. Но пусть мой внук
Услышит ваш приветный шум, когда,
С приятельской беседы возвращаясь,
Веселых и приятных мыслей полон,
Пройдет он мимо вас во мраке ночи
И обо мне вспомянет.

...I CAME BACK AGAIN 425

                              ...On the border
Of grandfather's old lands, in that same place,
Right where the road climbs up into the mountain,
All potholed by the rainfall, there three pines
Do stand — the first off farther, the two others
Right close together — here, when I would pass them,
When I'd ride by on horseback in the moonlight,
Their rustling treetops whisperings, well-known, soft,
Would send me greetings then. On that same pathway,
When I rode past them now they stood before me
And I saw them again. They're just the same still,
Still whisp'ring in my ear the same soft greetings,
But now, about their roots ancient and withered,
(Where everything before was bare and naked)
But now a new young grove is growing up,
A family of green, its bushes thickening,
Sheltering beneath like children. Further off,
Their brooding gloomy friend is still there, standing
Like some old bachelor, and all around
Him, still, all is deserted...
                              Greetings, youngsters!
So young, and so unknown to me! I won't
Be blessed to see your greening growth in fullness
When you outgrow and pass my old companions,
And hide their ancient heads with your new boughs
From sight to passersby. But, one day, may
My grandson hear your greeting whispered soft,
When riding back from chatting at a friend's house,
Filled in his heart with happy, pleasant musings,
And, passing by your shade in gloom of nighttime,
Then think of me, remembering.

Self-portrait in a fur hat

ИЗ «ЕГИПЕТСКИХ НОЧЕЙ»

Поэт идет — открыты вежды,
Но он не видит никого;
А между тем за край одежды
Прохожий дергает его...
«Скажи: зачем без цели бродишь?
Едва достиг ты высоты,
И вот уж долу взор низводишь
И низойти стремишься ты.
На стройный мир ты смотришь смутно;
Бесплодный жар тебя томит;
Предмет ничтожный поминутно
Тебя тревожит и манит.
Стремиться к небу должен гений,
Обязан истинный поэт
Для вдохновенных песнопений
Избрать возвышенный предмет».
— Зачем крутится ветр в овраге,
Подъемлет лист и пыль несет,
Когда корабль в недвижной влаге
Его дыханья жадно ждет?
Зачем от гор и мимо башен
Летит орел, тяжел и страшен,
На чахлый пень? Спроси его.
Зачем арапа своего
Младая любит Дездемона,
Как месяц любит ночи мглу?
Затем, что ветру и орлу
И сердцу девы нет закона.
Таков поэт: как Аквилон
Что хочет, то и носит он —
Орлу подобно, он летает
И, не спросясь ни у кого,
Как Дездемона избирает
Кумир для сердца своего.

FROM EGYPTIAN NIGHTS

The poet walks...his eyes are open,
But no one else around he sees;
Yet, by him, tugging on his clothing,
A passerby his hem does seize.
"Explain your ceaseless, senseless wandering!
You've barely scrambled to the heights,
Already though, your gaze is dropping,
For quick descent your spirit cries.
You see the world of culture dimly;
A fruitless fever wears you down;
A minor object for a minute
Distracts you, tempts you, lures you out.
A genius ought to seek the heavens;
A real poet is obliged
For his inspiring compositions
To seek a subject that's inspired."
"Why does the wind swirl in the valley
And lift the leaves and raise the dust,
When stuck in doldrums ships do languish,
And wait for a slight breath with thirst?
Why, flying down from peaks that tower,
Do soaring, solemn eagles glower,
Then swoop down on a stunted stump?
Ask! Why such passion for her Moor?
Why does she love, young Desdemona,
The way the moon's in love with dark?
Because, in truth, a maiden's heart,
Like wind, like eagle, knows no owner.
The poet, like the wind, is thus:
He picks up anything he wants –
And, like an eagle, soars in flying,
And asks of no one what to do,
As Desdemona chooses blindly
An idol for her loving heart."

Когда за городом, задумчив, я брожу
И на публичное кладбище захожу,
Решетки, столбики, нарядные гробницы,
Под коими гниют все мертвецы столицы,
В болоте кое-как стесненные рядком,
Как гости жадные за нищенским столом,
Купцов, чиновников усопших мавзолеи,
Дешевого резца нелепые затеи,
Над ними надписи и в прозе и в стихах
О добродетелях, о службе и чинах;
По старом рогаче вдовицы плач амурный;
Ворами со столбов отвинченные урны,
Могилы склизкие, которы также тут
Зеваючи жильцов к себе на утро ждут, —
Такие смутные мне мысли всё наводит,
Что злое на меня уныние находит.
Хоть плюнуть да бежать...
                Но как же любо мне
Осеннею порой, в вечерней тишине,
В деревне посещать кладбище родовое,
Где дремлют мертвые в торжественном покое.
Там неукрашенным могилам есть простор;
К ним ночью темною не лезет бледный вор;
Близ камней вековых, покрытых желтым мохом,
Проходит селянин с молитвой и со вздохом;
На место праздных урн и мелких пирамид,
Безносых гениев, растрепанных харит
Стоит широко дуб над важными гробами,
Колеблясь и шумя...

WHEN PAST THE CITY GATES IN WISTFUL THOUGHT I ROAM

When past the city gates in wistful thought I roam,
When I the public graveyard enter, footsteps slown,
See grates, small obelisks, smart pedestals, graves arty,
'Neath which the corpses of the capital are rotting,
In this thick swamp somehow together tightly bound,
As greedy guests at beggars' dinners crowd around,
See sleeping bureaucrats' and merchants' mausoleums,
Cheap-cut clumsy attempts to imitate museums,
And read inscriptions on them, both in verse and prose,
Supposed good deeds, and who in rank and service rose...
The amorous laments of widows for old cuckolds,
The urns ripped off by thieves, the obelisks unbuckled,
The graves gone slippery, that also, slanting sheer,
Yawn, waiting for new guests next morning to appear,
Such dark and dire depressing thoughts then come upon me,
An evil fit descends of gloom and melancholy.
To hell with it, to flee!
                        And yet, how dear to me
When autumn twilight comes, in evening reverie,
To walk past country graves where all my kin are buried,
Where still in solemn grace the dead slumber unhurried,
Where there is space for all the simple gravestones bare,
Where no pale sneaking thieves attempts at them would dare,
Where by those age-old stones, by yellow moss all covered,
A peasant passes by, says prayers with sighs smothered,
Instead of pompous urns and petty pyramids,
And noseless geniuses and frayed Caryatids,
Above the solid graves an oak stands, broad boughs casting,
With quivering, rustling leaves...

Отцы пустынники и жены непорочны,
Чтоб сердцем возлетать во области заочны,
Чтоб укреплять его средь дольних бурь и битв,
Сложили множество божественных молитв;
Но ни одна из них меня не умиляет,
Как та, которую священник повторяет
Во дни печальные Великого поста;
Всех чаще мне она приходит на уста
И падшего крепит неведомою силой:
Владыко дней моих! дух праздности унылой,
Любоначалия, змеи сокрытой сей,
И празднословия не дай душе моей.
Но дай мне зреть мои, о Боже, прегрешенья,
Да брат мой от меня не примет осужденья,
И дух смирения, терпения, любви
И целомудрия мне в сердце оживи.

Our hermit fathers and our nuns blessèd and blameless,
To let their hearts fly up into the heavens nameless,
To keep their spirits strong, in storms of wind and war,
Composed a multitude of sacred hymns and lore.
But there's not one of them which gives me so much comfort
As one prayer our priest repeats and utters
Upon the melancholy days of Lenten Fast.
Unbidden, more than other prayers does it pass
My lips, bracing my fallen soul with strength mysterious:
"Lord of my days! Keep me from sloth that hides in bleakness,
From lust for power, and serpents therein hid,
Let not my tongue in idle gossip slip,
But, Lord, show me my own faults and transgressions,
And may my brother never hear my condemnations,
May I for grace, patience, and love forever strive,
And wisdom's innocence within my heart revive."

A Monk in his Cell

Напрасно я бегу к сионским высотам;
Грех алчный гонится за мною по пятам...
Так, ноздри пыльные уткнув в песок сыпучий,
Голодный лев следит оленя бег пахучий.

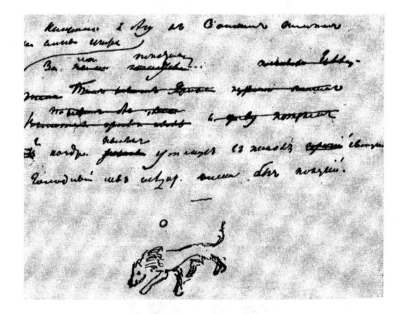

"In vain I seek to flee, to climb up Zion's heights"

In vain I seek to flee, to climb up Zion's heights,
For greedy sin pursues me at my heels, draws tight...
So, nostrils dusty drinking of quicksand shifting,
A hungry lion marks a deer's scent, sniffing.

(ИЗ ПИНДЕМОНТИ)

Не дорого ценю я громкие права,
От коих не одна кружится голова.
Я не ропщу о том, что отказали боги
Мне в сладкой участи оспоривать налоги
Или мешать царям друг с другом воевать;
И мало горя мне, свободно ли печать
Морочит олухов, иль чуткая цензура
В журнальных замыслах стесняет балагура.
Все это, видите ль, *слова, слова, слова*... **
Иные, лучшие мне дороги права;
Иная, лучшая потребна мне свобода:
Зависеть от царя, зависеть от народа—
Не все ли нам равно? Бог с ними!
                                        Никому
Отчета не давать, себе лишь самому
Служить и угождать, для власти, для ливреи
Не гнуть ни совести, ни помыслов, ни шеи;
По прихоти своей скитаться здесь и там,
Дивясь божественным природы красотам,
И пред созданьями искусств и вдохновенья
Трепеща радостно в восторгах умиленья,
        Вот счастье! вот права...

***Hamlet.* Примечание Пушкина

FROM PINDEMONTE*

I do not value much those rights hailed with such din
From which so many people's heads just seem to spin.
I don't complain and grouse about the gods' sharp practice
Denying me sweet rights to argue about taxes,
Or make it hard for Tsars to war with Tsars.
It little riles me if the press is free to charge
And torment idiots, or tender censors' humors
Offend themselves in every ragsheet's rumors.
Oh! Can't you see that all of this is "words, words, words?"
By other, better rights my soul gets stirred,
Another, better sort of freedom I am seeking.
Depend upon the Tsar? Depend upon the people?
Isn't it all the same? Who cares?
        No, to none
To have to give account! Only myself alone to
Serve, to powers that be and servants at their beck,
Bend neither thoughts, nor conscience, nor my neck,
But, flitting here and there as my whims may incline,
Enthralled by beauties of great nature most divine,
Before creations of fine arts and inspiration
To quiver joyously in deeply moved elation...
   —That's happiness!... Those are rights!...

---

*The Veronese poet Ippolito Pindemonte (1753–1828) wrote two books of Arcadian verse, *Le stanze* and *Poesie campestri,* and translated Homer's *Odyssey* into Italian. By presenting this poem as a "translation," Pushkin hoped to avoid problems with the censors. However, this poem was banned from publication until long after Pushkin's death.

** *Hamlet* (Pushkin's own footnote; see *Hamlet,*- Act II , sc. ii, at 194)

ЭЛЕГИЯ

Безумных лет угасшее веселье
Мне тяжело, как смутное похмелье.
Но, как вино — печаль минувших дней
В моей душе чем старе, тем сильней.
Мой путь уныл. Сулит мне труд и горе
Грядущего волнуемое море.

Но не хочу, о други, умирать;
Я жить хочу, чтоб мыслить и страдать,
И ведаю, мне будут наслажденья
Меж горестей, забот и треволненья:
Порой опять гармонией упьюсь,
Над вымыслом слезами обольюсь,
И может быть — на мой закат печальный
Блеснет любовь улыбкою прощальной.

ELEGY

The faded gaiety of past years' frenzies
Clouds up my heart, as if hung over, heavy.
But like a wine, of days gone by the woe,
While aging in my soul, with time does stronger grow.
My way ahead is bleak. Of work and gieving
The ocean of my future worries, heaving.

But, oh my friends, I do not want to die;
I want to live, to ponder, wrack, and pine.
I know there will be moments of elation
Amidst my mourning, cares, and tribulation,
When reveling I'll drink harmony again,
And art forth from my eyes new tears will send,
And it may pass, on my sad twilight dying,
That love may blaze its rays in farewell smiling.

Брожу ли я вдоль улиц шумных,
Вхожу ль во многолюдный храм,
Сижу ль меж юношей безумных,
Я предаюсь моим мечтам.

Я говорю: промчатся годы,
И сколько здесь ни видно нас,
Мы все сойдем под вечны своды —
И чей-нибудь уж близок час.

Гляжу ль на дуб уединенный,
Я мыслю: патриарх лесов
Переживет мой век забвенный,
Как пережил он век отцов.

Младенца ль милого ласкаю,
Уже я думаю: прости!
Тебе я место уступаю:
Мне время тлеть, тебе цвести.

День каждый, каждую годину
Привык я думой провождать,
Грядущей смерти годовщину
Меж их стараясь угадать.

И где мне смерть пошлет судьбина?
В бою ли, в странствии, в волнах?
Или соседняя долина
Мой примет охладелый прах?

И хоть бесчувственному телу
Равно повсюду истлевать,
Но ближе к милому пределу
Мне всё б хотелось почивать.

И пусть у гробового входа
Младая будет жизнь играть,
И равнодушная природа
Красою вечною сиять.

WHEN THROUGH THE NOISY STREETS I WANDER

When through the noisy streets I wander,
Walk in cathedral's throng that teems,
And sit by crazy youths, I ponder
And give myself up to my dreams.

And then I say: the years are passing,
And multitudes though we seem here
We'll all pass 'neath the vaults e'erlasting
And someone's hour's already near...

I see an oak alone in autumn:
This forests' patriarch, I think,
Will quite outlive my time forgotten
As he my father's time outlived.

When I caress a child's head tender,
I think already: Farewell soon:
To you my place I now surrender:
For I must wither, you must bloom.

Each day and year now I'm amassing,
I like to see off in my mind,
Guessing the dates of my own passing,
Trying the right one to divine.

And where will fate send me my dying?
In battle, wanderings, or waves?
Or will the valley nearby lying
Receive my ashes in its graves?

For though the body without feeling
Will wither anywhere and keep,
Yet closer to a place endearing
Is where I feel I'd rather sleep.

I'd like, if by my graveyard's entrance,
A sweet young life would bloom and play,
And nature, shining with indifference,
Forever beauty would display.

Exegi Monumentum...

Я памятник себе воздвиг нерукотворный,
К нему не зарастет народная тропа,
Вознесся выше он главою непокорной
    Александрийского столпа.

Нет, весь я не умру — душа в заветной лире
Мой прах переживет и тленья убежит —
И славен буду я, доколь в подлунном мире
    Жив будет хоть один пиит.

Слух обо мне пройдет по всей Руси великой,
И назовет меня всяк сущий в ней язык,
И гордый внук славян, и финн, и ныне дикой
    Тунгус, и друг степей калмык.

И долго буду тем любезен я народу,
Что чувства добрые я лирой пробуждал,
Что в мой жестокий век восславил я Свободу
    И милость к падшим призывал.

Веленью Божию, о Муза, будь послушна,
Обиды не страшась, не требуя венца;
Хвалу и клевету приемли равнодушно,
    И не оспоривай глупца.

Exegi Monumentum...

I've built myself a monument mere hands can't topple.
The people's path to it won't be o'ergrown with grass.
For it has raised itself above the crown unconquered
        Where Alexander's column stands.

No, I won't fully die: my soul, in sacred lyre,
Will yet survive my dust, and, despite with'ring, thrive:
I'll glorious be as long's in moonlit world entire
        One single bard is still alive.

Word about me will pass through all of Russia mighty.
My name in every one of her tongues will be penned:
By Slav's proud grandson, and by Finn, by savage, flighty
        Tungus, and Kalmyk, of steppes the friend.

And many years will I be favored with the people
For waking up good feelings by my lyre's thrall,
Because in my cruel age I praised and gloried Freedom,
        For mercy to the fallen called.

Be to the Lord's command, oh Muse, forever heeding,
Fear not offense and shame, care not for glory's rule,
Take praise and calumny indifferently, not needing —
        And never argue with a fool.

ТРУД

Миг вожделенный настал: окончен мой труд многолетний.
Что ж непонятная грусть тайно тревожит меня?
Или, свой подвиг свершив, я стою, как поденщик ненужный,
Плату приявший свою, чуждый работе другой?
Или жаль мне труда, молчаливого спутника ночи,
Друга Авроры златой, друга пенатов святых?

LABOR
(upon completion of *Eugene Onegin*)

Finally, now the time's come! I have finished my many years' labor.
Why, strange and secret, does sadness so trouble me now?
Is it, the deed being done, that I stand like a day-worker, useless,
Having been given my pay, foreign to all other work?
Or do I pine for my work, for my silent companion at nighttimes,
Friend of my dawns swathed in gold, friend of my home's holy shrine?

Page from the Manuscript of *Eugene Onegin*

ЕВГЕНИЙ ОНЕГИН (Отрывки из романа)

Pétri de vanité, il avait encore plus de cette espèce d'orgueil qui fait avouer avec la même indifférence les bonnes comme les mauvaises actions, suite d'un sentiment de supériorité peut-être imaginaire.

[Tiré d'une lettre particulière]

Не мысля гордый свет забавить,
Вниманье дружбы возлюбя,
Хотел бы я тебе представить
Залог достойнее тебя,
Достойнее души прекрасной,
Святой исполненной мечты,
Поэзии живой и ясной,
Высоких дум и простоты;
Но так и быть — рукой пристрастной
Прими собранье пестрых глав,
Полусмешных, полупечальных,
Простонародных, идеальных,
Небрежный плод моих забав,
Бессонниц, легких вдохновений,
Незрелых и увядших лет,
Ума холодных наблюдений
И сердца горестных замет.

EUGENE ONEGIN (Excerpts from the novel)

Steeped in vanity, he also had that particular type of pride which makes one confess with the same indifference good acts as well as bad, due to a possibly imaginary feeling of superiority.

[Taken from a private letter]

For smiles from lofty halls not daring,
But caring just for friendship true,
I wish I here could be presenting
A gift much worthier of you,
More worthy of a soul that's lovely,
In whom there dwells a holy dream
Of poetry that's clear and lively,
With lofty thoughts, simplicity.
But be it so, with your hand biased
Accept these brightly colored songs,
Half-humorous, half sad indeed,
Part folksy, and yet part ideal,
The breezy fruit of my free fun,
My sleepless nights, light inspirations,
My youth naïve, now faded far,
My intellect's cold observations,
And grieving notes straight from my heart.

Глава I.

И жить торопится и чувствовать спешит.
　　Кн. Вяземский

I «Мой дядя самых честных правил,
　　Когда не в шутку занемог,
　　Он уважать себя заставил
　　И лучше выдумать не мог.
　　Его пример другим наука;
　　Но, Боже мой, какая скука
　　С больным сидеть и день и ночь,
　　Не отходя ни шагу прочь!
　　Какое низкое коварство
　　Полуживого забавлять,
　　Ему подушки поправлять,
　　Печально подносить лекарство,
　　Вздыхать и думать про себя:
　　Когда же черт возьмет тебя?»

II Так думал молодой повеса,
　　Летя в пыли на почтовых,
　　Всевышней волею Зевеса
　　Наследник всех своих родных.
　　Друзья Людмилы и Руслана!
　　С героем моего романа
　　Без предисловий, сей же час
　　Позвольте познакомить вас.
　　Онегин, добрый мой приятель,
　　Родился на брегах Невы,
　　Где, может быть, родились вы
　　Или блистали, мой читатель;
　　Там некогда гулял и я:
　　Но вреден север для меня.

Chapter I

To live it hurries and to feel it flies...
— Prince Vyazemsky

I   "My uncle, man of rules, most honest,
When he fell ill beyond all joke,
Respect for himself forced upon us
(Better than that could not be hoped)
Let others learn from his example,
But Lord, how deathly dull to sample
The patient's sickbed night and day,
And never take a step away!
What execrably base dissembling
To keep someone half-dead amused,
Prop up his pillows, sadly brood,
With melancholy bring him medicine,
Sigh — as you ask yourself — all through —
When will the Devil will come for you!"

II   Such were the thoughts of our young scapegrace,
Flying on post-coaches through dust,
By Zeus Almighty's sudden grace
The heir of all the family trust.
My friends of *Ruslan and Lyudmila*!
Allow me, to my novel's hero,
Without more rigmarole or fuss,
To introduce you, all at once.
Onegin — my good pal in "Peter"* —
Was born there, on the Nevá's banks.
Where you were also born, perhaps,
Or else just sparkled, my dear reader.
I strolled there, had my flings, before,
But I'm allergic to the North.

*as the Russians themselves call their most graceful of cities

III Служив отлично-благородно,
Долгами жил его отец,
Давал три бала ежегодно
И промотался наконец.
Судьба Евгения хранила:
Сперва *Madame* за ним ходила,
Потом *Monsieur* ее сменил.
Ребенок был резов, но мил.
Monsieur l'Abbé, француз убогий,
Чтоб не измучилось дитя,
Учил его всему шутя,
Не докучал моралью строгой,
Слегка за шалости бранил
И в Летний сад гулять водил.

IV Когда же юности мятежной
Пришла Евгению пора,
Пора надежд и грусти нежной,
Monsieur прогнали со двора.
Вот мой Онегин на свободе;
Острижен по последней моде,
Как *dandy* лондонский одет –
И наконец увидел свет.
Он по-французски совершенно
Мог изъясняться и писал;
Легко мазурку танцевал
И кланялся непринужденно;
Чего ж вам больше? Свет решил,
Что он умен и очень мил.

III   By serving honestly and nobly,
　　　His father lived, from debt to debt,
　　　And gave three balls a year— and so he
　　　Did squander all, broke in the end.
　　　But fate was kind to our Eugene:
　　　At first *Madame* looked after him;
　　　Monsieur then came and took her place.
　　　The boy was frisky, but quite nice.
　　　Monsieur l'Abbé, a threadbare Frenchman,
　　　To keep the lad from suffering,
　　　While teaching, joked of everything,
　　　On morals strict and dull not dwelling.
　　　He'd slightly scold each impish lark,
　　　And walk him in the Summer Park.

IV   But when that age of youthful madness,
　　　Rebelllious, to Yevgeny came,
　　　That times of hopes and tender sadness,
　　　They kicked Monsieur right out the gate.
　　　Now my Onegin's free and dashing,
　　　His hair cut to the latest fashion,
　　　And like a London dandy dressed,
　　　He joined society at last.
　　　In French he absolutely brightly
　　　Could speak and write most fluently,
　　　And danced mazurkas easily,
　　　And bowed with grace and ease unfrightened.
　　　What need one more? Society
　　　Ruled him quite smart and quite a dear.

V   Мы все учились понемногу
    Чему-нибудь и как-нибудь,
    Так воспитаньем, слава Богу,
    У нас немудрено блеснуть.
    Онегин был, по мненью многих
    (Судей решительных и строгих),
    Ученый малый, но педант,
    Имел он счастливый талант
    Без принужденья в разговоре
    Коснуться до всего слегка,
    С ученым видом знатока
    Хранить молчанье в важном споре
    И возбуждать улыбку дам
    Огнем нежданных эпиграмм.

VI Латынь из моды вышла ныне:
    Так, если правду вам сказать,
    Он знал довольно по-латыни,
    Чтоб эпиграфы разбирать,
    Потолковать об Ювенале,
    В конце письма поставить *vale*,
    Да помнил, хоть не без греха,
    Из Энеиды два стиха.
    Он рыться не имел охоты
    В хронологической пыли
    Бытописания земли;
    Но дней минувших анекдоты
    От Ромула до наших дней
    Хранил он в памяти своей.

V   We all did study (more or less so)
    Something or other at some time.
    In education, God be praised, though,
    With us, it isn't hard to shine!
    Onegin was (such was the ruling
    Of many judges strict, unmoving)
    Just somewhat learnèd, yet a pedant.
    He had a very happy talent,
    Quite naturally, with a light touch,
    To chat of all things *en passant*,
    And looking sage, like a savant,
    Hear weightiest disputes and hush,
    And then incite smiles from *les dames*
    With sparks from surprise epigrams.

VI Latin has now gone out of fashion.
    Well, if I have to tell you true,
    He barely knew enough of Latin
    In epigraphs to have some clue,
    To speak of Juvenal not wincing,
    And write "*vale*," at letter's ending,
    And knew, fibbing not much, I hope,
    Two lines from the *Aeneid* by rote.
    He really did not have much passion
    To scour great tomes on ancient times,
    Leaf through vast tracts with dust begrimed,
    Yet various snips of history passing,
    From Romulus to the last word,
    Were in his memory preserved.

VII Высокой страсти не имея
    Для звуков жизни не щадить,
    Не мог он ямба от хорея,
    Как мы ни бились ,отличить.
    Бранил Гомера, Феокрита;
    Зато читал Адама Смита
    И был глубокий эконом,
    То есть, умел судить о том,
    Как государство богатеет,
    И чем живет, и почему
    Не нужно золота ему,
    Когда *простой продукт* имеет.
    Отец понять его не мог
    И земли отдавал в залог.

VIII Всего, что знал еще Евгений,
    Пересказать мне недосуг;
    Но в чем он истинный был гений,
    Что знал он тверже всех наук,
    Что было для него измлада
    И труд, и мука, и отрада,
    Что занимало целый день
    Его тоскующую лень,—
    Была наука страсти нежной,
    Которую воспел Назон,
    За что страдальцем кончил он
    Свой век блестящий и мятежный
    В Молдавии, в глуши степей,
    Вдали Италии своей.

VII But lacking in that lofty passion
That for sweet sounds would give up life,
From trochees couldn't tell an iamb,
However much we'd beat and try.
He panned Homer, Theocritus,
But read with pleasure Adam Smith,
And was a deep economist,
That is, he could the reasons list
By which a nation thrives and prospers,
What makes it live, get rich, and grow,
And why it has no need of gold,
When it makes good cheap, basic products.
His father couldn't understand,
And went and mortgaged off his land.

VIII All my Yevgeny knew's quite tedious:
Retelling it would bore me too.
But where he really was a genius,
And better than all science knew,
What, since he was a little boy,
Had been his labor, bane, and joy,
What occupied entire days
When he in torpor sad would laze,
Was that same art of passions tender,
Which Ovid used to celebrate,
For which, a traitor to the state,
He ended his bright age a rebel,
In bare Moldavian steppes and scree,
So far from his dear Italy.

X Как рано мог он лицемерить,
Таить надежду, ревновать,
Разуверять, заставить верить,
Казаться мрачным, изнывать,
Являться гордым и послушным,
Внимательным иль равнодушным!
Как томно был он молчалив,
Как пламенно красноречив,
В сердечных письмах как небрежен!
Одним дыша, одно любя,
Как он умел забыть себя!
Как взор его был быстр и нежен,
Стыдлив и дерзок, а порой
Блистал послушною слезой!

XI Как он умел казаться новым,
Шутя невинность изумлять,
Пугать отчаяньем готовым,
Приятной лестью забавлять,
Ловить минуту умиленья,
Невинных лет предубежденья
Умом и страстью побеждать,
Невольной ласки ожидать,
Молить и требовать признанья,
Подслушать сердца первый звук,
Преследовать любовь, и вдруг
Добиться тайного свиданья...
И после ей наедине
Давать уроки в тишине!

X   How he learned to dissemble early!
     To hide his hopes, feign jealousy,
     Shatter belief, then force believing,
     Then seem to sigh most gloomily,
     Then seem now haughty, now submissive,
     Now full of care, and now indifferent!
     How languid, too, his silence was!
     How fiery his eloquence!
     And, in his love letters, how reckless,
     Breathing of love and nothing else!
     How well he could forget himself!
     How quick and tender were his glances,
     Now shy, now brazen, and sometimes
     With an obedient tear he'd shine!

XI   How well he modeled innovation,
     Could joke, with innocence bemuse,
     Then scare with studied desperation,
     With pleasant flattery amuse,
     Alertly seize first tenderness,
     Defeat a young girl's prejudice
     With passion and intelligence,
     Against her will gain a caress,
     Demanding, wheedling her confession,
     Snoop as her heart skipped gingerly,
     Pursue her love, then suddenly
     Obtain a secret trysting session,
     Then, catching her now her on her own,
     Give lessons in the silence lone!

[«АХ, НОЖКИ, НОЖКИ!»]

XXIX Во дни веселий и желаний
Я был от балов без ума:
Верней нет места для признаний
И для вручения письма.
О вы, почтенные супруги!
Вам предложу свои услуги;
Прошу мою заметить речь:
Я вас хочу предостеречь.
Вы также, маменьки, построже
За дочерьми смотрите вслед;
Держите прямо свой лорнет!
Не то...не то, избави Боже!
Я это потому пишу,
Что уж давно я не грешу.

XXX Увы, на разные забавы
Я много жизни погубил!
Но если б не страдали нравы,
Я балы б до сих пор любил.
Люблю я бешенную младость
И тесноту, и блеск, и радость,
И дам обдуманный наряд;
Люблю их ножки; только вряд
Найдете вы в России целой
Три пары стройных женских ног.
Ах! Долго я забыть не мог
Две ножки...Грустный, охладелый,
Я всё их помню, и во сне
Они тревожат сердце мне.

["The Pedal Digression"]

XXIX On days of joys and of obsessions
  Balls used to make me lose my mind:
  There's no place better for confessions
  Or slipping love notes, you will find.
  Attention, husbands most respected!
  I'm at your service, please, expect it!
  Please mark it well, my little speech,
  My warning's meant to keep your peace.
  You, Mummies, too, be strict! Get with it!
  Watch carefully your daughter's steps,
  And hold on tight to your lorgnettes!
  If not, if not...oh Lord forbid it!
  I'm telling all this only since
  It's long ago since I last sinned.

XXX Alas, on various amusements
  I've wasted much, for good or ill.
  If only morals would permit it
  I would be crazy for balls still.
  I love their youthfulness and madness,
  Their crowding, and their spark, their gladness,
  The gowns the crafty ladies spout!
  I love their feet also – yet doubt–
  Search all of Russia, you won't find there
  Three pairs of lovely ladies' feet.
  Oh! I could not forget indeed
  Two sweet feet...Sad now, colder,
  I still remember. In my dreams
  They still trouble my heart, it seems.

XXXI Когда ж и где, в какой пустыне,
Безумец, их забудешь ты?
А, ножки, ножки! где вы ныне?
Где мнете вешние цветы?
Взлелеяны в восточной неге,
На северном, печальном снеге
Вы не оставили следов:
Любили мягких вы ковров
Роскошное прикосновенье.
Давно ль для вас я забывал
И жажду славы и похвал,
И край отцов, и заточенье?
Исчезло счастье юных лет,
Как на лугах ваш легкий след.

XXXII Дианы грудь, ланиты Флоры
Прелестны, милые друзья!
Однако ножка Терпсихоры
Прелестней чем-то для меня.
Она, пророчествуя взгляду
Неоцененную награду,
Влечет условною красой
Желаний своевольный рой.
Люблю ее, мой друг Эльвина,
Под длинной скатертью столов,
Весной на мураве лугов,
Зимой на чугуне камина,
На зеркальном паркете зал,
У моря на граните скал.

XXXI Oh, when and where, and in what desert
       Oh madman, where will you forget?
       Oh sweet feet, sweet feet that I treasured!
       Where now do you spring flowers tread?
       In Far East's bliss caressed so gently,
       In sad North's snows, you evidently,
       Could not so much as leave a trace!
       You loved the feel, softer than lace,
       Of carpets sumptuously mild.
       How long since I for you those days
       My thirst for glory and for praise
       Forgot? — and home and exile wild?
       My joy of younger years has passed
       Like your light footsteps on the grass.

XXXII Diana's breast, and Flora's cheeks
       Delight the soul, my dear, dear friends,
       However, Terpsichore's feet
       To me are more enchanting yet.
       How she to prophesying glances
       Hints at your yet unmeasured chances
       And with of beauty but a sign
       Stirs, swarms, Desire's capricious mind!
       Nymph-like Elvina, how I love her!
       Under long table's tablecloth
       On lawns'–in springtimes–well kept swathe,
       Warmed at the fireplace-screen in winter,
       On ballrooms' shimmering parquet floor,
       On granite cliffs perched by the shore.

XXXIII Я помню море пред грозою:
Как я завидовал волнам,
Бегущим бурной чередою
С любовью лечь к ее ногам!
Как я желал тогда с волнами
Коснуться милых ног устами!
Нет, никогда средь пылких дней
Кипящей младости моей
Я не желал с таким мученьем
Лобзать уста младых Армид,
Иль розы пламенных ланит,
Иль перси, полные томленьем;
Нет, никогда порыв страстей
Так не терзал души моей!

XXXIV Мне памятно другое время!
В заветных иногда мечтах
Держу я счастливое стремя...
И ножку чувствую в руках;
Опять кипит воображенье,
Опять ее прикосновенье
Зажгло в увядшем сердце кровь,
Опять тоска, опять любовь!..
Но полно прославлять надменных
Болтливой лирою своей;
Они не стоят ни страстей,
Ни песен, ими вдохновенных:
Слова и взор волшебниц сих
Обманчивы... как ножки их.

XXXIII Before the lightning, I remember
So envying the waves at sea,
Racing, in stormy ranks assembled,
With love to lie down at your feet!
I wished — as rush! — wave crashes, hisses,
To cover those sweet feet with kisses!
No, never in my wildest days,
A-boil with youth's mad glow and craze,
Was ever I so wracked with fire
To kiss bewitching young girls' lips,
Their rosy flaming cheeks, their hips,
Their fingers, languid with desire,
No, ne'er so much did passion's gust
So tear and rip my soul with lust!

XXXIV Another time now I'm remembering!
Sometimes, in my most cherished dreams,
I hold her happy stirrup, trembling,
And in my hands, I feel her feet:
Again, imagination's boiling,
Again slight touch, all passions roiling,
The blood burns in my faded heart,
Again I grieve, again I love!
But no more praising haughty maidens
With my incessant, babbling lyre!
They're worth nor songs nor passion's fire,
Of which they're yet the inspiration.
These witches' words and gazes sweet
Are trickery... just like their feet.

XLVI Кто жил и мыслил, тот не может
В душе не презирать людей;
Кто чувствовал, того тревожит
Призрак невозвратимых дней:
Тому уж нет очарований.
Того змия воспоминаний,
Того раскаянье грызет.
Все это часто придает
Большую прелесть разговору.
Сперва Онегина язык
Меня смущал; но я привык
К его язвительному спору,
И к шутке, с желчью пополам,
И злости мрачных эпиграмм.

XLVII Как часто летнею порою,
Когда прозрачно и светло
Ночное небо над Невою
И вод веселое стекло
Не отражает лик Дианы,
Воспомня прежних лет романы,
Воспомня прежнюю любовь,
Чувствительны, беспечны вновь,
Дыханьем ночи благосклонной
Безмолвно упивались мы!
Как в лес зеленый из тюрьмы
Перенесен колодник сонный,
Так уносились мы мечтой
К началу жизни молодой.

XLVI Whoever lives and thinks can't help but
       Despise most people in his soul.
       Whoever feels, is e'er perturbèd
       By specters of lost days of old:
       No more enchantments from a temptress,
       Instead, the serpent of remembrance
       Gnaws ceaselessly with cruel remorse.
       Quite often this accords, of course,
       Enormous charm to conversations.
       At first Onegin's biting tongue
       Embarrassed me; then I was drawn
       To his sarcastic condemnations,
       Got used to jokes and gall by halves,
       And gloomy bitter epigrams.

XLVII How often, in the summer nights,
       When, with a faint transparent glow,
       The sky o'er Nevá's banks still lights,
       And on its happy, glassy flow
       Diana's face is not reflected,
       By love affairs of old affected,
       By early love's sweet memories,
       We'd feel again, carefree, at ease,
       We'd drink kind night's breath to the lees.
       And in that blissful stillness pale,
       As if to forest green from jail
       A drowsy convict's just released —
       So we were borne back in a dream
       To life's beginnings young and keen.

XLVIII С душою, полной сожалений,
И опершися на гранит,
Стоял задумчиво Евгений,
Как описал себя пиит.
Все было тихо; лишь ночные
Перекликались часовые;
Да дрожек отдаленный стук
С Мильонной раздавался вдруг;
Лишь лодка, веслами махая,
Плыла по дремлющей реке:
И нас пленяли вдалеке
Рожок и песня удалая...
Но слаще, средь ночных забав,
Напев Торкватовых октав!

"And leaning on the granite bank"
Pushkin (at left) and Onegin on the Palace Embankment in St. Petersburg

XLVIII So, as regret in his soul seethed,
And leaning on the granite bank,
Yevgeny stood in reverie,
As "poet" paints himself, in prank...
And all was quiet; just night watchmen
Saluted to each other, lonesome,
And distant drozhkys' hoofbeats pound
From the Millionaya* did sound.
Drifting that sleepy flow along,
A rowboat lazed, its oars becalmed,
While from a distance we were charmed
By horns blown, then a rousing song...
Yet sweeter, midst the joys night brings,
Torquato Tasso's octave sings!

* The Millionaya, an elegant and fashionable street in St. Petersburg runs beside the Winter Palace from Palace Square to the Field of Mars.

XLIX Адриатические волны,
      О Брента! нет, увижу вас
      И, вдохновенья снова полный,
      Услышу ваш волшебный глас!
      Он свят для внуков Аполлона;
      По гордой лире Альбиона
      Он мне знаком, он мне родной.
      Ночей Италии златой
      Я негой наслажусь на воле,
      С венецианкою младой,
      То говорливой, то немой,
      Плывя в таинственной гондоле;
      С ней обретут уста мои
      Язык Петрарки и любви.

L.   Придет ли час моей свободы?
      Пора, пора! — взываю к ней;
      Брожу над морем, жду погоды,
      Маню ветрила кораблей.
      Под ризой бурь, с волнами споря,
      По вольному распутью моря
      Когда ж начну я вольный бег?
      Пора покинуть скучный брег
      Мне неприязненной стихии,
      И средь полуденных зыбей,
      Под небом Африки моей,
      Вздыхать о сумрачной России,
      Где я страдал, где я любил,
      Где сердце я похоронил.

XLIX　O billows of the Adriatic!
　　　　O Brenta! No, I'll see you yet!
　　　　With inspiration once more frantic,
　　　　I'll hear your magic cherishèd,
　　　　Your murmur, hallowed to Apollo's
　　　　Grandsons, which my own heart knows
　　　　Through Albion's proud lyre, and loves.
　　　　Gold Italy's nights sensuous
　　　　In freedom's bliss I'll revel in,
　　　　With a Venetian beauty young,
　　　　Who'll babble sometimes, then hush, numbed,
　　　　In a mysterious gondola:
　　　　With her my lips will soon acquire
　　　　The tongue of Petrarch and love's fire.

L.　　　But is my freedom's hour approaching?
　　　　It's time! It's time! I call to it!
　　　　Above the seashore I pace, roaming,
　　　　I wave to sails, wait for my wind.
　　　　Ah! Cloaked in storms, with waves disputing,
　　　　On oceans' crossroads, wild, free, gloomy,
　　　　When will I make my free escape!
　　　　It's time this dull land to forsake,
　　　　This earth, which is my enemy,
　　　　And then, by southern ripples sweet,
　　　　My Africa's clear skies beneath,
　　　　To sigh for gloomy Russia's lee,
　　　　Where I so suffered, loved so hard,
　　　　Where I did bury my own heart.

LV Я был рожден для жизни мирной,
Для деревенской тишины:
В глуши звучнее голос лирный,
Живее творческие сны.
Досугам посвятясь невинным,
Брожу над озером пустынным,
И *far niente** мой закон.
Я каждым утром пробужден
Для сладкой неги и свободы:
Читаю мало, долго сплю,
Летучей славы не ловлю.
Не так ли я в былые годы
Провел в бездействии, в тени
Мои счастливейшие дни?

LVI Цветы, любовь, деревня, праздность,
Поля! я предан вам душой.
Всегда я рад заметить разность
Между Онегиным и мной,
Чтобы насмешливый читатель
Или какой-нибудь издатель
Замысловатой клеветы,
Сличая здесь мои черты,
Не повторял потом безбожно,
Что намарал я свой портрет,
Как Байрон, гордости поэт,
Как будто нам уж невозможно
Писать поэмы о другом,
Как только о себе самом.

LV I was just born for this life peaceful,
For stillness pastoral, it seems...
My lyre in backwoods rings out clearer,
More life's in my creative dreams.
To leisures innocent, devoted,
Across a lonely lake I'm roaming,
And *far niente** is my law.
Each morning I wake up and yawn
With the sweet bliss of ease and freedom.
I read a little, sleep a lot,
And fleeting fame I have forgot.
In former years, was I not leading
Just such a life? Neath shade I'd laze...
The happiest of all my days!

LVI O flowers, love, sweet sloth, and country
Fields, with you my soul does dwell!
I'm always glad of contrasts sundry
Between Onegin and myself,
So that some ever-mocking reader —
Or publisher and eager feeder
Of most deliberate calumnies –
Would not spot here my qualities,
Would not proclaim, incorrigible,
That I my portrait scribbled here,
Like Byron, bard of pride, most dear,
As though it were impossible
To write a poem on anything –
Except about oneself to sing.

---

* Italian — to do nothing.

LVII Замечу кстати: все поэты —
Любви мечтательной друзья.
Бывало, милые предметы
Мне снились, и душа моя
Их образ тайный сохранила;
Их после Муза оживила:
Так я, беспечен, воспевал
И деву гор, мой идеал,
И пленниц берегов Салгира.
Теперь от вас, мои друзья,
Вопрос нередко слышу я:
«О ком твоя вздыхает лира?
Кому, в толпе ревнивых дев,
Ты посвятил ее напев?

LVIII Чей взор, волнуя вдохновенье,
Умильной лаской наградил
Твое задумчивое пенье?
Кого твой стих боготворил?»
И, други, никого, ей-Богу!
Любви безумную тревогу
Я безотрадно испытал.
Блажен, кто с нею сочетал
Горячку рифм: он тем удвоил
Поэзии священный бред,
Петрарке шествуя вослед,
А муки сердца успокоил,
Поймал и славу между тем;
Но я, любя, был глуп и нем.

LVII I note in passing that all poets
      Are friends of dreamy wistful love.
      I used to dream of love's sweet objects:
      My soul had visits from above,
      Then kept these images in hiding;
      Then, afterwards, my Muse revived them:
      So, I might spin a carefree reel
      Of mountain maiden*, my ideal,
      Or slave-girls by the Salgir River**.
      But now, my friends, I hear too often
      A question always in the offing:
      "For whom now does your lyre quiver?
      From whom, midst crouds of jealous swains,
      Have you poured forth new sweet refrains?

LVIII Whose glance excites your inspiration,
      Invokes a dear caress inside?
      With wistful pensive incantation
      Whom has your verse now deified?"
      And friends, the truth is, no one, honest!
      My crazy loves' wild cares aren't missed.
      I've suffered quite enough, and pined.
      Blessed is a poet who's combined
      Love's ache with Rhythm's, doubling thus
      Poetry's sacred ravings free!
      As Petrarch did before, so he
      Becalms his heartswell torturous,
      And all the while gains great repute.
      My love was foolish, though, and mute.

---

*Refers to *The Prisoner of the Caucasus*.
**Refers to *The Fountain of Bakhchisarai*; the Tatar Khans' harem was on the banks of the Salgir River in Bakhcisarai, on the Crimean Peninsula.

ГЛАВА ВТОРАЯ

O rus! (Hor.)

VII От хладного разврата света
Еще увянуть не успев,
Его душа была согрета
Приветом друга, лаской дев;
Он сердцем милый был невежда,
Его лелеяла надежда,
И мира новый блеск и шум
Еще пленяли юный ум;
Он забавлял мечтою сладкой
Сомненья сердца своего;
Цель жизни нашей для него
Была заманчивой загадкой,
Над ней он голову ломал
И чудеса подозревал.

VIII Он верил, что душа родная
Соединиться с ним должна,
Что, безотрадно изнывая,
Его вседневно ждет она;
Он верил, что друзья готовы
За честь его принять оковы,
И что не дрогнет их рука
Разбить сосуд клеветника;
Что есть избранные судьбами,
Людей священные друзья;
Что их бессмертная семья
Неотразимыми лучами,
Когда-нибудь нас озарит
И мир блаженством одарит.

Chapter II

O rus! (Oh, the country!) Horace

VII   From this world cold, depraved, deformed,
Having no chance to wither yet,
His soul was cosseted and warmed
By friends, by girlish tenderness,
In matters of the heart knew nothing,
Hope comforted his heart's young running,
New spark and bustle in this world
Still kept his youthful spirit thrilled.
He stilled, with daydreams sweet, amusing,
The doubts he felt deep in his heart.
The goal for him of this life hard
Was an enigma, mist alluring...
On it he pondered all the time,
In all things miracles did find.

VIII   A kindred soul, he was believing,
Was meant to meet him on life's way,
That joylessly alone and grieving
She waited for him every day,
And that his friends were true, and ready
To don, for his name's sake, chains heavy.
Unwavering would be their hand
Against which slander could not stand,
That by the Fates there had been chosen
For us alone, some holy friends,
A family that never ends,
Whose light uncanny's always glowing,
Whose rays will someday shine on us,
And to the world bring blessedness.

IX Негодованье, сожаленье,
    Ко благу чистая любовь
    И славы сладкое мученье
    В нем рано волновали кровь.
    Он с лирой странствовал на свете;
    Под небом Шиллера и Гете
    Их поэтическим огнем
    Душа воспламенилась в нем;
    И муз возвышенных искусства,
    Счастливец, он не постыдил:
    Он в песнях гордо сохранил
    Всегда возвышенные чувства,
    Порывы девственной мечты
    И прелесть важной простоты.

X   Он пел любовь, любви послушный,
    И песнь его была ясна,
    Как мысли девы простодушной,
    Как сон младенца, как луна
    В пустынях неба безмятежных,
    Богиня тайн и вздохов нежных.
    Он пел разлуку и печаль,
    И *нечто*, и *туманну даль*,
    И романтические розы;
    Он пел те дальные страны,
    Где долго в лоно тишины
    Лились его живые слезы;
    Он пел поблеклый жизни цвет
    Без малого в осьмнадцать лет.

IX   And indignation and compassion
      And purest love for doing good,
      For glory's agony sweet passion,
      From early days roused up his blood,
      With lyre his wandering ways did ply
      Neath Goethe's and 'neath Schiller's sky,
      Exposed to their poetic fire
      Which then his own soul did inspire.
      The Muses of their arts exalted
      He, happily, did not disgrace,
      In all his cantos, full of grace,
      He keep his feelings lofty, vaulted
      Sky-high with gusts of virgin dreams,
      With charming, simple, serious scenes.

X   He sang of love, to love submissive,
      And clear and limpid was his tune,
      As innocent maids' thoughts are, pensive,
      Or boyish dreams are, or the moon
      In heaven's desert calm appearing,
      Goddess of tender sighs and secrets.
      He sang of partings and of griefs,
      Of "something".... "Distant, misty heaths..."
      And — of course — roses (most romantic).
      He sang of a lost distant shore
      Where, wrapped in silence, long before,
      His tears rolled down his cheeks quite frantic...
      He sang of life's frayed, yellowed page,
      While scarcely eighteen years of age.

XI В пустыне, где один Евгений
Мог оценить его дары,
Господ соседственных селений
Ему не нравились пиры;
Бежал он их беседы шумной.
Их разговор благоразумный
О сенокосе, о вине,
О псарне, о своей родне,
Конечно, не блистал ни чувством,
Ни поэтическим огнем,
Ни остротою, ни умом,
Ни общежития искусством;
Но разговор их милых жен
Гораздо меньше был умен.

XII Богат, хорош собою, Ленский
Везде был принят как жених;
Таков обычай деревенский;
Все дочек прочили своих
За *полурусского соседа*;
Взойдет ли он, тотчас беседа
Заводит слово стороной
О скуке жизни холостой;
Зовут соседа к самовару,
А Дуня разливает чай,
Ей шепчут: «Дуня, примечай!»
Потом приносят и гитару:
И запищит она (Бог мой!):
Приди в чертог ко мне златой!..

XI   But in that desert where Yevgeny
Alone could recognize his gift,
Landowning neighbors' feasts of plenty
Were horrors he would rather miss.
He fled from all their noisy chatter,
From their good-natured, endless prattle
Of wine, of bringing the hay in,
About their kennels and their kin,
Which doubtless did not shine with feeling,
Nor with the spark of poetry,
Or wit, or clever repartee,
And with no hint of art was breathing...
But as for what their dear wives said —
T'was even less intelligent!

XII   But Lensky, being rich and handsome,
Was thought a suitor everywhere.
All planned—such is the country custom—
To hitch up, to their daughters fair,
This new-neighbor, this "semi-Russian".
If he walked in, at once discussion
Was focused only on the theme
How dull unmarried life did seem...
Round samovar they'd sit at tea,
While Dunya poured it clumsily,
They'd whisper "Dunya, carefully!"
Then bring out her guitar, so she
(Good God!) could shriek and caterwaul:
"Come, darling, to my golden hall!"

XIII Но Ленский, не имев конечно,
Охоты узы брака несть,
С Онегиным желал сердечно
Знакомство покороче свесть.
Они сошлись. Волна и камень,
Стихи и проза, лед и пламень
Не столь различны меж собой.
Сперва взаимной разнотой
Они друг другу были скучны;
Потом понравились; потом
Съезжались каждый день верхом
И скоро стали неразлучны.
Так люди (первый каюсь я)
От *делать нечего* друзья.

XIV Но дружбы нет и той меж нами.
Все предрассудки истребя,
Мы почитаем всех нулями,
А единицами — себя.
Мы все глядим в Наполеоны;
Двуногих тварей миллионы
Для нас орудие одно;
Нам чувство дико и смешно.
Сноснее многих был Евгений;
Хоть он людей, конечно, знал
И вообще их презирал,--
Но (правил нет без исключений)
Иных он очень отличал
И вчуже чувство уважал.

XIII   But Lensky, having no desire,
Of course, to put on marriage chains,
With all his heart wished to draw nigher
To Onegin – and become his friend.
They got quite close, though wave and stone,
And ice and fire, and prose and poem
Are not so different as they were.
At first, these differences disturbed,
They thought each other dull, then drolly
They rather liked each other, then
Together daily riding went,
Were soon inseparable wholly.
So we (I will confess first too)
Make friends from having *naught to do*.

XIV   But no such friendship our dear land knows...
Though prejudice we've killed and shun,
We think of all others as zeroes,
And of ourselves alone as one.
We all would be Napoleons,
Two-legged beasts, in millions,
At our command keep but as tools.
Feelings for us are quaint, for fools.
Yevgeny had far less objections
Than most, though he knew people well,
And so despised them, truth to tell,
But (there's no rule without exceptions)
Some he distinguished quite a lot,
Respecting feelings he'd forgot.

XV Он слушал Ленского с улыбкой.
Поэта пылкий разговор,
И ум, еще в сужденьях зыбкий,
И вечно вдохновенный взор, –
Онегину всё было ново;
Он охладительное слово
В устах старался удержать
И думал: глупо мне мешать
Его минутному блаженству;
И без меня пора придет;
Пускай покамест он живет
Да верит мира совершенству;
Простим горячке юных лет
И юный жар и юный бред.

XVI Меж ими всё рождало споры
И к размышлению влекло:
Племен минувших договоры,
Плоды наук, добро и зло,
И предрассудки вековые,
И гроба тайны роковые,
Судьба и жизнь в свою чреду,
Все подвергалось их суду.
Поэт в жару своих суждений
Читал, забывшись, между тем
Отрывки северных поэм,
И снисходительный Евгений,
Хоть их не много понимал,
Прилежно юноше внимал.

XV He heard out Lensky's feelings smiling.
 The poet's passion, feeling, ire,
 His wavering judgments undecided,
 And look, as if forever inspired.
 Onegin thought it fresh, appealing...
 Cold quips, a poet's hope congealing,
 He did his best never to vent,
 And thought "it's silly to prevent
 His momentary state of blessing.
 He'll learn, even unhelped by me,
 But just for now I'll let him be
 Believing in the world's perfection.
 So let's forgive a fevered youth
 Young fever and young nonsense too."

XVI Disputes between them, often heated,
 Arose, and led to thoughtfulness.
 The ancient pacts of bygone peoples,
 The ways of virtue, wickedness,
 The fruits of knowledge, prejudice,
 The secrets of the grave, of death,
 And Fate, and life, all one by one,
 Before their court in turn did come.
 Our bard, who found his own thoughts heady,
 Recited, read, waving his hands,
 Extracts of poems from Northern lands.
 Yevgeny listened, condescending,
 Though comprehending fitfully,
 He'd listen quite assiduously.

XVII Но чаще занимали страсти
Умы пустынников моих.
Ушед от их мятежной власти,
Онегин говорил об них
С невольным вздохом сожаленья.
Блажен, кто ведал их волненья
И наконец от них отстал;
Блаженней тот, кто их не знал,
Кто охлаждал любовь — разлукой,
Вражду — злословием; порой
Зевал с друзьями и с женой,
Ревнивой не тревожась мукой,
И дедов верный капитал
Коварной двойке не вверял.

XVIII Когда прибегнем мы под знамя
Благоразумной тишины,
Когда страстей угаснет пламя
И нам становятся смешны
Их своевольство иль порывы
И запоздалые отзывы, —
Смиренные не без труда,
Мы любим слушать иногда
Страстей чужих язык мятежный,
И нам он сердце шевелит.
Так точно старый инвалид
Охотно клонит слух прилежный
Рассказам юных усачей,
Забытый в хижине своей.

XVII   More often, though, the human passions
      Distracted our young hermits' minds.
      Onegin spoke of them as passing,
      Their violent power left behind—
      Yet with unbidden sighs regretful:
      Blessed is he, who's left their fretful
      Grip, of passions weary grown,
      Blessed he, who them has never known,
      Who has cooled off his love in parting,
      His hate, with bitter words, not strife,
      Yawned with his friends, sometimes, or wife,
      From jealous fits was never smarting,
      And never staked his parents' all
      Upon some deuce's treacherous fall.

XVIII   When we ourselves flee towards the banner
      Of reasonable tranquility,
      And when our passion's spark grows dimmer,
      And sillier, now, seem to be
      Our passions' gusts and willful longings,
      Their quirky and belated callings,
      Which we ourselves could scarecely tame,
      We sometimes like to hear the tale
      Of other people's stormy passions,
      And let our heart be stirred by it.
      Just so, an aged invalid
      Will eagerly bend his attentions,
      Being forgot, in bare hut cooped,
      To tales told by some mustached youth.

XIX Зато и пламенная младость
     Не может ничего скрывать.
     Вражду, любовь, печаль и радость
     Она готова разболтать.
     В любви считаясь инвалидом,
     Онегин слушал с важным видом,
     Как, сердца исповедь любя,
     Поэт высказывал себя;
     Свою доверчивую совесть
     Он простодушно обнажал.
     Евгений без труда узнал
     Его любви младую повесть,
     Обильный чувствами рассказ,
     Давно не новыми для нас.

XX   Ах, он любил, как в наши лета
     Уже не любят; как одна
     Безумная душа поэта
     Еще любить осуждена:
     Всегда, везде одно мечтанье,
     Одно привычное желанье,
     Одна привычная печаль.
     Ни охлаждающая даль,
     Ни долгие лета разлуки,
     Ни музам данные часы,
     Ни чужеземные красы,
     Ни шум веселий, ни науки
     Души не изменили в нем,
     Согретой девственным огнем.

XIX But young men's fiery rowdiness
     Can never hold back anything:
     Of hatred, love, grief, happiness,
     Their ready tongue keeps babbling.
     Thinking himself in love a cripple,
     Onegin heard, sage-faced, unquivering,
     The poet tell all of himself,
     In love with his own heart's distress,
     As he his over-trusting conscience
     With bare simplicity released.
     Yevgeny recognized with ease
     The tale of his young love's experience,
     The feelings full, splendiferous,
     That long since aren't new for us.

XX   Oh, he did love, as we already
     No longer love, as only bards'
     Insane poetic souls unsteady
     Condemned to love forever are!
     Just dreaming, always, everywhere,
     One wish just haunting, always there,
     One ever-present, endless grief.
     No distance cools, far though she be,
     Nor many years of being parted,
     Nor hours devoted to the Muse,
     Nor foreign beauties' tempting hues,
     Nor science, nor good cheer light-hearted,
     Could tame his soul's dear love inspired,
     Warmed with an innocent, pure fire.

| XXI | Чуть отрок, Ольгою пленненый,
Сердечных мук еще не знав,
Он был свидетель умиленный
Ее младенческих забав;
В тени хранительной дубравы
Он разделял ее забавы,
И детям прочили венцы
Друзья-соседы, их отцы.
В глуши, под сению смиренной,
Невинной прелести полна,
В глазах родителей, она
Цвела, как ландыш потаенный,
Незнаемый в траве глухой
Ни мотыльками, ни плечой.

| XXIII | Всегда скромна, всегда послушна,
Всегда как утро весела,
Как жизнь поэта простодушна,
Как поцелуй любви мила;
Глаза, как небо, голубые,
Улыбка, локоны льняные,
Движенья, голос, легкий стан,
Всё в Ольге...но любой роман
Возьмите и найдете верно
Ее портрет: он очень мил,
Я прежде сам его любил,
Но надоел он мне безмерно.
Позвольте мне, читатель мой,
Заняться старшею сестрой.

XXI.   While still a boy, with Olga taken,
       Still ignorant of heartfelt pains,
       He was a witness charmed, elated,
       To all her childish, playful games.
       Beneath the safe shades of the forest
       He shared her happiness and frolics.
       Their wedding wreathes by now were made
       By parents, friends from near estates.
       Plain, backwoods-raised, far from the city,
       Thus graced with charming purity,
       In her own parents' eyes it seemed
       She bloomed like hidden valley-lilies,
       That under thick weeds no one sees,
       Not even butterflies and bees.

XXIII Forever meek, forever humble,
       Forever happy as the dawn,
       As poets are, sincere and simple,
       As dear as kisses of first love,
       Her eyes as light blue as the sky,
       Her flaxen locks in curls, her smile,
       Her voice, light step, lithe frame, her look,
       All Olga's features…But take any book —
       All novels do her portrait paint:
       The picture's nice, it must be said.
       I used to love it once myself,
       But now I've grown quite sick of it.
       Dear reader, let me, anyhow,
       Turn to her elder sister now.

XXV Итак, она звалась Татьяной.
Ни красотой сестры своей,
Ни свежестью ее румяной
Не привлекла б она очей.
Дика, печальна, молчалива,
Как лань лесная боязлива,
Она в семье своей родной
Казалась девочкой чужой.
Она ласкаться не умела
К отцу, ни к матери своей;
Дитя сама, в толпе детей
Играть и прыгать не хотела
И часто целый день одна
Сидела молча у окна.

XXVI Задумчивость, ее подруга
От самых колыбельных дней,
Теченье сельского досуга
Мечтами украшала ей.
Ее изнеженные пальцы
Не знали игл; склонясь на пяльцы,
Узором шелковым она
Не оживляла полотна.
Охоты властвовать примета,
С послушной куклою дитя
Приготовляется шутя
К приличию — закону света,
И важно повторяет ей
Уроки маменьки своей.

XXV   And so, Tatyana was her first name:
        Neither her sister's beauty prized,
        Nor fresh and rosy cheeks aflame
        Would ever draw you to her eyes.
        Savage, and saddened, and withdrawn,
        As frightened as a forest fawn,
        She seemed in her own family
        A foundling child, an alien being.
        No cuddles could this girl display
        To Dad or Mom. Instead she'd pout,
        A child alone in childish crowd.
        She didn't want to skip and play;
        She'd sit, and let whole days just wane
        While staring out the windowpane.

XXVI And thoughtfulness was her best friend
        Since first in cradles she was laid;
        T'would to her rural rest extend
        Sweet flights that dreams did decorate...
        Her tender, fragile fingers graceful
        Knew not the needle or the lace-frame,
        No silken pattern did she weave
        To make a piece of linen breathe.
        Showing the urge to domination,
        With an obedient doll, a child,
        While playing, does prepare the while
        For well-brought up subordination,
        And solemnly to it repeats
        Laws, lessons that her Mommy speaks.

XXVII Но куклы даже в эти годы
Татьяна в руки не брала;
Про вести города, про моды
Беседы с нею не вела.
И были детские проказы
Ей чужды: страшные рассказы
Зимою в темноте ночей
Пленяли больше сердце ей.
Когда же няня собирала
Для Ольги на широкий луг
Всех маленьких ее подруг,
Она в горелки не играла,
Ей скучен был и звонкий смех,
И шум их ветреных утех.

XXVIII Она любила на балконе
Предупреждать зари восход,
Когда на бледном небосклоне
Звезд исчезает хоровод,
И тихо край земли светлеет,
И, вестник утра, ветер веет,
И всходит постепенно день.
Зимой, когда ночная тень
Полмиром доле обладает,
И доле в праздной тишине,
При отуманенной луне,
Восток ленивый почивает,
В привычный час пробуждена
Вставала при свечах она.

XXVII   But even in her girlish days
        Tatyana never touched a doll.
        Whatever fashions were the rage
        Were never shared with dolls at all.
        The usual childish escapades
        To her were foreign. Frightful tales
        Instead, through winter nights' bleak dark,
        Were all that thrilled her youthful heart.
        When Nanny gathered Sister Olga
        And all her little friends around
        To meadows greening in a crowd,
        She played no "hide and seek," unbothered.
        Dull to her did their laughs resound;
        Dull did their silly pleasures sound.

XXVIII   She loved, upon the balcony,
        To wait the coming of the dawn.
        When first in the pale firmament
        The dance of stars goes faint, is gone,
        With quiet light Earth's edges glow,
        And morning's herald wind, does blow,
        And gradually the day grows bright.
        In winter, when the shades of night
        Take over, lengthening half the world,
        When longer, in a languourous fit,
        The quiet moon is wrapped in mist,
        Until the lazy East is stirred,
        In waking, she would make a rite
        Of getting up by candlelight.

XXIX Ей рано нравились романы;
Они ей заменяли всё;
Она влюблялася в обманы
И Ричардсона, и Руссо.
Отец ее был добрый малый,
В прошедшем веке запоздалый;
Но в книгах не видал вреда;
Он, не читая никогда,
Их почитал пустой игрушкой
И не заботился о том,
Какой у дочки тайный том
Дремал до утра под подушкой.
Жена ж его была сама
От Ричардсона без ума.

"Carpe Diem"

XXIX She was quite early fond of novels
They replaced all, were all she'd know.
She fell in love with tricks and troubles
Of Richardson and of Rousseau.
Her father wasn't a bad fellow,
Though in the previous century wallowed.
In books he didn't see much harm,
Though he himself read not at all,
He thought of them as toys, as shallow,
And wouldn't give a second look
To check what kind of secret book,
Dozed with his daughter 'neath a pillow.
Meanwhile, his wife, for quite some time,
For Richardson quite lost her mind.

XXX Она любила Ричардсона
Не потому, чтобы прочла,
Не потому, чтоб Грандисона
Она Ловласу предпочла;
Но в старину княжна Алина,
Ее москоская кузина,
Твердила часто ей об них,
В то время был еще жених
Ее супруг, но по неволе;
Она вздыхала по другом,
Который сердцем и умом
Ей нравился гораздо боле:
Сей Грандисон был славный франт,
Игрок и гвардии сержант.

XXXI Как он, она была одета
Всегда по моде и к лицу;
Но, не спросясь ее совета,
Девицу повезли к венцу.
И, чтоб ее рассеять горе,
Разумный муж уехал вскоре
В свою деревню, где она,
Бог знает кем окружена,
Рвалась и плакала сначала,
С супругом чуть не развелась;
Потом хозяйством занялась,
Привыкла и довольна стала.
Привычка свыше нам дана:
Замена счастию она.

XXX Mum had been fond of Richardson
(Whom she in fact had never read)
Not because she thought Grandison
Another Lovelace, better yet,
But in her time Princess Alina,
Her Moscow cousin, wouldn't leave her
Alone—with talk of nothing else...
Her husband now was still back then
Her fiancé, against her will;
She'd pined for someone else, more dear,
In heart and spirit far more near,
She liked him much, much better still...
That Grandison was a gay fop,
A gambler, sergeant in the Guards.

XXXI She dressed up just like him, alluring,
In perfect style and fit, of course,
But no one asked for her opinion:
They dragged her to the church by force.
And hoping to relieve her mourning
Her husband shrewdly took her shortly
Off to his country seat where she
Bereft, stuck in obscurity,
At first, wept, raged, and wailed, tormented,
And very nearly got divorced,
Then drowned her woes in household chores,
Then with new habits grew contented.
From on high Habit comes to us
—And it replaces happiness.

ГЛАВА III

> Elle était fille, elle était amoureuse.
>
> --Malfilâtre

XV Татьяна, милая Татьяна!
С тобой теперь я слезы лью;
Ты в руки модного тирана
Уж отдала судьбу свою.
Погибнешь, милая; но прежде
Ты в ослепительной надежде
Блаженство темное зовешь,
Ты негу жизни узнаешь,
Ты пьешь волшебный яд желаний,
Тебя преследуют мечты:
Везде воображаешь ты
Приюты счастливых свиданий;
Везде, везде перед тобой
Твой искуситель роковой.

XVI Тоска любви Татьяну гонит,
И в сад идет она грустить,
И вдруг недвижны очи клонит,
И лень ей далее ступить.
Приподнялася грудь, ланиты
Мгновенным пламенем покрыты,
Дыханье замерло в устах,
И в слухе шум, и блеск в очах...
Настанет ночь; луна обходит
Дозором дальный свод небес,
И соловей во мгле древес
Напевы звучные заводит.
Татьяна в темноте не спит
И тихо с няней говорит:

CHAPTER III.

> She was a girl, she was in love.
>
> --Malfilâtre

XV   Tatyana, oh my dear Tatyana!
I cry with you in sympathy;
You're captive to a stylish tyrant;
You've given him your destiny.
You're doomed, my sweetheart, yet – one instant –
Enjoy your blinding hope resplendent,
And call your darkest error bliss:
If there is joy in life— it's this.
You drink desire's magic poison
And let yourself be chased by dreams:
No matter where you go, it seems
You've found a place for sweet liason,
And everywhere, it seems, you walk,
Your fateful ravisher does stalk.

XVI   The grief of love pursues Tatyana;
She seeks her garden out to pine,
And suddenly her own eyes fail her,
She cannot walk, can't even try...
Her breast is heaving, cheeks are blushing,
With momentary fire flushing,
Her breath right on her lips does freeze,
No sound she hears, no sight she sees...
The night has come, the moon goes strolling,
Inspecting all of heaven's arc.
The nightingale in forest dark
Melodious refrains is tolling.
Yet Tanya in the dark can't sleep,
Must with her nanny softly speak:

XVII «Не спится, няня: здесь так душно!
Открой окно да сядь ко мне».
— Что, Таня, что с тобой? — «Мне скучно,
Поговорим о старине».
— О чем же, Таня? Я, бывало,
Хранила в памяти не мало
Старинных былей, небылиц
Про злых духов и про девиц;
А нынче все мне тёмно, Таня:
Что знала, то забыла. Да,
Пришла худая череда!
Зашибло... — «Расскажи мне, няня,
Про ваши старые года:
Была ты влюблена тогда?»

XVIII — И, полно, Таня! В эти лета
Мы не слыхали про любовь;
А то бы согнала со света
Меня покойница свекровь. —
«Да как же ты венчалась, няня?»
— Так, видно, Бог велел. Мой Ваня
Моложе был меня, мой свет,
А было мне тринадцать лет.
Недели две ходила сваха
К моей родне, и наконец
Благословил меня отец.
Я горько плакала со страха,
Мне с плачем косу расплели
Да с пеньем в церковь повели.

XVII   "I can't sleep, nanny: it's so stuffy!
Open the window, sit by me."
"What's wrong, Tanya?" "I'm bored...it's nothing.
Let's talk of how things used to be."
"Of what things, Tanya? When I was younger
I once had memorized a number
Of old-wives' yarns and fairy tales,
Of evil spirits and fair maids,
But all grows dark in me, has vanished;
Yes, I've forgot all I once knew,
Yes, time's brought me a real to-do!
I've gone all blank..." "But tell me, nanny
About the days when you were young:
Back then were you ever in love?"

XVIII   "What nonsense, Tanya! Don't be silly!
Back then we'd never heard of love;
My mother-in-law really
Would have hounded me and chased me off!"
"How then did you get married, Nyanya?"
"It was God's will, I guess. My Vanya
Was younger e'en than me, my dear,
And I 'd just reached my thirteenth year.
Two weeks the matchmaker kept seeking
To close the deal with all my kin.
My Dad agreed, and blessed me then,
And scared, I started bitter weeping.
As they undid my braids, I lurched,
They sang, and led me off to church.

XIX И вот ввели в семью чужую...
Да ты не слушаешь меня... —
«Ах, няня, няня, я тоскую,
Мне тошно, милая моя:
Я плакать, я рыдать готова!..»
— Дитя мое, ты нездорова;
Господь помилуй и спаси!
Чего ты хочешь, попроси...
Дай окроплю святой водою,
Ты вся горишь... — «Я не больна:
Я... знаешь, няня... влюблена».
— Дитя мое, господь с тобою! —
И няня девушку с мольбой
Крестила дряхлою рукой.

XX «Я влюблена», — шептала снова
Старушке с горестью она.
— Сердечный друг, ты нездорова.
«Оставь меня: я влюблена».
И между тем луна сияла
И томным светом озаряла
Татьяны бледные красы,
И распущенные власы,
И капли слез, и на скамейке
Пред героиней молодой,
С платком на голове седой,
Старушку в длинной телогрейке;
И все дремало в тишине
При вдохновительной луне.

Tatyana

EUGENE ONEGIN (EXCERPTS) CHAPTER 3

XIX To a strange family they brought me...
— But you aren't listening to me—"
"Oh, nanny, nanny. I'm distraught. See
How I'm sick, my sweet, can't breathe,
I'm going to weep and sob — I will!"
"Oh my dear child, I see you're ill;
'Lord save us! Mercy! Hear our call!'
Whatever you might need at all...
Here, let me sprinkle holy water —
You have a fever." "I'm well enough:
You know what, nanny?...I'm in love."
"Lord bless you, sweetie, what's the matter?"
And nanny prayed, crossed herself fast,
Above her girl with shaky hand.

XX "Oh, I'm in love!" again she whispered,
To Nanny in a grieving voice.
"My dearest heart, you're sick. Now listen!"
"Leave me alone! I am in love!"
And all the while the moon was gleaming,
Its murky, dreamy light was beaming
Upon Tatyana's beauty pale,
Her loose hair tossing in a gale
Of teardrops, as her nanny sat
With our young heroine did fret,
Her bonnet wrapped round her grey head,
A long wool warmer round her back.
As all in peaceful sleep did seem
The moon inspired all to dream.

XXI И сердцем далеко носилась
Татьяна, смотря на луну...
Вдруг мысль в уме ее родилась...
«Поди, оставь меня одну.
Дай, няня, мне перо, бумагу,
Да стол подвинь; я скоро лягу;
Прости». И вот она одна.
Все тихо. Светит ей луна.
Облокотясь, Татьяна пишет,
И все Евгений на уме,
И в необдуманном письме
Любовь невинной девы лышит.
Письмо готово, сложено...
Татьяна! для кого ж оно?

XXV Кокетка судит хладнокровно,
Татьяна любит не шутя
И предается безусловно
Любви, как милое дитя.
Не говорит она: отложим —
Любви мы цену тем умножим,
Вернее в сети заведем;
Сперва тщеславие кольнем
Надеждой, там недоуменьем
Измучим сердце, а потом
Ревнивым оживим огнем;
А то, скучая наслажденьем,
Невольник хитрый из оков
Всечасно вырваться готов.

XXI   And as her heart raced, pounding tighter,
       Tatyana gazed up at the moon...
       And then a thought arose inside her...
       "Go now, and leave me, please, alone.
       And, Nanny, give me pen and paper,
       I'll lie down soon — but move this table.
       Goodbye." She's left alone. Deep night.
       And all is still. The moon shines bright,
       On elbows perched, Tatyana, seething
       Writes, just Yevgeny on her mind,
       With thoughtless words her soul unwinds
       A letter chaste, with pure love breathing.
       The letter's written, folded, sealed...
       Tatyana! Who's it for, my dear?

XXV   A flirt judges cold-bloodedly,
       Tatyana's love is artless, wild,
       Gives all her heart entirely
       To love, like an enchanting child.
       She doesn't reason: "let's delay,
       Let's raise love's price, and catch our prey
       By teasing mixed with flattery,
       At first, let's prick his vanity,
       And then allow some hope to soar,
       Then shock his heart with scorn and ire,
       Wake it again, with jealous fire,
       Or else, by pleasure growing bored,
       A clever captive ever strains
       And strives to break free from his chains."

XXVI Еще предвижу затрудненья:
Родной земли спасая честь,
Я должен буду, без сомненья,
Письмо Татьяны перевесть.
Она по-русски плохо знала,
Журналов наших не читала
И выражалася с трудом
На языке своем родном,
Итак, писала по-французски...
Что делать! Повторяю вновь:
Доныне дамская любовь
Не изъяснялася по-русски,
Доныне гордый наш язык
К почтовой прозе не привык.

XXXI Письмо Татьяны предо мною;
Его я свято берегу,
Читаю с тайною тоскою
И начитаться не могу.
Кто ей внушал и эту нежность,
И слов любезную небрежность?
Кто ей внушал умильный вздор,
Безумный сердца разговор,
И увлекательный и вредный?
Я не могу понять. Но вот
Неполный, слабый перевод,
С живой картины список бледный
Или разыгранный Фрейшиц
Перстами робких учениц:

XXVI Now I foresee another problem:
To save my native land's good name
I'll be obliged from French to Russian
Tatyana's letter to translate.
For she knew Russian rather badly.
She read no modish journals, sadly,
And words with ease could never come
To her in her own native tongue...
And so — in French, her heart's address...
Alas! I can't complain enough!
Till now, alas, a woman's love
In Russian never was expressed.
Our language proud still nothing knows
Of writing notes in postal prose.

XXXI Tatyana's letter lies before me:
I treasure it with all my heart,
And read with secret melancholy
And canot read its words enough.
Who first instilled in her such sweetness?
Such tender words, dear indiscreetness,
Such deeply moving foolishness,
Such mad and heartfelt openness,
Such dangerous, yet charming rapture?
I cannot comprehend. Yet here's
A partial, feeble, rendering,
A pallid print of a live picture,
A *Freischütz** sight-read, halting, poor,
By schoolgirl fingers, shy, unsure:

---

*Carl Maria von Weber's romantic opera *Der Freischütz* and various arrangements of it for piano (particularly of its celebrated overture) were all the rage in Russia.

ПИСЬМО ТАТЬЯНЫ К ОНЕГИНУ

Я к вам пишу — чего же боле?
Что я могу еще сказать?
Теперь, я знаю, в вашей воле
Меня презреньем наказать.
Но вы, к моей несчастной доле
Хоть каплю жалости храня,
Вы не оставите меня.
Сначала я молчать хотела;
Поверьте: моего стыда
Вы не узнали б никогда,
Когда б надежду я имела
Хоть редко, хоть в неделю раз
В деревне нашей видеть вас,
Чтоб только слышать ваши речи,
Вам слово молвить, и потом
Все думать, думать об одном
И день и ночь до новой встречи.
Но говорят, вы нелюдим;
В глуши, в деревне все вам скучно,
А мы... ничем мы не блестим,
Хоть вам и рады простодушно.

Зачем вы посетили нас?
В глуши забытого селенья
Я никогда не знала б вас,
Не знала б горького мученья.
Души неопытной волненья
Смирив со временем (как знать?),
По сердцу я нашла бы друга,
Была бы верная супруга
И добродетельная мать.
Другой!.. Нет, никому на свете
Не отдала бы сердца я!

TATYANA'S LETTER TO ONEGIN

I'm writing you – can I do further?
Is there a thing more need be said?
And now, I know, it's in your power
To punish me with your contempt.
But you, in seeing how I suffer,
Will keep a jot of sympathy,
And you will not abandon me.
At first I wanted to keep silent.
Believe me, of the shame that burned
Inside me you'd have never learned
Had I had hope– even most slightly,
If only even once a week,
In this poor place to take a peek
At you, to listen to you speaking,
But say one word to you, and then
To think, both day and night, of when
Oh when?–oh when we'll next be meeting.
But people say that you are shy,
That in these boondocks you're bored silly.
And we…in nothing do we shine,
Though glad to see you, rather simply.

Oh why did you come visit us?
Here in this god-forsaken village
I never would have suffered thus.
I never would have seen your visage.
In time, perhaps, I'd tame the heaving
Of my naive heart (who can tell?),
I'd find a friend fit to my nature
And would have been a good spouse, faithful,
And mother kind – for someone else
Than you! No! I'd have never rendered
My heart to anyone but you!

То в вышнем суждено совете...
То воля неба: я твоя;
Вся жизнь моя была залогом
Свиданья верного с тобой;
Я знаю, ты мне послан Богом,
До гроба ты хранитель мой...
Ты в сновиденьях мне являлся,
Незримый, ты мне был уж мил,
Твой чудный взгляд меня томил,
В душе твой голос раздавался
Давно... нет, это был не сон!
Ты чуть вошел, я вмиг узнала,
Вся обомлела, запылала
И в мыслях молвила: вот он!
Не правда ль? я тебя слыхала:
Ты говорил со мной в тиши,
Когда я бедным помогала
Или молитвой услаждала
Тоску волнуемой души?
И в это самое мгновенье
Не ты ли, милое виденье,
В прозрачной темноте мелькнул,
Приникнул тихо к изголовью?
Не ты ль, с отрадой и любовью,
Слова надежды мне шепнул?
Кто ты, мой ангел ли хранитель,
Или коварный искуситель:
Мои сомненья разреши.
Быть может, это все пустое,
Обман неопытной души!
И суждено совсем иное...
Но так и быть! Судьбу мою
Отныне я тебе вручаю,
Перед тобою слезы лью,
Твоей защиты умоляю...

Tatyana Weeping

That's in the highest court intended;
It's Heaven's will! I'm yours, I'm true!
My whole life was but preparation
For our first meeting planned by Fate.
I know that you're God's visitation,
That you will keep me to my grave.
You came to me when I was dreaming:
Unseen, you were already dear.
Your wondrous look my heart did sear,
And in my soul your voice was pealing
Long since!...No, that was not a dream!
You first walked in, and flash! I knew you!
I froze and blazed inside – all through,
And in my thoughts murmured: "It's him!"
I heard you! Isn't it the truth?
In stillness did you speak to me
When I would work to help the poor
Or with a prayer try to soothe
The grief my soul felt secretly?
And, in that flash of recognition,
Was it not you, oh dearest vision,
That slipped in through the darkness clear,
Caressed my pillow, softly moving?
Wasn't it you, with joy and loving
That whispered hope into my ear?
Who are you? Say! My guardian angel?
Or a seducing, tempting devil?
I beg of you: my doubts relieve!
Perhaps this all is empty ravings
That inexperienced souls deceive,
And something different is what's fated.
No matter what, from this day forth
I hand my fate into your keeping.
Before you all my tears I pour:
For your protection I am pleading;

Вообрази: я здесь одна,
Никто меня не понимает,
Рассудок мой изнемогает,
И молча гибнуть я должна.
Я жду тебя: единым взором
Надежды сердца оживи,
Иль сон тяжелый перерви,
Увы, заслуженным укором!

   Кончаю! Страшно перечесть...
Стыдом и страхом замираю...
Но мне порукой ваша честь,
И смело ей себя вверяю...

I'm all alone – can you not see?
In this place no one understands me.
My reason's weakened, felt but faintly,
And I must perish silently.
I wait for you: one look would serve
Restore the hope that's in my heart,
Or tear my heavy dream apart,
Alas, with a rebuke deserved!

      I'm finished! To re-read I dread.
Both shame and fear my spirit rivet.
Your honor, though, stands in my stead,
And boldly I entrust you with it.

ГЛАВА IV

La morale est dans la nature des choses.
                                    Necker.

VII Чем меньше женщину мы любим,
     Тем легче нравимся мы ей
     И тем ее вернее губим
     Средь обольстительных сетей.
     Разврат, бывало, хладнокровной
     Наукой славился любовной,
     Сам о себе везде трубя
     И наслаждаясь не любя.
     Но эта важная забава
     Достойна старых обезьян
     Хваленых дедовских времян:
     Ловласов обветшала слава
     Со славой красных каблуков
     И величавых париков.

VIII Кому не скучно лицемерить,
     Различно повторять одно,
     Стараться важно в том уверить,
     В чем все уверены давно,
     Всё те же слышать возраженья,
     Уничтожать предрассужденья,
     Которых не было и нет
     У девочки в тринадцать лет!
     Кого не утомят угрозы,
     Моленья, клятвы, мнимый страх,
     Записки на шести листах,
     Обманы, сплетни, кольца, слезы,
     Надзоры теток, матерей,
     И дружба тяжкая мужей!

CHAPTER IV

Morality is in the nature of things.
                                    Necker.

VII   The less it is we love a woman,
          With more ease we appeal to her,
          The more unerringly she's ruined,
          In our seductive nets held firm.
          Before, debauchery cold-hearted,
          As amatory art was touted;
          Its "artists"could not boast enough
          Of taking pleasure without love.
          But that amusement, puffed and storied,
          Is worthy only of old apes,
          From Grandpa's vaunted times, in capes.
          Dilapidated now's the glory
          Of those Lovelaces stuffed and rigged,
          With bright red heels and fancy wigs.

VIII   For whom's hypocrisy not boring?
          Repeating the same game and show,
          With fervor feigned belief imploring
          In what we're certain long ago!
          To hear the very same objections,
          Demolish the same preconceptions,
          Which can't be found around the world
          In the least thirteen year old girl!
          Who of false threats does not grow weary?
          Of prayers, quickly fading fears, and oaths?
          And — on six pages — "little notes"
          Lies, gossip, rings, and moments teary,
          Mom, Aunties, watching carefully,
          And husbands' heavy amity!

IX Так точно думал мой Евгений.
　　Он в первой юности своей
　　Был жертвой бурных заблуждений
　　И необузданных страстей.
　　Привычкой жизни избалован,
　　Одним на время очарован,
　　Разочарованный другим,
　　Желаньем медленно томим,
　　Томим и ветреным успехом,
　　Внимая в шуме и в тиши
　　Роптанье вечное души,
　　Зевоту подавляя смехом:
　　Вот как убил он восемь лет,
　　Утратя жизни лучший цвет.

X В красавиц он уж не влюблялся,
　　А волочился как-нибудь;
　　Откажут — мигом утешался;
　　Изменят — рад был отдохнуть.
　　Он их искал без упоенья,
　　А оставлял без сожаленья,
　　Чуть помня их любовь и злость.
　　Так точно равнодушный гость
　　На *вист* вечерний приезжает,
　　Садится; кончилась игра:
　　Он уезжает со двора,
　　Спокойно дома засыпает
　　И сам не знает поутру,
　　Куда поедет ввечеру.

IX Just such was my Yevgeny's thinking,
    He too, in the first bloom of youth,
    Once fell, was stormy errors' victim,
    Felt untamed passions, wild, uncouth.
    A little spoiled by life-long habit
    For one thing for a while enchanted,
    Soon disillusioned by what's new,
    With slow desire wearied through,
    Yet of flippant success grown weary,
    Hearing in silence and through noise
    His soul's ever-complaining voice,
    Suppressed by laughter, and yawns bleary:
    He killed off eight whole years this way,
    Wasting his life's best bloom away.

X   He fell no more in love with beauties,
    But chased them anyhow, he guessed,
    Took comfort fast on their refusing,
    When cheated on, was glad to rest.
    He'd seek them out without elation,
    Leave them, and feel no hesitation,
    No twinge of their last love and spite.
    Just so, a guest indifferent might
    Drive up, for evening whist appearing,
    Sit down, then, when the game was done,
    Ride homewards, horses at a run,
    To calm sleep drifting, disappearing,
    Himself not sure, when daylight came,
    Where he'd next ride when daylight waned.

XI Но, получив посланье Тани,
Онегин живо тронут был:
Язык девических мечтаний
В нем думы роем возмутил;
И вспомнил он Татьяны милой
И бледный цвет, и вид унылый;
И в сладостный, безгрешный сон
Душою погрузился он.
Быть может, чувствий пыл старинный
Им на минуту овладел;
Но обмануть он не хотел
Доверчивость души невинной.
Теперь мы в сад перелетим,
Где встретилась Татьяна с ним.

XII Минуты две они молчали,
Но к ней Онегин подошел
И молвил: «Вы ко мне писали,
Не отпирайтесь. Я прочел
Души доверчивой признанья,
Любви невинной излиянья;
Мне ваша искренность мила;
Она в волненье привела
Давно умолкнувшие чувства;
Но вас хвалить я не хочу;
Я за нее вам отплачу
Признаньем также без искусства;
Примите исповедь мою:
Себя на суд вам отдаю.

XI But Tanya's missive then receiving,
Onegin was quite moved within.
Her words of tender girlish dreaming
A swarm of thoughts provoked in him.
Remembering Tanya's face endearing,
Her skin so pale, her air so grieving,
In blameless dream delightedly,
He let his soul sink blissfully.
Perhaps he felt old feelings' panging,
For just a minute in him heave...
But he did not wish to deceive
Or leave an innocent soul hanging.
Now to that garden let's fly fleet
Where with Tatyana he did meet.

XII They stood in silence two whole minutes.
Then up to her Onegin went.
And softly said: "To me you've written.
Do not deny it. I have read
Your over-trusting soul's confession
Of love, its innocent profession.
Your heartfelt truth to me is dear,
You've made old feelings in me rear
Which long ago I chose to stifle.
But I don't want to praise you though.
Instead, I in exchange do owe
You just as artless an avowal.
So listen now; I give myself
For you to judge as I confess.

XIII Когда бы жизнь домашним кругом
Я ограничить захотел;
Когда б мне быть отцом, супругом
Приятный жребий повелел;
Когда б семейственной картиной
Пленился я хоть миг единый, —
То верно б кроме вас одной
Невесты не искал иной.
Скажу без блесток мадригальных:
Нашед мой прежний идеал,
Я, верно б, вас одну избрал
В подруги дней моих печальных,
Всего прекрасного в залог,
И был бы счастлив...сколько мог!

XIV Но я не создан для блаженства;
Ему чужда душа моя;
Напрасны ваши совершенства:
Их вовсе недостоин я.
Поверьте (совесть в том порукой),
Супружество нам будет мукой.
Я, сколько ни любил бы вас,
Привыкнув, разлюблю тотчас;
Начнете плакать: ваши слезы
Не тронут сердца моего,
А будут лишь бесить его.
Судите ж вы, какие розы
Нам заготовит Гименей
И, может быть, на много дней.

XIII   If, wrapped in a domestic garland,
        I'd limit my life's liberty,
        If being father, being husband,
        By pleasant Fate were granted me,
        Were I by family portraits tempted
        Just for a moment, brief and splendid,
        I doubt that I would ever choose
        Another bride on earth but you.
        I'll spare you madrigals and sparkles:
        If I sought my ideal of old,
        I'd seek to be with you alone,
        As helpmeet of my melancholy,
        My gage of all that's virtuous, good,
        And would be happy...as I could.

XIV   But not for bliss was my creation.
        No, bliss is foreign to my soul.
        In vain is your complete perfection;
        I'm quite unworthy of it all.
        Trust me (my conscience pledged in honor)
        Our marriage would become a torture.
        However much I loved you true.
        Accustomed, I'd cease loving soon.
        Then you'd start weeping; your tears, pouring,
        Would touch me no more in my heart,
        Instead would make it mad and hard.
        So think what roses Hymen's storing
        In wait for us – yourself decide –
        Perhaps for days and days gone by.

XV Что может быть на свете хуже
    Семьи, где бедная жена
    Грустит о недостойном муже
    И днем и вечером одна;
    Где скучный муж, ей цену зная
    (Судьбу, однако ж, проклиная),
    Всегда нахмурен, молчалив,
    Сердит и холодно-ревнив!
    Таков я. И того ль искали
    Вы чистой, пламенной душой,
    Когда с такою простотой,
    С таким умом ко мне писали?
    Ужели жребий вам такой
    Назначен строгою судьбой?

Natalya and Pushkin's shade

XVI Мечтам и годам нет возврата;
    Не обновлю души моей...
    Я вас люблю любовью брата
    И, может быть, еще нежней.
    Послушайте ж меня без гнева:
    Сменит не раз младая дева
    Мечтами легкие мечты;
    Так деревцо свои листы
    Меняет с каждою весною.
    Так, видно, небом суждено.
    Полюбите вы снова: но...
    Учитесь властвовать собою;
    Не всякий вас, как я, поймет;
    К беде неопытность ведет».

XV   For what on earth is sadder, really,
      Than a poor wife trapped in her home,
      For her unworthy husband grieving,
      And night and day left all alone.
      Where her dull husband knows she's worthy,
      But still, his fate regretting, cursing,
      Forever silently does brood,
      Enraged, by jealousy made cool?
      That's me. Was that whom you were seeking
      With such a pure and fiery soul,
      With such simplicity, so bold,
      When you wrote me with such deep meaning?
      How could it be you were so picked,
      Appointed to a fate so strict?

XVI   The months and years are not returning.
      My soul won't be renewed and freed.
      I love you with a brother's yearning,
      Perhaps, more tenderly, indeed.
      So listen to me without raging,
      Not merely once will a young maiden
      Replace light dreams but with light dreams.
      Just so, each greening tree its leaves
      Replaces at each springtime's coming.
      It seems that must be Heaven's will.
      You'll love again one day. But still...
      Learn self-control, act more becoming.
      Not all, like I, will understand.
      In grief the inexperienced land."

XX Гм! гм! Читатель благородный,
    Здорова ль ваша вся родня?
    Позвольте: может быть, угодно
    Теперь узнать вам от меня,
    Что значит именно *родные*.
    Родные люди вот какие:
    Мы их обязаны ласкать,
    Любить, душевно уважать
    И, по обычаю народа,
    О Рождестве их навещать
    Или по почте поздравлять,
    Чтоб остальное время года
    Не думали о нас они...
    Итак, дай Бог им долги дни!

XXI Зато любовь красавиц нежных
    Надежней дружбы и родства:
    Над нею и средь бурь мятежных
    Вы сохраняете права.
    Конечно так. Но вихорь моды,
    Но своенравие природы,
    Но мненья светского поток...
    А милый пол, как пух, легок.
    К тому ж и мнения супруга
    Для добродетельной жены
    Всегда почтенны быть должны;
    Так ваша верная подруга
    Бывает в миг увлечена:
    Любовью шутит сатана.

XX   Hmm! Hmm! Pray tell now, gentle reader.
        How do they do, your clan so dear?
        Allow me, if it's quite convenient,
        To make a little lesson clear.
        What does that mean, *our near and dear ones?*
        Our near and dear ones are just these ones:
        The ones we are obliged to kiss,
        Caress and love, and warmly miss,
        Also, by custom, in good cheer,
        On Christmas we must pay them calls,
        If not, at least must mail them cards,
        So all the rest of all the year
        They will not think of us a mite...
        And so, God grant them health, long life!

XXI   And yet the love of tender beauties
        Than friends' or family's love's more firm.
        To love, amidst life's worst storms furious
        Your right forever is confirmed.
        Of course...Yet...Trust in fashion's whirlwinds?
        And nature's whims, ever indifferent?...
        Care what the *beau monde* terms not right?...
        When the fair sex is feather-light...
        Besides, good husbands' judgments always
        For all good wives should always be
        Considered most respectfully;
        —That's your mistress ever-faithful
        Sometimes — like that — is torn away:
        For Satan likes with love to play.

XXII Кого ж любить? Кому же верить?
Кто не изменит нам один?
Кто все дела, все речи мерит
Услужливо на наш аршин?
Кто клеветы про нас не сеет?
Кто нас заботливо лелеет?
Кому порок наш не беда?
Кто не наскучит никогда?
Призрака суетный искатель,
Трудов напрасно не губя,
Любите самого себя,
Достопочтенный мой читатель!
Предмет достойный: ничего
Любезней верно нет его.

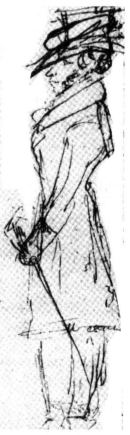

Pushkin on a stroll in Mikhailovsk

XXII Whom shall we love? And whom believe?
      Who never will betray our trust?
      Who measures all our words and deeds
      As our own yardstick measures us?
      Who never — ever — slanders us?
      Who always takes good care of us?
      Who doesn't think our flaws a sin?
      Who never bores, day out, day in?
      There's no point specters vainly seeking,
      Do not waste time in futile stress.
      Instead, just always love yourself,
      My most respected, noble reader!
      A worthwhile object, it would seem;
      There's none that's nicer, probably.

ГЛАВА V

> О, не знай сих страшных снов
> Ты, моя Светлана!
> —Жуковский

XXV Но вот багряною рукою
    Заря от утренних долин
    Выводит с солнцем за собою
    Веселый праздник именин.
    С утра дом Лариной гостями
    Весь полон; целыми семьями
    Соседи съехались в возках,
    В кибитках, в бричках и в санях.
    В передней толкотня, тревога;
    В гостиной встреча новых лиц,
    Лай мосек, чмоканье девиц,
    Шум, хохот, давка у порога,
    Поклоны, шарканье гостей,
    Кормилиц крик и плач детей.

XXVIII И вот из ближнего посада
    Созревших барышень кумир,
    Уездных матушек отрада,
    Приехал ротный командир;
    Вошел...Ах, новость, да какая!
    Музыка будет полковая!
    Полковник сам ее послал.
    Какая радость: будет бал!
    Девчонки прыгают заране;
    Но кушать подали. Четой
    Идут за стол рука с рукой.
    Теснятся барышни к Татьяне;
    Мужчины против; и, крестясь,
    Толпа жужжит, за стол садясь.

CHAPTER V

> Never know such frightful dreams,
> Oh, my dear Svetlana!
> —Zhukovsky

XXV   But stretching out with purple hands,
With sunshine gaily in its train,
The light from morning valleys spans
On Tanya's nameday holiday.
All morning to the Larin house
Guests kept arriving; family crowds,
Neighbors that came in wagon trains,
Carriages, coaches, sleds, and wains,
In the foyer, they push and jostle,
The guest hall with new faces fills,
The bark of lapdogs, kiss of girls,
Noise, laughter, crush and crowded bustle
The bows, foot-scraping of the guests,
The cries of children, nursemaids' yells.

XXVIII   But from his quarters not too far off
The older girls' joy, idol, pride,
The joy of all the district's mamas,
The troop commander has arrived,
Brings news that's absolutely super!
The regiment will give us music!
The colonel sent the band himself.
Oh what a joy! A ball is set!
With joy the girls all quiver, bouncing,
But dinner's served, and all in pairs
Go hand in hand, sit in their chairs,
Around Tatyana girlfriends crowding,
Across from them, the men. Then crossing
Themselves, the crowd sits, buzzing.

XXIX На миг умолкли разговоры;
Уста жуют. Со всех сторон
Гремят тарелки и приборы
Да рюмок раздается звон.
Но вскоре гости понемногу
Подъемлют общую тревогу.
Никто не слушает, кричат,
Смеются, спорят и пищат.
Вдруг двери настежь. Ленский входит,
И с ним Онегин. «Ах, творец! —
Кричит хозяйка: — наконец!»
Теснятся гости, всяк отводит
Приборы, стулья поскорей;
Зовут, сажают двух друзей.

XXX Сажают прямо против Тани,
И, утренней луны бледней,
И трепетней гонимой лани,
Она теменеющих очей
Не подымает: пышет бурно
В ней страстный жар; ей душно, дурно:
Она приветствий двух друзей
Не слышит, слезы из очей
Хотят уж капать; уж готова
Бедняжка в обморок упасть;
Но воля и рассудка власть
Превозмогли. Она два слова
Скозь зубы молвила тишком
И усидела за столом.

XXIX   All conversation's ceased one instant,
As mouths do chew. And all around
The plates and cutlery are whirring
We hear the glasses clink, resound,
But bit by bit the guests bestir,
Begin to make themselves be heard,
Yet no one listens, all just shout,
And laugh and argue, squeak and pout.
The doors swing open suddenly;
Onegin follows Lensky in.
The hostess cries: "Lord! Where've you been?"
The guests crowd in more, hurriedly,
The plates and chairs are moved aside
To seat the two friends side by side.

XXX   They're seated right across from Tanya,
Who, paler than the morning moon,
More shaky than a hunted fawn
With darkened eyes as if to swoon
Cast down, in stormy passion seething,
Sits feverishly, has trouble breathing,
And cannot hear her two friends' greeting;
Out of her eyes tears could come streaming,
And now she seems about to faint,
But by sheer will she holds back tears,
And forces herself to stay here,
Her feelings checked by mind's constraint,
She murmurs two words through her teeth,
And somehow kept still in her seat.

XXXI Траги-нервических явлений,
Девичьих обмороков, слез
Давно терпеть не мог Евгений:
Довольно их он перенес.
Чудак, попав на пир огромный,
Уж был сердит. Но, девы томной
Заметя трепетный порыв,
С досады взоры опустив,
Надулся он и, негодуя,
Поклялся Ленского взбесить
И уж порядком отомстить.
Теперь, заране торжествуя,
Он стал чертить в душе своей
Карикатуры всех гостей.

XXXII Конечно, не один Евгений
Смятенье Тани видеть мог;
Но целью взоров и суждений
В то время жирный был пирог
(К несчастию, пересоленный)
Да вот в бутылке засмоленной,
Между жарким и бланманже,
Цимлянское несут уже;
За ним строй рюмок узких, длинных,
Подобно талии твоей,
Зизи, кристалл души моей,
Предмет стихов моих невинных,
Любви приманчивый фиал,
Ты, от кого я пьян бывал!

XXXI All types of tragic nervous scenes
      Or maidens' fainting spells, and tears,
      Had long been shunned by our Eugene–
      He'd seen enough, over the years!
      A misfit, dragged to this great party,
      In cranky mood, and yet remarking
      This young maid's pining, trembling state,
      Annoyed, he tried to look away,
      And fumed at awkward circumstance,
      Vowed he'd embarass Lensky back,
      And really be avenged at last.
      And now, victorious in advance,
      He started drawing in his head
      Caricatures of all the guests.

XXXII Eugene was not the sole one there
      That for poor Tanya's plight had eyes,
      Yet all attention, thoughts, and stares
      Just then were fixed on a fat pie
      (Unfortunately, over-salted),
      But then the bottle got uncorked
      Between the roast and blanc-mangé,
      Then they brought in the cheap champagne,
      And row on row of long thin glasses
      Whose waists were delicate as yours,
      Zizi, you crystal of my soul,
      Sweet object of slight verse in passing,
      Enticing vial of pure love,
      Whose very being made me drunk!

XXXIV Пошли приветы, поздравленья;
Татьяна всех благодарит.
Когда же дело до Евгенья
Дошло, то девы томный вид,
Ее смущение, усталость
В его душе родили жалость:
Он молча поклонился ей,
Но как-то взор его очей
Был чудно нежен. Оттого ли,
Что он и вправду тронут был,
Иль он, кокетствуя, шалил,
Невольно ль, иль из доброй воли,
Но взор сей нежность изъявил:
Он сердце Тани оживил.

XLI Однообразный и безумный,
Как вихорь жизни молодой,
Кружится вальса вихорь шумный;
Чета мелькает за четой.
К минуте мщенья приближаясь,
Онегин, втайне усмехаясь,
Подходит к Ольге. Быстро с ней
Вертится около гостей,
Потом на стул ее сажает,
Заводит речь о том, о сем;
Спустя минуты две потом
Вновь с нею вальс он продолжает;
Все в изумленье. Ленский сам
Не верит собственным глазам.

XXXIV   Congratulations, nameday greetings…
Tatyana thanked all one by one,
When it was Eugene's turn for speaking
He saw her langourous and wan,
Worn out, embarassed looks of grieving,
And in his heart they stirred up pity:
He only bowed as she went by,
And yet the soft look in his eyes
Was wondrous-tender…Was it because
Indeed his heart was truly touched,
Or did he just flirt over-much?
Unconsciously, or with good heart?
Still, tenderness his eyes implied
To see them Tanya's heart revived.

XLI   Unvarying, yet wild and crazy,
Like to the whirlwind of young life,
The waltzes' noisy whirl keeps racing,
And pairs keep flitting, flashing by.
His moment of revenge approaching,
Onegin, hiding inner gloating,
Goes up to Olga in a whir,
Spins round the other guests with her,
Then sits her down in manner charming,
Begins to talk of this and that,
And after two minutes of chat,
Again begins more frenzied waltzing.
All are amazed; though Lensky tries,
He can't believe his very eyes.

XLIV Буянов, братец мой задорный,
К герою нашему подвел
Татьяну с Ольгою; проворно
Онегин с Ольгою пошел;
Ведет ее, скользя небрежно,
И, наклонясь, ей шепчет нежно
Какой-то пошлый мадригал,
И руку жмет — и запылал
В ее лице самолюбивом
Румянец ярче. Ленский мой
Все видел: вспыхнул, сам не свой;
В негодовании ревнивом
Поэт конца мазурки ждет
И в котильон ее зовет.

XLV Но ей нельзя. Нельзя? Но что же?
Да Ольга слово уж дала
Онегину. О Боже, Боже!
Что слышит он? Она могла...
Возможно ль? Чуть лишь из пеленок,
Кокетка, ветреный ребенок!
Уж хитрость ведает она,
Уж изменять научена!
Не в силах Ленский снесть удара;
Проказы женские кляня,
Выходит, требует коня
И скачет. Пистолетов пара,
Две пули — больше ничего —
Вдруг разрешат судьбу его.

XLIV   Buyanov, my too-fervent brother,
        Presented to our hero then
        Both sisters, Olga and Tatyana:
        Onegin nimbly grasped the hand
        Of Olga, led her, gliding, easy,
        Bending, cooing, whispering teasing
        Tenderness or trite sentiment,
        And pressed her hand– and then she went
        Red in the face from boastful blushing,
        As her cheeks reddened, Lensky watched,
        And saw it all, and raged in shock;
        In jealous indignation, rushing,
        The poet frets till dance's end,
        Calls her for the cotillion then.

XLV.   But no, she can't. She can't? Why not?
        Olga already gave her word
        To our Eugene. Oh God! Oh God!
        Could it be true what he's just heard?
        From baby clothes but barely slippingá
        She's now a flirting, fickle vixen!
        Already she is cunning, sly,
        Already she can cheat and lie!
        Lensky cannot abide it, bristlesá
        And curses women's cruel caprices,
        Storms out, demands his horse, and leaves,
        And rides off. Now a pair of pistols —
        Two bullets — no more's left to state —
        Will suddenly decide his fate.

ГЛАВА VI

Là sotto i giorni nubilosi e brevi,
Nasce una gente a cui l'morir non dole.

Petrarca

XIX Весь вечер Ленский был рассеян,
То молчалив, то весел вновь;
Но тот, кто музою взлелеян,
Всегда таков: нахмуря бровь,
Садился он за клавикорды
И брал на них одни аккорды,
То, к Ольге взоры устремив,
Шептал: не правда ль? я счастлив.
Но поздно; время ехать. Сжалось
В нем сердце, полное тоской;
Прощаясь с девой молодой,
Оно как будто разрывалось.
Она глядит ему в лицо.
«Что с вами?» — «Так». — И на крыльцо.

XX Домой приехав, пистолеты
Он осмотрел, потом вложил
Опять их в ящик и, раздетый,
При свечке, Шиллера открыл;
Но мысль одна его объемлет;
В нем сердце грустное не дремлет:
С неизъяснимою красой
Он видит Ольгу пред собой.
Владимир книгу закрывает,
Берет перо; его стихи,
Полны любовной чепухи,
Звучат и льются. Их читает
Он вслух, в лирическом жару,
Как Дельвиг пьяный на пиру.

The poet Schiller

CHAPTER VI

There, where the winter days are brief and cloudy,
People are born who feel no pain in dying.
Petrarch

XIX All evening Lensky was distracted.
At times he'd hush, then joke again.
But one on whom the Muse has acted
Is ever thus. Brows knit in pain,
He sat down to the clavichords,
But kept on playing only chords.
Then whispered stares at Olga, asking;
"In truth, am I not really happy?"
Tis late, though, time to ride off. Aching,
His heart, expanded, full of grief,
Took final leave of his maid sweet.
He seemed to feel it tearing, breaking.
Her eyes straight into his eyes bored:
"What's wrong?" -- "Nothing." And out the door.

XX Once home, he got his pistols ready,
And looked them over, placed them back
Into their box, finished undressing,
Read Schiller's verse by candlelight,
And yet one thought alone consumed him.
No slumber came to his heart gloomy.
With beauty words could not explain,
The face of Olga did not wane
From shining full before him. Closing
His book, he grasped his pen. His verse,
Full of love's nonsense, silly words,
Poured forth, and sang out, while he, glowing,
Read them aloud, in lyric trance,
Like Delvig, drunken at a dance.

XXI Стихи на случай сохранились;
     Я их имею; вот они:
     «Куда, куда вы удалились,
     Весны моей златые дни?
     Что день грядущий мне готовит?
     Его мой взор напрасно ловит,
     В глубокой мгле таится он.
     Нет нужды; прав судьбы закон.
     Паду ли я, стрелой пронзенный,
     Иль мимо пролетит она,
     Всё благо: бдения и сна
     Приходит час определенный;
     Благословен и день забот,
     Благословен и тьмы приход!

XXII Блеснет заутра луч денницы,
     И заиграет яркий день;
     А я, быть может, я гробницы
     Сойду в таинственную сень,
     И память юного поэта
     Поглотит медленная Лета,
     Забудет мир меня; но ты
     Придешь ли, дева красоты,
     Слезу пролить над ранней урной
     И думать: он меня любил,
     Он мне единой посвятил
     Рассвет печальный жизни бурной!..
     Сердечный друг, желанный друг,
     Приди, приди: я твой супруг!..»

XXI   By chance his poem's in my keeping
       Right here. I've kept it — lucky thing:
       "Where, where've you gone off, flying, fleeting,
       My golden, happy days of spring?"
       What has the next day fixed to send me?
       I look in vain for answers ready.
       The secret lurks in night's deep murk.
       No matter — let just Fate's law work.
       Whether I fall, shot by a bullet,
       Or whether it sweeps whistling past,
       God bless: of wakefulness and sleep
       That hour always comes appointed.
       Blessed be both cares of sunny day
       And night that takes the light away!

XXII   Soon dawn's sweet rays will come up sparkling,
       And bright the light of day will play.
       Soon I perhaps within the coffin's
       Mysterious vestibule will lay.
       And a young poet's memory
       Will sink to Lethe gradually.
       The world will quite forget my shade.
       But will you come here, lovely maiden,
       To shed a tear o'er my urn early,
       And think: "he loved me once, kept faith,
       To me alone did dedicate
       His life's brief dawn, sad hurly-burly,
       Oh heart's own friend, oh dreamed-of friend!
       Come, come to me! I'm your spouse to the end!"

XXIII Так он писал *темно и вяло*
(Что романтизмом мы зовем,
Хоть романтизма тут нимало
Не вижу я; да что нам в том?)
И наконец перед зарею,
Склонясь усталой головою,
На модном слове *идеал*
Тихонько Ленский задремал;
Но только сонным обаяньем
Он позабылся, уж сосед
В безмолвный входит кабинет
И будит Ленского воззваньем:
«Пора вставать: седьмой уж час.
Онегин верно ждет уж нас».

XXIV   Но ошибался он: Евгений
Спал в это время мертвым сном.
Уже редеют ночи тени
И встречен Веспер петухом;
Онегин спит себе глубоко.
Уж солнце катится высоко,
И перелетная метель
Блестит и вьется; но постель
Еще Евгений не покинул,
Еще над ним летает сон.
Вот наконец проснулся он
И полы завеса раздвинул;
Глядит — и видит, что пора
Давно уж ехать со двора.

XXIII   And on he scribbled: "darkly", "fading"
         (Romanticism that is called —
         Though what's romantic in this vaguely? —
         Not that we care too much at all).
         And finally just at the dawning,
         He let his tired head slip, and yawning,
         Over "ideal", word *à la mode*,
         Quietly Lensky, nodded, dozed,
         But just as charming sleep embraced him,
         Immediately his neighbor entered
         His room, saw him in slumber rendered,
         And woke up Lensky with words bracing:
         "Seven o'clock! Get up! Enough!
         No doubt Onegin waits for us!"

XXIV   But he was wrong. Just then, Yevgeny
         Slept like a dead man, without qualm,
         With shades of night already thinning,
         The cock roused morning star from calm.
         Onegin slept on, by and by,
         The sun's already climbed up high,
         Snow flurries having swirled and swept,
         Snow sparkling, winding round, and yet
         Yevgeny's still in bed, a-slumbering,
         Fast sleep still hovers over him.
         And finally he stirred within
         His room, opened his curtains broadly,
         Looks out, and sees he's rather late.
         It's time to race out from his gate.

XXV Он поскорей звонит. Вбегает
К нему слуга француз Гильо,
Халат и туфли предлагает
И подает ему белье.
Спешит Онегин одеваться,
Слуге велит приготовляться
С ним вместе ехать и с собой
Взять также ящик боевой.
Готовы санки беговые.
Он сел, на мельницу летит.
Примчались. Он слуге велит
Лепажа стволы роковые
Нести за ним, а лошадям
Отъехать в поле к двум дубкам.

XXVI Опершись на плотину, Ленский
Давно нетерпеливо ждал;
Меж тем, механик деревенский,
Зарецкий жернов осуждал.
Идет Онегин с извиненьем.
«Но где же, -- молвил с изумленьем
Зарецкий, -- где ваш секундант?»
В дуэлях классик и педант,
Любил методу он из чувства,
И человека растянуть
Он позволял -- не как-нибудь,
Но в строгих правилах искусства,
По всем преданьям старины
(Что похвалить мы в нем должны).

XXV He quickly rings. Rushing in briskly,
     Monsieur Guillot, his servant comes,
     Gives him his bathrobe, socks, and slippers,
     And also brings his pants and trunks.
     Onegin hurries up in dressing,
     Orders his servant to get ready
     To ride as well and also bring
     His duelling-box along with him.
     The racing-sleighs have since been readied.
     He gets on, to the mill raced off.
     Arrived. Tells his valet, straight off,
     To bear Lepage's* barrels deadly
     And follow him, then towards two oaks
     Through fields to lead the horses, yoked.

XXVI Upon the dam's rim, losing patience,
     Lensky just waited, stamped his foot.
     The while, discussing mills and grainage,
     Zaretsky, the mechanic, stood.
     Onegin comes and gives excuses.
     "But where" – Zaretsky almost loses
     His temper – "is your second?"
     In duels, for classic rules a pedant,
     He loved method with all his heart.
     And wouldn't let someone get killed
     Just any sort of way you will,
     But by the strictest rules of art
     As practiced once in olden days
     (For which we ought to give him praise).

---

* Jean Le Page was a famous Parisian gunsmith. Pushkin used a Lepage in his own fatal duel with Georges D'Anthès.

XXVII «Мой секундант? — сказал Евгений, —
Вот он: мой друг, monsieur Guillot.
Я не предвижу возражений
На представление мое:
Хоть человек он неизвестный,
Но уж конечно малый честный».
Зарецкий губу закусил.
Онегин Ленского спросил:
«Что ж, начинать?» — «Начнем, пожалуй» —
Сказал Владимир. И пошли
За мельницу. Пока вдали
Зарецкий наш и честный малый
Вступили в важный договор,
Враги стоят, потупя взор.

Lensky

XXVIII Враги! Давно ли друг от друга
Их жажда крови отвела?
Давно ль они часы досуга,
Трапезу, мысли и дела
Делили дружно? Ныне злобно,
Врагам наследственным подобно,
Как в страшном, непонятном сне,
Они друг другу в тишине
Готовят гибель хладнокровно...
Не засмеяться ль им, пока
Не обагрилась их рука,
Не разойтиться ль полюбовно?..
Но дико светская вражда
Боится ложного стыда.

Onegin

XXVII   Yevgeny answered then: "My second?
        He's here. My friend, Monsieur Guillot.
        I can't imagine much objection
        To this idea of mine, you know.
        Though he's unknown, I'll say in earnest.
        At least, of course, he's somewhat honest."
        Zaretsky bit his lip and gasped.
        Onegin turned to Lensky, asked:
        "Well, should we start?" "Perhaps, why not?"
        Vladimir said, and they were gone
        Beyond the mill, while further on
        Zaretsky and the "honest, somewhat"
        Engaged in pacts upon the snows.
        With lowered eyes, there stood the foes.

XXVIII Foes! How long since from each other
        This thirst for blood drove them apart?
        Has it been long since they like brothers
        Shared common meals, thoughts, cares, and heart?
        And now look at them! Cold and crude,
        Like enemies from an ancient feud,
        In stillness staring, how they seem,
        As if in strange and jumbled dream,
        In cold blood plan each other's doom...
        Could they not smile and show restraint
        Before with blood their hands got stained?
        Why not part friends, make up for good?
        But cruel society's to blame.
        It fears admitting to false shame.

XXIX Вот пистолеты уж блеснули.
Гремит о шомпол молоток.
В граненый ствол уходят пули,
И щелкнул в первый раз курок.
Вот порох струйкой сероватой
На полку сыплется. Зубчатый,
Надежно ввинченный кремень
Взведен еще. За ближний пень
Становится Гильо смущенный.
Плащи бросают два врага.
Зарецкий тридцать два шага
Отмерил с точностью отменной,
Друзей развел по крайний след,
И каждый взял свой пистолет.

XXX «Теперь сходитесь».
                Хладнокровно,
Еще не целя, два врага
Походкой твердой , тихо, ровно
Четыре перешли шага,
Четыре смертные ступени.
Свой пистолет тогда Евгений,
Не преставая наступать,
Стал первый тихо подымать.
Вот пять шагов еще ступили,
И Ленский, жмуря левый глаз,
Стал также целить — но как раз
Онегин выстрелил... Пробили
Часы урочные: поэт
Роняет молча пистолет,

XXIX The pistols are drawn out, shine glowing,
The mallet clangs against the rod,
Through barrels' facets bullets go in,
The first clicks sound from the guns' cock.
Into the pan in streamlets greyish,
The powder's poured, and without flourish,
The jagged-edged-flint's fast secured.
Not far away, by a stump moored,
Guillot looks on and waits, and fidgets.
The enemies cast down their cloaks.
Counting thirty-two steps by rote,
Zaretsky marked and measured, rigorous,
Brought over, to each bound, each friend,
And each one raised his pistol then.

XXX "Now take your paces."
                         Still not aiming,
Cold-bloodedly, with steady walk,
The enemies are hushed, are pacing,
And each one then four steps did stalk,
Four fatal fateful steps – and ready.
Lifting his pistol first, and steady,
Yevgeny, still relentlessly,
Advanced five steps more silently,
And held his gun up with a glower,
And Lensky, squinting his right eye,
Began to aim – just at the time
Onegin fired...Struck has the hour!
The time appointed him has run:
The poet, silenced, drops his gun,

XXXI На грудь кладет тихонько руку
И падает. Туманный взор
Изображает смерть, не муку.
Так медленно по скату гор,
На солнце искрами блистая,
Спадает глыба снеговая.
Мгновенным холодом облит,
Онегин к юноше спешит,
Глядит, зовет его... напрасно:
Его уж нет. Младой певец
Нашел безвременный конец!
Дохнула буря, цвет прекрасный
Увял на утренней заре,
Потух огонь на алтаре!..

XXXII Недвижим он лежал, и странен
Был томный мир его чела.
Под грудь он был навылет ранен;
Дымясь из раны кровь текла.
Тому назад одно мгновенье
В сем сердце билось вдохновенье,
Вражда, надежда и любовь,
Играла жизнь, кипела кровь,--
Теперь, как в доме опустелом,
Все в нем и тихо и темно;
Замолкло навсегда оно.
Закрыты ставни, окна мелом
Забелены. Хозяйки нет.
А где, Бог весть. Пропал и след.

XXXI His arm placed gently on his breast,
He falls down. And his misty look
Expresses no more pain, but death.
So, from a snowy, hilly nook,
Down slopes where sunshine, sparkling shines,
A lump of snow falls, slow, sometimes.
As if flooded by sudden cold,
Onegin runs to his friend old,
Looks, calls the youngster, but in vain.
He's gone. His youthful poet friend
Has met with an untimely end.
The storm's blown out, sweet color's waned,
Snuffed is the altar at its dawn;
The flame that burned there once is gone!

XXXII He moved not anymore, and strange
The languid look on his brow seemed.
His breast shot through at point-blank range,
As from his wound blood poured and steamed.
Past just one moment's expiration,
Where once this heart held inspiration,
Where hate, and hope, and love did grow,
And life did play, and hot blood flow,
Now, as if in a house abandoned,
What was in there's now stilled and dark.
Forever vanished is the spark,
The windows chalked, the shutters fastened.
The mistress of the house has left.
For where, God knows. No clue. Bereft.

XXXIII Приятно дерзкой эпиграммой
Взбесить оплошного врага;
Приятно зреть, как он, упрямо
Склонив бодливые рога,
Невольно в зеркало глядится
И узнавать себя стыдится;
Приятней, если он, друзья,
Завоет сдуру: это я!
Еще приятнее в молчанье
Ему готовить честный гроб
И тихо целить в бледный лоб
На благородном расстоянье;
Но отослать его к отцам
Едва ль приятно будет вам.

XXXIV Что ж, если вашим пистолетом
Сражен приятель молодой,
Нескромным взглядом, иль ответом,
Или безделицей иной
Вас оскорбивший за бутылкой,
Иль даже сам в досаде пылкой
Вас гордо вызвавший на бой,
Скажите: вашею душой
Какое чувство овладеет,
Когда недвижим, на земле
Пред вами, с смертью на челе,
Он постепенно костенеет,
Когда он глух и молчалив
На ваш отчаянный призыв?

XXXIII With biting epigrams it's pleasant
To dare and tempt a downcast foe;
It's nice to see, how he, face reddened,
Horns bent down, stubborn, full of woe,
Looks in his mirror by constraint,
And by his own face is ashamed.
Better yet, friends, if then he'll cry
And howl with folly: "Oh! T'is I!"
It's even better still, in silence,
Preparing him an honest grave,
Gun calmly at his forehead aimed,
While keeping a respectful distance.
But once he's lying in a pall
You'll hardly find it fun at all.

XXXIV What if, by virtue of your pistol,
Your young acquaintance gets cut down
For glance immodest, answer silly,
Repeating nonsense, anyhow,
Offending you over a bottle,
Even if he, quarrelsome and idle,
Himself sends you a glove and bow,
Say, in your soul, at this point now,
What feeling would begin to quicken,
When motionless, and on the ground
Before you, death stamped on his brow,
He'd gradually start to stiffen,
When he'd go deaf, and no more stirred,
When, desperate, your cry's not heard?

XXXV В тоске сердечных угрызений,
Рукою стиснув пистолет,
Глядит на Ленского Евгений.
«Ну, что ж? убит», — решил сосед.
Убит!.. Сим страшным восклицаньем
Сражен, Онегин с содроганьем
Отходит и людей зовет.
Зарецкий бережно кладет
На сани труп оледенелый;
Домой везет он страшный клад.
Почуя мертвого, храпят
И бьются кони, пеной белой
Стальные мочат удила,
И полетели, как стрела.

XXXVI Друзья мои, вам жаль поэта:
Во цвете радостных надежд,
Их не свершив еще для света,
Чуть из младенческих одежд,
Увял! Где жаркое волненье,
Где благородное стремленье
И чувств и мыслей молодых,
Высоких, нежных, удалых?
Где бурные любви желанья,
И жажда знаний и труда,
И страх порока и стыда,
И вы, заветные мечтанья,
Вы, призрак жизни неземной,
Вы, сны поэзии святой!

XXXV Reproachful, grieving, his heart aching,
Clutching the pistol in his hand,
Looking at Lensky stood Yevgeny.
"Oh, well, killed," Zaretsky deadpanned.
Killed! To hear this dread word uttered,
Onegin, shocked, inwardly shuddered,
Stepped back and called the others there.
Upon the sled then, full of care,
Zaretsky lays the corpse, now frozen,
Brings home the frightful load to rest.
Somehow it seems the horses sense
A dead man, and they snort, mouths foaming,
And dribbling on their bits of steel,
Like arrows shot, they fly and reel.

XXXVI My friends, you're for the poet grieving:
His flowering and happy hopes
For this world still so uncompleted,
Still barely out of baby clothes,
Are gone! Where now, hot agitation?
Where now's his noble aspiration,
Feelings and thoughts of youth sublime,
Lofty and tender, brave and kind?
Where vanished, love's desire tempestuous,
And lust for knowledge and for work,
And fear of vice, shame, sin, and murk?
Where now, dear dreams impetuous,
Where, ghost from earthly life set free?
Where, dreams of holy poetry?

XXXVII

    Быть может, он для блага мира
Иль хоть для славы был рожден;
Его умолкнувшая лира
Гремучий, непрерывный звон
В веках поднять могла. Поэта,
Быть может, на ступенях света
Ждала высокая ступень.
Его страдальческая тень,
Быть может, унесла с собою
Святую тайну, и для нас
Погиб животворящий глас,
И за могильною чертою
К ней не домчится гимн времен,
Благословение племен.

XXXVIII. XXXIX

    А может быть и то: поэта
Обыкновенный ждал удел.
Прошли бы юношества лета:
В нем пыл души бы охладел.
Во многом он бы изменился,
Расстался б с музами, женился,
В деревне счастлив и рогат
Носил бы стеганый халат;
Узнал бы жизнь на самом деле,
Подагру в сорок лет имел,
Пил, ел, скучал, толстел, хирел,
И наконец в своей постеле
Скончался б посреди детей,
Плаксивых баб и лекарей.

XXXVII

 Perhaps he had been born for glory,
To bring great blessings to the world.
Perhaps a grand, resounding story,
His lyre, now silent, wrapped up, furled,
Would have passed down. Perhaps the poet,
Though he himself would never know it,
Would climb high this world's ladder great.
Perhaps his martyred, suffering shade
Removed from us, in disappearing,
A sacred secret, full of joys,
A lively and life-giving voice,
And he's beyond the grave, not hearing
The reach of hymns of later days,
Of peoples' blessings, tears, and praise.

XXXVIII. XXXIX

Or else our bard awaited, likely,
A fate more ordinary still.
The years of youth would pass by lightly,
The passion in his soul would chill.
He would be changed in much that mattered,
Abandoning the Muse, get married,
A cuckold, happy, out of town,
Wearing a quilted dressing gown,
Would learn what real life's made of yet:
Have gout at forty, bored, would dither,
Would drink, eat, get too fat, then wither,
And finally, in his own bed,
He'd die, amidst his kids in ranks,
And weepy women's wails, and quacks.

XL Но что бы ни было, читатель,
Увы, любовник молодой,
Поэт, задумчивый мечтатель,
Убит приятельской рукой!
Есть место; влево от селенья,
Где жил питомец вдохновенья,
Две сосны корнями срослись;
Под ними струйки извились
Ручья соседственной долины.
Там пахарь любит отдыхать,
И жницы в волны погружать
Приходят звонкие кувшины;
Там у ручья в тени густой
Поставлен памятник простой.

XL Whatever might have been, dear reader,
    This young lover, alas, it's sad,
    This poet, thoughtful, pensive dreamer,
    Was killed, and by his friend's own hand!
    Left of his village, there's a spot,
    Where this inspired son's not forgot.
    Two pines right there their roots entwine.
    Beneath them rushing waters wind,
    Weaving the brooks of neighboring valleys.
    There plowmen often like to rest
    And reaping-maids to white waves' crest
    Come, dip their clinking pitchers, dally.
    There, by the brook, beneath thick shade,
    A simple monument's been made.

ГЛАВА СЕДЬМАЯ

...

Гоненье на Москву! что значит видеть свет!
Где ж лучше?
              Где нас нет.
                           Грибоедов

XXXIII Когда благому просвещенью
Отдвинем более границ,
Современем (по расчисленью
Философических таблиц,
Лет чрез пятьсот) дороги, верно,
У нас изменятся безмерно:
Шоссе Россию здесь и тут,
Соединив, пересекут.
Мосты чугунные чрез воды
Шагнут широкою дугой,
Раздвинем горы, под водой
Пророем дерзостные своды,
И заведет крещеный мир
На каждой станции трактир.

XXXIV Теперь у нас дороги плохи,
Мосты забытые гниют,
На станциях клопы да блохи
Заснуть минуты не дают;
Трактиров нет. В избе холодной
Высокопарный, но голодный
Для виду прейскурант висит
И тщетный дразнит аппетит,
Меж тем как сельские циклопы
Перед медлительным огнем
Российским лечат молотком
Изделье легкое Европы,
Благословляя колеи
И рвы отеческой земли.

CHAPTER SEVEN

...

You've toured the world – so Moscow earns your scorn!
What place is better?
                There from whence we've gone.
                      —Griboyedov

XXXIII   When to enlightenment our nation
         Begins its mighty bounds to pass,
         In time (by my own calculation
         Of *philosophic tabulae*,
         Five hundred years from now), then roadways
         Will likely be transformed for always:
         Broad highways will cross Russia's space:
         United, to and fro, we'll race.
         We'll bridge great spans with steel and copper,
         Casting a broad and mighty arc.
         And we'll move mountains, tunnels dark
         We'll dig with daring underwater.
         And Christendom will then set up
         At every station-house a pub.

XXXIV   But still – for now –our roads are awful:
         Forgotten bridges rot for years.
         At station-houses bedbugs woeful
         And fleas deny one minute's sleep.
         There are no pubs. In cold huts tawdry,
         With snobby airs, though very hungry,
         A menu's put up just for show,
         To tease one's vainly happy hope,
         As all the while some peasant Cyclop,
         Above a fire's sullen glimmer,
         Is fixing with a Russian hammer
         The light and graceful wheel of Europe,
         Blessing the potholes, muck, ruts, sand,
         And ditches of our Fatherland.

XXXV Зато зимы порой холодной
Езда приятна и легка.
Как стих без мысли в песне модной,
Дорога зимняя гладка.
Автомедоны наши бойки,
Неутомимы наши тройки,
И версты, теша праздный взор,
В глазах мелькают, как забор.
К несчастью, Ларина тащилась,
Боясь прогонов дорогих,
Не на почтовых, на своих,
И наша дева насладилась
Дорожной скукою вполне:
Семь суток ехали оне.

XXXVI Но вот уж близко. Перед ними
Уж белокаменной Москвы,
Как жар, крестами золотыми
Горят старинные главы.
Ах, братцы! как я был доволен,
Когда церквей и колоколен,
Садов, чертогов полукруг
Открылся предо мною вдруг!
Как часто в горестной разлуке,
В моей блуждающей судьбе,
Москва, я думал о тебе!
Москва... как много в этом звуке
Для сердца русского слилось!
Как много в нем отозвалось!

XXXV But still, at least, in winter chilly,
 Then travelling is smooth and light.
 Thoughtless as verse in hit song silly,
 You glide on winter roads in flight.
 Our happy charioteers heroic
 Race indefatigable troiki,
 The milestones, idly gazed at, charm,
 Flash by our eyes like fence's bars.
 But Mrs. Larin was employing
 — Fearing the bills that speed incurs —
 Alas! — not post-horses, but hers!
 And so our maiden's stuck enjoying
 The endless long dull road's delights:
 They rode for seven days and nights.

XXXVI But now they're near. Before them, glistening,
 Already white-stoned Moscow runs,
 Like fire, with golden crosses quivering,
 Its ancient domes gleam in the sun.
 Oh brothers! How my heart was happy
 To see the churches, bell-towers clanging,
 The gardens', courtyards', crescents' sweep,
 Before me opened suddenly!
 How often in my exile, grieving,
 Throughout my errant odyssey,
 Have I thought, Moscow, but of thee!
 Moscow! How Russian hearts are heaving
 At all that merges in that sound!
 How much in us it makes resound!

XXXVII

Вот, окружен своей дубравой,
Петровский замок. Мрачно он
Недавнею гордится славой.
Напрасно ждал Наполеон,
Последним счастьем упоенный,
Москвы коленопреклоненной
С ключами старого Кремля:
Нет, не пошла Москва моя
К нему с повинной головою.
Не праздник, не приемный дар,
Она готовила пожар
Нетерпеливому герою.
Отселе, в думу погружен,
Глядел на грозный пламень он.

XXXVIII

Прощай, свидетель падшей славы,
Петровский замок. Ну! не стой,
Пошел! Уже столпы заставы
Белеют; вот уж по Тверской
Возок несется чрез ухабы.
Мелькают мимо будки, бабы,
Мальчишки, лавки, фонари,
Дворцы, сады, монастыри,
Бухарцы, сани, огороды,
Купцы, лачужки, мужики,
Бульвары, башни, казаки,
Аптеки, магазины моды,
Балконы, львы на воротах
И стаи галок на крестах.

XXXVII

Here, by a wooded grove surrounded,
Petrovsky Castle glory claims.
With gloom its proud captor confounded,
Napoleon here did wait in vain,
With last success drunk to the lees,
For Moscow grovelling on her knees,
From Kremlin keys wrapped in a bow,
But no, my Moscow wouldn't go
To him, head bent submissively.
No feasts, no welcome gifts arrived.
Instead, it set a blaze sky-high;
The hero watched impatiently.
From here, wrapped in ambition dread.
He watched the terrible flame spread.

XXXVIII

Farewell, witness of fallen glory,
Petrovsky Castle! Well? Don't stop!
Let's go! Look how the gateposts storied
Gleam white! On down Tverskaya they trot,
Their sleigh-coach through the potholes drags,
Flashes past sentry-boxes, hags,
Street urchins, shops, street-lamps with sparks,
And monasteries, grand halls, parks,
Bukharans, sleds, neat garden plots,
Merchants, sad hovels, peasants cassocked,
Great boulevards and towers – and Cossacks,
And pharmacies, and fashion shops,
Porched gates, which lions guard with claws,
And crosses crowned with flocks of daws.*

---

*This line was deemed impious by the censor, and forbidden for decades.

LI   Ее привозят и в Собранье.
     Там теснота, волненье, жар,
     Музыки грохот, свеч блистанье,
     Мельканье, вихорь быстрых пар,
     Красавиц легкие уборы,
     Людьми пестреющие хоры,
     Невест обширный полукруг,
     Всё чувства поражает вдруг.
     Здесь кажут франты записные
     Свое нахальство, свой жилет
     И невнимательный лорнет.
     Сюда гусары отпускные
     Спешат явиться, прогреметь,
     Блеснуть, пленить и улететь.

LII У ночи много звезд прелестных,
     Красавиц много на Москве.
     Но ярче всех подруг небесных
     Луна в воздушной синеве.
     Но та, которую не смею
     Тревожить лирою моею,
     Как величавая луна,
     Средь жен и дев блестит одна.
     С какою гордостью небесной
     Земли касается она!
     Как негой грудь ее полна!
     Как томен взор ее чудесный!..
     Но полно, полно; перестань:
     Ты заплатил безумству дань.

"The night has many stars delightfu

LI   They bring her into the Assembly.
     The crushed, excited buzz, the heat,
     The music's crash, candle-gleams trembling,
     The flashing pairs in whirlwind fleet,
     The beauties' graceful, light attire,
     The gallery's bright-colored choir,
     The débutantes half-moon so thick,
     All strike the senses to the quick.
     The foppish dandies here are flaunting
     Their brazenness with waistcoats new,
     And lorgnettes they're not looking through.
     Hussars on leave are prancing, vaunting,
     They rush to show up, seize the day,
     To sparkle, shine, then run away.

LII The night has many stars delightful,
     And many beauties Moscow boasts,
     But, brighter than all *belles* at nightfall,
     The moon, in heaven's blue, soft glows.
     Yet she alone, whom I'm not daring
     To stir up through my lyre-playing,
     Majestic as the moon does roam,
     Amidst the wives and maids alone.
     With what unmatched celestial pride
     Upon mere Earth her footsteps stride!
     And with what bliss her bosom teems!
     Her languid look's the stuff of dreams!
     Enough, enough, now, stop and rest!
     To madness you have paid your debt.

LIII Шум, хохот, беготня, поклоны,
Галоп, мазурка, вальс... Меж тем,
Между двух теток у колонны,
Не замечаема никем,
Татьяна смотрит и не видит,
Волненье света ненавидит;
Ей душно здесь... она мечтой
Стремится к жизни полевой,
В деревню, к бедным поселянам,
В уединенный уголок,
Где льется светлый ручеек,
К своим цветам, к своим романам
И в сумрак липовых аллей,
Туда, где *он* являлся ей.

LIV Так мысль ее далече бродит:
Забыт и свет и шумный бал,
А глаз меж тем с нее не сводит
Какой-то важный генерал.
Друг другу тетушки мигнули
И локтем Таню враз толкнули,
И каждая шепнула ей:
— Взгляни налево поскорей. —
«Налево? где? что там такое?"
— Ну, что бы ни было, гляди...
В той кучке, видишь? впереди,
Там, где еще в мундирах двое?...
Вот отошел... вот боком стал...» —
«Кто? толстый этот генерал?»

LIII Noise, laughter, footsteps, bowing, bustling,
The galope, the mazurka, waltz.
Between two Aunties by the columns,
As no one looks at her at all,
Tatyana looks on, nothing seeing,
She loathes this social whirl, is seething,
She can't breathe here, and in a dream,
She flies again to field and stream,
To her own country, its poor farmers,
To her secluded little nook,
Right by the light, clear rushing brook,
To her old flowers, her old novels,
Back to the linden alleys' gloom,
Where once before her *he* did loom.

LIV And so her thoughts roam way off, distant,
Forget the loud, dull social whirl,
Yet someone eyes her every instant:
It's some important general.
The aunts wink at each other, knowing,
Each then Tatyana starts elbowing,
Each whispers then right in her ear:
"Look to the left. Look quick, my dear."
"Look left? Where? Why there? What's the matter?"
"Never mind that, just look with care...
See that bunch, right in front, right there?...
Where those two uniforms sit chattering?"...
He's moved now, see? He's turned aside."
"You mean that portly general?"

LV　　　Но здесь с победою поздравим
　　　　Татьяну милую мою...

EUGENE ONEGIN (EXCERPTS) CHAPTER 7 571

LV   But dear Tatyana sweet we now
     With victory congratulate...

ГЛАВА ВОСЬМАЯ

Fare thee well, and if for ever
Still for ever fare thee well.

Byron

X
Блажен, кто смолоду был молод,
Блажен, кто вовремя созрел,
Кто постепенно жизни холод
С летами вытерпеть умел;
Кто странным снам не предавался,
Кто черни светской не чуждался,
Кто в двадцать лет был франт иль хват,
А в тридцать выгодно женат;
Кто в пятьдесят освободился
От частных и других долгов,
Кто славы, денег и чинов
Спокойно в очередь добился,
О ком твердили целый век:
N. N. прекрасный человек.

XI
Но грустно думать, что напрасно
Была нам молодость дана,
Что изменяли ей всечасно,
Что обманула нас она;
Что наши лучшие желанья,
Что наши свежие мечтанья
Истлели быстрой чередой,
Как листья осенью гнилой.
Несносно видеть пред собою
Одних обедов длинный ряд,
Глядеть на жизнь, как на обряд,
И вслед за чинною толпою
Идти, не разделяя с ней
Ни общих мнений, ни страстей.

CHAPTER VIII

Fare thee well, and if for ever
Still for ever fare thee well.

Byron

X Blest he who in his youth was youthful,
Blest who matured when it was time,
Blest he who, gradually rueful,
Grew used to this life's chilly clime,
Who never by strange dreams was troubled,
Who never shunned smart stylish rabble,
At twenty, was a fop or blade,
At thirty, married, had it made,
Who, reaching fifty, lived in freedom
From personal and other debts,
Had fame, rank, funds with interest,
Which he was always calm in seeking,
Whom all did praise – his whole life's span:
"N.N.'s a perfectly nice man."

XI And yet it's sad to think how vainly
Our joyous youth was given us,
How hour by hour was spent betraying
It – till it in turn betrayed our trust.
That all our noblest aspirations,
Our freshest dreams and expectations,
Did wither one by one and pall,
Like rotting leaves by end of fall,
What dread to see our future bound
Only by meals in endless line,
To see just ritual in life,
To mingle with the proper crowd
And ape them, while with them you share
Nor thoughts, nor passions – and don't care.

XII Предметом став суждений шумных,
Несносно (согласитесь в том)
Между людей благоразумных
Прослыть притворным чудаком,
Или печальным сумасбродом,
Иль сатаническим уродом,
Иль даже Демоном моим.
Онегин (вновь займуся им),
Убив на поединке друга,
Дожив без цели, без трудов
До двадцати шести годов,
Томясь в бездействии досуга
Без службы, без жены, без дел,
Ничем заняться не умел.

XIII Им овладело беспокойство,
Охота к перемене мест
(Весьма мучительное свойство,
Немногих добровольный крест).
Оставил он свое селенье,
Лесов и нив уединенье,
Где окровавленная тень
Ему являлась каждый день,
И начал странствия без цели,
Доступный чувству одному;
И путешествия ему,
Как всё на свете, надоели;
Он возвратился и попал,
Как Чацкий, с корабля на бал.

XII If you're the butt of noisy gossip,
     It's awful (surely you'll agree)
     When people you respect as honest
     Call all your quirks fake flippancy,
     Call you a melancholy madman,
     Satanic ogre, ugly phantom,
     The very *Demon* of my poem.
     Onegin (I'll return to him),
     Killing his own friend in a duel,
     Attaining without work or goals
     To naught, though twenty six years old,
     In leisured idleness still stewing,
     Having no cares, career, or wife,
     Could not do anything in life.

XIII And restlessness soon quite bestirred him,
       He yearned for someplace new, fresh air,
     (A quality most disconcerting,
     Which some of us must choose to bear).
     And so he left his village rural,
     His woods and wheatfields so secluded,
     Where every day a bloody shade
     Before his vision ever stayed,
     And he began an aimless voyage,
     Which really only had one feeling,
     And travels soon enough were seeming,
     Like all in life, quite dull and cloying,
     So back he came to some fine hall,
     Like Chatsky* — straight from boat to ball.

---

* Chatsky, the hero of Alexander Griboedov's verse play *Woe from Wit,* came back to Moscow suddenly after three years abroad— feeling like a foreigner at home.

XIV Но вот толпа заколебалась,
По зале шепот пробежал...
К хозяйке дама приближалась,
За нею важный генерал.
Она была нетороплива,
Не холодна, не говорлива,
Без взора наглого для всех,
Без притязаний на успех,
Без этих маленьких ужимок,
Без подражательных затей...
Всё тихо, просто было в ней,
Она казалась верный снимок
Du comme il faut... (Шишков, прости:
Не знаю, как перевести.)

XVII «Ужели, — думает Евгений: —
Ужель она? Но точно... Нет...
Как! из глуши степных селений...»
И неотвязчивый лорнет
Он обращает поминутно
На ту, чей вид напомнил смутно
Ему забытые черты.
«Скажи мне, князь, не знаешь ты,
Кто там в малиновом берете
С послом испанским говорит?»
Князь на Онегина глядит.
— Ага! давно ж ты не был в свете.
Постой, тебя представлю я. —
«Да кто ж она?» — Жена моя. —

XIV   But soon the crowd began to waver
Through the salon a whisper ran...
Up to the hostess came a lady,
By her, a well-known general.
She walked unhurriedly and grandly,
And was not cold, yet was not chatty,
Cast no rude looks at everyone,
Claimed not her place beneath the sun,
Cared not for posing, phony frillage,
For little imitative tics...
Just calm and quiet in her mixed.
She seemed the very perfect image
Du comme il faut...(Shishkov, forgive:
Your Slavicisms help won't give)*.

XVII   Yevgeny wonders, "Could it be?
It can't be her! It is! No! ...Yet
How? From those barren plains and fields..."
And he an ever-fixed lorgnette
Keeps focused on her every second,
On she, whose traits did vaguely beckon
With memories from long ago.
"Please tell me, Prince, do you** not know
Who in that raspberry beret
Chats with the envoy fresh from Spain?"
The Prince looks at Onegin then
"Aha! You've not been out of late.
"I'll introduce you, if you like."
"But who is she, though?" "She's my wife."

*Admiral Alexander Shishkov, 1754-1841, President of the Academy of Sciences, railed against the oversue of French and German words in Russian.

**The prince is adressed by the familiar pronoun ты, used for family or friends.

XVIII «Так ты женат! не знал я ране!
Давно ли?» — Около двух лет. —
«На ком?» — На Лариной. — «Татьяне!»
— Ты ей знаком? — «Я им сосед».
—О, так пойдем же. — Князь подходит
К своей жене и ей подводит
Родню и друга своего.
Княгиня смотрит на него...
И что ей душу ни смутило,
Как сильно ни была она
Удивлена, поражена,
Но ей ничто не изменило:
В ней сохранился тот же тон,
Был так же тих ее поклон.

XIX Ей-ей! не то, чтоб содрогнулась
Иль стала вдруг бледна, красна...
У ней и бровь не шевельнулась;
Не сжала даже губ она.
Хоть он глядел нельзя прилежней,
Но и следов Татьяны прежней
Не мог Онегин обрести.
С ней речь хотел он завести
И — и не мог. Она спросила,
Давно ль он здесь, откуда он
И не из их ли уж сторон?
Потом к супругу обратила
Усталый взгляд; скользнула вон...
И недвижим остался он.

XVIII   "I didn't know that you were married!
How long?" "About two years."
"To whom?" "Miss Larin." "To Tatyana!"
"You know her then?" "I lived quite near."
"Oh, then come on". The prince approaches
His wife, and brings along in bunches
His kith and kin and his old friend.
The princess looks at him again...
Whatever in her heart was raging,
No matter how her soul was wracked,
How she was shocked, taken aback,
No sign of it she was betraying:
She acted as if nothing's wrong,
Her curtsey kept its tranquil calm.

XIX   Indeed! No trace of flutter, shiver,
She didn't start, pale, blush, or slip,
Even her eyebrow didn't quiver,
She didn't even bite her lip.
Though he looked at her through and through,
Of the Tatyana he once knew
No traces could Onegin find.
To speak to her once more he tried
But...but...could not. She just kept asking:
How long's he here, from whence come back?
Not from our parts by any chance?
Then to her husband she was casting
A tired look, slipped from the room...
Onegin froze and could not move.

XXVII Но мой Онегин вечер целый
Татьяной занят был одной,
Не этой девочкой несмелой,
Влюбленной, бедной и простой,
Но равнодушною княгиней,
Но неприступною богиней
Роскошной, царственной Невы.
О люди! все похожи вы
На прародительницу Эву:
Что вам дано, то не влечет,
Вас непрестанно змий зовет
К себе, к таинственному древу;
Запретный плод вам подавай,
А без того вам рай не рай.

XXVIII Как изменилася Татьяна!
Как твердо в роль свою вошла!
Как утеснительного сана
Приемы скоро приняла!
Кто б смел искать девчонки нежной
В сей величавой, в сей небрежной
Законодательнице зал?
И он ей сердце волновал!
Об нем она во мраке ночи,
Пока Морфей не прилетит,
Бывало, девственно грустит,
К луне подъемлет томны очи,
Мечтая с ним когда-нибудь
Свершить смиренный жизни путь!

XXVII   Onegin spent all evening yearning,
         Just by Tatyana occupied,
         Not more that girl he knew, uncertain,
         In love, unhappy without pride,
         But an indifferent, haughty princess,
         But an impregnable grand goddess
         Of the Nevá, of regal fame.
         Oh people! You are all the same!
         You're like our first ancestress Eve:
         What you've been given you prize not,
         The snake tempts with what others got,
         The snake calls to that fateful tree;
         Forbidden food you crave and miss—
         Or Heaven no more heaven is.

XXVIII   But oh, how changed Tatyana seems!
         How fixed she seems in her new role!
         How her restricting rank that gleams
         Has silenced all her habits old!
         Who'd dare to seek that sweet girl tender
         In this so unconcerned majestic
         Lawgiver of the drawing room?
         And once he used to make her swoon!
         She used to dream of him all night—
         Till Morpheus came and brought her sleep,
         She'd sit alone in girlish grief,
         Lift to the moon her languid eyes,
         "Just let me be with him!"... She'd pray
         To walk with him life's humble way.

XXIX Любви все возрасты покорны;
Но юным, девственным сердцам
Ее порывы благотворны,
Как бури вешние полям:
В дожде страстей они свежеют,
И обновляются, и зреют —
И жизнь могущая дает
И пышный цвет и сладкий плод.
Но в возраст поздний и бесплодный,
На повороте наших лет,
Печален страсти мертвой след:
Так бури осени холодной
В болото обращают луг
И обнажают лес вокруг.

XXX Сомненья нет: увы! Евгений
В Татьяну как дитя влюблен;
В тоске любовных помышлений
И день и ночь проводит он.
Ума не внемля строгим пеням,
К ее крыльцу, стеклянным сеням
Он подъезжает каждый день;
За ней он гонится как тень;
Он счастлив, если ей накинет
Боа пушистый на плечо,
Или коснется горячо
Ее руки, или раздвинет
Пред нею пестрый полк ливрей,
Или платок подымет ей.

XXIX To love all ages are submissive,
      And yet to young and virgin hearts
      Its sudden gusts are beneficial,
      As to the fields spring tempests are.
      They freshen in the rain of passion,
      They are renewed, matured, refashioned,
      Then life gives powerfully, in truth,
      Both splendid color and sweet fruit.
      But in late years love's misbegotten,
      Fruitless, past turning point of age,
      Sad then is deadened passion's trace:
      Just so the chilly storms of autumn
      A swamp make of a meadow green,
      And strip a forest of its gleam.

XXX   But there's no doubt! Alas! Yevgeny
      Loves Tanya like a lovelorn child.
      In melancholy loving frenzy
      He whiles away both day and night,
      Hears not his mind scold strict remonstrance,
      Up to her doors, her mirrored entrance,
      He drives up desperate every day,
      And haunts her like a ghostly shade.
      He's happy if by chance he's wrapping
      Her boa's fur round her shoulder-blades,
      Or if with warmth he does but graze
      Her hand, or if he aids her passing,
      Parting bright seas of liveries,
      Or picks up her dropped handkerchief.

XXXI Она его не замечает,
Как он ни бейся, хоть умри.
Свободно дома принимает,
В гостях с ним молвит слова три,
Порой одним поклоном встретит,
Порою вовсе не заметит:
Кокетства в ней ни капли нет —
Его не терпит высший свет.
Бледнеть Онегин начинает:
Ей иль не видно, иль не жаль;
Онегин сохнет, и едва ль
Уж не чахоткою страдает.
Все шлют Онегина к врачам,
Те хором шлют его к водам.

XXXII А он не едет; он заране
Писать ко прадедам готов
О скорой встрече; а Татьяне
И дела нет (их пол таков);
А он упрям, отстать не хочет,
Еще надеется, хлопочет;
Смелей здорового, больной,
Княгине слабою рукой
Он пишет страстное посланье.
Хоть толку мало вообще
Он в письмах видел не вотще;
Но, знать, сердечное страданье
Уже пришло ему невмочь.
Вот вам письмо его точь-в-точь.

XXXI But she ignores him, doesn't notice.
Though he might die – she still won't see.
Receives him freely as a hostess,
Politely says a word – or three –
Sometimes just curtseys are her greeting,
Sometimes completely isn't seeing,
There's not a drop in her that flirts –
Society this fault forbids.
Onegin soon becomes quite pale;
She can't see – or else pities not:
Onegin drops, has almost got
Consumption, now is truly ill,
To doctors our Onegin's sent,
Who all a spa do recommend .

XXXII But he's not going. He's quite ready
To meet his forefathers today.
And yet Tatyana's calm and steady,
Cares not (the fair sex is that way);
But he is stubborn, not desisting,
But hoping still, ever persisting,
Bolder than healthy men, though ill,
He writes now to the princess still,
His hand that's weak writes passionately.
Although most times in letters he
Saw little sense, reason, or need,
Yet his heart's suffering, indeed,
Was just no more to be endured:
Here is his letter word for word.

ПИСЬМО ОНЕГИНА К ТАТЬЯНЕ

Предвижу все: вас оскорбит
Печальной тайны объясненье.
Какое горькое презренье
Ваш гордый взгляд изобразит!
Чего хочу? с какою целью
Открою душу вам свою?
Какому злобному веселью,
Быть может, повод подаю!

Случайно вас когда-то встретя,
В вас искру нежности заметя,
Я ей поверить не посмел:
Привычке милой не дал ходу;
Свою постылую свободу
Я потерять не захотел.
Еще одно нас разлучило...
Несчастной жертвой Ленский пал...
Ото всего, что сердцу мило,
Тогда я сердце оторвал;
Чужой для всех, ничем не связан,
Я думал: вольность и покой
Замена счастью. Боже мой!
Как я ошибся, как наказан.

Нет, поминутно видеть вас,
Повсюду следовать за вами,
Улыбку уст, движенье глаз
Ловить влюбленными глазами,
Внимать вам долго, понимать
Душой всё ваше совершенство,
Пред вами в муках замирать,
Бледнеть и гаснуть... вот блаженство!

"No, every moment seeing you..."

ONEGIN'S LETTER TO TATYANA

I foresee all: you'll take offense
At secret sorrow's revelation.
What scorn, what bitter condemnation
Are in your look so proud and tense!
What do I want? And for what reason
Do I pour forth my soul to you?
What gaiety and gloating teasing
From my appeal, perhaps, ensue!

By chance, somehow, at our first meeting
The spark of warmth within you seeing,
I dared not trust that it could be.
I didn't keep my own dear custom,
I didn't want to lose my freedom,
My stale and loathsome liberty.
Another thing drove us apart:
Lensky, unhappy victim, fell,
From all things dearest to my heart
I ripped my heart away back then.
Stranger to all, and friend to nothing,
I thought remaining free and calm
Was joy's replacement! Oh my God!
How wrong I was! How I've been punished!

No, every moment seeing you,
Just watching everywhere you go,
Your lips that smile, your eyes that move,
Seeing with eyes in love, aglow.
To hear and hear you, understand,
With all my soul, your sweet perfection,
In agonies before you stand,
Turn pale and swoon! What bliss! What blessing!

И я лишен того: для вас
Тащусь повсюду наудачу;
Мне дорог день, мне дорог час:
А я в напрасной скуке трачу
Судьбой отсчитанные дни.
И так уж тягостны они.
Я знаю: век уж мой измерен;
Но чтоб продлилась жизнь моя,
Я утром должен быть уверен,
Что с вами днем увижусь я...

Боюсь: в мольбе моей смиренной
Увидит ваш суровый взор
Затеи хитрости презренной —
И слышу гневный ваш укор.
Когда б вы знали, как ужасно
Томиться жаждою любви,
Пылать — и разумом всечасно
Смирять волнение в крови;
Желать обнять у вас колени,
И, зарыдав, у ваших ног
Излить мольбы, признанья, пени,
Все, все, что выразить бы мог,
А между тем притворным хладом
Вооружать и речь и взор,
Вести спокойный разговор,
Глядеть на вас веселым взглядом!..
Но так и быть: я сам себе
Противиться не в силах боле;
Все решено: я в вашей воле,
И предаюсь моей судьбе.

But everywhere, deprived of these,
Hoping to see you, I roam, listless,
Each day is dear, each hour's dear
To me, but I in boredom useless
Do waste the days Fate's counted me.
They're burdensome enough, indeed.
Short spans, I know, life's measured distance,
Yet, to keep going and endure,
Each morning I need reassurance
I'll see you in the afternoon.

I fear how my entreaty humble
Will seem to your regard severe.
You'll see but tricks of clever cunning –
Alas, your vexed rebuke I hear!
If you but knew what t'is to suffer
The awful ache and thirst of love,
To blaze – yet stifle every hour
With logic –- passion in my blood,
To want to grasp your knees, and weeping,
Break down and bawl, cast at your feet,
Pour forth confessions, prayers, pleading,
Express all, all, both sad and sweet,
Yet coolness all the while to feign,
With caution speech and glance to arm,
To keep up conversation calm,
Mere cheerful glance at you maintain!
Let it be so. I'm in no state
To fight this further. For good or ill
The die is cast. I'm in your will,
And give myself up to your fate.

XXXIII Ответа нет. Он вновь посланье:
Второму, третьему письму
Ответа нет. В одно собранье
Он едет; лишь вошел...ему
Она навстречу. Как сурова!
Его не видят, с ним ни слова;
У! Как теперь окружена
Крещенским холодом она!
Как удержать негодованье
Уста упрямые хотят!
Вперил Онегин зоркий взгляд:
Где, где смятенье, состраданье?
Где пятна слез?...Их нет, их нет!
На сем лице лишь гнева след...

XXXIV Да, может быть, боязни тайной,
Чтоб муж иль свет не угадал
Проказы, слабости случайной...
Всего, что мой Онегин знал...
Надежды нет! Он уезжает,
Свое безумство проклинает --
И, в нем глубоко погружен,
От света вновь отрекся он.
И в молчаливом кабинете
Ему припомнилась пора,
Когда жестокая хандра
За ним гналася в шумном свете,
Поймала, за ворот взяла
И в темный угол заперла.

XXXIII No answer came....Another letter..
A second, then a third — in vain.
No answer came. Then to some dinner
He went, had scarce walked in — again
She walks straight by, severely,
Says not one word and doesn't see him.
Oh! Wrapped in cold! She looks so cross,
As harsh as January's frost!
Just barely holding indignation
In check, her stubborn stiff lips seem!
Onegin fixes a look keen...
Where's sympathy? Where's consternation?
No hint of tears? No, none at all!
Just rage on that face casts a pall.

XXXIV Or maybe she just fears in secret,
Lest husband — or the world — find out
Her escapade, or sudden weakness...
Onegin knows this game throughout...
No! There's no hope! He drove off, hurried,
Was moping, his own madness cursing,
And deeper in it he did sink,
Again abjured society.
Now, in his little study quiet,
The feeling rose again within
Of cruel depression seizing him,
As earlier, 'midst modish riot,
It grabbed his collar, took firm hold,
And locked him up in a dark hole.

XXXV Стал вновь читать он без разбора.
Прочел он Гиббона, Руссо,
Манзони, Гердера, Шамфора,
Madame de Staël, Биша, Тиссо,
Прочел скептического Беля,
Прочел творенья Фонтенеля,
Прочел из наших кой-кого,
Не отвергая ничего:
И альманахи, и журналы,
Где поученья нам твердят,
Где нынче так меня бранят,
А где такие мадригалы
Себе встречал я иногда:
E sempre bene, господа.

XXXVI И что ж? Глаза его читали,
Но мысли были далеко;
Мечты, желания, печали
Теснились в душу глубоко.
Он меж печатными строками
Читал духовными глазами
Другие строки. В них-то он
Был совершенно углублён.
То были тайные преданья
Сердечной, темной старины,
Ни с чем не связанные сны,
Угрозы, толки, предсказанья,
Иль длинной сказки вздор живой,
Иль письма девы молодой.

XXXV And so he read again at random,
      And leafed through Gibbon and Rousseau,
      Manzoni, Herder, and Chamfort,
      Madame de Staël, Bichat, Tissot,
      And read the skeptic works of Bayle,
      The works also of Fontenelle,
      He even read some of our stuff —
      And didn't care, and made no fuss:
      Thick journals, almanacs, he read,
      Where everyone so loves to preach,
      Where now at me they sometimes screech,
      Or madrigals sing, au contraire,
      I've seen their paeans there now and then.
      E sempre bene, gentlemen.

XXXVI And yet? Although his eyes were reading,
      His thoughts were ever far away.
      And dreams, desires, inner grieving,
      Deep furrows in his heart did lay.
      Between the lines in his books printed
      He read -- with eyes now of the spirit --
      Far different lines, and in these he
      Submerged himself in reverie.
      Sometimes he'd see old tales, collections,
      Of heartfelt, ancient history.
      At times confused dreams he did see,
      Threats, meanings, plots, and dire predictions,
      An endless fable's lively whirl,
      The letter of a tender girl.

XXXVII И постепенно в усыпленье
 И чувств и дум впадает он,
 А перед ним воображенье
 Свой пестрый мечет фараон.
 То видит он: на талом снеге,
 Как будто спящий на ночлеге,
 Недвижим юноша лежит,
 И слышит голос: «что ж? убит».
 То видит он врагов забвенных,
 Клеветников, и трусов злых,
 И рой изменниц молодых,
 И круг товарищей презренных,
 То сельский дом — и у окна
 Сидит *она*...и всё она!

XXXVIII Он так привык теряться в этом,
 Что чуть с ума не своротил
 Или не сделался поэтом.
 Признаться: то-то б одолжил!
 А точно: силой магнетизма
 Стихов российских механизма
 Едва в то время не постиг
 Мой бестолковый ученик.
 Как походил он на поэта,
 Когда в углу сидел один,
 И перед ним пылал камин,
 И он мурлыкал: *Benedetta*
 Иль *Idol mio*, и ронял
 В огонь то туфлю, то журнал.

XXXVII So he through fading soft sensation
  His thoughts and feelings lulled to sleep.
  For him, then, his imagination
  Began its colored cards to deal.
  And so he sees on snowfall melted,
  As though but sleeping in a shelter,
  A youth just lying very still,
  And hears a voice: "Oh well! He's killed."
  And then he sees old foes forgotten,
  Both slanderers and cowards cruel,
  Of femmes fatales a swarming pool,
  And old companions, hated, rotten...
  Then country home, then window where
  She sits and sits...still waiting there!

XXXVIII He got so used to such discomfort
  He very nearly lost his mind,
  Or else nearly became a poet.
  (Now that would be a welcome sign!)
  In truth, as though by magnetism
  Russian verse-writing mechanisms
  Almost saw him who could not learn
  From hopeless case to poet turned.
  How he a poet then resembled,
  Alone in his dark corner there,
  Watching the hearth blaze up and blare
  And purring, murmuring "*Benedetta,*"
  Or "*Idol mio,*" then to flames threw
  His paper – or sometimes his shoe!

XXXIX Дни мчались; в воздухе нагретом
       Уж разрешалася зима;
       И он не сделался поэтом,
       Не умер, не сошел с ума.
       Весна живит его: впервые
       Свои покои запертые,
       Где зимовал он, как сурок,
       Двойные окна, камелек
       Он ясным утром оставляет,
       Несется вдоль Невы в санях.
       На синих, иссеченных льдах
       Играет солнце; грязно тает
       На улицах разрытый снег.
       Куда по нем свой быстрый бег

XL   Стремит Онегин? Вы заране
       Уж угадали; точно так:
       Примчался к ней, к своей Татьяне
       Мой неисправленный чудак.
       Идет, на мертвеца похожий.
       Нет ни одной души в прихожей.
       Он в залу; дальше: никого.
       Дверь отворил он. Что ж его
       С такою силой поражает?
       Княгиня перед ним, одна,
       Сидит, не убрана, бледна,
       Письмо какое-то читает
       И тихо слезы льет рекой,
       Опершись на руку щекой.

XXXIX   Time raced, and soon the air was thawing
And melting sullen wintertime.
And he did not become a poet,
Or die, and didn't lose his mind.
The spring brought him to life; one day
He stirred from his locked hideaway,
From hibernating marmot-like,
By double-windows' fireside,
And one clear morning went off riding
His sleigh along the Nevá's banks.
On ice floes' blue blocks, cut-out flanks,
The sun is sparkling, sun is shining,
On dirty slush of melting snows,
On shoveled streets where his sled goes.

XL   But where's he going? Right! Amazing!
Of course you've guessed it long before,
To her, to his Tatyana racing,
Flies my eccentric unreformed.
Walks in, half-dead, with corpse's pallor,
No living soul is in her parlor;
Into her hall...there's no one there.
Opens a door: the whole place–bare...
Then what a sight his senses shatter!
The princess, pale, before him sits
Alone; her hair disheveled is...
She's reading, reading, someone's letter,
And softly tears flow down her cheek,
Which she leans softly on hands weak.

XLI О, кто б немых ее страданий
В сей быстрый миг не прочитал!
Кто прежней Тани, бедной Тани
Теперь в княгине б не узнал!
В тоске безумных сожалений
К ее ногам упал Евгений;
Она вздрогнула и молчит;
И на Евгения глядит
Без удивления, без гнева...
Его больной, угасший взор,
Молящий вид, немой укор,
Ей внятно всё. Простая дева,
С мечтами, сердцем прежних дней,
Теперь опять воскресла в ней.

XLII Она его не подымает
И, не сводя с него очей,
От жадных уст не отымает
Бесчувственной руки своей...
О чем теперь ее мечтанье?
Проходит долгое молчанье,
И тихо наконец она:
«Довольно; встаньте. Я должна
Вам объясниться откровенно.
Онегин, помните ль тот час,
Когда в саду, в аллее нас
Судьба свела, и так смиренно
Урок ваш выслушала я?
Сегодня очередь моя.

XLI Oh, who to her mute grief's so hardened
     That in a flash could not perceive?
     Who my old Tanya, my poor Tanya,
     Now in this princess could not see?
     In crazy heartache wistful, saddened,
     Yevgeny's at her feet, abandoned...
     She shudders, sees, and cannot speak,
     Looks at Onegin, looks that shriek,
     Without a trace of shock or rage,
     Can see his sick, drawn, vanquished look,
     Imploring, haggard, mute reproof...
     She understands. My simple maid,
     With dreams and heart of former days
     Lives, resurrected in her gaze.

XLII She lets him lie by her, not moving;
     She doesn't tear away her eyes.
     His hungry lips she's not removing
     From her limp arm, which lifeless lies.
     Of what now is it that she's dreaming?
     A silence goes by, endless seeming,
     Then softly she speaks up at last:
     "Enough. Please rise. For now I must
     Explain myself to you completely.
     Onegin, you remember when
     We in my garden walkway spent
     An hour entwined by Fate? Meekly
     I heard the lesson you did teach...
     Today it is my turn to preach:

XLIII   Онегин, я тогда моложе,
        Я лучше, кажется, была,
        И я любила вас; и что же?
        Что в сердце вашем я нашла?
        Какой ответ? одну суровость.
        Не правда ль? Вам была не новость
        Смиренной девочки любовь?
        И нынче — Боже! — стынет кровь,
        Как только вспомню взгляд холодный
        И эту проповедь... Но вас
        Я не виню: в тот страшный час
        Вы поступили благородно,
        Вы были правы предо мной.
        Я благодарна всей душой...

XLIV   Тогда — не правда ли? — в пустыне,
        Вдали от суетной молвы,
        Я вам не нравилась... Что ж ныне
        Меня преследуете вы?
        Зачем у вас я на примете?
        Не потому ль, что в высшем свете
        Теперь являться я должна;
        Что я богата и знатна,
        Что муж в сраженьях изувечен,
        Что нас за то ласкает двор?
        Не потому ль, что мой позор
        Теперь бы всеми был замечен
        И мог бы в обществе принесть
        Вам соблазнительную честь?

XLIII Onegin, back then I was younger,
       A better person too, it seems,
       And I did love you. What resulted?
       What from your heart did I then reap?
       What answer? Just severity.
       Right? You found nothing new indeed
       In a submissive young girl's love.
       And even now – Lord! – still my blood
       Runs cold, recalling your look glacial,
       And then your sermon! ... But I
       Don't blame you. In that hour dire
       You acted fairly, decent, graceful,
       Correct towards me, I must avow.
       With all my soul I'm grateful now.

XLIV   Back then – right? – in our barren desert,
       Far from this noise and vanity,
       You didn't like me. Now what's different?
       What makes you chase now after me?
       Why now am I your goal, your prize?
       Is it you know that I'm obliged
       To be in high society,
       That now I'm rich nobility,
       That from the wars my husband's crippled,
       For which the court caresses us.
       Is it that you'd be famous thus,
       My shame through everywhere would ripple,
       And bring you in society
       More rakish notoriety?

XLV Я плачу... если вашей Тани
Вы не забыли до сих пор,
То знайте: колкость вашей брани,
Холодный, строгий разговор,
Когда б в моей лишь было власти,
Я предпочла б обидной страсти
И этим письмам и слезам.
К моим младенческим мечтам
Тогда имели вы хоть жалость,
Хоть уважение к летам...
А нынче! — что к моим ногам
Вас привело? какая малость!
Как с вашим сердцем и умом
Быть чувства мелкого рабом?

XLVI А мне, Онегин, пышность эта,
Постылой жизни мишура,
Мои успехи в вихре света,
Мой модный дом и вечера,
Что в них? Сейчас отдать я рада
Всю эту ветошь маскарада,
Весь этот блеск, и шум, и чад
За полку книг, за дикий сад,
За наше бедное жилище,
За те места, где в первый раз,
Онегин, видела я вас,
Да за смиренное кладбище,
Где нынче крест и тень ветвей
Над бедной нянею моей...

XLV I'm weeping…if you still are holding
     Your Tanya in your memory,
     Then know: the sharp bite of your scolding,
     Your cold, severe, strict homily,
     If I had power to command it,
     I'd choose over offensive passion,
     And all your letters and your tears…
     Back then for girlish dreams at least
     You had a bit of pity, slightly,
     At least respect for tender years.
     But now? What's brought you to my feet?
     How could it be? A merest trifle?
     How could you with your heart and mind
     Be slave to feelings shallow? Why?

XLVI For all this pomp to me, Onegin,
     This tinsel of a hated life,
     My triumphs in the *beau monde's* whirlwind,
     My fancy home and evenings' style –
     Who needs them? Would I could exchange them,
     These rags in which I'm masquerading,
     And all this glitter, noise, and smoke,
     For my old books, my yard o'ergrown,
     For our poor dwelling solitary,
     For those same places dear where I,
     Onegin, first on you laid eyes,
     And for the humble cemetery,
     Where o'er her cross, 'neath branches' shade,
     My nanny to her rest was laid.

XLVII А счастье было так возможно,
Так близко!.. Но судьба моя
Уж решена. Неосторожно,
Быть может, поступила я:
Меня с слезами заклинаний
Молила мать; для бедной Тани
Все были жребии равны...
Я вышла замуж. Вы должны,
Я вас прошу, меня оставить;
Я знаю: в вашем сердце есть
И гордость и прямая честь.
Я вас люблю (к чему лукавить?),
Но я другому отдана;
Я буду век ему верна».

XLVIII Она ушла. Стоит Евгений,
Как будто громом поражен.
В какую бурю ощущений
Теперь он сердцем погружен!
Но шпор незапный звон раздался,
И муж Татьянин показался,
И здесь героя моего,
В минуту, злую для него,
Читатель, мы теперь оставим,
Надолго... навсегда... За ним
Довольно мы путем одним
Бродили пó свету. Поздравим
Друг друга с берегом. Ура!
Давно б (не правда ли?) пора!

XLVII   Yet happiness had been so close by,
So possible. But my fate's now
Decided. Rashly incautious I,
Perhaps acted, accepting vows:
My Mom with tears did plead, imploring...
For her poor Tanya, all ignoring,
All choices seemed about the same...
So I got married in this way.
You must, I beg you, leave entirely,
I know your heart has dignity,
And pride, and straight integrity.
I love you (what's the point in lying?)...
I'm given, though, to someone else,
And I'll be faithful unto death."

XLVIII   She leaves. Yevgeny's left alone
As if by lightning he'd been struck.
What feelings in a seething storm
His heart is plunged into with shock.
But sudden spurs sound sharply, clonking,
In comes Tatyana's husband walking...
Yet from our hero now we go,
Now — in this minute full of woe —
Yes, reader, now — our leave we're taking,
For long...forever. We have passed
Together with him a long path,
Long voyage. Let's congratulate
Each other on landfall! Hooray!
Long overdue! (Wouldn't you say?)

XLIX Кто б ни был ты, о мой читатель,
Друг, недруг, я хочу с тобой
Расстаться нынче как приятель.
Прости. Чего бы ты за мной
Здесь ни искал в строфах небрежных,
Воспоминаний ли мятежных,
Отдохновенья ль от трудов,
Живых картин, иль острых слов,
Иль грамматических ошибок,
Дай Бог, чтоб в этой книжке ты
Для развлеченья, для мечты,
Для сердца, для журнальных сшибок
Хотя крупицу мог найти.
За сим расстанемся, прости!

L Прости ж и ты, мой спутник странный,
И ты, мой верный идеал,
И ты, живой и постоянный,
Хоть малый труд. Я с вами знал
Всё, что завидно для поэта:
Забвенье жизни в бурях света,
Беседу сладкую друзей.
Промчалось много, много дней
С тех пор, как юная Татьяна
И с ней Онегин в смутном сне
Явилися впервые мне —
И даль свободного романа
Я сквозь магический кристалл
Еще не ясно различал.

XLIX   Whoever, reader, you might be,
            Both friend or foe, my leave I take,
            Today, at least, with amity.
            Farewell. Whatever in my wake
            You once did seek in stanzas careless,
            Whether remembrances rebellious,
            Or rest from labours unperturbed,
            Or lively pictures, witty words,
            Or else, perhaps, mistakes in grammar,
            God grant, in this brief book you gleaned
            Food for amusement, for your dream,
            Your heart, or journalistic scandal,
            A grain, let's hope, you here could find,
            And so, I wave farewell, goodbye!

L   Goodbye to you too, strange companion,
            And you as well, ideal so true,
            And you, my lively, dear and constant,
            Though little, work. I've known with you
            All that a poet ought to envy,
            Oblivion from this world's frenzy,
            Sweet conversation with a friend.
            It has been many days on end
            Since first my virginal Tatyana –
            Onegin too, in blurried dream –
            Began at first to come to me,
            And my free novel's free expansion,
            As through a magic crystal's gleam,
            Was still not clearly to be seen.

LI Но те, которым в дружной встрече
Я строфы первые читал...
Иных уж нет, а те далече,
Как Сади некогда сказал.
Без них Онегин дорисован.
А та, с которой образован
Татьяны милый идеал...
О много, много рок отъял!
Блажен, кто праздник жизни рано
Оставил, не допив до дна
Бокала полного вина,
Кто не дочел ее романа
И вдруг умел расстаться с ним,
Как я с Онегиным моим.

КОНЕЦ

LI   But those for whom, in friendly trysting,
My early stanzas I once read...
"They are no more, and some are distant,"
As once the poet Saadi said.
Onegin's been sketched in without them.
And she, that one in whom I found, in
Truth, Tatyana's perfect grace?
Oh how much Fate did take away!
Blest he who early left life's party
Before he could drink up in time
His goblet, brimming full of wine,
Who did not read all of life's novel,
Who how to part at once well knew,
As I from my Onegin do.

THE END

МОЙ ТАЛИСМАН

Храни меня, мой талисман,
Храни меня во дни гоненья,
Во дни раскаянья, волненья:
Ты в день печали был мне дан.

Когда подымет океан
Вокруг меня валы ревучи,
Когда грозою грянут тучи,
Храни меня, мой талисман.

В уединенье чуждых стран,
На лоне скучного покоя,
В тревоге пламенного боя
Храни меня, мой талисман.

Священный сладостный обман,
Души волшебное светило...
Оно сокрылось, изменило...
Храни меня, мой талисман.

Пускай же ввек сердечных ран
Не растравит воспоминанье.
Прощай, надежда; спи, желанье;
Храни меня, мой талисман.

Deliver me, my talisman,
Deliver me from fear and fleeing,
Days of remorse and worry healing:
On a sad day you touched my hand.

When rising by the ocean strand
The waves around me crash in pounding,
And when with lightning clouds are sounding,
Deliver me, my talisman.

Lost in seclusion, in strange lands,
In boredom's lull my bosom taming,
In the alarm of battle flaming,
Deliver me, my talisman.

You are my soul's own magic lamp,
You sweet and sacred trickery,
When you drop down, are flickering!
Deliver me, my talisman.

Wounds of the heart help me withstand
Forever; bad memories burn with fire!
Farewell, fond Hope; and sleep, Desire;
Deliver me, my talisman.

Во времена сталинского террора, когда миллионы гибли в лагерях и тюрьмах, НКВД выполняло ежедневную квоту арестов обычно в три часа ночи, чтобы захватить своих жертв врасплох, неспособными к сопротивлению. Вообразите себе: вас в полусонном, полушоковом состоянии палачи в штатском тащат из постели, ничего не объясняя, только проклиная. Больше уже никогда вы, наверное, не увидите свой дом и близких, осталось только несколько секунд, и беспощадное колесо истории унесет вас в пропасть...Что вы сделаете? Великий русский поэт Анна Андреевна Ахматова вспоминала, что в эти последние свободные секунды у многих русских была чуть ли не инстинктивная реакция — схватить и положить в карман книжку стихов Пушкина.

МОЙ ТАЛИСМАН

В годы холодной войны, когда один мой друг, ныне живущий в Англии, рискуя жизнью, перебирался из Восточной Германии в Западную, он ничего с собой не взял — кроме карманного томика стихов Пушкина. Такие томики в годы Отечественной войны находили и в окопах Сталинграда и Курска, и в противотанковых рвах под Ленинградом, на полях сражений от Арктики до Черного моря и от Волги до Эльбы, нередко простреленные пулями и искореженные шрапнелью. Так близко к сердцу находится Пушкин — и так глубоко связан с «загадочной русской душой».

> Небесного земли свидетель,
> Воспламененною душой,
> Я пел на троне добродетель
> С ее приветною красой.
> Любовь и тайная свобода
> Внушали сердцу гимн простой
> И неподкупный голос мой
> Был эхо русского народа.

Пушкинская «любовь и тайная свобода», свобода души, неотнимаемая мирской властью, были и остаются для русского сердца лучом света во тьме, священным талисманом при всех перипетиях судьбы. Нынче в России (по крайней мере, в Москве) снесены памятники большевикам, как раньше были снесены статуи царей; непонятно пока еще, кто встанет на их место. Но у памятников Пушкину — а их в России больше пятисот — даже в самые леденящие морозы всегда есть живые цветы.

Для русских Пушкин — первый и величайший гений, путеводная звезда русской культуры, создатель самогó русского литературного языка. Гоголь, Толстой, Достоевский и Чехов, гении русской литературы, которые известны на Западе, все признали себя литературными должниками Пушкина. Для Гоголя «Пушкин есть явление чрезвычайное и, может быть, единственное явление русского духа». Для Достоевского «Пушкин — вершина художественного совершенства». Толстой не раз утверждал, что все читатели обязаны читать и перечитывать «Повести Белкина» Пушкина как образец высшего литературного мастерства. И Толстой дал высшую похвалу Чехову, назвав его «Пушкиным в прозе». И действительно, Чехов унаследовал от

Пушкина многие черты, которые нам на Западе кажутся «чеховскими»: конфликты, страсти и эмоции, переданные с изящной краткостью и иронией — всё пропитано теплейшим сердоболием и сочувствием, отсутствует проповедь или «учение». Для русских поэтов от Лермонтова, Фета и Тютчева до Блока, Белого, Мандельштама, Ахматовой, Цветаевой и Есенина глубочайшее преклонение перед Пушкиным является своего рода религией. Пушкин истинно был «Пророком» русской литературы; он по сей день «глаголом жжет сердца людей». Но, хотя русские единогласно провозглашают Пушкина величайшим гением своей литературы, Пушкин куда менее известен у нас на Западе, чем его великие наследники. Несравненное мастерство пушкинского слога ускользает от перевода. В результате даже западная интеллигенция зачастую считает Пушкина чем-то вроде «либреттиста» Чайковского. Потеря так же велика, как если, например, считать Шекспира только «либреттистом» Верди.

Трудно передать иностранцам пушкинское волшебство. Его можно сравнить со светлым гением Моцарта: невероятные подвиги труда, его безупречная, беззаботная грация, легкость, моментально завораживающая власть над душами, теплота, юмор, страстность, бесконечная музыкальность, чуть ли не детская игривость, ритмичная и лирическая изобретательность — и все это в сочетании с божественной мудростью, рожденной из тончайшей духовной чистоты. Пушкинскую прелесть и прямоту тем труднее перевести на чужой язык, чем таинственно прозрачнее и энергичнее оригинал.

> Когда бы все так чувствовали силу
> Гармонии! Но нет: тогда б не мог
> И мир существовать; никто б не стал
> Заботиться о нуждах низкой жизни;
> Все предались бы вольному искусству.
> Нас мало избранных, счастливцев праздных,
> Пренебрегающих презренной пользой,
> Единого прекрасного жрецов.

Эти последние слова Моцарта в пушкинском «Моцарте и Сальери» говорят и об уникальности Пушкина, и вообще об одиночестве гения в окружающем мире. Но как помочь англоязычным читателям почувствовать силу пушкинской гармонии? В предисловии к своему знаменитому переводу «Евгения Онегина» Набоков так выразил обоснованные страхи многих ученых:

> Можно ли перевести стихотворение Пушкина, пусть "Евгений Онегин» или любое другое с определенной ритмикой? Безусловно, нет. Воспроизвести рифмы и в то же время перевести все стихотворение математически невозможно. Но, потеряв рифму, стихотворение теряет свою прелесть, свое цветение, которое не восстановят ни сноски на полях, ни алхимия учености.

Поэтому Набоков решил нам завещать как можно более дословный перевод, извиняясь заранее, что «для моего идеала дословности я принес в жертву всё: элегантность, музыкальность, прозрачность, изящество, свежую современность и даже иногда грамматику». Но при всем уважении к несравненному стилисту и ученому, нельзя так «дословно» перевести Пушкина. Получается совершенно безжизненный музейный экспонат, приколотый под стеклом с аккуратненькой этикеткой известным специалистом по бабочкам, но без намека на неописуемую грацию живой бабочки в полете.

Невозможно понять Пушкина без его музыки. Не только Чайковский, но и Мусоргский, Римский-Корсаков, Рахманинов, Прокофьев, Глинка, Глазунов и многие другие просто не могли не положить пушкинские строки на музыку. Ведь музыка уже живет в его стихах, кружится в их созвучиях:

> Буря мглою небо кроет,
> Вихри снежные крутя;
> То, как зверь, она завоет,
> То заплачет, как дитя.

Пушкин воистину был высочайшим жрецом "Единого Прекрасного" Пифагора. Как известно, пифагорейцы лечили больных поэзией, веря в целительную силу строк из «Илиады» и

«Одиссеи» Гомера, правильно прочитанных вслух. Как Гомер, Пушкин извлекает невыразимую силу из самого звучания слов, как и из их смысла, от их напева, движения, магического заклинания, очарования.

Однако русский язык, со своими тонкими интонациями, намного богаче английского в естественных рифмах. И слишком много переводчиков метались от Харибды «дословности» к Сцилле слепого сохранения рифм Пушкина, принося при этом в жертву естественность и непринужденность пушкинского языка. Многие видные ученые, такие как Арндт, Джонстон, Дойч и Фален, нам завещали переводы в рифмах, чем заслужили похвалу и уважение. Но, увы, зачастую, чем легче и одновременно величественнее рифмы звучат в русском оригинале, тем принужденнее и неуместнее они звучат в переводе, где выбранные рифмы напоминают скорее оперетту или варьете, чем поэзию, и отнюдь не имеют ничего общего с Пушкиным. Вот почему иногда использование приблизительной рифмы (вроде Ейтса или Дилана Томаса) вместо возможных абсурдных результатов слишком строгой рифмы, решает много проблем. Внутренний слух улавливает желаемый ассонанс и ритм без потери свежести оригинала. Но есть другая проблема: расхождение в количестве слогов в русских и английских синонимах. Посмотрим, например, на первое четверостишие, пожалуй, самого известного любовного стихотворения в русском языке. Дословно на английском оно звучит так:

> I remember a wonderful moment:
> You appeared before me
> Like a fleeting vision,
> A genius of pure beauty.

Но дословный перевод не способен передать волшебство этого чудного мгновенья. Флобер прочел полученный от своего друга И.С. Тургенева перевод в прозе, и сказал только: «Il est plat, votre poète» («ваш поэт пресен»). Сохранение волшебства требует от переводчика так называемой в английском «вольности поэта»: изредка добавляя или удаляя по необходимости, с благоговейной осторожностью, кое-какие слова, чтобы сохранить пифагорейскую силу, заклятье талисмана, вшитые в ритм оригинала. Иногда, видимо, только легкие вольности в выражении точнейшей правды спасают высшую поэтическую истину:

Я помню чудное мгновенье:	A wondrous moment I remember:
Передо мной явилась ты,	Before me once you did appear:
Как мимолетное виденье,	A fleeting vision you resembled
Как гений чистой красоты.	Of beauty's genius pure and clear.

Сам Пушкин в его стихотворных переводах придерживался «вольности поэта». Обычно иностранные стихи, переведенные Пушкиным на русский язык, «что-то теряют в оригинале». Даже в переводах Гёте, Ариосто, Шекспира и Шенье он подходил к текстам скорее как к темам для вариации и игры, чем как к академическим задачам для воспроизведения. Сравните, например, следующие строки малоизвестного (но популярного в то время) английского поэта Брайана Уолтера Проктора, писавшего под псевдонимом «Барри Корнуалл», с «переводом» Пушкина.

Текст Корнуалла	«Перевод» Пушкина
Inesilla! I am here!	Я здесь, Инезилья,
Thy own cavalier	Я здесь под окном.
Is now beneath thy lattice playing	Объята Севилья
Why art thou delaying?	И мраком и сном.
He hath ridden many a mile	Исполнен отвагой,
But to see thy smile	Окутан плащом,
The young light on the flowers is shining	С гитарой и шпагой
Yet he is repining.	Я здесь под окном.

Пушкинский перевод поет, танцует; он, как видно, не только живее оригинала, но сразу нас переносит в Испанию, в страну его мечты, где «Ночной зефир/Струит эфир/Шумит/ Бежит/ Гвадалквивир». Еще одной заветной мечтой поэта всю жизнь было паломничество в Италию, «свят[ую] для внуков Аполлона». Творенья Пушкина содержат более 90 цитат из Данте, Ариосто, Тассо, Петрарки и других на свободном итальянском языке. При такой любви Пушкина к итальянской культуре, чувствуется, что Пушкин впитал в себя дух Возрождения, идеалы, выраженные в книге «Придворный» Бальдассара Кастильоне:

> Принимая во внимание то, как возникает грация (не говорю только об унаследовании оной от звезд), нахожу это правило наиболее универсальным практически во всех вещах человеческих, сказанных либо сделанных. Следует избегать как острейшего, опаснейшего рифа в море любой искусственности и вместо этого сохранить во всем (пожалуй, тут изобретаю новое слово) некую sprezzatura (беспечность, непринужденность, легкость, самоуничижение, отречение), которая скрывает собственное свое мастерство, как будто все, что делается и говорится, получается слегка, непринужденно, даже без созерцания. От этого как раз рождается грация. Ведь все понимают трудности исполнения тяжелейших вещей, и легкость в их исполнении следственно вызывает высочайшее восхищение. Напротив, громоздкая и демонстративная вымученность, будто художник себя форсирует, вырывая волосы с головы, кажется экстремально дурным тоном, из-за чего мы не воспринимаем грацию в данной работе, даже если она является шедевром. А истинно только то искусство, которое не кажется «искусством». (*Il Libro del Cortigiano*, I, xxvi. Пер. с итал. *Д. Л.*).

Творчество Пушкина пронизано этой невыразимой sprezzatura. «Беспечное мастерство» сразу проникает в душу, доверительно, как слова ближайшего друга, наполняет сердце теплом, как «янтарным блеском», которым заполнена комната, когда он будит свою любовь в «Зимнем утре». Именно этим теплом и грацией он и воплощает невыразимую, не понимаемую, все понимающую, любящую «русскую душу» — и она становится универсальной. Достоевского особенно поражала эта «всемирная отзывчивость Пушкина».

Великий римский поэт Теренций учил: «Ничто человеческое мне не чуждо». И Пушкин согласился: «мне не скучно ни с кем, начиная с будочника и до царя». Создатель русского литературного языка любил общение с иностранцами, легко щеголял французскими, английскими, итальянскими, немецкими словами. Он был знатоком и балета, и балов, и подобных французскому кружеву хитросплетений Двора и при этом он любил крестьянские ярмарки, а однажды специально обучил попугая губернатора Бессарабии ругаться, как матрос, как раз перед приездом архиепископа. Его «Отцы пустынники и жены непорочны», возможно, самая возвышенная молитва в стихах, когда бы то ни было написанная, и в то же время Пушкин писал стихи для мальчишников, которые цензура, пожалуй, по сей день не пропустила бы.

Принимая все, не отвергая ничего, он встречался и посвящал стихи одновременно графиням и их служанкам, царям и рабам, дворцам, и тюрьмам и баракам. В городе или в деревне, в лесах, полях, горах, у бурного моря, у нежного ручья, в сражениях, на кладбищах, в сумасшедшем доме, в борделях, в игорных залах... Читатель не может не замечать, как Пушкин одновременно везде свой, словно у себя дома, и при этом везде чужой.

Не случайно он воспевал «опыт, сын ошибок трудных, и гений, парадоксов друг». Ведь все герои Пушкина — трехмерные, богаты внутренними конфликтами, тем, что Колридж назвал «сознательным диссонансом». Парадокс вездесущ в пушкинской sprezzatura. И его творения являются «энциклопедией русской жизни» (по мнению критика Белинского) и одновременно диалогом разных воплощений самого поэта (в виде персонажей). Лицейский друг, поэт Вильгельм Кюхельбекер, воскликнул: «Татьяна — это же Пушкин!» А другой друг Пушкина, великий польский поэт Адам Мицкевич, говорил в своих лекциях, что Пушкин воплощен и в Ленском, и в Онегине. Правы оба. Но в результате такой искренней парадоксальности возникла основа великой традиции русской литературы: сердечная объективность, пропитанная духовностью, душевной теплотой, состраданием.

Царь Александр I отправил «солнце русской поэзии» в ссылку и держал его в глухой деревне под домашним арестом два года после перлюстрации письма, где поэт с некоей иронией сболтнул другу, что «пишу пестрые строфы романтической поэмы — и беру уроки чистого афеизма у глухого философа, молодого англичанина». В письме поэт признался: «читаю Шекспира и Библию, святой дух иногда мне по сердцу, но предпочитаю Гёте и Шекспира». И в самом деле, Пушкин был настолько впечатлен «Фаустом» Гёте, что он во время этой ссылки написал «Сцены из Фауста». Он очень гордился позже подарком — пером, присланным ему Гёте. Несомненно, два национальные поэта имеют много общего. Оба — изобретатели современных литературных идиом их родных языков, оба — романтики, оба — в высочайшей степени музыкальны и недаром переложены на музыку бессмертными композиторами, оба считаются выразителями лучших черт национальной «души». Можно даже сказать, что оба драматизировали и достоинства, и недостатки своих стран. Но, при всем восхищении Гёте Пушкин, похоже, не разделял дидактического прагматизма «веймарского мудреца». Возьмем, например, стихотворение Гёте «Вода и Вино»:

Von Wasser allein wird man stumm.
Das beweisen im Wasser die Fische.
Von Wein allein wird man dumm
Das beweisen die Herren am Tische.
Und drum, um keines von beiden zu sein
Trink ich mit wasser vermischt mein Wein.

От воды остаешься немым,
Молчаливым в воде, как все рыбы;
От вина остаешься тупым:
На людей за столом посмотри ты.
Итак, как я сам ни такой, ни другой,
Смешиваю я вино с водой. (Перевод с немецкого Д.Л.)

Портрет Гёте. Рисунок А. С. Пушкина

Восемнадцатилетний Пушкин возмущенно ответил своему кумиру:

Вода и вино

Люблю я в полдень воспаленный
Прохладу черпать из ручья
И в роще тихой отдаленной
Смотреть, как плещет в брег струя.
Когда ж вино в края поскачет,
Напенясь в чаше круговой,
Друзья, скажите, — кто не плачет,
Заране радуясь душой?

> Да будет проклят дерзновенный,
> Кто первый грешною рукой,
> Нечестьем буйным ослепленный,
> О горе!... смесил вино с водой!
> Да будет проклят род злодея!
> Пускай не будет в силах пить,
> Или, стаканами владея,
> Лафит с цымлянским различить!

Читатель, возможно, удивится чему-то совсем macho в нем, т.е. нестесненной мужественности его голоса. У Пушкина, как у его другого кумира, Шекспира, герои поражают своей силой, даже в их колебаниях. Прислушиваясь к Пушкину, внимаем то ликующий, то печальный голос мужчины, всегда уверенного в собственной мужественности, мужчины, который при бесконечных изменениях настроений всегда чувствует в себе и Бога, и озорного мальчишку. Он настолько в единстве со своей мужественностью, что способен прославлять и принимать в себе женственность; Пушкин даже как-то нарисовал автопортрет в женском облике. Пожалуй, его лучшие строки — о любви. Иначе говоря, Пушкин был всегда влюблен, не только в женщин, но и в природу, в искусство — в саму жизнь. Любить для него было так же необходимо и естественно, как дышать:

> И сердце вновь горит и любит оттого,
> Что не любить оно не может.

Пушкин однажды, рассуждая в письме о природе первой любви, иронизировал, что его невеста Наталья Гончарова «замечу в скобках — моя сто тринадцатая любовь». (Сам замечу в скобках, что разные ученые, почему-то принимая эту шутку за статистику, чуть ли не написали 113 томов «расследования» этой ветреной фразочки, не понимая игривого *bon mot*)... Но ведь суть не в этом:

> Друзья! Не все ль одно и то же:
> Забыться праздною душой
> В блестящей зале, модной ложе
> Или в кибитке кочевой?

По сути Пушкин был всегда влюблен не только в «деву минуты», но в божественную энергию, которую она в нем рождала. Любая женщина, воспетая Пушкиным, стала для него «музой» или (как Гёте завершил свой «Фауст», «das Ewig-Weibliche») «той вечной женственностью». Уже двести лет во все мрачные времена русская душа никогда не забывает пушкинскую «способность легкую страдать» и утешается чистотой пушкинского возвышения женственности. Каким-то чудом его страсть только углубляется при чуть ли не самоуничижительной воздушности, с которой он признает капризность своего каприза:

Не смею требовать любви.
Быть может, за грехи мои,
Мой ангел, я любви не стою!
Но притворитесь! Этот взгляд
Все может выразить так чудно!
Ах, обмануть меня не трудно!..
Я сам обманываться рад!

По-настоящему «обманутый» таких строк не напишет! Но в то же время обманываться, умиляться, чувствовать головокружение, будто от лишнего бокала вина, от влюбленности — как раз сущность пушкинской отзывчивости и сострадания. Он предпочитал искреннюю уязвимость высокопарным одам. Он даже однажды ругал Вяземского за сверхсложность и надуманность: «Поэзия, прости Господи, должна быть глуповата!» Как утешно, когда поэт воспевает родное несовершенство с таким совершенством! Как хорошо в плохие времена иметь теплого друга, который не прячется за своим гением, но всегда с нами слегка подшучивает! Ведь в конце концов, только принимая и любя несовершенство любимой, мы возвышаемся над влюбленностью, не требующей усилий, и приходим к настоящей, несказанной любви, с ее глубокими, таинственными противоречиями. С утонченной болью Пушкин даже раскрывает тайну грустной супружеской неги:

О, как мучительно тобою счастлив я,
Когда, склоняяся на долгие моленья
Ты предаешься мне нежна без упоенья,
Стыдливо-холодна, восторгу моему
Едва ответствуешь, не внемлешь ничему
И оживляешься потом всё боле, боле —
И делишь наконец мой пламень поневоле!

Любовь, иногда даже эротика — сердцевина пушкинской sprezzatura. Но, воспевая «всё про любовь да про любовь», Пушкин довольно-таки задевал тех, кто предпочел бы, чтобы он был более политичным. Некоторые советские ученые и критики, такие как Вересаев и ему подобные, чуть ли не осуждали Пушкина за антисоветское поведение. Вересаев жаловался, что «в вопросах политических, общественных, религиозных Пушкин был неустойчив, колебался, в разные годы был себе противоположен». Итак, советские пропагандисты воспевали до небес автора «Пророка», «Анчара» и «Послания в Сибирь», но не могли простить ему сердечного сочувствия, не только к заключенным декабристам, но и к тем, кто был «на службе царской» («Бог помочь вам, друзья мои»), к солдатам противника («Делибаш»), а не только к «своим» русским войскам. Другой великий русский поэт Александр Блок восхищался этим стихотворением: в нем Пушкин тончайшими линиями, словно легким прикосновением показывает всю бессмысленность войны. Но в эпоху жестоких идеологий такая «всемирная отзывчивость» воспринималась как государственная измена. Ведь в вересаевское время давали «10 лет без права переписки» за такие «политически-неустойчивые» высказывания:

> Не дорого ценю я громкие права,
> От коих не одна кружится голова.
> Я не ропщу о том, что отказали боги
> Мне в сладкой участи оспаривать налоги
> Или мешать царям друг с другом воевать;
> И мало горя мне, свободно ли печать
> Морочит олухов, иль чуткая цензура
> В журнальных замыслах стесняет балагура.
> Все это, видите ль, «слова, слова, слова».
> Иные, лучшие мне дороги права,
> Иная, лучшая потребна мне свобода:
> Зависеть от царя, зависеть от народа —
> Не все ли нам равно? Бог с ними!

Такие стихи пугают и царей, и наркомов. Чтобы бороться с такой «контрреволюционной» ересью, Вересаеву пришлось изобрести «поразительное несоответствие между живой личностью поэта и ее отражением в его творчестве», чтобы (неудобного) «живого

Пушкина» очернить пасквилем. Но как раз душа поэта и его творчество неразделимы. И как бы она ни была неудобна властям, «иная, лучшая свобода» Пушкина — свобода души — поддерживает русский народ, не знающий другого рода свободы, через поколения. Его «политически неустойчивое» возвышение чувств дышит свежим воздухом, надеждой, счастьем. А воспевая причудливость человеческую, Пушкин напоминает нам, как Оскар Уайльд, что «жизнь слишком важна, чтобы ее воспринимать всерьез». Поэта не устраивают холодный материализм, жесткая расчетливость и преднамеренность во всем, тяжелое (как бы «самодержавное» или, позже, «советское»), т.е. «серьезное» отношение к жизни — как у Германна в «Пиковой даме». Поэт (награждая счастьем героя-повесу в «Метели») вместо этого выбирает «ветреность, непростительную ветреность», выбирает дорогу таинственную, причудливую, духовную, «женственную», путь настроений, путь луны.

Твое унынье безрассудно.
Ты любишь горестно и трудно,
А сердце женское — шутя.
Взгляни: под отдаленным сводом
Гуляет вольная луна;
На всю природу мимоходом
Равно сиянье льет она.
Заглянет в облако другое,
Его так пышно озарит —
И вот — уж перешла в другое;
И то не долго посетит.
Кто место в небе ей укажет,
Примолвя: там остановись!
Кто сердцу юной девы скажет:
Люби одно, не изменись?

Но луна, как сама любовь, капризничает, требует жертв. Иногда у Пушкина явление луны — признак мечтаний, печали, душевной тоски, одиночества. Но внутренний мир Пушкина ему важнее, чем место под солнцем, пусть даже солнцем всеобщей народной любви. Ни яркий день, ни ночь глухая не раскроют ту поэтическую истину, которая видна только в сумерках. Внутреннюю гармонию поэт находит в мягком сиянии звезд:

> Близ мест, где царствует Венеция златая,
> Один, ночной гребец, гондолой управляя,
> При свете Веспера по взморию плывет,
> Ринальда, Годфреда, Эрминию поет.
> Он любит песнь свою, поет он для забавы,
> Без дальних умыслов; не ведает ни славы,
> Ни страха, ни надежд, и, тихой музы полн,
> Умеет услаждать свой путь над бездной волн.
> На море жизненном, где бури так жестоко
> Преследуют во мгле мой парус одинокий,
> Как он, без отзыва утешно я пою
> И тайные стихи обдумывать люблю.

Но не все его песни были утешными, особенно в последние годы, задыхаясь в «свинском Петербурге», который он всё же любил («Люблю тебя, Петра творенье»). Читатель заметит, как «сверчок» (так друзья-«арзамасцы» его в молодости называли) уже меньше поет и больше горюет, превращается в более мрачного мужчину, осажденного скорбью («Воспоминание»), одержимого мыслями о безумии («Не дай мне Бог сойти с ума») и о смерти («Когда за городом, задумчив, я брожу»).

На самом деле этот «скорбный» мужчина присутствовал уже в его веселой молодости («Умолкну скоро я»; «Я пережил свои желанья»), когда он еще обучал попугаев ругать духовенство, волочился за красивыми цыганками и гнался за свежими устрицами... («Я жил тогда в Одессе пыльной»). В унынии поздних лет поэта некоторые винят его якобы легкомысленную жену, ее увлечение Дантесом, что привело в итоге к роковой дуэли. Другие — подавляющую атмосферу царского надсмотра, духоту, из-за которой поэт жаловался в последнем из его 78 писем жене: «Черт догадал меня родиться в России с душою и с талантом!»

Поэт поэта понимает. И Блок заметил, что «Пушкина убила не пуля Дантеса; он задохнулся от отсутствия воздуха». Сопровождая жену и сестер на бесконечных балах, облаченный в унизительный костюм камер-юнкера, поэт в суете царского Двора был в ловушке высшего света, блеск которого затмил самый его яркий бриллиант. Он мрачнел, видя как его жена кокетничала с другими мужчинами, покрасивее, подстать ее эгоистичному легкомыслию. Любить ее, но чувствовать себя нелюбимым, становилось невыносимым. За два года до смерти он уже писал:

Пора, мой друг, пора! покоя сердце просит —
Летят за днями дни, и каждый час уносит
Частичку бытия, а мы с тобой вдвоем
Предполагаем жить... И глядь — как раз — умрем.
На свете счастья нет, но есть покой и воля.
Давно завидная мечтается мне доля -
Давно, усталый раб, замыслил я побег
В обитель дальную трудов и чистых нег.

Но — опять парадокс! Ведь кто, кроме самой свободной души в порабощенной стране посмеет себя назвать «усталым рабом»? «Сознательный диссонанс», т.е. принятие парадокса — это суть поэтической истины. Китс знал, что «в Храме Неги / Грусть под вуалью царствует величаво». И у Пушкина: «печаль моя светла». Как мне кажется, его принципиально игривое отношение к жизни выражалось в некотором смысле игрой и со смертью. В молодости у Пушкина была дуэль из-за того, что в ресторане он заказал мазурку, а какой-то пьяный офицер хотел кадриль. Пушкин дал оппоненту выстрелить первым, но тот промахнулся, так как дуэль проходила в снежном буране на расстоянии 16 шагов. Тогда Пушкин предложил ему выстрелить с 12 шагов. Когда лицейский друг Кюхельбекер его вызвал за стишок о похмелье «...и кюхельбекерно, и тошно», Пушкин не стрелял, дал другу промахнуться, затем ему протянул руку и сказал: «Полно дурачиться, милый; пойдем чай пить!» На еще одной дуэли (которая, м.б., послужила сюжетом для повести «Выстрел»), пока противник целился в него с 12 шагов, он стоял, «выбирая из фуражки спелые черешни и выплевывая косточки». Его впечатленный противник сказал: «Вы стоите под пулей так же хорошо, как вы хорошо пишете». Поэт бросился ему на шею. А в «Делибаше» Пушкин советует: «Эй, казак, не рвися к бою». Но в единственной битве, в которой поэт участвовал, он сам был выведен насильно, когда «схватив пику подле одного из убитых казаков, устремился против неприятельских всадников».

Пушкин был смертельно ранен на дуэли в 37 лет. А всё же, как Пушкин мог себе позволить так рано погибнуть на дуэли? Как мог он допустить, чтобы мир был так рано лишен его гения? Может такое быть, что даже дуэль каким-то таинственным образом вплетена в самую суть его искусства, его души? Есть поразительные совпадения в «Евгении Онегине» между роковой дуэлью поэта Ленского с Онегиным и Пушкина с Дантесом. Обе дуэли были из-за оскорбленной чести поэта, обе случились точно в такое же время года, в снежном январе. Неужели Пушкин сам не задумывался над трагическим концом своего Ленского? Зачем Пушкин, такой суеверный, что он отвернулся от побега к заветным друзьям обратно в Михайловское, когда ему дорогу перебежал заяц, рискнул нарушить известную примету и, идя на дуэль, вернулся в дом, чтобы поменять шубу? Разве он хотел смерти?

Но не хочу, о други, умирать;
Я жить хочу, чтоб мыслить и страдать...

А почему уходя на дуэль в тот роковой день, он не взял свой перстень с бирюзой — талисман от насильственной смерти? Просто забыл? А, может, устал страдать, искал уже избавление? А, может, это все очередные легенды? Тайну не разгадать. Можно лишь сопереживать его мужественной готовности шагать навстречу смерти с тоской, но и с неким ветреным любопытством:

День каждый, каждую годину
Привык я думой провождать,
Грядущей смерти годовщину
Меж их стараясь угадать.

И где мне смерть пошлет судьбина?
В бою ли, в странствии, в волнах?
Или соседняя долина
Мой примет охладелый прах?

Если, как верят дзен-буддисты, его душа могла бы выбрать свою собственную судьбу, будто выбирая желаемый конец для героя романа или повести, то, мне кажется, Пушкин, вероятно, выбрал бы именно такой же конец — в зрелости, в гордости, в борьбе за честь. Уникально пушкинский парадокс: «Свой дар, как жизнь, я тратил без вниманья». Он так любил жизнь, что с ней расставался легко, смело шагнув навстречу горькой смерти, как молодой граф в «Выстреле», со сладким вкусом черешен во рту. Кстати, его почти последние слова на смертном ложе были: «Дайте морошки».

Даже в глубине его грустнейших, полных страдания страстей всегда чувствуется присутствие какого-то «друга», «наблюдателя», сочувственно и чуть сардонически всё замечающего. Он всегда как бы увлекается, даже в описании Онегина в минуты глубочайшей любовной тоски:

> Как походил он на поэта,
> Когда в углу сидел один,
> И перед ним пылал камин
> И он мурлыкал "Benedetta"
> Иль "Idol mio" и ронял
> В огонь то туфлю, то журнал.

Умея смеяться над самим собой, Пушкин был величайшим оптимистом. Его литературные наследники создали русской литературе мрачную репутацию, как в песне Гершвина: «больше мрачных туч, чем гарантировано в русской пьесе», но сам основатель русской литературы осмеливался иногда писать счастливые концы (что уже ересь для некоторых слишком политизированных критиков). И даже его несчастные финалы легко могли бы обернуться по-другому, как замечает его Татьяна:

> А счастье было так возможно,
> Так близко.

Набоков, кстати, даже выразил сомнения по поводу однозначности трагического окончания «Евгения Онегина».

> Рискуя разбить сердца поклонников «княгини Греминой» (так именно два «веселых ума», либреттисты Чайковского, назвали Татьяну), всё ж считаю себя обязанным заметить, что ее ответ Онегину отнюдь не звучит с такой величавой финальностью, как пишут комментаторы. Заметьте ее интонации, вздымающуюся грудь, прерывистую речь, страдание, горькость, трепет, восхищение, сладострастье, почти

соблазнительные enjambements, настоящая оргия намеков, заканчивая признаньем в любви, от которого, безусловно, опытное сердце Евгения радостно подпрыгивало. И что же завершает эти 12 рыдающих строк? Всего лишь пустой в звучании поверхностный выкрик добродетели, фальшиво повторяя свои готовые реплики!

Возможно, Набоков здесь заходит слишком далеко. Пушкин не Фальстаф. Честь для него не пустое слово, а, может быть, даже главное слово. Но мир Пушкина пропитан двойственностью и иронией. Он никогда не проповедует, не судит, вместо этого лишь указывает возможные выборы и последствия. Везде в его твореньях — перепутья, дороги, повороты в разные стороны. Некоторые из них серьезные, некоторые, напротив, ветреные, легкомысленные, как выбор героя повести «Метель». (Кстати, у Пушкина легкомысленному выбору, как бы покорности судьбе, чаще везет). Часто, предвещая открытия квантовой механики, Пушкин позволяет герою одновременно два противоположных выбора, невзирая на его знаменитую фразу в «Пиковой даме»: «Две неподвижные идеи не могут вместе существовать в нравственной природе, так же как два тела не могут в физическом мире занимать одно и то же место». Но Пушкин, со свойственной ему непринужденной легкостью, часто избегает следования своему собственному закону. В его мире, с одной стороны, всё неизбежно и никак не может быть иначе, а с другой стороны, всегда возможен любой выход на свете. В его мире, без наставления и проповеди, воля человеческая и случай, выбор и шанс, гармонично сплетаются в грациозный Танец Судьбы. И... «Скозь слезы улыбнуся я.»

Увы, Пушкин не преуспел в достижении желанного удела, не смог следовать примеру своего любимца, поэта Горация, и, будучи «рожден для жизни мирной, для деревенской тишины», совершить заветный «побег в обитель дальную трудов и чистых нег». Но даже «невыездной», в тщетных просьбах о поездке в Испанию, Италию, «к подножию ль стены далекого Китая, в кипящий ли Париж», часто даже не отпущенный царем в свою деревню, он всё же был всегда свободным душою, «иной, лучшей свободой». Даже его предчувствия смерти придали ему смиренное превышение грусти, высшую мудрость целомудрия. Одно из последних его стихотворений основано на великой оде Горация "Exegi Monumentum", в которой Гораций гордится величаво своим устойчивым литературным наследием:

Exegi monumentum aere perennius
Ragalique situ piramidum altius,
Quod non imber edax, non Aquilo impotens
Possit diruere aut innumerabilis
Annorum series et fuga temporum.
Non omnis moriar, multaque pars mei
Vitabit Libitinam: usque ego postera
Crescam laude recens, dum Capitolium
Scandet cum tacita virgine pontifex.
Dicar, qua violens obstrepit Aufidus
Et qua pauper aqaue Daunus agrestium
Regnavit populorum, ex humili potens,
Princeps Aeolium carmen ad Italos
Deduxisse modos. Sume superbiam
Quaesitam meritis et mihi Delphica
Lauro cinge volens, Melpomene, comam.

В знаменитом переводе М. В. Ломоносова эта, XXX ода Горация звучит так (для перевода на английский см. страницу 19):

Я знак бессмертия себе воздвигнул
Превыше пирамид и крепче меди,
Что бурный Аквилон стереть не может,
Ни множество веков, ни едка древность.
Не вовсе я умру, но смерть оставит
Велику часть мою, как жизнь скончаю.
Я буду возрастать повсюду славой,
Пока великий Рим владеет светом,
Где быстрыми шумит струями Авфид,
Где Давнус царствовал в простом народе,
Отечество мое молчать не будет,
Что мне беззнатный род препятством не был,
Чтоб внесть в Италию стихи Эольски,
И первому звенеть Алцейской лирой.
Взгордися праведной заслугой, муза,
И увенчай главу Дельфийским лавром.

Но Пушкин, в отличие от своего ментора Горация, уже не верил в мишуру тленной мирской власти. Его слава не зависит от какого бы то ни было Pontifex Maximus (Высшего Жреца римской империи). У Пушкина никакая империя не дает поэту духовную, внутреннюю, интуитивную «вечно женственную» силу, рожденную в горе и печали, но несущую радость, силу, живущую не под Царем-Солнцем, а скрытую под Луной.

> Нет, весь я не умру — душа в заветной лире
> Мой прах переживет и тленья убежит –
> И славен буду я, доколь в подлунном мире
> Жив будет хоть один пиит.

Вся великая поэзия — особенно поэзия Пушкина — является, в конце концов, памятником Любви — этой священной слабости, которая сильнее всего на свете. Ведь «великий Рим» уже давно не владеет светом, однако Гораций всё еще с нами. Исчезли весталки цезарей, но стихи, вдохновленные ими, еще живут... Так же Татьяна Пушкина (тоже, по-своему, весталка, давшая обет безлюбовному браку, «отдана» как монахиня изувеченному, толстому генералу) всегда будет близка сердцам миллионов, а ее любовь никогда не иссякнет. Они с Евгением напоминают безымянного юношу, утешенного Джоном Китсом в «Оде греческой вазе».

> Bold lover, never, never canst thou kiss,
> Though winning near the goal — yet, do not grieve;
> She cannot fade, though thou hast not thy bliss,
> For ever wilt thou love, and she be fair!

> Влюбленный пылкий, не дано тебе
> Коснуться уст ее — но не горюй.
> Навек живет в нетленной красоте
> Любви нетленной поцелуй. (Перевод с английского Д.Л.)

«Доколь в подлунном мире жив будет хоть один пиит», пока поэзия еще жива в наших душах, нам нужен Пушкин, поэт поэтов, поэт русской души. Нам нужен его пример, его выбор трудности и изгнания вместо компромисса в безупречной чести своего искусства. Не в пример Горацию, он не просил музу увенчать его главу лавровым венцом («Поэт, не дорожи любовию народной»). Напротив, он безмятежно принимал на себя горестные муки поэта, непонятого окружающим его миром, довольный своей истиной и тем, что служил Добру.

> И долго буду тем любезен я народу,
> Что чувства добрые я лирой пробуждал,
> Что в мой жестокий век восславил я свободу
> И милость к падшим призывал.
> Веленью Божию, о муза, будь послушна,
> Обиды не страшась, не требуя венца;
> Хвалу и клевету приемли равнодушно,
> И не оспоривай глупца.

Давно пора нам слышать чистый, неразмытый голос Пушкина на английском языке. Пусть эта книга поможет не знающим русский язык услышать, наконец, его музыку. Прошу прощения у всех читателей, уже благословленных знанием русского, уже знакомых с Пушкиным, за всё то невыразимое волшебство Пушкина, которое всё равно не может не пропадать в переводе. Но надеюсь, что и русскоязычным эта книга, может быть, поможет уловить иное сиянье ярчайшей звезды русского литературного небосвода, так, как порой бывает, что пролитие света с необычной стороны выявляет новые грани и отблески бриллианта.

Джулиан Лоуэнфэлд *Осень 2003*

Он сам себя увенчал венцом лавровым

К ДОРОГИМ РУССКИМ ЧИТАТЕЛЯМ!

Эти страницы жизни Пушкина я написал сначала по-английски, для англоязычного читателя, мало знакомого с поэтом. Когда меня просили перевести их на русский язык, признаюсь, я даже колебался — нужен ли перевод? Ведь многие факты, необходимые англоязычному читателю, скорее всего давно известны читателю русскому, воспитанному на Пушкине с детства. Поразмыслив, я все же пришел к выводу, что в двуязычной книге все ее компоненты должны присутствовать на обоих языках. А то, не дай Бог, меня еще могут обвинить в дискриминации! И заранее извиняюсь: русский язык мною страстно любим, но не родной... Если мой перевод с английского иногда невольно ведет к некоторому своеобразию конструкции русского предложения, пожалуйста, не обессудьте! (Или взгляните на английский текст). Все же главное в этой книге — стихи Пушкина и возможность любоваться чудными рисунками поэта.

Всю многогранность гения Пушкина, к сожалению, одна книга никогда не вместит. Более политически или философски настроенный читатель простит, надеюсь, мой уклон в бесподобную любовную лирику поэта. И, увы, я не смог в размерах этой книги, так, как хотелось бы, углубиться в бездонный духовный мир поэта. Простите меня и за некоторое повторение азов и неизбежное упрощение фактов, памятуя, что текст был рассчитан на англоязычного читателя и что я не русский и даже не американский пушкинист, а лишь американец, обожающий Пушкина...

ПРИМЕЧАНИЕ К ТЕКСТАМ

Ральф Уалдо Эмерсон заметил: «Глупая последовательность во всем — мелкий бес мелких умов». У Пушкина, как и у Шекспира, нет единого канонического издания, а существуют различные варианты публикаций. В этой книге я придерживался издания: Академия Наук СССР. Институт Русской Литературы (Пушкинский Дом). Пушкин, А.С. «Полное собрание сочинений» в 10 тт., издание третье. Издательство Академии Наук СССР, Москва, 1962.

INTRODUCTION

КРАТКАЯ БИОГРАФИЯ ПОЭТА

Что такое поэт? Человек, который пишет стихами? Нет, конечно. Он называется поэтом не потому, что он пишет стихами; но он пишет стихами, то есть приводит в гармонию слова и звуки, потому что он – сын гармонии, поэт.

А.А. Блок «О назначении Поэта»

1799–1811. Детство

Александр Сергеевич Пушкин родился в Москве 6 июня 1799 г. (или 26 мая 1799 года по юлианскому календарю, действовавшему в России до 1918 г. Далее в этой книге все даты последуют «по старому стилю», как сам Пушкин их прожил). Отец поэта, Сергей Львович Пушкин, был родом из прославленной, хотя и обедневшей дворянской семьи. Мать поэта, Надежду Осиповну, урожденную Ганнибал, называли "la belle créole" (прекрасной креолкой). Ее черный дед, Ибрагим Ганнибал, был похищен в детстве, вероятно, в центральной Африке, перевезен работорговцами к туркам, затем куплен и отправлен «подарком» императору Петру I. Петр крестил его, сделал талантливого мальчика своим секретарем, окружил атмосферой тепла и отеческой заботы, позднее отправил во Францию, где он изучил военные науки. Абрам стал главным фортификатором России и даже написал учебники на французском языке по математике и фортификации. Гордясь своим африканским происхождением, он позже выбрал себе фамилию в честь великого карфагенского полководца Ганнибала (одна из версий). Абрам закончил свою карьеру в звании генерал-аншефа императорской российской армии с наградами. Императрица Елизавета Петровна наделила его имениями, включая Михайловское в Псковской губернии. Итак, бывший раб стал русским дворянином и владельцем 800 крепостных (белых рабов). Пушкин унаследовал несколько физических черт своего африканского деда: полные губы, кудрявые волосы и смугловатую кожу. Чернильница на его письменном столе изображала статуэтку черного раба, выгружающего хлопок, и он любил шутить с легкой гордостью о своем «арапстве»:

Зачем твой дивный карандаш
Рисует мой арапский профиль?

В доме Пушкиных бывали поэты, писатели... Отца поэта уважали за образованность, за одну из лучших библиотек Москвы, преимущественно на французском языке; в литературных салонах он блистал остроумием и читал Мольера в лицах с живостью и изяществом. Дядя Пушкина Василий Львович был известным русским поэтом («Вы дядя мой и на Парнасе»). Мать поэта очень любила читать детям вслух, и Пушкин потом напишет: «Чтение — вот лучшее учение». Если бы не было в семье атмосферы любви к поэзии, великой европейской культуры и стиля исконно русской жизни мы бы не имели такого Пушкина. Но биографы поэта и мемуаристы обычно критикуют его родителей и, порой, не без основания. «Сергей Львович был нежный отец, но нежность его черствела ввиду выдачи денег. Вообще он был чрезвычайно скуп»,— вспоминал князь Петр Вяземский, друг поэта. Рассказывали, что случайная поломка какой-нибудь 35-копеечной рюмочки могла его взбесить на целый день. Отец «никогда не оказывал ни малейшей помощи своему сыну Александру, и... он едва ли получил от отца во всю свою жизнь до пятисот рублей ассигнациями, при всем том, тщеславие его тешили успехи своего сына, и он по-своему гордился ими», — писал биограф М. И. Семевский. Мать поэта, по мнению многих, была обаятельной, но капризной и не очень заботливой. «Она умела дуться по дням, месяцам и даже годам», — вспоминал муж сестры поэта Л.Н. Павлищев. Справедливости ради надо заметить, что любой матери было бы трудно управляться с восемью детьми (Александр был вторым; пятеро детей умерли в малолетстве). Но по какой-то причине она предпочитала младшего брата поэта — Льва — беспокойному, блестящему enfant terrible, Александру, с которым она бывала иногда холодна и неласкова. Только в последние годы ее жизни в отношениях между поэтом и его матерью появились теплота и, в некоторой степени, духовная связь. В глубочайшей любовной лирике Пушкина можно почувствовать и тоску, и жажду по материнской любви, которой ему не хватало в детстве. Может, он не случайно изобразил себя сиротой в почти автобиографичном «Русском Пеламе»?

> ...Пребывание мое под отеческою кровлею не оставило ничего приятного в моем воображении. Отец, конечно, меня любил, но вовсе обо мне не беспокоился и оставил меня на попечении французов, которых беспрестанно принимали и отпускали. Первый мой гувернер оказался пьяницей; второй, человек неглупый и не без сведений, имел такой бешеный нрав, что однажды чуть не убил меня поленом за то, что пролил я чернила на его жилет; третий, проживший у нас целый год, был совершенно сумасшедший.

Современные «семейные ценности» в пушкинские времена были не модны. Au contraire, легкое пренебрежение к родительским обязанностям, считалось аристократичным bon ton; как и то, что дети в доме должны быть «лишь видны, а не слышны». Ими часто занимались слуги, приглашенные гувернеры и гувернантки.

Недостаток родительского внимания маленький Саша чувствовал, но, в отличие от его современника Диккенса, детские переживания не стали главными темами его творчества. Вместо этого Пушкин предпочитал иногда держаться на некотором расстоянии от «родных»:

> Что значит именно родные?
> Родные люди вот какие:
> Мы их обязаны ласкать,
> Любить, душевно уважать,
> И, по обычаю народа,
> О Рождестве их навещать
> Или по почте поздравлять,
> Чтоб остальное время года
> Не думали о нас они...
> Итак, дай Бог им долги дни!

С. Л. Пушкин, отец поэта

Но Пушкин посвятил теплые стихи своей бабушке Марии Алексеевне Ганнибал и крепостной няне Арине Родионовне («Наперсница волшебной старины»). Однажды, гуляя с маленьким Сашей в Юсуповском саду, няня позабыла вовремя снять картузик с младенца при приближении государя, за что тотчас получила выговор от царя Павла I (предзнаменование, пожалуй, будущих проблем с властями). Именно няне с бабушкой он обязан чудесным знанием русского языка (в то время во многих дворянских семьях язык общения был французский; Татьяна пишет Онегину на французском, так как: «...Она по-русски плохо знала»). Каждое лето до Лицея он гостил в Захарове, имении Марии Алексеевны, недалеко от родового поместья царя Бориса Годунова. Ласки няни и бабушки объединились в восприятии маленького Саши с "призывом млечным" самого́ русского языка, с великим даром и тайной русских сказок и сказаний.

> Ах! Умолчу ль о мамушке моей,
> О прелести таинственных ночей,
> Когда в чепце, в старинном одеянье
> Она, духов молитвой уклоня,
> С усердием перекрестит меня
> И шепотом рассказывать мне станет
> О мертвецах, о подвигах Бовы.
> От ужаса не шелохнусь, бывало,
> Едва дыша, прижмусь под одеяло,
> Не чувствуя ни ног, ни головы.
> Под образом простой ночник из глины
> Чуть освещал глубокие морщины.

Няня

И без страшных сказок, кажется, Пушкин часто страдал бессонницей ("Мне не спится, нет огня»; «Воспоминание»). Может быть, бессонница – это "служебная болезнь" поэта? Однажды, когда ему было 7 лет, бабушка обнаружила, что он всю ночь до самой зари не спал, а бродил по дому, словно в трансе, повторяя: "Я пишу стихи". Со старшей сестрой Ольгой они часто играли, придумывая маленькие сценки в стихах. Самый ранний из сохранившихся стихов Пушкина, на французском, bien sûr, описывает провал его первой мировой première:

> Dis-moi, pourquoi L'Escamoteur
> Fût-il sifflé par le parterre?
> Hélas! C'est que son pauvre auteur
> L'escamota de Molière.

Уже в семь лет слышны первые нотки пушкинского голоса: самоуничижительное остроумие, чуть шаловливый юмор, таящий в себе тоску и внутреннее одиночество... Пожалуй, самый правдивый портрет поэта в детстве, это — описание мечтательной юности Татьяны в «Евгении Онегине» (гл. II, XXV-XXIX). Он обожал чтение и часто целыми сутками забывался в библиотеке отца: Гомер, Плутарх, Вергилий, Овидий, Тацит, Ювенал, Теренций, Светоний, Гораций, Монтень, Корнель, Расин, Мольер, Бомарше, Лакло, Сен-Прё, Ричардсон, Стерн, Дефо, Дидро, Вольтер, Руссо... Маленький Саша «глотал» одну книгу за другой, при этом не пропуская ни одного bon mot на литературных вечерах, которые устраивал отец. Француз Жилле заметил: «Какой чудный ребенок! Как рано он всё начал понимать! Дай Бог ему жить и жить, да вы увидите, что из него будет!» Уже в детстве Пушкин в таком совершенстве овладел французским языком, что лицейские товарищи потом прозвали его «французом». Взращенный певучими русскими сказками и присказками няни и бабушки, но непринужденно воспитанный в пьянящем блеске французского салона отца, он стал уникально способным преобразовать русский язык. Его невероятная восприимчивость и понимание, способность пребывать у себя дома одновременно в двух мирах — это всё даровано нам его детством. Как ни парадоксально, можно справедливо назвать «солнце русской поэзии» и чадом французского Просвещения.

Н.О. Пушкина, мать поэта

Вольтер

1811–1817. Лицей

Сначала родители хотели отправить Пушкина во французскую иезуитскую школу в Петербурге. Но в 1811 году царь Александр I решил основать в Царском Селе, приятном пригороде столицы, в здании, соединенном с императорским дворцом, элитарное учебное заведение, даровав ему свою личную библиотеку. Шесть лет учебы (без права выезда домой) предоставлялись бесплатно молодым дворянам, предназначенным «к важным частям службы государственной». Телесные наказания запрещались, что было в то время редкостью. Василий Пушкин, дядя поэта, отвез своего племянника в Петербург для вступительного экзамена (взяв в долг по пути 100 рублей, без отдачи, подаренные Пушкину тетушкой «на орехи»). Пушкин был принят в Лицей с 29 другими мальчиками 19 октября 1811 г. Эта дата станет святой для Пушкина на всю жизнь, годовщину ее поэт воспел в семи стихотворениях. Как только закончилась торжественная церемония инаугурации, юные лицеисты выбежали во двор и начался веселый бой снежками. С первых дней тесно связанные между собой лицеисты пробуждали друг в друге дух резвой мальчишеской вольности, радости, игривого соперничества и доброго юмора — всё это при неизменном благоговении перед высшими целями в жизни — свободы, чести, глубокой дружбы, преданности любви и искусству, которые потом назовут «лицейским духом».

> Друзья мои, прекрасен наш союз!
> Он, как душа, неразделим и вечен —
> Неколебим, свободен и беспечен,
> Срастался он под сенью дружных муз.
> Куда бы нас ни бросила судьбина
> И счастие куда б ни повело,
> Всё те же мы: нам целый мир чужбина;
> Отечество нам Царское Село.

Лицейские друзья, поэты Дельвиг и Кюхельбекер и любимый «Жанно», будущий декабрист Пущин, всегда были и оставались самыми близкими и дорогими ему до конца дней.

Довольно смелая программа обучения в Лицее включала в себя предметы: «1. грамматика: изучение русского, латинского, французского и немецкого языков; 2. нравственные науки: религия, философия, этика, логика; 3. математические и физические науки: алгебра, физика, тригонометрия; 4. исторические науки: история России и иностранных государств, география, хронология мира; 5. основательное знание литературы: чтение лучших авторов, правила критического анализа, риторики; 6. изобразительные искусства, к тому же гимнастика, каллиграфия, рисование, фехтование, танец, искусство верховой езды, плавание...»

> Мы все учились понемногу
> Чему-нибудь и как-нибудь...

Если бы Пушкин серьезнее относился к учебе, то он бы мог стать, как князь Горчаков, сначала первым в классе, а потом, чего доброго, канцлером русской империи. Некоторые либерально настроенные педагоги повлияли на мировоззрение Пушкина, особенно профессор нравственных наук Куницын, соединявший резкое осуждение крепостного права с учением о «естественном праве» и доктринами Адама Смита. Преподаватель французского был родным братом французского революционера Марата. Лицеисты близко к сердцу восприняли наполеоновское вторжение в Россию в 1812 г., Бородинскую битву, сожжение Москвы. Однажды, как рассказывал друг Пушкина Малиновский, они даже выбросили учебники французского в знак протеста.

Вы помните: текла за ратью рать,
Со старшими мы братьями прощались
И в сень наук с досадой возвращались,
Завидуя тому, кто умирать
Шел мимо нас...

В своих «Записках о Пушкине» Иван Пущин («Жанно») вспоминал молодого поэта, своего лучшего друга лицейских дней:

> Все мы видели, что Пушкин нас опередил, многое прочел, о чем мы и не слыхали, всё, что читал, помнил, но достоинство его состояло в том, что отнюдь не думал высказываться и важничать, как это бывает в те годы... Напротив, все научное он считал ни во что и как будто желал только доказать, что мастер бегать, прыгать через стулья или бросать мячик...

Действительно, Пушкин замечательно освоил фехтование и верховую езду, прекрасно плавал и подолгу ходил пешком, был страстным гимнастом и, даже чемпионом России в легком весе по «французскому боксу». Но и поэтический дар Пушкина также быстро стал заметен в соперничестве с другими лицейскими поэтами. Его первая публикация вышла в 1814 году, когда друзья тайком отправили его рукопись «К другу стихотворцу» в журнал «Вестник Европы» за подписью «Н.К.Ш.П.» (Пушкин — наоборот). В 1815 году, пока «голос мой отроческий зазвенел», Пушкин декламировал свои «Воспоминания в Царском Селе» на экзамене по русской литературе, на котором присутствовал самый известный в то время поэт России Гавриил Державин. От этого «сердце забилось упоительным восторгом... Не помню, как я кончил свое чтение; не помню, куда убежал. Державин был в восхищении: он меня требовал, хотел меня обнять... Меня искали, но не нашли».

Но, вообще, он не все предметы любил. Даже профессор Куницын жаловался: «Пушкин — весьма понятен, замысловат и остроумен, но крайне неприлежен». Пушкину, вместе с Пущиным и Малиновским, часто доставалось за какие-то проказы. За питье гоголь-моголя с ромом их наказали двухдневным лишением обедов и стоянием на коленях во время молитв. Молодой поэт «считал схоластику за вздор/ И прыгал в сад через забор», уходя с лицейской территории, прогуливая уроки и волочась за девушками (Mon Portrait). И «писал он везде, где мог, а всего более в математическом классе». Самая первая сохранившаяся рукопись стихотворения Пушкина уже о любви: «К Наталье» было написано в 1813 году молодой актрисе из крепостного театра графа Толстого. Пушкин написал более 120 стихотворений в лицейские годы, из них более двадцати были обращены к фрейлине Екатерине Бакуниной («Певец», «Дориде», «Друзьям»). В Лицее он также начал ироническую сказку-эпопею «Руслан и Людмила». На последнем году обучения Пушкин иногда пропускал уроки, чтобы общаться с гусарами, чьи полки располагались недалеко от Екатерининского дворца, для серьезных политических бесед и застолий. Одним из этих гусар был Петр Чаадаев, проницательный критик самодержавия и крепостного права, который познакомил молодого поэта с английским языком, философией Локка и Юма и свободолюбивой лирикой Байрона. В Царском Селе Пушкин также встречался и с великим русским историком и сентиментальным романистом Николаем Карамзиным и его женой Екатериной Андреевной, которую некоторые считают «утаенной любовью» Пушкина.

9 июня 1817 года Пушкин заканчивает лицей двадцать шестым из 29 воспитанников, с отличными оценками только по русскому и французскому языкам и фехтованию. Год спустя, когда Пушкин уже стал знаменитым, один из его преподавателей жаловался: «Да что он вам дался, — шалун был, и больше ничего!» (Ф. О. Калинин, учитель чистописания). Е. А. Энгельгардт, директор Лицея, высказал еще резче свою неприязнь к самому знаменитому ученику в лицейской характеристике Пушкина 1816 года:

> Высшая и конечная цель Пушкина — блистать, и именно поэзией; но едва ли найдет она у него прочное основание, потому что он боится всякого серьезного учения, и его ум, не имея ни проницательности, ни глубины, совершенно поверхностный, французский ум. Это еще самое лучшее, что можно сказать о Пушкине. Его сердце холодно и пусто: в нем нет ни любви, ни религии; может быть, оно так пусто, как никогда не бывало юношеское сердце.

В буддийской практике медитации такая «пустота» иногда являет собой высокую степень похвалы — достижение наивысшей стадии духовного совершенства. Возможно, что такая «пустота» или (другими словами) открытость пушкинского сердца сделала его идеальным проводником для возвышенных проявлений неистощимой небесной любви. Во всяком случае, эта «пустота» была его богатством, даром, который не мог быть захламлен обыкновенными какими-то «приспособлениями» к «важным частям службы государственной». Еще в Лицее он решил:

> Простите, хладные науки!
> Простите, игры первых лет!
> Я изменился, я поэт,
> В душе моей едины звуки
> Переливаются, живут.
> В размеры сладкие бегут.

1817–1820. Санкт-Петербург

По окончании Лицея Пушкин был определен в Коллегию иностранных дел, со скромным чином коллежского секретаря. «Вышед из лицея, я тотчас почти уехал в псковскую деревню моей матери. Помню, как обрадовался сельской жизни, русской бане, клубнике...» Ему было приятно видеться со своим черным двоюродным дедушкой и распивать с ним по шесть рюмок огненной домашней настойки. Вернувшись в Петербург, Пушкин жил, по последним данным, сначала в доме графа И. Апраксина (ныне кан. Грибоедова, 174), а потом, вместе со своими родителями, в тесной квартире на реке Фонтанке. Этажом выше жил лицеист граф Модест Корф. Пушкин однажды вызвал его на дуэль за то, что Корф позволил себе ударить крепостного «дядьку» Пушкина Никиту Козлова. Корф, кстати, был любимчиком директора Лицея Энгельгардта. Корф не жаловал своего соседа, а в своих воспоминаниях презрительно отзывался о семье поэта:

> Все семейство Пушкиных было какое-то взбалмошное. Отец его был довольно приятным собеседником, на манер старинной французской школы, с анекдотами и каламбурами, но в существе человеком самым пустым, бестолковым и бесполезным, особенно безмолвным рабом своей жены. Последняя была женщина неглупая, но эксцентрическая, вспыльчивая, до крайности рассеянная и особенно чрезвычайно дурная хозяйка. Дом их представлял всегда какой-то хаос: в одной комнате богатые старинные мебели, в другой пустые стены, даже без стульев, многочисленная, но оборванная и пьяная дворня, ветхие рыдваны с тощими клячами, пышные дамские наряды, вечный недостаток во всем, начиная от денег и до последнего стакана. Когда у них обедывало человека два-три, то всегда присылали к нам за приборами.

Возможно, Корф здесь нарочно преувеличивает (как и в других своих воспоминаниях о Пушкине). Но бесспорно, после пьянящей свободы и комфорта Лицея жизнь с родителями казалась полной ограничений и лишений. Позже, в письме к младшему брату Льву, Пушкин вспоминал: «Больной, когда в осеннюю грязь или в трескучие морозы я брал извозчика от Аничкова моста, (отец) вечно бранился за 80 коп. (которых, верно б, ни ты, ни я не пожалели для слуги)». Отцовская скупость провоцировала ответную реакцию: вызывающую беспечность сына в отношении денег. Из воспоминаний друга: «Однажды ему (Пушкину) случилось кататься на лодке в обществе, в котором находился Сергей Львович (отец поэта). Погода стояла тихая, а вода была так прозрачна, что виднелось самое дно. Пушкин вынул несколько золотых монет и одну за другою стал бросать в воду, любуясь падением и отражением их в чистой влаге».

Он не «горел» на службе, но страстно любил театр, оставив о нем замечательные заметки. И, естественно, увлекался хорошенькими актрисами. Например, Еленой Сосницкой, в любовные сети которой попался молодой Пушкин, «но взялся за ум и отделался стишком» («В альбом Сосницкой»). Как большинство молодых интеллектуалов того времени, он был либералом; в отличие от большинства либералов, однако, не был особенно фанатичен. Его друзья из литературного общества «Арзамас», в которое он вступил, прозвали его «Сверчком» — за привычку петь, оставаясь незамеченным, и за подход к жизни, который, на их взгляд, соответствовал более кузнечику, чем муравью. Он был членом свободолюбивого литературного клуба «Зеленая лампа», а также встречался с идеалистской дворянской молодежью и будущими декабристами.

Как-то вечером в доме Алексея Оленина, директора Публичной библиотеки и Академии, он впервые встретил прекрасную, кокетливую Анну Керн, против воли выданную замуж в 16 лет за грубого генерала, солдафона (старше ее на 35 лет). Она вспоминает:

> Завязался между нами шутливый разговор о том, кто грешник, а кто нет, кто будет в аду и кто попадет в рай. Пушкин сказал брату: «Во всяком случае, в аду будет много хорошеньких, там можно будет играть в шарады. Спроси у M-me Керн: хотела бы она попасть в ад?» Я отвечала очень серьезно и несколько сухо, что я да не желаю. «Ну, как же ты теперь, Пушкин?» — спросил брат. «Я раздумал, — ответил поэт, — я в ад не хочу, хотя там и будут хорошенькие женщины».

В 1819 году он потерял голову из-за Евдокии Голицыной, «Princesse Nocturne», которая устраивала салоны, обычно далеко переходящие за полночь.

> Где женщина — не с хладной красотой,
> Но с пламенной, пленительной, живой?
> Где разговор найду непринужденный,
> Блистательный, веселый, просвещенный?
> С кем можно быть не хладным, не пустым?
> Отечество почти я ненавидел —
> Но я вчера Голицыну увидел
> И примирен с Отечеством моим.

Пушкин посетил известную немецкую гадалку Александру Кирхгоф. Ее советы императору Александру I якобы помогли царю выстоять в самые критические моменты войны 1812 года. Мадам Кирхгоф предсказала Пушкину великую славу, две ссылки и долгую счастливую жизнь, если только на 37 году жизни «не случится с ним какой беды от белой лошади или белой головы, или белого человека (т.е. блондина), которых и должен он опасаться». Пушкин поверил без всяких сомнений ее предсказаниям — и они действительно все сбылись.

В то время по городу распространялись слухи о ветреном поэте-повесе, легко пренебрегающем запретами в отношении вина, женщин и песен. Энгельгардт, директор Лицея, как обычно, выражал свое недовольство: «Если б только этот бездельник захотел учиться, он был бы человеком выдающимся в нашей литературе!». Друг поэта Александр Тургенев отчаивался: «Праздная леность, как грозный истребитель всего прекрасного и всякого таланта, парит над Пушкиным... Пушкин по утрам рассказывает Жуковскому, где он всю ночь не спал; целый день делает визиты б...м или мне и княгине Голицыной, а ввечеру иногда играет в банк...» Поэт Батюшков ему отвечал: «Не худо бы Сверчка запереть в Гёттинген и кормить года три молочным супом и логикою». Но Пушкин, вполне счастливый, (см. стихи «Тургеневу»), «гулял», веселился и не раскаивался:

> Я люблю вечерний пир,
> Где веселье председатель,
> А свобода, мой кумир,
> За столом законодатель,
> Где до утра слово пей!
> Заглушает крики песен,
> Где просторен круг гостей,
> А кружок бутылок тесен.

На заре Пушкин взбадривал себя ледяной ванной, затем работал часами, часто еще лежа в кровати. Он дописывал «Руслана и Людмилу», ироническую русскую сказку в стихах, которая стала настоящей сенсацией, когда вышла в свет в 1820 году. Русская публика была очарована волшебным богатством и искрометностью пушкинского языка.

Соперники в искусстве брани,
Не знайте мира меж собой;
Несите мрачной славе дани
И упивайтеся враждой!
Пусть мир пред вами цепенеет,
Дивяся грозным торжествам:
Никто о вас не пожалеет,
Никто не помешает вам.
Соперники другого рода,
Вы, рыцари парнасских гор,
Старайтесь не смешить народа
Нескромным шумом ваших ссор;
Бранитесь — только осторожно.
Но вы, соперники в любви,
Живите дружно, если можно!
Поверьте мне, друзья мои:
Кому судьбою непременной
Девичье сердце суждено,
Тот будет мил назло вселенной;
Сердиться глупо и грешно.

Рыцарь с дамой

Поэт Жуковский, переводчик «Одиссеи» в величественный русский гекзаметр, отреагировал на «Руслана и Людмилу», подарив Пушкину свой портрет с надписью: «Победителю-ученику от побежденного учителя».

Многие из ближайших друзей Пушкина тех трех лет, проведенных в Петербурге, являлись членами революционных обществ. К неудобству советских биографов, сам Сверчок был слишком занят «стрекотанием», чтобы вступить в эти общества. При этом Пушкин сделал больше для их дела, чем сами его члены — своими популярными стихотворениями и острыми эпиграммами против правительства и министров (включая «Эпиграмму на Аракчеева», фактически управляющего правительством Александра I). Казалось, поэт не испытывал страха самовыражения. Пущин вспоминает, как однажды, в переполненном театре, Пушкин на рассказ о том, что в Летнем дворце медвежонок сорвался с цепи и чуть ли не погубил государя, отреагировал громким восклицанием: «Наконец-то нашелся в России человек, да и тот — медведь!» (Кстати, медвежонка казнили.)

На вечере, проходившем в комнате с видом на мрачный Михайловский дворец царя Павла I, Пушкина попросили выглянуть в окно и сымпровизировать стихотворение. Через несколько часов он уже набросал черновик оды «Вольность» — запрещенной в России до 1906 года. Эта ода и другие запрещенные стихи, такие, как «К Чаадаеву», «Деревня», быстро распространялись по стране, создавая сенсацию, вдохновляя тайные общества и диссидентов.

КРАТКАЯ БИОГРАФИЯ ПОЭТА

Александра I крайне взбесила ода «Вольность»: она не только содержала призыв к конституционной монархии, но и нарушала строжайшее табу, честно упоминая об убийстве Павла I, отца Александра I (в котором косвенно сам Александр был замешан). Агент тайной полиции делал попытки подкупить верного слугу Пушкина Никиту Козлова, чтобы получить запрещенные рукописи. Козлов отказался и сразу предупредил своего хозяина, который все сжег, и «...я жаждал Сибири или (Петропавловской) крепости для восстановления моей чести». Военный губернатор Петербурга Милорадович вызвал его на допрос. Пушкин, проявив истинное гражданское мужество, написал по памяти слово в слово свои самые вызывающие стихи против правительства в ставшую знаменитой «тетрадь Милорадовича». Очарованный и восхищенный храбростью и талантом молодого поэта, Милорадович отпустил Пушкина под честное слово. Царь, однако, не нашел в тетради ничего забавного и намеревался сослать Пушкина в Сибирь или на Соловки, за полярный круг в Белом море (где в советское время был построен страшный концентрационный лагерь). К счастью, в последнюю минуту, благодаря ходатайствам Милорадовича, Жуковского, Чаадаева и Карамзина, место ссылки оказалось более теплым: в юго-западную провинцию России под начальство генерала Ивана Никитича Инзова. 6 мая 1820 года, в день Вознесения Господня, Пушкин покинул Санкт-Петербург и выехал на юг. В своем эпилоге к «Руслану и Людмиле» Пушкин подвел итог своих бурных петербургских лет:

> Я славил лирою послушной
> Преданья темной старины.
> Я пел — и забывал обиды
> Слепого счастья и врагов,
> Измены ветреной Дориды
> И сплетни шумные глупцов.
> На крыльях вымысла носимый,
> Ум улетал за край земной;
> И между тем грозы незримой
> Сбиралась туча надо мной!..
> Я погибал... Святой хранитель
> Первоначальных бурных дней,
> О дружба, нежный утешитель
> Болезненной души моей!
> Ты умолила непогоду;
> Ты сердцу возвратила мир;
> Ты сохранила мне свободу,
> Кипящий младости кумир!

Александр I

1824–1826. Южная ссылка

После двухнедельной тряски по грязным, прославленным изрытостью дорогамоссийской империи Пушкин явился к генералу Инзову в Екатеринославль (современный Днепропетровск, город, известный своими «потемкинскими деревнями» — фасадами несуществующих дворцов, построенных специально для того, чтобы произвести впечатление на императрицу Екатерину II, проплывающую мимо на корабле). «Приехав в Екатеринославль, я соскучился, поехал кататься по Днепру, выкупался и схватил горячку», — написал он брату. И в постели, без присмотра, в забытьи его нашел генерал Николай Раевский, герой войны 1812 года. Он был в пути с двумя сыновьями и четырьмя дочерьми на кавказские минеральные воды, и Раевский упросил, чтобы генерал Инзов позволил Пушкину поехать с ними. Два месяца, проведенные на Кавказе, прогулки по горам и лечебная минеральная вода полностью восстановили здоровье и творческие силы поэта. Он позже вспоминал: «Источники, большею частию в первобытном своем виде, били, дымились и стекали с гор по разным направлениям, оставляя по себе белые и красноватые следы. Мы черпали кипучую воду ковшиком из коры или дном разбитой бутылки... Признаюсь: кавказские воды представляют ныне более удобностей; но мне было жаль их прежнего дикого состояния; мне было жаль крутых каменных тропинок, кустарников и неогороженных пропастей, над которыми, бывало, я карабкался».

Он вдохновился новой поэмой, «Кавказский пленник», про русского солдата, взятого в плен чеченцами и полюбившего чеченскую девушку. (Возможно, лучшим фильмом, посвященным современному конфликту в Чечне, является прекрасная экранизации поэмы, переложенной на современную действительность; фильм называется «Кавказский пленник», главные роли в нем сыграли Сергей Бодров и Олег Меньшиков.) Поэма обозначила развитие поэтического таланта Пушкина, в котором романтическая страстность сочеталась с характерным, словно влюбленным, вниманием к малейшим деталям:

> Казалось, пленник безнадежный
> К унылой жизни привыкал.
> Тоску неволи, жар мятежный
> В душе глубоко он скрывал.
> Влачася меж угрюмых скал
> В час ранней, утренней прохлады,
> Вперял он любопытный взор
> На отдаленные громады
> Седых, румяных, синих гор.
> Великолепные картины!

Престолы вечные снегов,
Очам казались их вершины
Недвижной цепью облаков,
И в их кругу колосс двуглавый,
В венце блистая ледяном,
Эльбрус огромный, величавый
Белел на небе голубом.
Когда, с глухим сливаясь гулом,
Предтеча бури, гром гремел,
Как часто пленник над аулом
Недвижим на горе сидел!
У ног его дымились тучи,
В степи взвивался прах летучий;
Уже приюта между скал
Олень испуганный искал;
Орлы с утесов подымались
И в небесах перекликались;
Шум табунов, мычанье стад
Уж гласом бури заглушались...
И вдруг на долы дождь и град
Из туч сквозь молний извергались;
Волнами роя крутизны,
Сдвигая камни вековые,
Текли потоки дождевые —
А пленник, с горной вышины,
Один, за тучей громовою,
Возврата солнечного ждал,
Недосягаемый грозою,
И бури немощному вою
С какой-то радостью внимал.

Николай Гоголь (для него Пушкин сыграл роль наставника) считал это путешествие переломным для Пушкина:

> Исполинский, покрытый вечным снегом Кавказ, среди знойных долин, поразил его; он, можно сказать, вызвал силу души его и разорвал последние цепи, которые еще тяготели на свободных мыслях. Его пленила вольная поэтическая жизнь дерзких горцев, их схватки, их быстрые, неотразимые набеги; и с этих пор кисть его приобрела тот широкий размах, ту быстроту и смелость, которая так дивила и поражала только начинающую читать Россию. Рисует ли он боевую схватку чеченца с казаком — слог его молния; он так же блещет, как сверкающие сабли, и летит быстрее самой битвы. Он один только певец Кавказа.

Пересекая Черное море, по дороге с Кавказа в Крым, на борту брига «Мингрелия», Пушкин «всю ночь не спал; луны не было, звезды блистали; передо мною, в тумане, тянулись полуденные горы...», и он написал свою замечательную, напоминающую Байрона элегию «Погасло дневное светило». Он писал домой брату:

> Корабль плыл перед горами, покрытыми тополями, виноградом, лаврами и кипарисами; везде мелькали татарские селения; он остановился в виду Юрзуфа. Там прожил я три недели. Мой друг, счастливейшие минуты жизни моей провел я посереди семейства почтенного Раевского. Я не видел в нем героя, славу русского войска, я в нем любил человека с ясным умом, с простой, прекрасной душою; снисходительного, попечительного друга, всегда милого, ласкового хозяина. Свидетель Екатерининского века, памятник 12 года; человек без предрассудков, с сильным характером и чувствительный, он невольно привяжет к себе всякого, кто только достоин понимать и ценить его высокие качества... Все его дочери — прелесть, старшая — женщина необыкновенная. Суди, был ли я счастлив: свободная, беспечная жизнь в кругу милого семейства; жизнь, которую я так люблю и которой никогда не наслаждался, — счастливое, полуденное небо; прелестный край; природа, удовлетворяющая воображение, — горы, сады, море!

В черновике письма своему другу Дельвигу он вспоминал:

> Я купался в море и объедался виноградом; я тотчас привык к полуденной природе и наслаждался ею со всем равнодушием и беспечностию неаполитанского lazzaroni (итал. — «лентяя»). Я любил, проснувшись ночью, слушать шум моря, — и заслушивался целые часы. В двух шагах от дома рос молодой кипарис; каждое утро я навещал его и к нему под конец привязался чувством, похожим на дружество.

Старший сын Раевского Александр взял Пушкина с собой в Бахчисарай посмотреть на дворец, принадлежавший когда-то хану крымских татар.

> В Бахчисарай приехал я больной. Я прежде слыхал о странном памятнике влюбленного хана. **** поэтически описывала мне его, называя la fontaine des larmes. Вошед во дворец, увидел я испорченный фонтан; из заржавой железной трубки по каплям падала вода. Я обошел дворец с большой досадою на небрежение, в котором он истлевает, и на полуевропейские переделки некоторых комнат. NN почти насильно повел меня по ветхой лестнице в развалины гарема и на ханское кладбище. Но не тем
>   В то время сердце полно было:
> лихорадка меня мучила. Растолкуй мне теперь, почему полуденный берег и Бахчисарай имеют для меня прелесть неизъяснимую? Отчего так сильно во мне желание вновь посетить места, оставленные мною с таким равнодушием? Или воспоминание самая сильная способность души нашей, и им очаровано все, что подвластно ему?

Пушкин вернулся к этому заржавевшему «фонтану слез» в поэме «Бахчисарайский фонтан»:

Я посетил Бахчисарая
В забвенье брошенный дворец.
Среди безмолвных переходов
Бродил я там, где, бич народов,
Татарин буйный пировал
И после ужасов набега
В роскошной лени утопал.
Еще поныне дышит нега
В пустых покоях и садах;
Играют воды, рдеют розы,
И вьются виноградны лозы,
И злато блещет на стенах.
Я видел ветхие решетки,
За коими, в своей весне,
Янтарны разбирая четки,
Вздыхали жены в тишине.
Я видел ханское кладбище,
Владык последнее жилище.
Сии надгробные столбы,
Венчанный мраморной чалмою,
Казалось мне, завет судьбы
Гласили внятною молвою.
Где скрылись ханы? Где гарем?
Кругом всё тихо, всё уныло,
Всё изменилось... Но не тем
В то время сердце полно было:
Дыханье роз, фонтанов шум
Влекли к невольному забвенью,
Невольно предавался ум
Неизъяснимому волненью,
И по дворцу летучей тенью
Мелькала дева предо мной...
....
Чью тень, о други, видел я?
Скажите мне: чей образ нежный
Тогда преследовал меня,
Неотразимый, неизбежный?

Была ли это Екатерина Раевская (считают, что этой «необыкновенной женщине» Пушкин посвятил «Редеет облаков летучая гряда»). А может, «образ нежный» — ее сестра Мария (позже преданная «жена декабриста», ссыльного Сергея Волконского, согласившаяся поехать к мужу в сибирскую ссылку)? Считается, что именно Мария Раевская — «одна любовь души моей», которой Пушкин, м.б. посвятил поэму «Полтава», и разные исследователи называют ее «утаенной любовью» Пушкина. Сама Мария Раевская написала: «Как поэт, Пушкин считал своим долгом быть влюбленным во всех хорошеньких женщин и девушек... В сущности, он обожал только свою музу и поэтизировал все, что видел».

Все эти версии об «утаенной любви», пожалуй, заслуживают отступления (Пушкин, осмелюсь сказать, простил бы меня, так как сам увлекался отступлениями — особенно об этом).

> Поговорим о странностях любви
> (Другого я не смыслю разговора).

Пушкин прежде всего — поэт любви. Ни один российский писатель, ни до, ни после Пушкина, не сумел так выразить океан любви в столь разных ее проявлениях. Любовь для него являлась непросто выбором, сколь неудержимой единой силой, для которой он родился, силой, которой он был лишь благословленным проводником. Любовь, всесторонняя и непредсказуемая, присутствует практически во всех его творениях. И все, что им написано, тоже в той или иной мере посвящено любви. Любовь с первого взгляда или после долгих лет дружбы, случайная или по чьему-то знакомству, эротическая или платоническая, сексуальная или духовная, ревнивая или спокойная, ироничная или все принимающая, печально-горькая или смиренная и безропотная, страстно-губительная или мягкая, верная и всепрощающая... всё в любви было его темами; любовь, в которой каждое счастливое мгновение, казалось, ведет к горю, а каждое горе — к счастью. Пушкин угадал ту таинственную сторону любви, которая противостоит всем точным определениям, потому что нет для нее ни рецепта, ни определения — ее можно только чувствовать. Любовь — загадка, которая определяет нас, и «нет истины, где нет любви».

Некоторые советские и поздние современные пушкинисты (как бы фрейдистские марксисты — или, пожалуй, наоборот) цепляются (от зависти?) к каждому имени в шуточно составленном так называемом «дон-жуанском списке» поэта. (Само существование «списка» едва ли можно было назвать политически корректным.) Но в море пролитых чернил на эти темы «леса не видно из-за деревьев» и главное остается незамеченным. Именно весь пушкинский «опыт — сын ошибок трудных» и даровал нам то божественное богатство любовной лирики, превосходящее все суждения. Нам всем следует перечитать письмо Пушкина, упрекающего своего друга, князя Вяземского, за интерес к мемуарам об интимной жизни Байрона:

> Оставь любопытство толпе и будь заодно с гением. Мы знаем Байрона довольно. Видели его на троне славы, видели в мучениях великой души, видели в гробе посреди воскресающей Греции. — Охота тебе видеть его на горшке. Толпа жадно читает исповеди, записки etc., потому что в подлости своей радуется унижению высокого, слабостям могущего. При открытии всякой мерзости она в восхищении: он мал, как мы, он мерзок, как мы! Врете, подлецы: он и мал и мерзок — не так, как вы — иначе.

Даже в своих ранних, более приземленных любовных стихах Пушкин находил ту единственную грань — чувство меры, которое он постиг у классиков еще в Лицее и библиотеке отца. Даже его юношеские (обычно полушутливые) оды женщинам «полусвета», как их тогда называли, были наполнены неким теплом и изяществом... нет ни малейшей вульгарности, которую Пушкин считал одним из наивысших и непростительных грехов. Но уже на юге, от Кавказа ли, что разорвал последние цепи его свободных мыслей, как предположил Гоголь, или же от таинства причастия души с молодым кипарисом на рассвете — возникла какая-то внутренная гармония... ярко родился новый поэт. И обновленный Пушкин, вернувшись из южных скитаний, уже был и оставался до самой смерти более духовным, задумчивым, проницательным и, при этом, непостижимым поэтом.

Тайна, безусловно, необходима великой поэзии. Любимый автор Пушкина, Шекспир, покрыл завесой тайны свою работу настолько, что Марк Твен однажды сострил по этому поводу: «Шекспир — самый знаменитый человек, которого никогда не было». Каким бы на самом деле ни был этот гений английского языка, часто сталкиваешься с ощущением, что он как автор предпочитает оставаться в тени; даже по его героям заметно это пристрастие к анонимности, как у короля Генриха V, бродящего инкогнито в своей армии накануне битвы при Агинкурте, или у его «причудливого герцога затемненных углов» в пьесе «Мера за меру». Даже его самые личные творения — сонеты — проливают мало света на автора: все внимание приковано к объекту любви поэта, к ее достоинствам:

> My mistress' eyes are nothing like the sun;
> Coral is far more red than her lips red;
> If snow be white, why then, her breasts are dun;
> If hair be wires, black wires grow on her head.
> I have seen roses damasked, red and white
> But no such roses see I in her cheeks;
> And in some perfumes there is more delight
> Than in the breath that from my mistress reeks.
> I love to hear her speak, yet well I know
> That music hath a far more pleasing sound;
> I grant I never saw a goddess go;
> My mistress, when she walks, walks on the ground:
> And yet, by heaven I think my love as rare
> As any she belied with false compare.
>   (*Sonnet CXXX*).

Ее глаза на звезды не похожи,
Нельзя уста кораллами назвать,
Не белоснежна плеч открытых кожа
И черной проволокой вьется прядь.
С дамасской розой алой или белой
Ты не сравнишь оттенок этих щек,
А тело пахнет так, как пахнет тело —
Не как фиалки нежной лепесток.
Ты не найдешь в ней совершенных линий,
Особенного света на челе.
Не знаю я, как шествуют богини,
Но милая шагает по земле.
Но все ж она уступит тем едва ли,
Кого в сравненьях пышных оболгали.
    (*Сонет CXXX. Пер. С.Я. Маршака*)

А у Пушкина загадка кроется не столько в *ее* качествах, сколько в *его* собственных переживаниях. Мы не узнаем даже, как она выглядит; она обрисовывается лишь тем, как она заставляет его чувствовать: иными словами, мы часто (так и задумано) не имеем ни малейшего понятия, о ком идет речь. (Во времена, когда брачные узы часто налагались без любви, рождалась неизбежно любовь вне этих уз. Некоторые из «любовий» Пушкина — несчастные в браке женщины, чью репутацию нельзя было подвергать опасности). Он часто вычеркивал целые строчки и четверостишия, которые могли компрометировать лицо, их вдохновившее (например, «Ненастный день потух; ненастной ночи мгла...»); многие стихи носили интимный характер и не предназначались для публикаций. Когда стихотворение «Редеет облаков летучая гряда» было опубликовано полностью, вопреки намерениям Пушкина, он пришел в негодование: упоминание об увлечении его возлюбленной вечерним небом скомпрометировало, как он считал, любительницу смотреть на звезды — Екатерину Раевскую (по одной из версий). Но по сути загадка и таинственность вызваны не практическими соображениями. В его тайне часто залог глубокой печали, неизбежной и неотделимой от самой любви.

Что в имени тебе моем?
Оно умрет, как шум печальный
Волны, плеснувшей в берег дальний,
Как звук ночной в лесу глухом.

Оно на памятном листке
Оставит мертвый след, подобный
Узору надписи надгробной
На непонятном языке.

КРАТКАЯ БИОГРАФИЯ ПОЭТА

Его стихи еще более совершенны потому, что они абсолютно независимы от тех, кому написаны: неважно, как она выглядела или что она сказала или сделала... Она просто есть — и этого достаточно. Детали и причины были бы излишни (а у Пушкина нет ничего лишнего). Как сказано в Талмуде: «Любовь, у которой есть причина, только длится, пока длится эта причина; а любовь безо всякой причины длится вечно, не зная конца». В этом Пушкин похож на Шекспира: сильнейшие чувства не нуждаются в обосновании. Но внимание Пушкина сосредоточено на субъективных чувствах и переходит к объективным качествам предмета любви только в том случае, когда кажется, что чувства на самом деле не так уж серьезны (например, «Признание», «Калмычке», «Подъезжая под Ижоры»). Даже в этом случае он нам дает лишь скелетные детали, при помощи которых отражаются его сердечные переживания... Итак, его поэзия уникально и непревзойденно передает — вместо ненужных деталей о возлюбленной — святое, истинное ощущение любви. И мы вовлекаемся еще глубже в саморазоблачения, переживания, ликования поэта. Он даже приглашает нас посмотреть, где он со своей любовью. И кажется самой Любовью «...Вся комната янтарным блеском озарена».

Правда, были и те, кому Пушкин писал посвящения или записывал стихи в альбомы. Но большинство даже этих произведений осветило любимых в каких-то блаженных, несказанных сумерках, в свете и цвете стихотворного Вермеера. И попытка угадать (в большей или меньшей степени), кому предназначался шедевр, все равно что обжечь этот божественный мрак светом прожектора... И в конце концов, зачем нам так нужно знать имя «утаенной любви» Пушкина? К чему такая страсть выяснять, кого поэт любил «с такой неизъяснимой страстью»:

Она одна бы разумела
Стихи неясные мои;
Одна бы в сердце пламенела
Лампадой чистою любви!
Увы, напрасные желанья.
Она отвергла заклинанья,
Мольбы, тоску души моей,
Земных восторгов излиянья,
Как божеству, не нужно ей!..

Cherchez la femme! Для русских «утаенная любовь» Пушкина — пожалуй, самая знаменитая женщина, которой никогда не было. И напрасно ее ищут в архивах... Она бессмертна... Она — Женщина.

Увы, идиллия Пушкина у южных морей и гор закончилась внезапно, как и сие отступление. В сентябре 1820 года Пушкин приступил к службе в степях Молдавии, на грязных улочках Кишинева, куда переехала канцелярия генерала Инзова. Делать там особенно было нечего; единственное, что его утешало, была сомнительная честь этих же скудных равнин — место ссылки римского поэта Овидия. В ноябре 1820 года Пушкин попросил разрешения посетить Каменку, украинское имение семьи Давыдовых, родственников генерала Раевского. Получив двухнедельный отпуск, он провел там шесть месяцев; генерал Инзов продлевал его пребывание как добродушный отец, написав Давыдовым: «До сего времени я был в опасении о г. Пушкине, боясь, чтобы он, невзирая на жестокость бывших морозов с ветром и метелью, не отправился в путь и где-нибудь при неудобствах степных дорог не получил несчастья. Но, получив почтеннейшее письмо Ваше... я спокоен и надеюсь, что Ваше превосходительство не позволит ему предпринять путь, доколе не получит укрепления в силах».

4 декабря 1820 года Пушкин написал Гнедичу (переводчику «Илиады» на русский язык): «Вот уже восемь месяцев, как я веду странническую жизнь, почтенный Николай Иванович. Был я на Кавказе, в Крыму, в Молдавии и теперь нахожусь в Киевской губернии, в деревне Давыдовых, милых и умных отшельников, братьев генерала Раевского. Время мое протекает между аристократическими обедами и демократическими спорами... веселая смесь умов оригинальных, людей известных в нашей России, любопытных для незнакомого наблюдателя. — Женщин мало, много шампанского, много острых слов, много книг, немного стихов». Большинство «оригинальных и известных умов» в этом имении состояли в тайных революционных обществах, а одна из немногих женщин, польская красотка Каролина Собаньская, была агентом тайной полиции. Пушкин, правда, не вступал ни в какие общества, но он распивал «много шампанского» с будущими декабристами за восстания в Испании, Португалии, Латинской Америке, Неаполе, Греции... все же продолжая работу над «Кавказским пленником», а затем — и «Бахчисарайским фонтаном».

Нельзя сказать, что старший брат Давыдова (тоже ветеран войны 1812 года) особенно нуждался в поводе для рюмки. Пушкин описывал его так: «...второй Фальстаф: сластолюбив, трус, хвастлив, не глуп, забавен, без всяких правил, слезлив и толст. Одно обстоятельство придавало ему прелесть оригинальную. Он был женат. Шекспир не успел женить своего холостяка. Фальстаф умер у своих приятельниц, не успев быть ни рогатым супругом, ни отцом семейства...» Кажется, у Пушкина был короткий роман с женой Давыдова, Аглаей (чья чрезмерная доступность вызвала со стороны поэта ряд едких эпиграмм на русском и на французском). А старшей дочери Давыдова Адели, которой было тогда 12 лет, он посвятил такую чудную безделушку:

Играй, Адель,
Не знай печали.
Хариты, Лель
Тебя венчали.
И колыбель
Твою качали.
Твоя весна
Тиха, ясна:
Для наслажденья
Ты рождена.
Час упоенья
Лови, лови!
Младые лета
Отдай любви,
И в шуме света
Люби, Адель,
Мою свирель.

Добрый Иван Никитич

В марте 1821 года Пушкин вернулся в Кишинев. Генерал Инзов, негодуя, что (как водится на Руси) месяцами не платили жалованья Пушкину, поселил его у себя в доме, заставленном экзотическими цветами и птицами. Пушкин относился с нежностью к Инзову, а «добрый Иван Никитич» боготворил его талант (даже такие запрещенные гимны свободе, как «Птичка» или «Узник») и смотрел сквозь пальцы на выходки и странности поэта. Кишинев являлся пограничным городом, его заполняли люди разных национальностей. Поэт, которого дразнили всю жизнь за его «африканство», был лишен предрассудков в отношении других народов: скорее — наоборот, чужая культура очаровывала, привлекала его внимание и симпатию. С тетрадкой в руках он бродил по городу то в феске и турецком халате, то в молдавской накидке, то в суровом наряде набожного хасида... У Пушкина, кстати, было несколько еврейских подруг. Сочувствие к еврейскому народу выражена в нескольких его произведениях (например, «Юдифь», «История села Горюхина»), а его сердобольное понимание переживаний еврейской семьи ясно отражено во фрагменте «В еврейской хижине лампада...». Пушкина страстно волновала борьба греков за независимость. Он и гречанкой увлекся, которая, по слухам, была любовницей Байрона («Гречанке»). А очарованный молодой цыганкой, он ушел с ней за табором. Его теплые воспоминания об этом приключении воспеты в поэме «Цыганы»:

Цыганы шумною толпой
По Бессарабии кочуют.
Они сегодня над рекой
В шатрах изодранных ночуют.
Как вольность, весел их ночлег
И мирный сон под небесами;
Между колесами телег,
Полузавешанных коврами,
Горит огонь; семья кругом
Готовит ужин; в чистом поле
Пасутся кони; за шатром
Ручной медведь лежит на воле.
Всё живо посреди степей:
Заботы мирные семей,
Готовых с утром в путь недальний,
И песни жен, и крик детей,
И звон походной наковальни.
Но вот на табор кочевой
Нисходит сонное молчанье,
И слышно в тишине степной
Лишь лай собак да коней ржанье.

Цыганка

Его любовные похождения, едкий ум и острое восприятие чести и собственного достоинства повлекли за собой немало дуэлей, около 20 — все бескровные, а иногда и комичные. Но его друг, полковник Липранди, вспоминал: «...Когда он становился лицом к лицу со смертью, когда человек обнаруживает себя вполне, Пушкин обладал в высшей степени невозмутимостью при полном сознании своей запальчивости, виновности, но не выражал ее. Когда дело дошло бы до барьера, к нему он являлся холодным, как лед». На одной дуэли, пока противник целился и готовился стрелять, Пушкин спокойно ел вишню, не уворачиваясь от выстрела, а сам не стрелял. В другой раз дуэль проходила в жуткую снежную бурю на расстоянии шестнадцати шагов: противник выстрелил и промахнулся, после чего Пушкин сознательно выстрелил в воздух и предложил противнику стреляться с двенадцати шагов. Тот ответил: «...Вы так же хорошо стоите под пулями, как хорошо пишете». И Пушкин бросился ему на шею... Время от времени Инзов пытался оградить своего подопечного от подобных приключений, заключая его под домашний арест, приводя его насильно в церковь. А Пушкин, вечный шутник, научил попугая Инзова богохульствам на разных языках, как раз перед приходом архиепископа, приглашенного на чай. Пушкин в это время пишет ироничную записку в стихах Давыдову:

> Я стал умен, я лицемерю,
> Пощусь, молюсь, и твердо верю,
> Что Бог простит мои грехи
> Как государь мои стихи.
> Говеет Инзов, и намедни
> Я променял парнасски бредни
> И лиру, грешный дар судьбы,
> На часослов и на обедни,
> Да на сушеные грибы.

В Кишиневе Пушкин, возможно иронизируя над навязываемой ему благочестивостью, написал «Гавриилиаду», «блистательное озорство», пародию на историю непорочного зачатия (не предназначенную никогда для публикации). Позже эта «шутка» чуть ли не стоила ему новой ссылки — по обвинению в богохульстве и атеизме. Однако Пушкин не так просто классифицируется. Разве истинный «богохульник» завершил бы свою «ересь» молитвой и обращением к ангелу?

> Но дни бегут, и время сединою
> Мою главу тишком посеребрит,
> И важный брак с любезною женою
> Пред алтарем меня соединит.
> Иосифа прекрасный утешитель!
> Молю тебя, колена преклоня,
> О рогачей заступник и хранитель,
> Молю — тогда благослови меня,
> Даруй ты мне беспечность и смиренье,
> Даруй ты мне терпенье вновь и вновь,
> Спокойный сон, в супруге уверенье,
> В семействе мир и к ближнему любовь!

Уже эти строки, в свете последних лет поэта, воспринимаются с грустью: шутила в итоге судьба — с ним. Но тогда он был еще, по сути, счастлив: в мае 1823 года Пушкин начал работу над своим великим романом в стихах «Евгений Онегин». Несколькими месяцами позже Пушкин написал своему другу, поэту Дельвигу: «Пишу теперь новую поэму, в которой забалтываюсь донельзя... Бог знает когда и мы прочитаем ее вместе». За время южной ссылки Пушкин создал несколько глав романа, завершив «Письмом Татьяны к Онегину». В июле 1823 года Пушкина перевели в Одессу, в подчинение к новому наместнику юга России, генерал-губернатору графу Михаилу Воронцову. В то время Одесса была «наполовину итальянским porto franco», все вывески были как на русском, так и на итальянском языках. Пушкин плескался в море, ходил в оперу и рестораны и дружил с бывшим морским пиратом, мавром Али, иногда мечтая о побеге из России.

Но, оставив нежную опеку генерала Инзова, «новая печаль мне сжала грудь — мне стало жаль моих покинутых цепей». И что еще очень расстраивало — жизнь в Одессе была намного дороже. Жалованье приходило нерегулярно, рукопись «Кавказского пленника» принесла ему только 500 рублей. (До 1828 года в России не существовало закона об авторских правах, и даже по его принятии закон так слабо применялся, что Пушкин был беззащитен перед массовыми неразрешенными перепечатками его творений, от которых он не получал ни копейки). Однако как первый в 19 веке профессиональный писатель России, «На конченную свою поэму я смотрю, как сапожник на пару своих сапог: продаю с барышом»; он заключил хорошую сделку за рукопись »Бахчисарайского фонтана»: три тысячи рублей, больше, чем жалованье за целых четыре года — и вскоре с размахом их истратил, как описано в одном из поэтических фрагментов, не вошедших в роман «Евгений Онегин» («Итак, я жил тогда в Одессе»). Живя в Одессе, Пушкин не раз мечтал убежать в Италию. Он давно увлекся итальянской культурой (начал учить «язык Италии златой» еще в Кишиневе) и Амалией Ризнич, итальянской красавицей еврейского происхождения, приехавшей в Одессу из Триеста вместе с мужем — скучным венецианским торговцем. Ризнич, считается, вдохновила поэта на стихи: «Простишь ли мне ревнивые мечты»; «В твою светлицу, друг мой нежный»; «Для берегов отчизны дальной»; »Под небом голубым страны своей родной» и «Заклинание» (хотя стихотворение на подобную тему есть у Барри Корнуела). Тем не менее, Ризнич в Одессе не задержалась надолго. А Пушкин вскоре уже снова потерял голову из-за Каролины Собаньской («Ночь»), подруги Витте, главы южной секретной полиции.

Считается, но не доказано, что в последние месяцы в Одессе любовью Пушкина стала другая польская красавица, графиня Елизавета Воронцова. Их отношения покрыты тайной и обросли легендами (вот еще одна кандидатка на роль его «утаенной любви»; есть более тридцати рисунков графини в рукописях поэта, правда, на многих она рядом с мужем). Их прогулки у моря увековечены в первой главе «Евгения Онегина» («Ах, ножки, ножки...», гл. I, XXIX-XXXIV). Правда, Набоков считал, что только одна из этих ножек, «взлелеянных в восточной неге», принадлежала Воронцовой, а другая — Марии Раевской. Говорят, что именно Воронцова подарила Пушкину то кольцо с надписью на иврите «симха» (радость), которое он бережно хранил всю свою жизнь. (Он завещал его поэту Жуковскому; тот передал его Тургеневу, а в 1917 году кольцо исчезло.) Якобы это кольцо — «талисман» поэта. Сестра Пушкина Ольга предполагала, что Воронцова писала Пушкину в дальнюю михайловскую ссылку и будто это стало поводом для стихотворения «Сожженное письмо». Но трудно представить, чтоб жена всесильного генерал-губернатора Бессарабии графа Воронцова писала опальному поэту, зная, что каждое письмо к нему перлюстрируется. К тому же у Андре Шенье, о котором Пушкин писал в Михайловском, тоже было стихотворение «Сожженное письмо», которого Пушкин не мог не знать. Стихотворение «Демон», согласно самому Пушкину, написано в Одессе как ответ поэта на психологический паралич, вызываемый сомнениями, цинизмом окружающих и отрицательными эмоциями. Но многие верят, что это стихотворение конкретно о старшем сыне генерала Раевского. Александр Раевский, в то время открытый, почти официальный любовник Воронцовой, якобы был одним из тех, кто умышленно «подставлял» Пушкина, распуская слухи об его увлечении графиней.

Отношения поэта с ее мужем, графом Воронцовым, были сложными, и скорее всего не из-за ревности. (Воронцов, сам известный своими многочисленными любовными похождениями, относился спокойно к интрижкам жены.) Строгий и формальный, Воронцов отождествлял себя с английскими лордами, с которыми он учился в Кембридже. Но показные английские манеры не мешали ему использовать жесткие русские методы при управлении югом российской империи: шпионство, интриги, репрессии. И хотя сам Воронцов пользовался служебным положением для собственной наживы в торговле («полу-купец»), он не поощрял привычку Пушкина писать стихи вместо официальных меморандумов. Он пытался заставить поэта выполнять свои бюрократические обязанности, готовить официальные доклады, например, о нашествии саранчи на Херсон. На что Пушкин отвечал в письме к его помощнику:

> Будучи совершенно чужд ходу деловых бумаг, не знаю, вправе ли я отозваться на предписание его сиятельства. Как бы то ни было, надеюсь на вашу снисходительность и приемлю смелость объясниться откровенно насчет моего положения. Семь лет я службою не занимался, не написал ни одной бумаги, не был в сношении ни с одним начальником. Эти семь лет, как вам известно, вовсе для меня не потеряны. Жалобы с моей стороны были бы неуместны. Я сам заградил себе путь и выбрал другую цель. Ради Бога, не думайте, чтоб я смотрел на стихотворство с детским тщеславием рифмача или как на отдохновение чувствительного человека: оно просто мое ремесло, отрасль честной промышленности, доставляющая мне пропитание и домашнюю независимость. Думаю, что граф Воронцов не захочет лишить меня ни того ни другого. Мне скажут, что я, получая 700 рублей, обязан служить. Вы знаете, что только в Москве или Петербурге можно вести книжный торг, ибо только там находятся журналисты, цензоры и книгопродавцы; я

поминутно должен отказываться от самых выгодных предложений единственно по той причине, что нахожусь за 2000 верст от столиц. Правительству угодно вознаграждать некоторым образом мои утраты, я принимаю эти 700 рублей не так, как жалование чиновника, но как паек ссылочного невольника. Я готов от них отказаться, если не могу быть властен в моем времени и занятиях.

Однако Сверчка вынуждали дать писменный отчет о саранче. Но не существует ни одной записи, подтверждающей, что этот отчет был когда-либо написан. Наоборот, легенда гласит, что его «меморандум» представлял собой стишки (часто используемые при преподавании русского языка иностранцам — для оттачивания бесконечных нюансов совершенных или несовершенных видов глаголов):

Саранча летела, летела,
   И села,
Сидела, сидела — все съела
   И вновь улетела.

Воронцов вызвал своего секретаря: «Вы, кажется, любите Пушкина; не можете ли вы склонить его заняться чем-нибудь путным, под руководством вашим? — Помилуйте, такие люди умеют быть только что великими поэтами, — ответил тот. — Так на что же они годятся? — сказал он». Естественно, Пушкин негодовал: «Воронцов — вандал, придворный хам и мелкий эгоист. Он видел во мне лишь коллежского секретаря, а я, признаюсь, думаю о себе что-то другое». Пушкин написал о графе несколько эпиграмм:

Полу-милорд, полу-купец,
Полу-мудрец, полу-невежда,
Полу-подлец, но есть надежда,
Что будет полным наконец.

Воронцов отправлял доносы в Петербург, характеризуя Пушкина как радикала и настаивая на том, чтобы поэта выслали из Одессы. Повод нашелся, когда полиция вскрыла личное письмо Пушкина лицейскому другу Кюхельбекеру (?), в котором он шутил: «Ты хочешь знать, что я делаю — пишу пестрые строфы романтической поэмы — и беру уроки чистого афеизма». Атеизм в царские времена был почти таким же тяжелым преступлением, как потом вероисповедание для большевиков. По приказу царя Александра I канцлером Нессельроде (еще одна мишень для насмешек и эпиграмм) было объявлено о решении лишить Пушкина государственного чина и полномочий и сослать в родительское имение псковской губернии Михайловское «под надзор местных властей». При переезде ему было приказано: «Нижеподписавшийся сим обязывается данному от г-на Одесского градоначальника маршруту без замедления отправиться к месту назначения в губернский город Псков, не останавливаясь нигде на пути по своему произволу; а по прибытии в Псков явиться к г-ну гражданскому губернатору. Одесса. 9 июля 1824». За день до отъезда Пушкин начал писать роскошное прощальное стихотворение «К морю». 31 июля 1824 года он отбыл на север. Ожидая новую упряжку лошадей в Могилеве, Пушкин узнал кадета лицейских времен. Пошли крепкие объятия, слезы, и поэта радостно затащили на славное экспромтное русское полуночное пиршество и чтение стихов; в четыре утра гуляки даже хотели искупать любимого певца в ванной с шампанским… Он добрался до дома родителей 9 августа 1824 года. Случилась вторая ссылка, предсказанная мадам Кирхгоф.

1824 –1826. Ссылка в Михайловское

На расстоянии тяжелого недельного пути от Москвы или Санкт-Петербурга, «…в забытой сей глуши, / В обители пустынных вьюг и хлада…», имение Михайловское представляло собой скромный деревянный барский дом, скудно окруженный избами для крепостных. Когда он приехал, вся семья была в столовой, а отец играл на гитаре. Но «пребывание среди семьи только усугубило мои огорчения… Мой отец имел слабость согласиться на выполнение обязанностей, которые во всех обстоятельствах поставили его в ложное положение по отношению ко мне; вследствие этого все то время, что я не в постели, я провожу верхом в полях. Все, что напоминает мне море, наводит на меня грусть — журчанье ручья причиняет мне боль в буквальном смысле слова. Думаю, что голубое небо заставило бы меня плакать от бешенства. Но, слава Богу, небо у нас сивое, а луна точно репка…» (см. «Ненастный день потух, ненастной ночи мгла…»). Но, по-видимому, отец Пушкина отказался (есть разные версии) от роли информатора и надсмотрщика над сыном и вскоре уехал. К ноябрю 1824 года вся семья покинула Михайловское, оставив поэта в блаженном одиночестве, в окружении лишь нескольких домашних слуг и Арины Родионовны, преданной няни. Он ее обожал с самого детства. Ее постоянная забота, добродушная ласка, напевная речь, полная присказок и поговорок, сделали ее олицетворением теплоты, истинно любящей душой, к которой он так тянулся. Он и называл ее «мама, мамушка»; после разорительных устриц и французских вин одесских ресторанов он восхищался ее простой гречневой кашей, вареными яйцами, печеной картошкой, соленьями, мочеными яблоками, ее славными ягодными вареньями и настойками. Пушкин написал другу в Одессу:

Нахожусь я в глухой деревне — скучно, да нечего делать; здесь нет ни моря, ни неба полудня, ни итальянской оперы. Но зато нет — ни саранчи, ни милордов Уоронцовых. Уединение мое совершенно — праздность торжественна. Вечером слушаю сказки моей няни, оригинала няни Татьяны; вы, кажется, раз ее видели, она единственная моя подруга — и с нею только мне не скучно.

Душевное тепло Арины Родионовны в ту унылую пору не раз воспето Пушкиным в таких стихах, как «Зимний вечер» и «Няне»; он упоминает о ней с любовью и в «Евгении Онегине», и во «Вновь я посетил». Пушкин записал десятки песен, которым она его научила, и еще семь сказок (три из них — «Сказка о царе Салтане», «Сказка о Балде» и «Сказка о мертвой царевне» — он переложил в стихи, сохранив элементы народной сказки и прелесть устных сказаний). Одна из няниных присказок стала основой вступления ко второму изданию «Руслана и Людмилы», с завораживающей первой строкой: «У лукоморья дуб зеленый». Кроме сказок и постоянного чтения книг, он утешался посещениями соседнего имения Прасковьи Александровны Осиповой-Вульф — Тригорское. Пушкин любил ее удивлять, внезапно запрыгивая через окно в столовую. Он дружил с ее младшим сыном Алексеем Вульфом, не говоря уже обо всех его хорошеньких сестричках:

> Чудо — жизнь анахорета!
> В Троегорском до ночи,
> А в Михайловском до света.
> Дни любви посвящены,
> Ночью царствуют стаканы,
> Мы же — то смертельно пьяны,
> То мертвецки влюблены.

В Тригорском Пушкин посвятил Александре (Алине) Осиповой, падчерице Прасковьи Александровны, свое «Признание». А в альбом Евпраксии Вулф («Зизи, кристалл души моей») он написал «Если жизнь тебя обманет». В Тригорском он вновь увидел красавицу-племянницу Прасковьи Александровны, Анну Петровну Керн, с которой познакомился шесть лет тому назад в Санкт-Петербурге. Накануне отъезда Керн в Ригу Пушкин вручил ей рукопись второй главы «Евгения Онегина». К ней был приложен листок со стихотворением «К***» («Я помню чудное мгновенье») — возможно, самое знаменитое стихотворение в русской поэзии, чудно переложенное на музыку другом поэта Глинкой (и многими другими композиторами).

Пушкин немного удивил сонного священника тригорской церкви, заказав ему службу за упокой души «болярина Георгия» (Байрона). Несмотря на некую беспечность в отношении веры, которая оказалась формальным поводом для второй ссылки, Пушкин любил ходить из Михайловского в местный Святогорский монастырь и навещать настоятеля отца Иоанна. Он проводил много времени в монастырской библиотеке, изучая старые свитки и летописи. Пушкин посещал монастырские ярмарки, гуляя в толпе, слушая рассказы и песни нищих слепцов, бродяг и юродивых. Все эти впечатления послужили материалом для трагедии «Борис Годунов», написанной белым стихом. Он просыпался до восхода солнца, ночью писал при свечах и порой не покидал своей маленькой комнаты целыми днями. Стихи лились. Он писал Николаю Раевскому: «Чувствую, что духовные силы мои достигли полного развития, я могу творить». 7 ноября 1825 года он написал Вяземскому: «Трагедия моя кончена; я перечел ее вслух, один, и бил в ладоши и кричал, ай да Пушкин, ай да сукин сын!» (Это, увы, почти единственные аплодисменты, которые ему было суждено услышать. Трагедия была опубликована в 1831 г., но запрещена для театральной постановки до 1866 г.) Хотя невероятно прекрасные, изящные, звонкие строки «Бориса Годунова» никогда не преодолевали языковой барьер, это произведение известно на Западе как основа величественной оперы Модеста Петровича Мусоргского. Невозможно в двух словах дать справедливую оценку «Борису Годунову», хотя сам Пушкин выразился кратко: «Судьба человеческая — судьба народная». По мнению многих, «Борис Годунов» является самой совершенной драмой на русском языке. Критик Белинский считал: «Словно гигант между пигмеями до сих пор высится между множеством quasi-русских трагедий пушкинский «Борис Годунов», в гордом и суровом уединении, в недоступном величии строгого художественного стиля, благородной классической простоты».

19 ноября 1825 года царь Александр I умер без наследника; эта новость дошла до Пушкина лишь в конце месяца. «Как верный подданный, должен я, конечно, печалиться о смерти государя; но, как поэт, радуюсь». Ожидали, что трон займет старший из оставшихся братьев, Константин, но он, женившись на польской католичке, в 1823 году отрекся от престола в пользу брата Николая. Не зная об этом, многие россияне отказывались присягать на верность Николаю I, считая Константина законным наследником. 14 декабря 1825 года произошло событие, которое потом назовут декабрьским восстанием: дворяне — члены тайных революционных обществ, офицеры и солдаты собрались на Сенатской площади в Петербурге, требуя «Константина и Конституции». Толпа отказалась расходиться, началась стрельба, был убит губернатор столицы Милорадович. Николай I приказал разогнать толпу картечью и «площадь была обагрена кровью». Полицейские потом «скоблили красный снег» и «побросали в ледяную Неву не только убитых, но и раненых». После полугодового следствия пять декабристов были повешены, а сто двадцать сосланы в Сибирь.

Пушкин, узнав о смерти Александра I, хотел бежать в Петербург. Он даже сделал себе поддельный паспорт для поездки. В нем было записано: «Алексей Хохлов, росту 2 арш. 4 вер. (примерно 164 см.), волосы темно-русые, глаза голубые, бороду бреет, лет 29». Но едва Пушкин двинулся в путь, как ему три раза, по легенде, перебежал дорогу заяц, а затем встретился священник. Этих плохих примет хватило суеверному (пусть и не самому верующему) поэту, чтобы вернуться домой. Предчувствуя возможность каких-то тревожных событий в Петербурге и ища утешения у Шекспира, Пушкин размышлял о странных случайностях и роли личности в истории:

> Перечитывая «Лукрецию», довольно слабую поэму Шекспира, я подумал: что, если б Лукреции пришла в голову мысль дать пощечину Тарквинию? быть может, это охладило б его предприимчивость и он со стыдом принужден был отступить? Лукреция б не зарезалась, Публикола (т.е. Коллатин —*Д.Л.*) не взбесился бы, Брут не изгнал бы царей, и мир и история мира были бы не те. Итак, республикою, консулами, диктаторами, Катонами, Кесарем мы обязаны соблазнительному происшествию, подобному тому, которое случилось недавно в моем соседстве, в Новоржевском уезде. Мысль пародировать историю и Шекспира мне представилась. Я не мог воспротивиться двойному искушению и в два утра написал эту повесть. Я имею привычку на моих бумагах выставлять год и число. «Граф Нулин» писан 13 и 14 декабря. Бывают странные сближения. (Заметка о «Графе Нулине», 1830 г.)

В «Графе Нулине» Пушкин иронизирует над своей современной Лукрецией, однако сочувствует ей и даже отождествляет с ней свое душевное состояние в строках о колокольчике:

> Она сидит перед окном;
> Пред ней открыт четвертый том
> Сентиментального романа:
> Любовь Элизы и Армана,
> Иль переписка двух семей.
> Роман классический, старинный,
> Отменно длинный, длинный, длинный,
> Нравоучительный и чинный,
> Без романтических затей.
> Наталья Павловна сначала
> Его внимательно читала,
> Но скоро как-то развлеклась
> Перед окном возникшей дракой
> Козла с дворовою собакой
> И ею тихо занялась.
> Кругом мальчишки хохотали.
> Меж тем печально, под окном,
> Индейки с криком выступали

КРАТКАЯ БИОГРАФИЯ ПОЭТА

Вослед за мокрым петухом;
Шла баба через грязный двор
Белье повесить на забор;
Погода становилась хуже:
Казалось, снег идти хотел...
Вдруг колокольчик зазвенел.
Кто долго жил в глуши печальной,
Друзья, тот, верно, знает сам,
Как сильно колокольчик дальный
Порой волнует сердце нам.
Не друг ли едет запоздалый,
Товарищ юности удалой?..

«Жанно» — И.И. Пущин

На рассвете 11 января 1825 года к Пушкину приехал любимый «Жанно», Иван Пущин. Пушкин услышал звон колокольчика и побежал прямо в ночной рубашке, босиком по снегу, чтобы обнять друга. Тут же их стала обнимать Арина Родионовна, даже не ведая, кто приехал. Пущин был членом тайного революционного общества и не хотел задерживаться более чем на день, чтобы не подвести ссыльного поэта.[1] Через некоторое время Пущин станет одним из декабристов, сосланных в Сибирь «как враг государства» (он пробыл там 30 лет). Но те объятия на заснеженном дворе длились дольше, чем все его годы ссылки; воспоминания о той встрече остались в стихотворении «Мой первый друг, мой друг бесценный!» И после того как Пущин был сослан, Пушкин, рискуя оказаться в третьей ссылке, отправил это стихотворение другу вместе со своим знаменитым «Посланием в Сибирь». Но дружба и поэзия в его воображении были неразрывны, и «Поэзия, как ангел-утешитель/ Спасла меня, и я воскрес душой». Другой близкий друг Пушкина, поэт Антон Дельвиг, также рискнул навестить его. Дельвиг приехал весной 1825 года и помог поэту отредактировать первую книгу его стихов.

---

1. Пущинские «Записки о Пушкине» наполнены человеческим теплом и высокими устремлениями, что и называлось «лицейским духом». Но многие игнорируют все, что добрый «Жанно» хотел сказать, кроме двух предложений о маленькой комнатке в доме Пушкина, в которой шили крепостные девушки. «Я тотчас заметил между ними одну фигурку, резко отличавшуюся от других... Он прозрел шаловливую мою мысль, улыбнувся значительно». Эта «фигурка» была Ольга Калашникова, миловидная дочка управляющего пушкинского поместья в Болдино. Советский поэт Михаил Дудин назвал их любовь, которая, несмотря на неравное положение (Ольга была крепостной Пушкиных), была открытой и взаимной, «чудо "чудного мгновенья"». Конечно, любовь национального поэта к простой крестьянке — подарок советской пропаганде. В 1826 году Ольга ждала ребенка от Пушкина и уехала рожать к родителям в Болдино. Ссыльный Пушкин смог лишь попросить друзей позаботиться о ней и о ребенке. Но маленький Павел умер вскоре после рождения. Как только Пушкин стал владельцем Болдино, он дал Ольге »отпускную« (свободу). Она вышла замуж за мелкого дворянина и уже сама владела крепостными. Пушкин стал заочным восприемником ее сына от нового мужа, и позже много раз помогал.

Пушкин выразил благодарность друзьям в своей элегии, воспевающей юбилей Лицея, «19 октября», классическое стихотворение, которое можно найти в каждом русском поэтическом сборнике. «19 октября» объединяет печальную роскошь осени с теплым ощущением от одинокого бокала вина, окрашивающего ностальгию ссыльного и согревающего его душу, полную надежд и тоски по лицейским друзьям.

> Пылай, камин, в моей пустынной келье;
> А ты, вино, осенней стужи друг,
> Пролей мне в грудь отрадное похмелье,
> Минутное забвенье горьких мук.
>
> Печален я: со мною друга нет,
> С кем долгую запил бы я разлуку,
> Кому бы мог пожать от сердца руку
> И пожелать веселых много лет.

Поэт, не получив прощения от царя, сам, с его характерной щедростью, прощает царю «неправое гоненье»:

> Он человек! Им властвует мгновенье.
> Он раб молвы, сомнений и страстей.
> Простим ему неправое гоненье:
> Он взял Париж, он основал Лицей.

4 сентября 1826 года императорский фельдъегерь привез Пушкину приказ немедленно явиться к императору Николаю I. Это было вскоре после его коронации в Москве. Вероятно, по дороге на эту судьбоносную встречу Пушкин сочинил великое воззвание о роли поэта как совести мира: «Пророк». Полное образов, взятых из VI главы книги пророка Исайи, оно как бы описывает операцию небесного хирурга, в результате которой поэт, «и празднословный и лукавый», вдруг превращается во всевидящий, всеслышащий источник божества, восприимчивый и полный сочувствия ко всей вселенной:

> И внял я неба содроганье,
> И горний ангелов полет,
> И гад морских подводный ход,
> И дольней лозы прозябанье.

«Пророк» — это первое из цикла стихотворений Пушкина о поэте и о самой поэзии (См. здесь раздел VIII, «Поэт», «Эхо», «Осень» и т.д.). «Пророк» возвышается над политикой, при этом призывая поэта к святой миссии в жизни:

> Восстань, пророк, и виждь, и внемли,
> Исполнись волею моей:
> И, обходя моря и земли,
> Глаголом жги сердца людей.

1826–1831. Москва и Санкт-Петербург

И наша дева насладилась
Дорожной скукою вполне:
Семь суток ехали оне.

Но вот уж близко. Перед ними
Уж белокаменной Москвы,
Как жар, крестами золотыми
Горят старинные главы.
Ах, братцы! Как я был доволен,
Когда церквей и колоколен,
Садов, чертогов полукруг
Открылся предо мною вдруг!
Как часто в горестной разлуке,
В моей блуждающей судьбе,
Москва, я думал о тебе!
Москва... Как много в этом звуке
Для сердца русского слилось!
Как много в нем отозвалось!

Николай I

Пушкин прибыл в Москву 8 сентября 1826 года и был немедленно доставлен в Чудов дворец к императору. После долгой дороги ему даже не дали возможности умыться и переодеться. Скрупулезное расследование дела об осужденных декабристах показало, что они все любили творения Пушкина. Многие из них, наивные идеалисты, не строили четких планов и не придерживались конкретной идеологии, кроме романтических надежд, зачастую вызванных пушкинскими стихами, найденными у большинства декабристов. Поэтому в Михайловское для расследования возможной бунтарской деятельности Пушкина был послан агент тайной полиции Бошняк. Оказалось, по его донесениям, что Пушкина любили местные крестьяне за веселый нрав и великодушие, правда, он имел странную привычку записывать рассказы стариков и народные сказки. С досадой донесли, что он равнодушен к политике и предпочитает проводить свое время, катаясь верхом, плавая или гуляя по окрестностям в широкополой соломенной шляпе и цветастой русской рубашке. Вот уж на самом деле, очень подозрительно!

Разговор с царем длился около трех часов. Пушкин не отрицал, что многие декабристы были его друзьями. Он также добавил, что обвинения, выдвинутые против них, его чувств дружбы не изменили. На вопрос, что бы он делал, находясь 14 декабря в Петербурге, поэт храбро и честно ответил, что был бы на площади со своими друзьями. Император приказал ему никогда более не писать против правительства, предоставлять персонально ему (царю) свои работы для цензуры, затем объявил, что он может идти и что ссылка его окончена. Чуть позже Николай заметил: «Сегодня я разговаривал с умнейшим мужем России». Однако вскоре за поэтом все-таки была установлена постоянная агентурная слежка (как любил повторять Пушкин: «Любит царь, да не любит псарь»). Почему Пушкина освободили из ссылки? Был ли это политический ход, неуверенная попытка нелюбимого правителя завоевать популярность? Пушкин ведь был тогда самым популярным поэтом России, любимцем обеих столиц. Когда поэт в доме у своего московского друга читал собравшимся гостям «Бориса Годунова», все были в восторге:

> Читал Пушкин превосходно, и чтение его, в противность тогдашнему обыкновению читать стихи нараспев и с некоторою вычурностью, отличалось, напротив, полною простотою. ...мы просто все как будто обеспамятели. Кого бросало в жар, кого в озноб. Волосы поднимались дыбом... кончилось чтение... начались объятия, поднялся шум, раздался смех, полились слезы, поздравления.

Но в этой восторженной толпе был информатор, и ему этот восторг не понравился. Пушкин получил выговор за то, что не показал пьесу царю до ее публичного чтения. Рисунки поэта того времени отражают постоянную память о повешенных и сосланных «друзьях, братьях, товарищах». Вместо этого, окруженный «шпионами, б...... и пьяницами», Пушкин уже тосковал по простоте и душевной чистоте деревенской жизни, по своей няне Арине Родионовне («Няне»). Старые и новые друзья, знакомство и дружба со ссыльным великим польским поэтом Адамом Мицкевичем и даже пестрая компания цыган не утешали поэта... В январе 1827 года полиция начала расследование по делу Пушкина за стихотворение «Андрей Шенье», которое содержало в себе провокационные строки:

> Разоблачался ветхий трон;
> Оковы падали. Закон,
> На вольность опершись, провозгласил равенство,
> И мы воскликнули: Блаженство!
> О горе! О безумный сон!
> Где вольность и закон? Над нами
> Единый властвует топор.
> Мы свергнули царей. Убийцу с палачами
> Избрали мы в цари. О ужас! О позор!

Пушкин был вынужден дать письменные показания под присягой и предъявить доказательства, что он эти строчки, давно прошедшие цензуру, написал задолго до декабря 1825 года и, таким образом, они ничего общего с восстанием декабристов не имели. И хотя было очевидно, что стихотворение посвящено великому поэту Андре Шенье, казненному в 1794 году во время террора Робеспьера, дело о стихотворении было закрыто лишь в июле 1828 года. Сегодня, конечно, эти строки воспринимаются как мрачное пророчество последствий большевистской революции.

Последовавшие после ссылки четыре года Пушкин проводил по нескольку месяцев то в Москве, то в Петербурге. Потеря ближайших друзей после подавления восстания декабристов усугубляла чувство одиночества и тоски поэта; всё чаще ему приходят мысли о доме, о жене, всё чаще ему хочется «…о невесте на досуге помышлять». В 1826 году он сделал предложение дальней родственнице Софи Пушкиной, но свадьба так и не состоялась. В мае 1827 года, перед тем как в очередной раз покинуть Москву и уехать в Петербург, повидаться с родителями, Пушкин написал в альбом своей новой возлюбленной Екатерине Ушаковой «В отдалении от вас». Ушакова обожала Пушкина и его стихи. Но в то же время, будучи блондинкой и очень суеверной особой, она боялась, что ее «белая голова» станет причиной смерти поэта, и существует мнение, что на предложение Пушкина ответила отказом. Они остались друзьями. В альбоме Ушаковой сохранилось множество рисунков Пушкина (часто причудливых) и его знаменитый так называемый «дон-жуанский список».

В Петербурге Пушкин продолжал работать над «Евгением Онегиным». Он возобновил отношения с Анной Петровной Керн и был неразлучен со своим лицейским другом Дельвигом. На годовщину со дня казни друзей-декабристов он пишет стихотворение «Арион». В июле 1827 г. в Михайловском он начинает исторический роман о своем великом прадеде «Арап Петра Великого»... Роман задумывался как история русского Отелло, написанная в прозе. Однако Пушкин отложил эту работу, хотя были готовы уже шесть глав. Решающая сцена показывает его неуверенность и сомнения при мысли о женитьбе. Мавр Ибрагим беседует с царем Петром:

> «…Если б и имел в виду жениться, то согласятся ли молодая девушка и ее родственники? моя наружность…
> — Твоя наружность! какой вздор! чем ты не молодец? Молодая девушка должна повиноваться воле родителей, а посмотрим, что скажет старый Гаврила Ржевский, когда я сам буду твоим сватом? — При сих словах государь велел подавать сани и оставил Ибрагима, погруженного в глубокие размышления.
> «Жениться! — думал африканец, — зачем же нет? ужели суждено мне провести жизнь в одиночестве и не знать лучших наслаждений и священнейших обязанностей человека потому только, что я родился под пятнадцатым градусом? Мне нельзя надеяться быть любимым: детское возражение! разве можно верить любви? разве существует она в женском, легкомысленном сердце? Отказавшись навек от милых заблуждений, я выбрал иные обольщения — более существенные. Государь прав: мне должно обеспечить будущую судьбу мою. Свадьба с молодою Ржевскою

присоединит меня к гордому русскому дворянству, и я перестану быть пришельцем в новом моем отечестве. От жены я не стану требовать любви, буду довольствоваться ее верностию, а дружбу приобрету постоянной нежностию, доверенностию и снисхождением».

В октябре 1827 года, меняя лошадей на станции Залазы, Пушкин вздрогнул от неожиданности, увидев полицейских, везших в Динабургскую крепость любимого лицейского друга, осужденного декабриста и поэта, Вильгельма Кюхельбекера. «Мы кинулись друг другу в объятия. Жандармы нас растащили». 19 октября 1827 года, несколькими днями позже, еще находясь под впечатлением встречи, Пушкин отметил юбилей Лицея стихами «Бог помочь вам, друзья мои».

Вернувшись в 1828 году в Петербург («Город пышный, город бедный»), Пушкин безответно ухаживал за Аннетой Олениной, сделал ей предложение, но получил отказ («Счастлив, кто избран своенравно»). В это время секретная полиция начала новое преследование Пушкина, на сей раз за богохульство, т.е. за авторство «Гавриилиады». Отец Аннеты был членом комиссии по делу о «Гавриилиаде». Тучи начали сгущаться над головой Пушкина («Предчувствие»); дело закрыл лишь Николай I, после того, как Пушкин отправил ему личное письмо, которое не сохранилось. Находясь под постоянной слежкой, Пушкин написал знаменитое стихотворение «Анчар». Характерно, что само стихотворение открыто не критикует самодержавие. Но мощные образы, сила и страстность языка заставляют читателя глубоко задуматься над проблемой зла, порождающего зло, и страшным итогом слепого повиновения жестокой власти.

В бессонных размышлениях («Воспоминание» и «Дар напрасный, дар случайный» — по случаю дня его рождения) ощущаются почти вселенское горе и одиночество, пережитые Пушкиным в 1828 году. Примерно тогда же Пушкин написал и стихотворение «Я вас любил», светлый, но глубоко печальный, прощальный подарок любви. Снова Пушкин не опаляет чудесного мрака, тонкого заката чувств яркими и ненужными деталями. Опять, совершенно не важно, кто была его возлюбленная; она — Женщина. И ясно чувствуется, что его глубокая, терпеливая любовь не встретила взаимности. Те, кто знаком со стихотворением У. Б. Ейтса "When you are old and grey", найдут там описание похожего настроения. Каким-то образом происходит, что сам процесс перехода любви в прошедшее время придает ей бессмертие, безграничную печаль, теплоту... Задумчивое сожаление, горе и настоящее благородство духа окрашены горько-сладкой иронией. И что утеряно — остается навсегда.

КРАТКАЯ БИОГРАФИЯ ПОЭТА

Несмотря на печаль и невзгоды, Пушкин в 1827 и 1828 годах продолжает работу над «Евгением Онегиным», завершая седьмую главу. В 1828 г. Пушкин также закончил «Полтаву», захватывающую повествовательную поэму (ее лучше знают на Западе как основу оперы Чайковского «Мазепа»). Марии, главной героине произведения, приходится делать нелегкий выбор между отцом и его смертельным врагом — своим мужем, с которым она убегает. Всё это на фоне разгрома шведского вторжения в Россию в 1709 году Петром Великим. На протяжении всего произведения, при всех конфликтах и поворотах, Пушкин показывает всевозможные варианты судьбы. Он дает нам героя — царя Петра, чье эксцентричное величие и упорство создают могучую нацию, но не без невинных жертв. Одновременно он рисует портрет злейшего врага Петра, жестокого украинского гетмана Мазепы, который борется со своей судьбой и — временами — со своей совестью.

Мазепа

Тиха украинская ночь.
Прозрачно небо. Звезды блещут.
Своей дремоты превозмочь
Не хочет воздух. Чуть трепещут
Сребристых тополей листы.
Но мрачны странные мечты
В душе Мазепы: звезды ночи,
Как обвинительные очи,
За ним насмешливо глядят.
И тополи, стеснившись в ряд,
Качая тихо головою,
Как судьи, шепчут меж собою.
И летней, теплой ночи тьма
Душна, как черная тюрьма.

Но власть развращает. И видно,

Что он не ведает святыни,
Что он не помнит благостыни,
Что он не любит ничего,
Что кровь готов он лить, как воду,
Что презирает он свободу,
Что нет отчизны для него.

Вскоре после окончания «Полтавы» Пушкин уехал в Москву. Там в декабре 1828 года у танцмейстера Иогеля он заметил шестнадцатилетнюю Наталью Николаевну Гончарову. «Когда я увидел ее в первый раз, красоту ее едва начинали замечать в свете. Я полюбил ее, голова у меня закружилась...» Но головокружение не мешало ему смотреть по сторонам. Спустя пару дней он снова уехал в Петербург, сделав по дороге остановку у друзей в Малинниках

(Тверской губернии), где опять слегка увлекся Алиной Осиповой и написал медитативный «Цветок». А в Петербурге он написал стихи-размышления «Брожу ли я вдоль улиц шумных».

В Москве в марте 1830 года Пушкин на балу снова увидел Наталью Гончарову. Через неделю он сделал ей предложение. Наталья, или «Таша», как называли ее, была самой младшей и, несомненно, самой хорошенькой из трех сестер. Ее мать, Наталья Ивановна Загряжская, была в свое время любовницей лихого конного офицера, фаворита Александра I и возлюбленного императрицы Елизаветы, убитого при таинственных обстоятельствах. Вскоре Наталью Ивановну выдали замуж за Николая Афанасьевича Гончарова, владельца поместья Полотняный завод под Калугой. Но отец Натальи страдал тяжелым алкоголизмом с припадками белой горячки. А дедушка Афанасий Николаевич проматывал колоссальное семейное состояние. Наталья Ивановна во всех горестях видела проявление воли Господней и стала религиозной фанатичкой, что не мешало ее не очень скрытым романам с поварами и кучерами. Наталья Ивановна была строгой, властной и удивительно капризной матерью. Но дочери были обучены французскому и танцам — главным двум навыкам, которые считались необходимыми для удачного замужества. Она надеялась поправить плачевное финансовое положение семьи, выдав замуж хорошенькую молодую Наталью Николаевну в Москве «на ярмарке невест». Но женихи не появлялись, так как у Натальи не было приданого. Семья Гончаровых видела серьезность намерений Пушкина. Но Наталью Ивановну не интересовали его гениальный дар и знаменитость. Она была настроена против «арапа», имевшего малые средства, но большие проблемы с правительством; ее также беспокоили легенды об его бурном любовном прошлом. Известно, что она диктовала дочке колкие высокомерно-заносчивые письма поэту (тон которых ее дочь смягчала нежными приписками в конце). Категорически требуя от дочери изображения холодного безразличия, она надеялась, что Пушкин уймется. Наталья Ивановна напрямик сказала ему, что рассчитывала на более «подходящую» партию. Но никто другой не появлялся, и Наталья Ивановна (на всякий случай), полуотклоняя предложения Пушкина, называла неясные причины. 1 мая 1829 года Пушкин ей писал:

> На коленях, проливая слезы благодарности, должен был бы вам писать теперь... Ваш ответ — не отказ, вы позволяете мне надеяться. Не обвиняйте меня в неблагодарности, если я все еще ропщу, если к чувству счастья примешиваются еще печаль и горечь; мне понятна осторожность и нежная заботливость матери! — Но извините нетерпение сердца больного, которому недоступно счастье. Я сейчас уезжаю и в глубине своей души увожу образ небесного существа, обязанного вам жизнью.

Пушкин уехал на юг. Его друг Николай Раевский, сын генерала, служил в русской армии, воевавшей в очередной раз на Кавказе. На одной из станций, меняя подводу, Пушкин был приглашен семьей калмыцких кочевников разделить с ними завтрак:

> Молодая калмычка, собою очень недурная, шила, куря табак. Я сел подле нее. «Как тебя зовут?» — ***. — «Сколько тебе лет?» — «Десять и восемь». — «Что ты шьешь?» — «Портка». — «Кому?» — «Себя». Она подала мне свою трубку и стала завтракать. В котле варился чай с бараньим жиром и солью. Она предложила мне свой ковшик. Я не хотел отказаться и хлебнул, стараясь не перевести духа. Не думаю, чтобы другая народная кухня могла произвести что-нибудь гаже. Я попросил чем-нибудь это заесть. Мне дали кусочек сушеной кобылятины; я был и тому рад. Калмыцкое кокетство испугало меня; я поскорее выбрался из кибитки и поехал от степной Цирцеи. («Путешествие в Арзрум»)

Повозка покатила на юг, Пушкин описал эту случайную встречу в стихотворении «Калмычке». Он сделал остановку у подножия горы Машук, чтобы попить минеральной воды там, где однажды он излечился и нашел вдохновение, а потом продолжил путь на юг в Чечню, делая заметки: «Черкесы нас ненавидят. Мы вытеснили их из привольных пастбищ; аулы их разорены, целые племена уничтожены. Они час от часу далее углубляются в горы и оттуда направляют свои набеги. Дружба мирных черкесов ненадежна: они всегда готовы помочь буйным своим единоплеменникам». (Задумывался ли кто-нибудь в Кремле над этими словами?) Возвращение в горы вдохновило его на несколько стихотворений, включая «Монастырь на Казбеке». Он примкнул к армии и принял участие в сражении, как раз, когда турки неожиданно атаковали казацкую передовую цепь. «...Он тотчас выскочил из ставки, сел на лошадь и мгновенно очутился на аванпостах. Опытный майор Семичев, посланный генералом Раевским вслед за поэтом, едва настиг его и вывел насильно из передовой цепи казаков в ту минуту, когда Пушкин, одушевленный отвагою, столь свойственной новобранцу-воину, схватив пику после одного из убитых казаков, устремился против неприятельских всадников». Эта турецкая кампания стала единственным путешествием Пушкина за границу; он заполнял тетрадь рисунками персидских придворных и непокорных турецких пленников. В Грузии, полон дум о Наталье Николаевне, он написал возвышенные стихи: «На холмах Грузии лежит ночная мгла». А как только приехал в Москву, бросился к ногам возлюбленной — но тщетно. Он писал своей будущей теще:

> Какие муки меня ждали по возвращении! Ваше молчание, ваша холодность, та рассеянность и то безразличие, с какими приняла меня м-ль Натали... Я не смел объясниться, — я уехал в Петербург со смертью в душе.

Пушкин решил найти утешение и по дороге на север остановился у друзей в Тверской губернии. В стихотворении «Подъезжая под Ижоры» Пушкин восстанавливает картину знакомства с Катенькой Вельяшевой, в которую он обещал «влюбиться до ноября». В заснеженных Малинниках он написал скорее сардоническое, нежели лирическое стихотворение «Зима. Что делать нам в деревне?». В нем тоска и хандра лечатся неожиданным появлением на горизонте милых девушек. Снова стоит жить, стихи льются, как музыка, и поэт снова погружается в веселье и удовольствия, флирт, танцы, намеки... а затем сладострастие и... «как жарко поцелуй пылает на морозе»... На какое-то время он, может быть, выбросил из головы мысли о «Карсе» и «маме Карса» — как он называл Наталью Николаевну и ее мать (в честь турецкой крепости, которая упорно держала долгую осаду российских войск).

В Петербурге он просил разрешения у царя об отъезде «К подножию ль стены далекого Китая, В кипящий ли Париж...» («Поедем, я готов; куда бы вы, друзья»). Ему было отказано. Бенкендорф негодовал, что Пушкин посмел уехать на Кавказ без его позволения. До самой смерти (даже при транспортировке гроба) все передвижения поэта были строго ограничены III отделением (тайной полицией). Путешествие за границу оставалось его самой заветной мечтой. Еще находясь в ссылке в Кишиневе, он мечтал присоединиться к Байрону в его борьбе за независимость Греции. В первой книге «Евгения Онегина» он мечтал об Италии и мечты перекладывал в стихи. Из Одессы в январе 1824 года он писал брату:

> ...Я дважды просил о своем отпуске — и два раза воспоследовал всемилостивейший отказ. Осталось одно - писать прямо на его имя — Такому-то, в Зимнем дворце, что против Петропавловской крепости, не то взять тихонько трость и шляпу и поехать посмотреть на Константинополь. Святая Русь мне становится невтерпеж.

А из Михайловского Пушкин умолял о разрешении поехать за границу на лечение (по медицинским показаниям); мать Пушкина тогда написала лично царю. Но ему было отказано снова, и на лечение его направили лишь в местную «столицу» — город Псков. Пушкин отвечал:

> Неожиданная милость его величества тронула меня несказанно, тем более что губернатор предлагал уже мне иметь жительство во Пскове, но я строго придерживался повеления высшего начальства. Я справлялся о псковских врачах; мне указали там на некоторого Всеволожского, очень искусного по ветеринарной части и известного в ученом свете по своей книге об лечении лошадей. Несмотря на все это, я решился остаться в Михайловском, тем не менее чувствуя отеческую снисходительность его величества.

В мае 1826 года он писал своему другу князю Вяземскому:

> Я, конечно, презираю отечество мое с головы до ног — но мне досадно, если иностранец разделяет со мною это чувство. Ты, который не на привязи, как можешь ты оставаться в России? если царь даст мне свободу, то я месяца не останусь. Мы живем в печальном веке, но когда воображаю Лондон, чугунные дороги, паровые корабли, английские журналы или парижские театры и бордели — то мое глухое Михайловское наводит на меня тоску и бешенство. В 4-ой песне «Онегина» я изобразил свою жизнь; когда-нибудь прочтешь его и спросишь с милою улыбкой: где ж мой поэт? в нем дарование приметно — услышишь, милый, в ответ: он удрал в Париж и никогда в проклятую Русь не воротится — ай да умница!

Но не суждено было. Ему удалось приблизиться к Англии не дальше московского Английского клуба. Когда кто-то пошутил о том, что нет нагляднее оксюморона, чем московский Английский клуб, Пушкин ответил: «Как же? А Императорское гуманитарное общество?» Итак, самый европейский из русских писателей был лишен возможности даже ненадолго побывать в Европе, о которой так мечтал. Интересно, что бы случилось, если бы Пушкину разрешили путешествовать? Русский художник Карл Брюллов вспоминал:

> Вскоре после того как я приехал в Петербург (осенью 1836 года), вечером, ко мне пришел Пушкин и звал к себе ужинать. Я был не в духе, не хотел идти и долго отнекивался, но он меня переупрямил и утащил с собой. Дети его уже спали, он их будил и выносил ко мне поодиночке на руках. Это не шло к нему, было грустно, рисовало передо мною картину натянутого семейного счастья. Я не утерпел и спросил его: «На кой черт ты женился?» Он мне отвечал: «Я хотел ехать за границу — меня не пустили, я попал в такое положение, что не знал, что мне делать, — и женился».

Зима 1830 года для Пушкина была особенно тревожной. Царский шпион и пропагандист Фаддей Булгарин распространял грязную клевету на Пушкина и его семью и писал очернительные статьи в «Северной пчеле», газете, которая полностью финансировалась тайной полицией. Пушкин парировал эпиграммой «На Булгарина» и стихотворением «Моя родословная». Его надежды жениться на Наталье Николаевне, казалось, уже разбились вдребезги. А в Петербурге он встретил свою старую пылкую любовь Каролину Собаньскую. 2 февраля 1830 года он набросал два письма ей, напоминающие по содержанию черновик в прозе письма Онегина к Татьяне. В одном из них: «Счастье так мало создано для меня, что я не признал его, когда оно было передо мною». В другом:

> Сегодня 9-я годовщина дня, когда я вас увидел в первый раз. Этот день был решающим в моей жизни. Чем более я об этом думаю, тем более убеждаюсь, что мое существование неразрывно связано с вашим; я рожден, чтобы любить вас и следовать за вами — всякая другая забота с моей стороны — заблуждение или безрассудство; вдали от вас меня лишь грызет мысль о счастье, которым я не сумел насытиться. Рано или поздно мне придется все бросить и пасть к вашим ногам.

Пушкин не отправил этих писем. Как считала Анна Ахматова, эти черновики служили чем-то вроде упражнений в сочинительстве: Собаньская совершенно явно не была создана для брака. На прощанье Собаньская просила поэта написать в ее альбом. И он создал дивные стихи: «Что в имени тебе моем?» В апреле 1830 г. Пушкин вернулся в Москву и все еще «со смертью в душе» снова предложил руку и сердце дочери «мамы Карса»:

> Только привычка и длительная близость могли бы помочь мне заслужить расположение вашей дочери; я могу надеяться возбудить со временем ее привязанность, но ничем не могу ей понравиться; если она согласится отдать мне свою руку, я увижу в этом лишь доказательство спокойного безразличия ее сердца. Но, будучи всегда окружена восхищением, поклонением, соблазнами, надолго ли сохранит она это спокойствие? Ей станут говорить, что лишь несчастная судьба помешала ей заключить другой, более равный, более блестящий, более достойный ее союз; — может быть, эти мнения и будут искренни, но уж ей они безусловно покажутся таковыми. Не возникнут ли у нее сожаления? Не будет ли она тогда смотреть на меня как на помеху, как на коварного похитителя? Не почувствует ли она ко мне отвращения? Бог мне свидетель, что я готов умереть за нее; но умереть для того, чтобы оставить ее блестящей вдовой, вольной на другой день выбрать себе нового мужа, — эта мысль для меня — ад.

Трудно представить более печальные слова предложения... в нем читается зловещее предчувствие того, что за этим последовало. Как же мог светлейший гений, «умнейший муж России», блестящее «солнце русской поэзии» так низко себя ценить? Почему, окруженный поклонницами, певец романтической любви так хотел жениться на девушке, которая относилась к нему с «холодным безразличием»?

Два года прошли, однако, и за это время Наталья Николаевна не получила другого предложения. И вскоре Пушкин размышлял в письме к княгине Вяземской: «Первая любовь всегда является делом чувствительности: чем она глупее, тем больше оставляет по себе чудесных воспоминаний. Вторая, видите ли, — дело чувственности. Параллель можно было бы провести гораздо дальше. Но у меня на это совершенно нет времени. Моя женитьба на Натали (это, замечу в скобках, моя сто тринадцатая любовь) решена». Помолвка была объявлена 6 мая 1830 года.

> Исполнились мои желанья. Творец
> Тебя мне ниспослал, тебя, моя Мадонна,
> Чистейшей прелести чистейший образец.

Но его будущая теща была сущим кошмаром. Она не оставляла попыток разрушить помолвку, требуя все время у поэта денег. 31 августа 1830 года он писал другу-издателю Плетневу:

> Милый мой, расскажу тебе всё, что у меня на душе: тоска, тоска... Дела будущей тещи моей расстроены. Свадьба моя отлагается день от дня далее. Между тем я хладею, думаю о заботах женатого человека, о прелести холостой жизни. К тому же московские сплетни доходят до ушей невесты и ее матери — отселе размолвки, колкие обиняки, ненадежные примирения — словом, если я и не несчастлив, по крайней мере не счастлив. Осень подходит. Это любимое мое время — здоровье мое обыкновенно крепнет — пора моих литературных трудов настает — а я должен хлопотать о приданом да о свадьбе, которую сыграем Бог весть когда. Все это не очень утешно. Еду в деревню, Бог весть буду ли там иметь время заниматься и душевное спокойствие, без которого ничего не произведешь, кроме эпиграмм на Каченовского.

В сентябре 1830 года Пушкин приехал в Болдино, Нижегородской губернии, чтобы войти во владение частью болдинского поместья, полученного в подарок от отца к женитьбе. Наталья Ивановна заявила, что на приданое дочери у нее денег нет. Пушкину необходимо было заложить имение, чтобы купить вместо семьи Гончаровых приданое Наталье Николаевне и покрыть свадебные расходы. Но вскоре в губернии вспыхнула эпидемия холеры. Объявили карантин, на дорогах установили посты, отрезавшие движение в Москву. Отсиживаясь в деревянном доме в Болдине, он писал другу Плетневу: «Около меня холера морбус. Знаешь ли, что это за зверь? того и гляди, что забежит он и в Болдино, да всех нас перекусает... Ты не можешь вообразить, как весело удрать от невесты, да и засесть стихи писать». Началась «Болдинская осень». Тремя месяцами позже он отчитывался издателю: «Я в Болдине писал, как давно уже не писал...» И правда, продуктивность и качество того, что вылетало тогда из-под пера Пушкина, потрясающи: несколько драматических сцен «Маленьких трагедий» — изумительные «Моцарт и Сальери», «Каменный гость», «Скупой рыцарь», «Пир во время чумы», несколько поэм, включая юмористическое произведение «Домик в Коломне». Кроме того, в Болдине он написал пять блестящих коротких рассказов, известных как «Повести Белкина», которые стали переломным моментом в истории российской литературы. Толстой называл повести лучшей прозой, когда-либо написанной на русском языке, и советовал молодым авторам: «Читайте и перечитывайте «Повести Белкина». Их должен изучать и изучать каждый писатель». В Болдине он также написал около тридцати стихотворений, среди них «Бесы»; «Элегия»; «Поэту»; «Мне не спится, нет огня»; «Заклинание»; «Для берегов отчизны дальной»; «Когда в объятия мои»; «Паж». В Болдине он также закончил (без «Письма Онегина к Татьяне») «Евгения Онегина», коронный венец русской литературы, после семи лет, четырех месяцев и семнадцати дней трудов и любви:

Миг вожделенный настал: окончен мой труд многолетний.
Что ж непонятная грусть тайно тревожит меня?
Или, свой подвиг свершив, я стою, как поденщик ненужный,
Плату приявший свою, чуждый работе другой?
Или жаль мне труда, молчаливого спутника ночи,
Друга Авроры златой, друга пенатов святых?

«Евгений Онегин» известен на Западе главным образом благодаря опере Чайковского, в которой, к сожалению, не присутствует главный герой романа — поэт-рассказчик Пушкин. Хотя музыка великолепно улавливает волшебство и богатство чувств, вызываемое пушкинскими стихами, она не способна заменить доброе сердце поэта, радушное человеколюбие, обрамленное печальным сюжетом поэмы. Для многих русских критиков «Евгений Онегин» — это история о так называемом «лишнем человеке», прообраз вечно неустроенных, недовольных русских интеллигентов. Но это только одна сторона медали. По другую сторону — за безответной любовью Татьяны и Онегина и упущенными возможностями, за трагическими недоразумениями и погубленной обществом дружбой, за всем этим несчастьем стоит в противовес сам поэт, вечно жизнерадостный, влюбленный... Он не сетует на судьбу. Даже трагедия для него становится метафорой, которая лишь делает глубже неизменную любовь к человечеству и природе, его мудрость и смирение — его поэтическое счастье. И то, что на поверхностный взгляд может казаться бесцельным отступлением, «в котором забалтываюсь донельзя», в действительности являет собой «энциклопедию русской жизни», в знаменитой фразе Белинского. Но эта энциклопедия не только русской жизни. Она воистину — вселенская.   Она — энциклопедия человеческого сердца.

Пушкин вернулся в Москву в декабре 1830 года, но из-за стычек с будущей тещей свадьба все время откладывалась. А в январе 1831 г. Пушкина постиг тяжелейший удар — смерть ближайшего друга Антона Дельвига. Боль Пушкина в эти дни была нескрываема, совсем не подобающая жениху. Из светского письма: «Пушкин женится на Гончаровой, entre nous, на бездушной красавице, и мне сдается, что он бы с удовольствием заключил отступной контракт». За неделю до свадьбы Пушкин пишет другу:

> Женат — или почти. Все, что бы ты мог сказать мне в пользу холостой жизни и противу женитьбы, все уже много передумано. Я хладнокровно взвесил выгоды и невыгоды состояния, мною избираемого. Молодость моя прошла шумно и бесплодно. До сих пор я жил иначе, как обыкновенно живут. Счастья мне не было. Il n'est de bonheur que dans les voies communes. (Счастье только на проторенных дорогах.) Мне за 30 лет. В тридцать лет люди обыкновенно женятся — я поступаю как люди и, вероятно, не буду в том раскаиваться. К тому же я женюсь без упоения, без ребяческого очарования. Будущность является мне не в розах, но в строгой наготе своей. Горести не удивят меня: они входят в мои домашние расчеты. Всякая радость будет мне неожиданностью.

За два дня до женитьбы он пишет издателю: «Взять жену без состояния — я в состоянии, но входить в долги для ее тряпок — я не в состоянии. Но я упрям и должен был настоять по крайней мере на свадьбе. Делать нечего: придется печатать мои повести». Уныние Пушкина не рассеял мальчишник, на котором он разрыдался, слушая вольные цыганские песни. День свадьбы 18 февраля 1831 года начался еще хуже: Наталья Николаевна заболела, будущая теща прислала Пушкину грубую записку с угрозой отменить свадьбу, если Пушкин не пришлет денег на экипаж. Но Пушкин и Наталья Николаевна тем не менее обвенчались в церкви Большого Вознесения в Москве у Никитских ворот. Во время церемонии невеста обронила кольцо жениха. Затем подул ветер, Евангелие упало с аналоя, а сквозняк задул у Пушкина свечу. Княгиня Долгорукая видела, как побледнел Пушкин и прошептал "Tous les mauvais augures!" («Все плохие предзнаменования!») Но потом поэт успокоился, улыбнулся и продолжал ритуал.

> Участь моя решена. Я женюсь... Та, которую любил я целые два года, которую везде первую отыскивали глаза мои, с которой встреча казалась мне блаженством — Боже мой - она... почти моя. Ожидание решительного ответа было самым болезненным чувством жизни моей. Ожидание последней заметавшейся карты, угрызение совести, сон перед поединком, — всё это в сравнении с ним ничего не значит. Жениться! Легко сказать — большая часть людей видят в женитьбе шали, взятые в долг, новую карету и розовый шлафрок. Другие — приданое и степенную жизнь... Третьи женятся так, потому что все женятся — потому что им 30 лет. Спросите их, что такое брак, в ответ они вам

скажут пошлую эпиграмму... Я женюсь, то есть я жертвую независимостию, моею беспечной, прихотливой независимостию, моими роскошными привычками, странствиями без цели, уединением, непостоянством. Я готов удвоить жизнь и без того неполную. Я никогда не хлопотал о счастии, я мог обойтись без него. Теперь мне нужно на двоих, а где мне взять его?» (Набросок повести «Участь моя решена. Я женюсь».)

1831–1837. Семейная жизнь. Санкт-Петербург

Некоторые комментаторы не воспринимают духовную, возвышенную сторону чувств Пушкина к Наталье Николаевне. А великая поэтесса Марина Цветаева судила (не без ревности?): «Было в ней одно: красавица. Только — красавица, просто — красавица, без корректива ума, души, сердца, дара. Голая красота, разящая, как меч. И — сразила». Владимир Соллогуб (с которым у Пушкина впоследствии чуть было не случилась дуэль из-за попыток привлечь внимание Натальи Николаевны) вспоминал: «Много видел я на своем веку красивых женщин... но никогда не видывал я женщины, которая соединила бы в себе законченность классически правильных черт и стана... все остальные даже из самых прелестных меркли как-то при ее появлении. На вид всегда она была сдержанна до холодности и мало вообще говорила...» Словно в противовес Соллогубу поэт Туманский писал: «Пушкина — беленькая, чистенькая девочка, с правильными чертами и лукавыми глазками, как у любой гризетки. Видно, что она неловка еще и неразвязна; а все-таки московщина отражается на ней довольно заметно. Что у нее нет вкуса, это было видно по безобразному ее наряду; что у нее нет ни опрятности, ни порядка, — о том свидетельствовали запачканные салфетки и скатерть и расстройство мебели и посуды».

Не сохранились письма Натальи Николаевны к Пушкину, но зато 78 писем Пушкина к Наталье Николаевне выжили. По их нежному, глубоко личному тону становится очевидно, что поэт, по крайней мере, в своей жене ценил не только ее наружность. Наоборот, его письма явно демонстрируют нежную дружбу, привязанность, симпатию, заботу, и действительно: «С твоим лицом ничего нельзя сравнить на свете, а душу твою люблю более твоего лица». Пушкина, пожалуй, и в самом деле глубоко трогала детская уязвимость любимой и он сочувствовал и жалел ее.

Молодожены сняли комнаты в доме Хитровой на Арбате. Именно там поэт Туманский посетил их и оказался одним из немногих, на кого Наталья Николаевна не произвела особого впечатления, как видно из его письма. Несмотря даже на плохие предзнаменования,

Пушкин искренне радовался семейной жизни. Через неделю после тревожной церемонии венчания он писал Плетневу:

> Я женат — и счастлив; одно желание мое, чтоб ничего в жизни моей не изменилось — лучшего не дождусь. Это состояние для меня так ново, что, кажется, я переродился.

Однако теща Пушкина не разделяла его радости. Она упрекала зятя в антиклерикализме, приказывая дочери строго придерживаться церковных служб, молитв и постов. Снова и снова она не уставала повторять, что ее дочь совершила трагическую ошибку, выйдя замуж за никчемного писаку, источник беспорядков, еретика и вольнодумца, одновременно выпрашивая у этой «ошибки» все большие суммы денег. Вскоре Пушкин не выдержал и покинул Москву с женой навсегда, написав на прощанье своей теще:

> Я вынужден уехать из Москвы во избежание неприятностей, которые под конец могли лишить меня не только покоя; меня расписывали моей жене как человека гнусного, алчного, как презренного ростовщика, ей говорили: ты глупа, позволяя мужу... и т. д. Согласитесь, что это значило проповедовать развод... Я проявил большое терпение и мягкость, но, по-видимому, и то и другое было напрасно.

В мае 1831 года молодожены переехали в дом Китаевой, маленький уютный домик у парка Летнего дворца в Царском Селе, недалеко от любимого поэтом Лицея. Каждое утро они с Натальей Николаевной совершали прогулки вокруг озера. Сестра Пушкина Ольга была рада, что «они, казалось, обожали друг друга». Поэт Жуковский писал: «Пушкин мой сосед, и мы видимся с ним часто. Женка его очень милое творение. И он к нею мне весьма нравится. Я более и более за него радуюсь тому, что он женат. И душа, и жизнь, и поэзия в выигрыше». В Царском селе Пушкин написал «Письмо Онегина к Татьяне» и несколько строф — до и после него — к теперь уже полностью законченному произведению «Евгений Онегин».

> ....Поминутно видеть вас,
> Повсюду следовать за вами,
> Улыбку уст, движенье глаз
> Ловить влюбленными глазами,
> Внимать вам долго, понимать
> Душой все ваше совершенство,
> Пред вами в муках замирать,
> Бледнеть и гаснуть... вот блаженство!

Свое новое «мучительное счастье» он выразил в стихотворении «Нет, я не дорожу мятежным наслажденьем», которое преподносит двусмысленный портрет Натальи Николаевны, как холодной в интимных отношениях, пока «И делишь наконец мой пламень поневоле!» Многие усматривают в этом стихотворении доказательство того, что Наталья Николаевна просто не любила своего мужа. Но нельзя так односторонне воспринимать стихотворение Пушкина... Для меня это стихотворение отражает сильнейшее притяжение его страстного «янь» и ее кокетливо-застенчивого «инь». Стоит заметить, что во время медового месяца в Царском Селе Пушкин написал самую счастливую, самую свою любимую «Сказку о царе Салтане».

Говорят, царевна есть,
Что не можно глаз отвесть.
Днем свет божий затмевает,
Ночью землю освещает —
Месяц под косой блестит,
А во лбу звезда горит.
А сама-то величава,
Выступает, будто пава;
Сладку речь-то говорит,
Будто реченька журчит.

Жена поэта

В 1831 году Пушкин написал аллегорию «Эхо» — о долге поэта отказаться от своего «я», чтобы слышать и отражать услышанное, быть «пустым», как эхо, в котором звучит Истина. Все еще скорбя по своему другу Дельвигу и другим друзьям по Лицею, он пишет меланхолично-философское стихотворение, 19 октября 1831 года, на двадцатилетнюю годовщину основания Лицея: «Чем чаще празднует Лицей».

Гуляя в парке Екатерининского дворца, Пушкин с женой встретили императорскую чету; они, по всем воспоминаниям, были просто очарованы Натали. Вскоре после этой встречи Николай I восстановил Пушкина в звании чиновника 10 класса, предоставил ему доступ к государственным архивам и позднее — к прославленной «библиотеке Вольтера» Екатерины Великой. Пушкин начал работу над новым трудом — историей Петра Великого (так и не законченной), а также над историей восстания Пугачева 1773-1775 годов — первой, по сути, русской гражданской войны. В ходе своих исследований Пушкин получил подарок от царя — «Свод Законов Российской Империи» и внимательно их изучил. Погружаясь в архивные документы, Пушкин стал воспринимать себя больше и больше не только как поэта, но и как историка, и все чаще стал обращаться к прозе. Восстания во Франции, Польше и крестьянские бунты в России вернули его интерес к темам личности и государства, контрастным проявлениям власти и мятежа, общества и восстания. Его следующий роман «Дубровский», написанный в 1832–1833 годах, объединил массу фактического материала, почти документального, включая письмо от его любимой няни Арины Родионовны, судебное разбирательство коррумпированного суда в Муромской губернии и жестокое преследование разорившегося бывшего дворянина, ставшего разбойником в Белоруссии. Однако он внезапно бросил работу, оставив ее, как и многие свои творения, прекрасно незавершенной, подобно греческим фрагментам. Может быть, Пушкин с трудом еще мог примирить в себе конфликт между романтической поэтической лирикой и прозой, которая (на его взгляд) должна быть как можно более беспристрастной.

Одним из новых друзей Пушкина, с которыми он сблизился в Царском Селе, был Николай Васильевич Гоголь, только что приехавший из провинции. Пушкин сразу же признал и поощрил талант Гоголя, помог ему опубликовать первые произведения. Гоголь обязан Пушкину идеями и сюжетами двух своих самых знаменитых произведений: комедии «Ревизор» и романа «Мертвые души». Пушкин оказал содействие Гоголю в получении должности профессора университета, редактировал несколько гоголевских «Петербургских повестей», включая «Нос», «Коляску», «Невский проспект», и письменно рекомендовал дать разрешение на театральную постановку «Ревизора». Гоголь не просто был благодарен Пушкину всю свою жизнь — он боготворил его как величайшего из поэтов.

Дочь Мария, первый ребенок Пушкина, родилась 19 мая 1832 года. По письмам Пушкина, да и по мнению многих, поэт был преданным отцом. Однако семейная жизнь в столице оказалась губительно дорогой, особенно, если учесть пристрастие Натальи Николаевны к дорогим нарядам и экипажам. Хотя Пушкин и гордился оглушительным успехом своей жены в петербургском свете, он с трудом мог себе позволить такие расходы (даже при том, что тетушка, Екатерина Ивановна Загряжская, часто дарила ей роскошные туалеты). А без меры кокетливая Наталья Николаевна неожиданно оказалась очень ревнивой. Осенью 1832 года Пушкин, будучи в Москве по издательским делам, написал жене:

> По пунктам отвечаю на твои обвинения. 1) Русский человек в дороге не переодевается и, доехав до места свинья свиньею, идет в баню, которая наша вторая мать. Ты разве не крещеная, что всего этого не знаешь? 2) В Москве письма принимаются до 12 часов — а я въехал в Тверскую заставу ровно в 11, следственно, и отложил писать к тебе до другого дня. Видишь ли, что я прав, а что ты кругом виновата?

виновата 1) потому, что всякий вздор забираешь себе в голову, 2) потому, что пакет Бенкендорфа (вероятно, важный) отсылаешь с досады на меня Бог ведает куда, 3) кокетничаешь со всем дипломатическим корпусом, да еще жалуешься... нечего тебе и писать. Мне без тебя так скучно, так скучно, что не знаю, куда головы преклонить... Прощай, мой ангел, целую тебя и Машу. Прощай, душа моя. Христос с тобою.

Наталья Николаевна родила Пушкину четырех детей, была привязана к мужу и, вероятно, благодарна ему за то, что он ввел ее в высший свет. Но она мало интересовалась поэзией, миром его идей и вообще искусством. Похоже, она мало ценила или даже не догадывалась о гениальности мужа. Ей было скучно, когда он уединялся и писал стихи или читал их с друзьями. Александра Смирнова, подруга Пушкина, утверждала, что как-то слышала от Натальи во время чтения мужа: «Ах, Пушкин, как ты надоел мне со своими стихами!» Лев Павлищев вспоминал, как «однажды на вопрос Баратынского, не помешает ли он ей, если прочтет в ее присутствии Пушкину новые стихотворения, Наталья Николаевна ответила: «Читайте, пожалуйста, я не слушаю». Однажды к Пушкину во сне пришли стихи и он проснулся вдохновленный. Наталья Николаевна его упрекнула: «Ночь создана на то, чтобы спать». Как заметил выдающийся пушкинист В. С. Непомнящий, после женитьбы Пушкин больше не писал любовной лирики.

Должно быть, в их отношениях был бессознательный дух соперничества; в ответ на его литературную славу она жаждала успеха в обществе, славы «первой красавицы» Петербурга. Сологуб очень точно сформулировал это как бы соперничество: «Ее блистательная красота рядом с его магическим именем». В 1833 году Пушкин писал другу Нащокину: «Жизнь моя в Петербурге ни то ни сё. Заботы о жизни мешают мне скучать. Но нет у меня досуга, вольной холостой жизни, необходимой для писателя. Кружусь в свете, жена моя в большой моде — все это требует денег, деньги достаются мне через труды, а труды требуют уединения». В мае 1833 г. у Пушкиных родился второй ребенок — сын Александр.

В 1833 году впервые был полностью опубликован «Евгений Онегин». В этом же году Пушкин начал собирать материалы для написания исторического романа о восстании Пугачева. 30 июля 1833 года он ходатайствовал о поездке по губерниям, в которых проходило восстание: «В продолжение двух последних лет занимался я одними историческими изысканиями, не написав ни одной строчки чисто литературной. Мне необходимо месяца два провести в совершенном уединении, дабы отдохнуть от важнейших занятий и кончить книгу, давно мною начатую, и которая доставит мне деньги, в коих имею нужду». Разрешение было получено.

Пушкин совершил утомительное путешествие по Казанской, Симбирской, Оренбургской и Уральской губерниям, по местам, где начиналось восстание, делая многочисленные пометки. По пути домой он сделал остановку в Болдине, чтобы записать свои впечатления, но испугался дурного предзнаменования, когда при въезде в имение ему перешел дорогу местный священник. По письму домой понятно, какие опасения закрутились в голове у Пушкина при виде этого попа:

> Недаром все эти встречи. Смотри, женка. Того и гляди избалуешься без меня, забудешь меня — искокетничаешься. Одна надежда на Бога да на тетку. Авось сохранят тебя от искушений рассеянности. Честь имею донести тебе, что с моей стороны я перед тобою чист, как новорожденный младенец. Дорогою волочился я за одними 70- и 80-летними старухами — а на молоденьких... 60-летних, и не глядел. В деревне... где Пугачев простоял шесть месяцев, имел я une bonne fortune — нашел 75-летнюю казачку, которая помнит это время, как мы с тобою помним 1830 год.

Вторая «Болдинская осень» Пушкина снова ознаменовалась феноменальным успехом в его творчестве. Он написал свою «Историю пугачевского бунта», две поэмы-сказки — «Сказка о рыбаке и рыбке» и «Сказка о мертвой царевне и семи богатырях» и свыше пятнадцати стихотворений, в том числе «Осень», величественные размышления о природе и ее влиянии на творчество. Там же написаны поэмы — «Анджело» (основана на его любимой пьесе Шекспира «Мера за меру», отдельные сцены из которой Пушкин перевел на русский язык) и «Медный всадник».

Величайшая поэма - «Медный всадник» — о том, как бедный конторский служащий в Петербурге потерял свой дом и невесту во время великого наводнения 7 ноября 1824 года и идет, убитый горем, к памятнику Петру Великому на Сенатской площади жаловаться «Медному всаднику». Царь Петр ведь убил его любовь и разрушил его жизнь, построив свою роскошную столицу на болоте у моря, не думая о будущих страданиях людей. Бедный чиновник (тоже Евгений) грозит царю: «Ужо тебе!» В ответ грозный всадник преследует несчастного стряпчего, который в конце концов сходит с ума и умирает на пустынном острове в устье Невы. «Медный всадник» — это гимн Петру и любви к его городу Санкт-Петербургу, но и одновременно обвинение в жестокости русского государства, олицетворенное в скульптуре самого гиганта Петра Великого, по существу, двуликого Януса. Тема потерянной любви вновь приобретает глубокое значение, показывая противоречие между природой самой власти и ее губительным, российским отношением к свободе и судьбе человека.

Судьба и свобода — темы еще одного шедевра, написанного в ту «Болдинскую осень». «Пиковая дама» стала поворотным моментом, поиском «безопасного риска», сказкой игрока (еще и с привидением), романтической интригой и веселым, почти сатирическим выявлением конфликтов между естественным и сверхъестественным, риском и определенностью, свободной волей и личной ответственностью, судьбой, милосердием и безумием. Хотя Пушкин сам любил играть в карты, в этой истории он превратил свой собственный неудачный опыт заядлого игрока во что-то более глубокое. Риск в игре становится мощной метафорой в определении самой жизни как игры и саморазрушительной силы жестоких амбиций. По словам Достоевского, это «вершина художественного совершенства» (что оказало огромное влияние на собственные великие произведения Достоевского «Игрок» и «Преступление и наказание»). Старая княгиня Голицына стала прототипом жестокой графини, обладавшей роковой тайной трех верных карт. Другие усматривали в капризной графине черты тетки или матери Натальи Николаевны. Но неужели нет там искорки сочувствия Пушкина к жене в описании героини Лизаветы Ивановны, так жестоко угнетаемой графиней?

> Графиня ***, конечно, не имела злой души; но была своенравна, как женщина, избалованная светом, скупа и погружена в холодный эгоизм, как и все старые люди, отлюбившие в свой век и чуждые настоящему. Она участвовала во всех суетностях большого света, таскалась на балы, где сидела в углу, разрумяненная и одетая по старинной моде, как уродливое и необходимое украшение бальной залы; к ней с низкими поклонами подходили приезжающие гости, как по установленному обряду, и потом уже никто ею не занимался. У себя принимала она весь город, наблюдая строгий этикет и не узнавая никого в лицо. Многочисленная челядь ее, разжирев и поседев в ее передней и девичьей, делала, что хотела, наперерыв обкрадывая умирающую старуху. Лизавета Ивановна была домашней мученицею. Она разливала чай и получала выговоры за лишний расход сахара; она вслух читала романы и виновата была во всех ошибках автора; она сопровождала графиню в ее прогулках и отвечала за погоду и за мостовую. Ей было назначено жалованье, которое никогда не доплачивали; а между тем требовали от нее, чтоб она одета была, как и все, то есть как очень немногие. В свете играла она самую жалкую роль. Все ее знали и никто не замечал; на балах она танцевала только тогда, как недоставало vis-à-vis, и дамы брали ее под руку всякий раз, как им нужно было идти в уборную поправить что-нибудь в своем наряде. Она была самолюбива, живо чувствовала свое положение и глядела кругом себя, — с нетерпением ожидая избавителя; но молодые люди, расчетливые в ветреном своем тщеславии, не удостоивали ее внимания, хотя

> Лизавета Ивановна была сто раз милее наглых и холодных невест, около которых они увивались. Сколько раз, оставя тихонько скучную и пышную гостиную, она уходила плакать в бедной своей комнате, где стояли ширмы, оклеенные обоями, комод, зеркальце и крашеная кровать и где сальная свеча темно горела в медном шандале!

В эпилоге к «Пиковой даме» Лизавета Ивановна, кажется, становится похожей на саму графиню. Это ведь не в повести, а только в опере Чайковского она бросается в ледяную Неву: либо Чайковский предпочел «патетику», либо двусмысленная ирония не является грандиозным оперным решением.

В то время как творческий гений Пушкина раскрывался в Болдине, Наталья Николаевна, уже не робкая и кроткая девушка, писала ему, хвастаясь, как она покорила сердца всех мужчин, в том числе и самого царя. 11 октября 1833 года Пушкин отвечал ей: «...не стращай меня, будь здорова, смотри за детьми, не кокетничай с царем...» Через три недели он оторвался от работы над «Медным всадником» и написал домой:

> Вчера получил я, мой друг, два от тебя письма. Спасибо; но я хочу немножко тебя пожурить. Ты, кажется, не путем искокетничалась. Смотри: недаром кокетство не в моде и почитается признаком дурного тона. В нем толку мало. Ты радуешься, что за тобою, как за сучкой, бегают кобели, подняв хвост трубочкой и понюхивая тебе задницу; есть чему радоваться! ... легко за собою приучить бегать холостых шаромыжников; стоит разгласить, что-де я большая охотница. Вот вся тайна кокетства. *Было бы корыто, а свиньи будут.* К чему тебе принимать мужчин, которые за тобою ухаживают? ... Теперь, мой ангел, целую тебя как ни в чем ни бывало; и благодарю за то, что ты подробно и откровенно описываешь мне свою беспутную жизнь... Да, ангел мой, пожалуйста не кокетничай. Я не ревнив, да и знаю, что ты во все тяжкое не пустишься; но ты знаешь, как я не люблю всё, что пахнет московской барышнею, все, что не comme il faut, всё, что vulgar... Если при моем возвращении я найду, что твой милый, простой, аристократический тон изменился, разведусь, вот те Христос, и пойду в солдаты с горя!

Пушкин вернулся в Петербург ночью 21 ноября 1833 года. Натальи Николаевны дома не было, она была на балу. Он нашел ее экипаж у бального крыльца и спрятался в нем, послав слугу сказать ей, что дома произошло что-то чрезвычайное. Когда она не пришла немедля (ее пригласили на мазурку), Пушкин разволновался и разгневался. Наконец, в роскошном розовом платье, она села в экипаж, и Пушкин ее «увез к себе, как улан уездную барышню с именин городничихи».

Некоторое творческое равновесие, восстановленное в Болдине, было вновь сорвано двумя серьезными ударами судьбы. Публикация «Медного всадника» была запрещена цензурой (полная версия произведения была напечатана лишь в 1917 году). Но, что еще тяжелее, накануне нового 1834 года Пушкин получил придворное звание камер-юнкера, «что довольно неприлично для моего возраста». Но «Двору хотелось, чтобы Наталья Николаевна танцевала в Аничковом» (личной резиденции царя). Это означало, что Пушкин со своей женой приглашался теперь на все придворные мероприятия — к удовольствию Натальи Николаевны и к его отчаянию. Ему была противна его камер-юнкерская форма, а бальные платья жены и ее популярность губительно сказывались не только на кармане Пушкина, но и на его душевном состоянии. Он снова начал играть в карты и появились карточные долги (после трехлетнего перерыва, когда, женившись, он бросил играть, хотя однажды заявлял английскому путешественнику Томасу Райксу: «Я скорее умру, чем брошу играть»).

К марту 1834 года: «Моя «Пиковая дама» в большой моде. Игроки понтируют лишь на тройку, семерку и туза!» Все же карты не стали утешением, когда его жена была королевой на всех балах, в то время как он сам мрачно скучал в углу в своем лакейском костюме. Он так ненавидел свой костюм, что однажды попытался прийти на придворную церемонию в простом вечернем платье, за что получил официальный выговор. Это уязвило его еще больше. В дневнике он с горечью писал: «Я могу быть подданным, даже рабом, — но холопом и шутом не буду и у царя небесного... Праздников будет на полмиллиона. Что скажет народ, умирающий с голода?.. В государе много от прапорщика и совсем немного от Петра Великого».

В 1834 г. Наталья Николаевна танцевала в Аничковом каждый день по два раза — в 12 часов и снова в 8 часов вечера. Гоголь переживал за своего друга и наставника: «Пушкина нигде не встретишь, как

только на балах. Так он протранжирит всю жизнь свою, если только какой-нибудь случай и более необходимость не затащат его в деревню». Напуганный слухами об увлечении жены царем, Пушкин отправляет ее и детей в деревню, в родовое поместье Гончаровых, Полотняный завод, недалеко от Москвы². Мучения, которые он испытывал летом 1834 года, и нестерпимое желание сбежать из этого «свинского Петербурга» можно ясно почувствовать в стихотворении, написанном тогда: «Пора, мой друг, пора! Покоя сердце просит...» Увезя жену к родным, подальше от дворца, Пушкин испытал некоторое облегчение, о чем свидетельствует стихотворение «Я возмужал среди печальных бурь», написанное в то же время.

Ожесточилось перлюстрирование его писем. Даже одно его письмо жене передали лично царю. В нем Пушкин писал: «Видел я трех царей: первый [Павел I] велел снять с меня картуз и пожурил за меня мою няньку; второй [Александр I] меня не жаловал; третий, хоть и упек меня в камер-пажи под старость лет, но променять его на четвертого не желаю; от добра добра не ищут». Письмо вызвало официальное предупреждение против lèse-majesté — («пренебрежительное отношение к Его Величеству»). Пушкин записал в дневнике: «Однако какая глубокая безнравственность в привычках нашего правительства! Полиция распечатывает письма мужа к жене и приносит их читать царю (человеку благовоспитанному и честному), и царь даже не стыдится в этом признаться... Что ни говори, мудрено быть самодержавным». (Заметьте, что опять, как в «19 октября», гонимый поэт всё же сочувствует его гонителю-царю. Его способность сочувствовать, совмещенная с острой, меткой, неуловимой легкостью всегда поражают — как и в его стихах, так и в его прозе.)

И все же он писал письма жене, уже понимая, что они будут прочитаны:

---

2 Была ли у Натальи Николаевны любовная связь с императором? До сих пор неизвестно; пусть так и останется. А.П. Арапова — ее дочь от второго брака, намекала в своих сплетнических мемуарах, что она родилась в результате связи матери с царем. Но это уже было через много лет после смерти Пушкина. Возможно, это самолюбивая попытка Араповой подняться выше по социальной лестнице. Историки всерьез не воспринимают ее воспоминания. Тем не менее, опасения Пушкина в отношении намерений царя были не лишены оснований: Николай I слыл донжуаном (Глава XV романа Л. Толстого «Хаджи-Мурат» описывает, как царь пытался соблазнить женщину в дальней комнатке Зимнего дворца, которая и существовала специально для этих целей).

Ты так давно, так давно ко мне не писала, что, несмотря на то, что беспокоиться по-пустому я не люблю, но я беспокоюсь. Здорова ли ты и дети? спокойна ли ты? Я тебе не писал, потому что был зол — не на тебя, на *других*. Одно из моих писем попало полиции и так далее... Тайна семейственных сношений проникнута скверным и бесчестным образом... Никто не должен знать, что может происходить между нами; никто не должен быть принят в нашу спальню. Без тайны нет семейственной жизни... а свинство уж давно меня ни в ком не удивляет...

...Свинство так меня охолодило, что я пера в руки взять был не в силе. Мысль, что кто-нибудь нас с тобой подслушивает, приводит меня в бешенство à la lettre (фр. «буквально»). Без политической свободы жить очень можно; без семейственной неприкосновенности (inviolabilité de la famille) невозможно: каторга не в пример лучше. Это писано не для тебя; а вот что пишу для тебя. Начала ли ты железные ванны? есть ли у Маши новые зубы?.. Будь здорова, умна, мила, не езди на бешеных лошадях, за детьми смотри, чтоб за ними няньки их смотрели, пиши ко мне чаще... «Петр I» идет; того и гляди напечатаю 1-й том к зиме. На того я перестал сердиться, потому что, toute réflexion faite не он виноват в свинстве, его окружающем. А живя в нужнике, поневоле привыкнешь к говну, и вонь его тебе не будет противна, даром что gentleman. Ух, кабы мне удрать на чистый воздух!

Летом 1834 года Пушкин отправил официальную просьбу об отставке и разрешении уехать; он хотел на какое-то время переехать с семьей в деревню. Но все напрасно: Наталья Николаевна была категорически против планов мужа, а царь пригрозил отказать Пушкину в доступе к государственным архивам, что было бы ударом для него, так как история Петра Великого была еще не готова. Пушкина вынудили забрать заявление, и надзор за ним стал строже. Примерно в это время Пушкин написал: «Не дай мне Бог сойти с ума».

Получив разрешение хоть иногда выезжать в Болдино, Пушкин поехал туда снова в надежде на еще одну чудотворную осень. Но печаль так поглотила его, что он не мог писать. 25 сентября 1834 года Пушкин сообщил Наталье: «Вот уж скоро две недели, как я в деревне, а от тебя еще письма не получил. Скучно, мой ангел. И стихи в голову нейдут; и роман не переписываю. Читаю Вальтер Скотта и Библию, а всё об вас думаю... Видно, нынешнюю осень мне долго в Болдине не прожить...» Роман, который он «переписывал», назывался «Капитанская дочка»; работой над ним Пушкин был поглощен до октября 1836 года.

В свое последнее пребывание в Болдине Пушкин написал только одну, правда, великую «Сказку о золотом петушке», основанную на легенде об арабском астрологе из новелл «Альгамбры» Вашингтона Ирвинга. Эта сказка — яркое изображение безнравственного влияния власти, ее жестокости и похоти. Но это и история о волшебном подарке, превращенном алчностью в проклятье. А все так искусно замаскировано, так весело и незаметно, как и сама сказка, что даже царь разрешил ее опубликовать, запретив только (мнимое lèse-majesté) припев Петушка:

> И кричит: Кири-ку-ку.
> Царствуй, лежа на боку!

Пушкин вернулся в Петербург. Ситуация с деньгами становилась все хуже. Наталья Николаевна, несмотря на возражения Пушкина, привезла двух своих старших сестер, Екатерину и Александру, чтобы ввести их в свет. И Пушкину пришлось перевезти возросшее семейство в бо́льшую, и, естественно, более дорогую квартиру. Теперь, в бесконечном круговороте постоянных балов, приемов и вечеринок, из которых состояла их жизнь в Петербурге, Пушкин оказался вынужденным сопровождать уже не одну, а трех дам. Пушкин мрачно заметил: «Я думал, что мои расходы из-за этого утроятся — и что ты думаешь? Они увеличились в десять раз». Он возлагал большие материальные надежды на выход «Истории пугачевского бунта», которая была опубликована в декабре 1834 года. Однако российский читатель был не готов к нейтральному взгляду Пушкина на историю восстания. Критики-либералы ругали Пушкина за мало романтизированные портреты мятежников, за откровенный показ порочного и деспотичного беззакония бунтарей. Однако консерваторов, во главе с Сергеем Уваровым, министром образования, книга задела честной оценкой жестокостей и некомпетентности царского правительства, которые и вызвали восстание, неумело и жестоко подавленное. (Несмотря на провал «Истории пугачевского бунта», он потом напишет на ее основе роман — «Капитанская дочка»ю) Поэт нам оставил заметку в дневнике о блестящей карьере Уварова: «Он начал тем, что был сутенером, потом стал нянькой детей министров, затем сразу попал в президенты Академии наук». На злобную критику в свой адрес он ответил стихотворением об Уварове, известном взяточнике и воре государственного имущества, «На выздоровление Лукулла». Словно ему не хватало проблем, у Пушкина появился новый влиятельный враг. Его «Путешествие в Арзрум» было задержано цензурой, как и второе издание «Повестей Белкина». А дома Пушкин не мог найти покоя, потому что его жена и две ее сестры были поглощены светской жизнью. Даже больная мать Пушкина жаловалась в январе 1835 года:

Натали выезжает и танцует ежедневно со своими сестрами. Только и слышишь разговору, что о праздниках, балах и спектаклях. Она привезла ко мне Машу, которая настолько привыкла видеть только изящно одетых, что, увидев меня, начала громко кричать; ее спросили, почему она не хотела поцеловать бабушку; она ответила, что у меня скверный чепчик и скверное платье.

В мае 1835 года у Пушкина родился сын Григорий. Семья росла... «Живу на 33 буквы русского языка...», но цензура усложняла творческую жизнь Пушкина; в это время ему было отказано в издании собственного литературного журнала. За четыре года семейной жизни в столице долг Пушкина превысил 60 000 рублей. В отчаянье он снова направил просьбу об отъезде в деревню на несколько лет, написав графу Бенкендорфу 1 января 1835 года:

> У меня нет состояния; ни я, ни моя жена не получили еще той части, которая должна нам достаться. До сих пор я жил только своим трудом. Мой постоянный доход — это жалованье, которое государь соизволил мне назначить. В работе ради хлеба насущного, конечно, нет ничего для меня унизительного; но привыкнув к независимости, я совершенно не умею писать ради денег; и одна мысль об этом приводит меня в полное бездействие. Жизнь в Петербурге ужасающе дорога... Ныне я поставлен в необходимость покончить с расходами, которые вовлекают меня в долги и готовят мне в будущем только беспокойство и хлопоты, а может быть — нищету и отчаяние. Три или четыре года уединенной жизни в деревне снова дадут мне возможность по возвращении в Петербург возобновить занятия, которыми я еще обязан милостям его величества.

Но царю нравилось присутствие Натальи Николаевны на балах, а граф Бенкендорф не хотел отпускать Пушкина из-под надзора. Зная, как много значит для Пушкина его историческое исследование, он подтвердил, что, если Пушкин уедет, он не только потеряет жалованье, но и навсегда лишится доступа к государственным архивам. В итоге царь согласился выдать Пушкину заем на 30 000 рублей, с условием приостановления его жалованья в течение следующих шести лет. Но царского займа не было достаточно, он мгновенно ушел на уплату старых срочных долгов и — еще более срочных — новых (одна шляпка обходилась Наталье Николаевне в 250 рублей). Осенью 1835 года Пушкин уехал в Михайловское, надеясь завершить «Капитанскую дочку». Оттуда он написал Наталье Николаевне:

> Ты не можешь вообразить, как живо работает воображение, когда сидим одни между четырех стен или ходим по лесам, когда никто не мешает нам думать, думать до того, что голова кружится. А о чем я думаю? Вот о чем: чем нам жить будет? Отец не оставит мне имения; он его уже вполовину промотал; ваше имение на волоске от погибели. Царь мне не позволяет ни записаться в помещики, ни в журналисты. Писать книги для денег, видит Бог, не могу. У нас ни гроша верного дохода, а верного расхода 30 000. Что из этого будет, Бог знает. Покамест грустно. Поцелуй-ка меня, авось горе пройдет. Да лих, губки твои на 400 верст не оттянешь... Кстати: пришли мне, если можно, Essays de M. Montaigne — 4 синих книги, на длинных моих полках. Отыщи. Сегодня погода пасмурная. Осень начинается... Я много хожу, много езжу верхом на клячах, которые очень тому рады, ибо им за то дается овес, к которому они не привыкли. Ем я печеный картофель, как маймист, и яйца всмятку, как Людовик XVIII. Вот мой обед. Ложусь в 9 часов; встаю в 7. Теперь требую от тебя такого же подробного отчета. Целую тебя, душа моя, и всех ребят, благословляю вас от сердца. Будьте здоровы.

Однако все эти «думы» продолжали тяготить его, и через несколько дней он снова пишет домой:

> В Михайловском нашел я все по-старому, кроме того, что нет уж в нем няни моей и что около знакомых старых сосен поднялась, во время моего отсутствия, молодая сосновая семья, на которую досадно мне смотреть, как иногда досадно мне видеть молодых кавалергардов на балах, на которых уже не пляшу.

Эти настроения составляют часть знаменитейшей философской элегии «Вновь я посетил...», которая была написана в дни прогулок по Михайловскому:

> ...Вновь я посетил
> Тот уголок земли, где я провел
> Изгнанником два года незаметных.
> Уж десять лет ушло с тех пор — и много
> Переменилось в жизни для меня,
> И сам, покорный общему закону,
> Переменился я — но здесь опять
> Минувшее меня объемлет живо,
> И кажется, вечор еще бродил
> Я в этих рощах.
> ...Вот опальный домик,
> Где жил я с бедной нянею моей.
> Уже старушки нет — уж за стеною
> Не слышу я шагов ее тяжелых,
> Ни кропотливого ее дозора.

> Вот холм лесистый, над которым часто
> Я сиживал недвижим — и глядел
> На озеро, воспоминая с грустью
> Иные берега, иные волны...

По крайней мере, в этой элегии (чей свободный белый стих является водоразделом в русской поэзии) Пушкин превозмог печаль и мысли о своей смерти в трогательном воспевании обновленной природы, приветствуя новые поколения, как символ вечности жизни.

> Теперь младая роща разрослась,
> Зеленая семья; кусты теснятся
> Под сенью их как дети. А вдали
> Стоит один угрюмый их товарищ,
> Как старый холостяк, и вкруг него
> По-прежнему все пусто.
> Здравствуй, племя
> Младое, незнакомое! Не я
> Увижу твой могучий поздний возраст,
> Когда перерастешь моих знакомцев
> И старую главу их заслонишь
> От глаз прохожего. Но пусть мой внук
> Услышит ваш приветный шум, когда,
> С приятельской беседы возвращаясь,
> Веселых и приятных мыслей полон,
> Пройдет он мимо вас во мраке ночи
> И обо мне вспомянет.

Новые беды поджидали его в Петербурге. Среди «молодых кавалергардов на балах, на которых уже не пляшу», появился красивый блондин, француз Жорж Дантес. «Шуан» (роялист), покинувший Францию после революции 1830 года, Дантес в России был принят на службу в лейб-гвардии гусарский полк (и успел заработать за короткое время службы 44 выговора). Дантес слыл «мальчиком-игрушкой» у барона Геккерна, голландского посла. Геккерн «усыновил» Дантеса, когда «ребенку» стукнуло 24 года (хотя в то время официально Голландия еще не утвердила этого). Существует множество доказательств их гомосексуальных отношений, включая страстную переписку между Геккерном и Дантесом. Дантес заслужил славу покорителя женских сердец — яркий гусар-красавчик, искусный танцор, пижонски причесанный и одетый. Ну, а если к этому добавить не поддающееся объяснению cachet француза в обществе галломанов, нетрудно понять его головокружительный успех в свете; ему покровительствовала даже императрица. Помимо своей популярности, Дантес купался в «папочкиных» деньгах. Он был, в общем, полной противоположностью Пушкину и идеально подходил бы, с точки зрения «мадам Карс», ее дочери. Ничего удивительного нет в том, что Дантес совершенно вскружил голову Наталье Николаевне (и двум ее сестрам тоже).

Поздней осенью 1835 года Дантес возжелал достичь совершеннейшего триумфа в обществе: соблазнить и завоевать первую красавицу Петербурга Натали Пушкину. То, что она была замужем за «солнцем русской поэзии», его не волновало. Он не знал русского совсем (да ему и не надо было — кроме нескольких строевых команд и бранных слов). Даже его французский был заурядным; он ничего не читал, поэзия же была для него китайской грамотой. Но Дантес утверждал потом, что он завоевал сердце Натали недолгой осадой, постепенно убеждая ее в «родстве душ»... Возможно, так и было. В любом случае — она поверила ему или, по меньшей мере, ей льстило, что Дантес ухаживал за ней и умолял ее почти, можно сказать, как Онегин — Татьяну. Как сказал Шекспир («Ромео и Джульета», Акт II, сцена ii, 92-93) «сам Юпитер, говорят, над заверениями любовников смеется». К 20 января 1836 года Дантес написал барону Геккерну, что он (не называя имени) полюбил первую красавицу столицы и «она меня тоже любит, но мы не можем видеться, так как ее муж отвратительно ревнив». Стала ли Наталья Николаевна любовницей Дантеса? Много лет спустя в Париже, на этот вопрос друга Пушкина Соболевского Дантес ответил «Само собой разумеется». Но утверждения Дантеса вполне могли быть лишь гусарским бахвальством. Впрочем, какие бы ни были у них отношения, нам в этой истории важно то, что Наталья Николаевна даже не пыталась утаивать от мужа своего флирта с красивым кавалергардом.

Она продолжала этот флирт даже в тяжелые дни, когда умирала мать поэта — Надежда Осиповна. Старая подруга Пушкина по Михайловскому, Зизи, вспоминала: «Пушкин чрезвычайно был привязан к своей матери, которая, однако, предпочитала ему второго своего сына (Льва), и потом до такой степени, что каждый успех старшего делал ее к нему равнодушнее и вызывал с ее стороны сожаление, что успех этот не достался ее любимцу. Но последний год ее жизни, когда она была больна несколько месяцев, Александр Сергеевич ухаживал за нею с такой нежностью и уделял ей от малого своего состояния с такой охотой, что она узнала свою несправедливость и просила у него прощение, сознаваясь, что она не умела его ценить». Анна Керн (которая всегда была искренним другом семьи Пушкиных) вспоминала:

> ...Я его еще раз встретила с женою у родителей, незадолго до смерти матери и когда она уже не вставала с постели, которая стояла посреди комнаты, головами к окнам: они сидели рядом на маленьком диване у стены, и Надежда

Осиповна смотрела на них ласково, с любовью, а Александр Сергеевич держал в руке конец боа своей жены и тихонько гладил его, как будто тем выражая ласку к жене и ласку к матери. Он при этом ничего не говорил. Наталья Николаевна была в папильотках: это было перед балом.

Мать Пушкина скончалась 29 марта 1836 года. Он сам хоронил ее, проделав путь в 400 верст по размытым весенним таяньем снегов дорогам, к семейной могиле Ганнибалов в Святогорском монастыре, недалеко от Михайловского. Похоронив мать, он заплатил монастырю за свою будущую могилу — рядом с ней. Зизи пишет: «После похорон он был чрезвычайно расстроен и жаловался на судьбу: она и тут его не пощадила, дав ему такое короткое время пользоваться нежностью материнскою, которой до того времени он не знал. Между тем, как он сам мне рассказывал, нашлись люди в Петербурге, которые уверяли, что он при отпевании тела матери неприлично весел был».

В 1836 году царь дал, наконец, разрешение Пушкину на издание собственного ежеквартального журнала «Современник» (он проходил 4 цензуры). В апреле 1836 года вышел первый номер журнала, в котором были: «Путешествие в Арзрум», несколько стихов Пушкина, а также первая публикация «Носа» Гоголя. К сожалению, тираж был небольшим, а критики (недруги Пушкина, возглавляемые Булгариным и Уваровым) были жестоки. Весь 1836 год для Пушкина превратился в финансовую катастрофу. «Современник» боролся за существование и за увеличение тиража. И Пушкин не имел ни рубля дохода за свои публикации, так как печатался только в собственном журнале. 27 мая 1836 года родилась младшая дочь Наталья. К семейным заботам добавились еще долги брата и отца. Он был вынужден общаться с ростовщиками, занимать деньги; дела его шли так плохо, что ему даже чуть ли не приходилось отказывать себе в покупке книг! Правда, у него уже были новые выгодные договоры с издателями на будущее.

Мне кажется, что биографы переживают больше о финансах поэта, чем сам поэт. Каким бы безрадостным ни было материальное положение Пушкина, надо помнить, однако, что многие представители русского дворянства годами жили в долг, это было не только достаточно распространено, а, в какой-то степени, даже стильно. «Служив отлично-благородно / Долгами жил его отец». И хотя Пушкин однажды шутливо заметил: «Пишу по той же причине, что певец поет, булочник печет, а лекарь морит — ради денег», в нем всегда оставался тот юноша, который бросал золотые монеты в канал, чтобы полюбоваться их блеском под водой. Он был готов к тому, что его труды могли не пройти четырехслойную цензуру, которой они подвергались. Из-за цензуры многое осталось ненапечатанным при его жизни. Но красоты и художественная чистота для поэта всегда были гораздо важнее дохода. Будучи «тихой музы полн» («Близ мест, где царствует Венеция златая»), он всегда мог найти счастье в самом себе («Поэт! Не дорожи любовию народной...»).

Что заставляет считать 1836 год самым мучительным в жизни Пушкина — это его совершеннейшее одиночество. Глубоко переживая смерть матери, потеряв семейный покой и чувство свободы, он больше чем когда-либо тосковал по лицейским друзьям, по Дельвигу: «Никто на свете не был мне ближе Дельвига. С ним толковал обо всем, *что душу волнует, что сердце томит*». Тосковал и о Пущине, о Кюхельбекере, сосланным в Сибирь. К концу 1836 года Пушкин был фактически во всем поднадзорным: «Шпионы у нас подобны букве «*ять*». Они беззвучны, бесполезны и вездесущи».

Пока Пушкин не находил себе места и не знал, как ему унять боль и ревность, терзающие душу, Дантес находил Натали на каждом балу. Наталья Николаевна не изменяла свой образ жизни. А, в лучших гусарских традициях, Дантес ухаживал одновременно за Натали, ее сестрой Екатериной, за княжной Барятинской... и не забывал своего «отца».

Летом 1836 года Наталья Николаевна сняла дорогую дачу в модном пригороде Петербурга, на Каменном острове (полк Дантеса располагался совсем рядом). Оправившись после родов, она с сестрами и Дантесом любила совершать прогулки верхом. А Пушкин тогда на даче уже писал глубочайшие стихи о смерти, о душе, о вере, о своем поэтическом наследии: «Напрасно я бегу к сионским высотам»; «Отцы пустынники и жены непорочны»; «Когда за городом, задумчив, я брожу»; «Из Пиндемонти» и «Памятник». Этот так называемый «Каменноостровский цикл», может быть, вершина всего, что создано в русской поэзии. Там же он завершал работу над «Капитанской дочкой», которая была напечатана в декабре 1836 года в «Современнике». Многие считают это произведение лучшим романом, когда-либо написанным на русском языке. Захватывающий сюжет о взрослении и любви среди мятежей, гражданской войны, лишения свободы, предательства и смерти — сделал этот роман классикой. Журнал раскупался мгновенно. В романе Пушкин пророчески предостерегает: «Не приведи Бог видеть русский бунт, бессмысленный и беспощадный!» Знаменитый российский критик Белинский называет роман «чудом художественного мастерства», а гениальный Гоголь сказал:

Сравнительно с «Капитанскою дочкой» все наши романы и повести кажутся приторной размазней... Чистота и безыскусственность взошли в ней на такую высокую степень, что сама действительность кажется перед нею искусственной и карикатурной.

Но Пушкину, увы, не пришлось закончить другую необыкновенную повесть (начатую в 1835 году в Михайловском). «Египетские ночи» — очаровательное искусное сплетение поэзии и прозы, смешивающее российскую реальность с идеями итальянского Ренессанса и затрагивающее автобиографические темы борьбы поэта за свободу среди равнодушно-враждебного «света». Поэтическая импровизация в повести — о природе любви: ее самопожертвование, сладострастие, возвышенная жестокость, необъяснимое волшебство и сила, олицетворенные в египетской мифической Клеопатре.

> Кто к торгу страстному приступит?
> Свою любовь я продаю;
> Скажите: кто меж вами купит
> Ценою жизни ночь мою?

19 октября 1836 года — день 25-й годовщины Лицея — «промчалась четверть века!». В то утро Пушкин, своего рода летописец Лицея, начал писать, но не успел закончить, стихи к традиционному праздничному обеду. На встрече он прочитал только:

> Была пора: наш праздник молодой
> Сиял, шумел и розами венчался,
> И с песнями бокалов звон мешался,
> И тесною сидели мы толпой.
> Тогда, душой беспечные невежды,
> Мы жили все и легче и смелей,
> Мы пили все за здравие надежды
> И юности, и всех ее затей.
>
> Теперь не то: разгульный праздник наш
> С приходом лет, как мы, перебесился,
> Он присмирел, утих, остепенился,
> Стал глуше звон его заздравных чаш;
> Меж нами речь не так игриво льется,
> Просторнее, грустнее мы сидим,
> И реже смех средь песен раздается,
> И чаще мы вздыхаем и молчим.

Но как только он начал читать, «слезы покатили из глаз его. Он положил бумагу на стол и отошел в угол комнаты на диван. Другой товарищ уже прочел за него». Этот лицейский день был необыкновенно плодотворным. Он закончил «Капитанскую дочку» и подписал — «19 окт. 1836». В этот же день Пушкин написал своему старому другу Петру Чаадаеву, отвечая на его «Философическое письмо», обличающее власть, крепостное право, прогнившее раболепие перед грубой силой и отсутствие цивилизованного общества в России. Чаадаев винил во всех этих болезнях общества православную церковь и наследие Византии. Само намерение написать письмо Чаадаеву, которого объявили сумасшедшим и посадили под строжайший домашний арест, было смелым и рискованным. Но откровенный диспут с другом был превыше всего:

> Благодарю за брошюру, которую вы мне прислали. Я с удовольствием перечел ее, хотя очень удивился, что она переведена и напечатана. Я доволен переводом: в нем сохранена энергия и непринужденность подлинника. Что касается мыслей, вы знаете, я далеко не во всем согласен с вами. Нет сомнения, что схизма (разделение церквей) отъединила нас от остальной Европы и что мы не принимали участия ни в одном из великих событий, которые ее потрясали, но у нас было свое особое предназначение. Это Россия, это ее необъятные пространства поглотили монгольское нашествие. Татары не посмели перейти наши западные границы и оставить нас в тылу. Они отошли к своим пустыням, и христианская цивилизация была спасена. Для достижения этой цели мы должны были вести совершенно особое существование, которое, оставив нас христианами, сделало нас, однако, совершенно чуждыми христианскому миру, так что нашим мученичеством энергичное развитие католической Европы было избавлено от всяких помех. Вы говорите, что источник, откуда мы черпали христианство, был нечист, что Византия была достойна презрения и презираема и т.п. Ах, мой друг, разве сам Исус Христос не родился евреем? И разве Иерусалим не был притчею во языцех? Евангелие от этого разве менее изумительно? ...Согласен, что наше духовенство отстало. Но оно никогда не пятнало себя такими низостями папизма и, конечно, никогда не вызвало бы реформации в тот момент, когда человечество больше всего нуждалось в духовном единстве. Что же касается нашей исторической ничтожности, то я решительно не могу с Вами согласиться... Пробуждение России, развитие ее могущества, ее движение к единству... как, неужели все это не история, а лишь бледный и полузабытый сон? А Петр Великий, который один есть целая история! А Екатерина II, которая поставила Россию на пороге Европы? А Александр, который привел вас в Париж? и (положа руку на сердце) разве не находите вы чего-то значительного в теперешнем положении России, чего-то такого, что поразит будущего историка? Думаете ли вы, что он поставит нас вне Европы?

Хотя лично я сердечно привязан к государю, я далеко не восторгаюсь всем, что вижу вокруг себя; как литератора — меня раздражают, как человека с предрассудками — я оскорблен, — но клянусь честью, что ни за что на свете я не хотел бы переменить отечество или иметь другую историю, кроме истории наших предков, такой, какой нам Бог ее дал... Но, поспорив с вами, я должен вам сказать, что многое в вашем послании глубоко верно. Действительно, нужно сознаться, что наша общественная жизнь — грустнейшая вещь. Что это отсутствие общественного мнения, равнодушие ко всему, что является долгом, справедливостью и истиной, циничное презрение к человеческой мысли и достоинству — поистине могут привести в отчаяние.

От этого отчаяния Пушкин страстно желал скрыться, уехать в деревню. Но он был в западне «золотой клетки». 20 октября 1836 года он писал отцу: «Я рассчитывал побывать в Михайловском — и не мог. Это расстроит мои дела по меньшей мере еще на год. В деревне я бы много работал; здесь я ничего не делаю, а только исхожу желчью». В эти месяцы травля Пушкина Булгариным и Уваровым усилилась. В «Северной пчеле» Булгарина всё чаще можно было прочесть, что дар Пушкина кончился. Поэт Жуковский негодовал: «Наши врали-журналисты, писали, что Пушкин иссяк».

> Я слышу вкруг меня жужжание клеветы,
> Решенья глупости лукавой,
> И шепот зависти, и легкой суеты
> Укор веселый и кровавый.

Сплетни о Наталье Николаевне и Дантесе становились главной темой светской черни, вызывая едва скрываемую насмешку многих. Существуют разные версии того, что происходило потом. Якобы 2 ноября 1836 года Дантес имел тайное свидание с Натальей Николаевной и грозил убить себя, если она откажется стать его любовницей. Предположительно, она ответила бледным подражанием — отказом в прозе Татьяны Онегину: «Вы владеете моим сердцем, остальное мне не принадлежит». Что на самом деле произошло во время той встречи, если таковая и была, мы никогда не узнаем. Но свет безжалостно ловил все слухи и злорадствовал.

4 ноября 1836 года Пушкин и его друзья получили анонимные «дипломы» на французском, утверждающие Пушкина в звании «коадъютора великого магистра Ордена Рогоносцев и историографа ордена». Эти «дипломы», однако, намекали, что Пушкину наставил рога не Дантес, а Николай I. Пушкин подверг документ тщательному анализу. «По виду бумаги, по слогу письма,

по тому, как оно было составлено, я с первой же минуты понял, что оно исходит от иностранца, от человека высшего общества, от дипломата», иными словами, от барона Геккерна. Анна Ахматова утверждает, что Пушкин был прав и что он привел веские доказательства царю. Ведь барон искренне ненавидел Пушкина из-за своего «сына» — кроме того, он не меньше Пушкина ревновал «любимца» к его новому увлечению, которое их могло разлучить. Ахматова настаивает, что письма были «отводом глаз» для Геккерна. В такое время Пушкину, может быть, следовало бы уехать подальше с семьей или хотя бы отослать жену к родным, таким образом положив конец отношениям Натальи Николаевны и с царем с Дантесом. Но это было невозможно. Другие пушкинисты уверяют, что «дипломы» не могли быть отправлены Геккерном, потому что, как они утверждают, эта шалость могла бы повлечь за собой скандал. Какими бы ни были мотивы и кто бы ни писал эти «дипломы», рискуя своим положением, они распространяли клевету не только на национального поэта России, но и на честь двух монархов. (В дипломе упоминался князь Нарышкин, муж любовницы Александра I, таким образом намекая, что Пушкин — муж любовницы Николая I.) Так рисковать мог только тот, кто занимал достаточно высокое положение в правительстве, чтобы чувствовать себя в безопасности, или человек со статусом дипломатической неприкосновенности. Все «дипломы» были написаны печатными буквами. Много лет спустя император Александр II сказал в узком кругу приближенных: «Ну, вот теперь известен автор анонимных писем, которые были причиной смерти Пушкина. Это — Нессельроде» (канцлер, близкий друг Геккерна).

Вечером 4 ноября 1836 г. Пушкин говорил Наталье Николаевне о «дипломе». Она рассказала, по-видимому, свою версию событий 2 ноября, согласно которой Дантес был чуть ли не хищником, а она была жертвой — и примерной женой (со слов кн. Взяемской). Но она показала Пушкину несколько любовных записок Дантеса. Пушкин читал их... И понял, что она их принимала и хранила...

Пушкин вызвал Дантеса на дуэль. Барон Геккерн на следующий день пришел к Пушкину, подтвердил получение вызова по поручению своего «сына», однако запросил двухнедельную отсрочку. Начались переговоры, и дуэли удалось избежать, так как Дантес, к удивлению всего петербургского общества, объявил о своей помолвке с Екатериной Гончаровой, сестрой Натальи Николаевны. По-видимому, Пушкину намекнули, что его своячница беременна от Дантеса, и поэт, очень неохотно, отозвал свой вызов на дуэль. Он поставил одно условие — никаких контактов в дальнейшем между семьями Пушкина и Геккернов. Но «Приготовление приданого очень занимает и поглощает мою жену и ее сестер, но меня они злят, так как мой дом превращен в модную белошвейную лавку». 10-го января 1837 года Дантес и Екатерина Николаевна обвенчались. Пушкин шутил по этому поводу, интересуясь, какое подданство теперь Екатерине Николаевне лучше подходит: французское, голландское или русское?

Однако Дантес продолжал ухаживания за Натальей Николаевной, как и раньше бросал в ее сторону долгие «многозначительные» взгляды... она краснела, опускала глазки и танцевала с ним. Дантес делал неприличные намеки даже в присутствии Пушкина. Злобный слух распространился по Петербургу о том, что Дантес женился на Екатерине только для того, чтобы спасти честь Натальи Николаевны. На самом деле Дантес делал всё возможное, чтобы только скомпрометировать ее честь полностью. Пушкин больше не мог этого выносить. 26 января 1837 года он послал барону Геккерну письмо, которое, он был уверен, должно было спровоцировать дуэль:

> Поведение вашего сына было мне известно уже давно и не могло быть для меня безразличным. Я довольствовался ролью наблюдателя, готовый вмешаться, когда сочту это своевременным. Случай, который во всякое другое время был бы мне крайне неприятен, весьма кстати вывел меня из затруднения; я получил анонимные письма. Я увидел, что время пришло, и воспользовался этим. Остальное вы знаете: я заставил вашего сына играть роль столь жалкую, что моя жена, удивленная такой трусостью и пошлостью, не могла удержаться от смеха, и то чувство, которое, быть может, и вызывала в ней эта великая и возвышенная страсть, угасло в презрении самом спокойном и отвращении вполне заслуженном. Я вынужден признать, барон, что ваша собственная роль была не совсем прилична. Вы, представитель коронованной особы, вы отечески сводничали вашему сыну. По-видимому, всем его поведением (впрочем, в достаточной степени неловким) руководили вы. Это вы, вероятно, диктовали ему пошлости, которые он отпускал, и нелепости, которые он осмеливался писать. Подобно бесстыжей старухе, вы подстерегали мою жену по всем углам, чтобы говорить ей о любви вашего незаконнорожденного или так называемого сына; а когда, заболев сифилисом, он должен был сидеть дома, вы говорили, что он умирает от любви к ней; вы бормотали ей: верните мне моего сына. Вы хорошо понимаете, барон, что после всего этого я не могу терпеть, чтобы моя семья имела какие бы то ни было сношения с вашей. Только на этом условии согласился я не давать ходу этому грязному делу и не обесчестить вас в глазах дворов нашего и вашего, к чему я имел и возможность и намерение. Я не желаю, чтобы моя жена выслушивала впредь ваши отеческие увещания. Я не могу позволить, чтобы ваш сын, после своего мерзкого поведения, смел разговаривать с моей женой, и еще того

менее — чтобы он отпускал ей казарменные каламбуры и разыгрывал преданность и несчастную любовь, тогда как он просто плут и подлец. Итак, я вынужден обратиться к вам, чтобы просить вас положить конец всем этим проискам, если вы хотите избежать нового скандала, перед которым, конечно, я не остановлюсь.

На этот раз от дуэли отвертеться уже было невозможно. 26 января 1836 г. Пушкин получил вызов на дуэль от Дантеса. Она произошла на следующий день, 27 января 1837 года. Собираясь на дуэль, Пушкин не надел свой талисман от насильственной смерти, подаренный ему ближайшим московским другом Нащокиным. В дверях он остановился и вернулся, чтобы надеть медвежью шубу. Поэту была хорошо известна примета — «возвращаться назад — к неудаче», и всё же... По дороге на дуэль сани Пушкина разминулись с каретой Натальи Николаевны, которая возвращалась после катания с гор. Но Наталья Николаевна была близорукой, а он смотрел в другую сторону — последний символ их отношений...

Дуэль между Пушкиным и Дантесом на заснеженном берегу Чёрной речки недалеко от Петербурга имела неимоверное сходство с дуэлью поэта Ленского с Онегиным. Обе происходили в январе; в обоих случаях поэт противостоял повесе и причина дуэлей была одна: оскорблённая честь поэта. Как Татьяна и Ольга, Наталья Николаевна и Екатерина Николаевна были сёстрами. Пушкин и Ленский использовали одну модель пистолетов «Лепаж» (См. «Евгений Онегин», глава VI, xxv)... (Дантес стрелял из пистолета немецкого оружейнного мастера Ульбриха, одолженного у Эрнеста де Баранта, сына французского посла, который три года спустя сразится на дуэли с другим великим поэтом России, Михаилом Лермонтовым, используя тот же самый «роковой ствол».)

Неужели Пушкин не задумался над параллелями? Неужели он забыл пророчество мадам Кирхгоф? Почему же ровно на 37-м году своей жизни он ввязался в дуэль с блондином? Как писала Зизи, которая приехала погостить в Петербург как раз за несколько дней до дуэли, Пушкин признался ей в своём желании искать исход даже в смерти. Однако слова Зизи противоречат (а может, и нет?) строкам, написанным незадолго до этого:

О нет, мне жизнь не надоела,
Я жить люблю, я жить хочу,
Душа не вовсе охладела,
Утратя молодость свою.

В этих строках чувствуется душевное смятение поэта: восклицание «О нет» звучит словно в ответ на внутренний голос, говорящий «да».

Утром в день дуэли Пушкин казался счастливым больше, чем обычно в последние дни. Он даже пел... Он написал письмо в связи с выходом нового выпуска «Современника». Он вёл себя не как человек, предвидевший свою смерть. И всё же, по настоянию Пушкина дуэль состоялась с десяти шагов, почти в упор — «чем кровавее, тем лучше», и он не надел (забыл?) перстень-талисман от насильственной смерти. Дантес выстрелил первым: пуля разорвала брюшную полость и раздробила кости бедра. Рана была смертельной. Лёжа на снегу и истекая кровью, не в силах подняться из-за страшной боли, Пушкин настоял, чтобы ему тем не менее дали возможность сделать выстрел. Его пуля задела правую руку Дантеса и отскочила от пуговицы, сбив его с ног, но не более. Думая, что Дантес убит, Пушкин воскликнул: «Странно, я думал, что мне доставит удовольствие его убить, но я чувствую теперь, что нет...»

Раненого поэта принесли домой, его осмотрели восемь врачей, включая доктора Арендта, личного врача царя. Врачи подтвердили, что рана смертельна. Пушкин их поблагодарил. Как писал Жуковский: «Умирающий исповедовался и причастился с глубоким чувством». В тот же вечер Пушкин вызвал Данзаса и продиктовал список всех долгов, включая те, что не имели письменных подтверждений, и подписал его. Снова приехал Арендт с запиской от Николая I, в которой царь просил поэта «умереть христианином. О жене и детях не беспокойся. Я их беру на свое попечение». Пушкин просил Арендта благодарить царя, передать просьбу о прошении и о снисходительности к секунданту, своему лицейскому товарищу Данзасу (дуэли, хотя и были часты, всё же по закону считались серьёзным преступлением в России). Несмотря на потерю крови и мучительную боль, он продолжал еще жить в течение 46 часов после дуэли. Доктор Арендт сказал: «Я был в тридцати сражениях и видел много умирающих, но ничего не видел подобного». Пушкин благословил своих детей и сказал Наталье Николаевне по-французски: «Поезжай в деревню, носи по мне траур два года, и потом, если пожелаешь, выходи опять замуж, но не за пустозвона». Он прошептал, обводя глазами книжные полки: «Прощайте, друзья!» Рядом с ним неотлучно находились поэт Жуковский и врач Даль, известный составитель словаря (с которым он еще мог шутить, что в первый раз — и, к сожалению, в последний — в своей жизни он позволяет себе обращение с ним на «ты»). И всё же даже в эти минуты он был одинок и снова вспомнил о друзьях-лицеистах: «Как жаль, что нет теперь здесь ни Пущина, ни Малиновского, мне бы легче было умирать». Незадолго до смерти он попросил морошки; Наталья Николаевна покормила его с ложечки. Он умер 29 января 1837 года в 2:45 пополудни. Даже время смерти привлекает внимание: злой дух графини в «Пиковой Даме» фатально появился в 2:45 во мраке ночи. Светлый дух Пушкина покинул его тело, когда еще не начало заходить зимнее солнце.

Наталья Николаевна была в истерике, кричала: «Я убила моего мужа! Я причина его смерти!» Поэтесса Анна Ахматова, оглядываясь на столетие назад, с негодованием согласилась: «Она всегда делала, что хотела и никогда не заботилась о его чувствах. Она разорила его, лишала его душевного спокойствия; не пускала в дом его умирающую мать, хотя привела своих двух сестёр; нанимала самые дорогие дачи и дома; забывала его адрес, когда он путешествовал; непрестанно делилась с ним своими любовными победами, жалуясь при этом Дантесу на его ревнивость. Потом она сделала мужа своим наперсником во всей ситуации, что и вызвало трагедию». Но сам Пушкин не жаловался, а был с ней ласковым до конца, настаивая на смертном одре, что «моя жена невинна». Он и не позволил своим друзьям отомстить барону Геккерну и Дантесу, сказав: «Не мстить за меня; я всё простил». Сдался ли он хладнокровно судьбе, которую когда-то ему предсказали?

После того, как остановили часы и все вышли из комнаты, поэт Жуковский остался. Он писал позже отцу Пушкина:

> Когда все ушли, я сел перед ним и долго, один смотрел ему в лицо. Никогда на этом лице я не видал ничего подобного тому, что было в нем в эту первую минуту смерти. Голова его несколько наклонилась; руки, в которых было за несколько минут какое-то судорожное движение, были спокойно протянуты, как будто упавшие для отдыха, после тяжелого труда. Но что выражалось на его лице, я сказать словами не умею. Оно было для меня так ново и в то же самое время так знакомо! Это был не сон и не покой. Это не было выражение ума, столь прежде свойственное этому лицу; это не было также выражение поэтическое. Нет! Какая-то глубокая, удивительная мысль на нем развивалась, что-то похожее на видение, на какое-то полное, глубокое, удовольствованное знание. Всматриваясь в него, мне все хотелось спросить: что видишь, друг? И что бы он отвечал мне, если бы мог на минуту воскреснуть?.. Я уверяю тебя, что никогда на лице его не видал я выражения такой глубокой, величественной мысли. Она, конечно, проскакивала в нем и прежде. Но в этой чистоте обнаружилась только тогда, когда все земное отделилось от него с прикосновением смерти. Таков был конец нашего Пушкина.

Глубокий шок сковал столицу при вести о смерти Пушкина. Тысячи людей оплакивали его, тысячи купили его работы, принеся доходы, во много раз превышающие его долги. Общественность была возмущена, что иностранец, любимец Двора, убил национального поэта. Многие понимали, что власти, которые так терзали поэта при жизни, в какой-то степени были виновны в его смерти. Молодой поэт Михаил Лермонтов очень точно выразил народное негодование в своём стихотворении «Смерть Поэта»:

> ...Вы, жадною толпой стоящие у трона,
> Свободы, Гения и Славы палачи!
> Таитесь вы под сению закона,
> Пред вами суд и правда — все молчи!
> Но есть и Божий суд, наперсники разврата!
>
> Есть грозный суд: он ждет;
> Он не доступен звону злата,
> И мысли и дела он знает наперед.
> Тогда напрасно вы прибегнете к злословью:
> Оно вам не поможет вновь,
> И вы не смоете всей вашей черной кровью
> Поэта праведную кровь!

Гоголь написал в более мягкой форме: «Вся моя радость и удовольствие жизни умерли вместе с ним. Я никогда больше не написал ни одной строчки, не видя его перед собой и спрашивая себя: а что бы он сказал на это? Понравилось бы ему? Заставило бы это его смеяться?»

Тысячи людей собрались возле дома Волконской на набережной реки Мойки (ныне Мойка, 12) недалеко от Зимнего дворца, серьёзно обеспокоив царя и графа Бенкендорфа, которые опасались повторения декабрьского восстания. Ответили они на это, как всегда, репрессиями. Упоминания о смерти поэта в прессе были строго запрещены. Только одной газете («Литературные прибавления», 1837 г., № 5, 30 января) удалось поместить некролог, написанный В.Ф. Одоевским: «Солнце нашей поэзии закатилось! Пушкин скончался!» Главный редактор Краевский был немедленно вызван для объяснений, и ему был объявлен выговор лично Бенкендорфом:

> К чему эта публикация о Пушкине? Что это за черная рамка вокруг известия о кончине человека не чиновного, не занимавшего никакого положения на государственной службе? —Солнце русской поэзии? — Ха! Помилуйте, что это за чин? за что такая честь?

Сначала Наталья Николаевна отправила пригласительные билеты для отпевания в Исаакиевском соборе (тогда расположенном в Адмиралтействе, а не на нынешнем месте). Но отпевание в соборе отменилось, по-видимому, оттого, что Митрополит Серафим отказался служить панихиду (по законам православной церкви дуэлянты, как и самоубийцы, не заслуживали христианского погребения). На теле поэта уже начали появляться признаки разложения, когда император Николай I проявил участие и дал личное разрешение на отпевание Пушкина в придворной Конюшенной церкви, недалеко от Зимнего дворца, о чем, как писал Жуковский, «даже и помыслить не могли» (при советской власти церковь превратили в таксомоторный парк). Отпевание в придворной церкви сделало прощание с Пушкиным актом государственного национального значения. Тогда, кроме ранее приглашенных Натальей Николаевной, были разосланы билеты государственным чиновникам, генералитету и дипломатическому корпусу. Таким образом, обвинения властей в несправедливом переносе отпевания поэта в другую церковь — необоснованы. Кстати, в Петербурге не было ни одной церкви, которая могла бы вместить тысячи скорбящих.

Однако традиционное внесение гроба в церковь было отменено. Его перенесли из квартиры на Мойке в ночь на 1 февраля 1837 года. Солдатские пикеты блокировали улицы. Вспоминаются печальные слова Вяземского: «у гроба собрались в бóльшем количестве не друзья, а жандармы…» Утром 1 февраля состоялась панихида. Учащимся, студентам и преподавателям запретили пропускать занятия для участия в похоронах. Тем не менее, полиция с трудом сдерживала толпу вокруг церкви. Вход был только по билетам. Но толпы неприглашенных ждали молча, простаивая несколько часов на ледяном холоде около церковных дверей.

Чтобы избежать дальнейших проявлений народных чувств, под покровом глубокой ночи 3 февраля 1837 года быстрые полицейские сани с гробом (в засмоленном ящике) выехали в направлении Святогорского монастыря. Приказом III отделения запрещалось оказывать и по дороге и на месте захоронения какие-либо почести поэту. На одной из станций под Петербургом жена цензора Никитенко увидела эти сани и спросила о них у стоявших рядом крестьян. Ей ответили: «Да, вишь, какой-то Пушкин убит, и мчат его в рогоже и соломе, прости Господи, как собаку». Было разрешено сопровождать траурный поезд только двоим: старому другу Пушкина Александру Тургеневу и жандарму Ракееву. Но при гробе неотлучно находился преданный слуга Пушкина (от колыбели до могилы) Никита Козлов, который «от горя три дня не ел и не пил».

«Солнце русской поэзии» похоронили в ледяной земле рассветного часа 6 февраля 1837 года. Никто из псковичей, кроме двух дочерей Прасковьи Осиповой-Вульф и нескольких крепостных, не постоял над могилой поэта.

Наталья Николаевна с маленькими детьми навестила могилу мужа только дважды. Первый раз в 1841 году, когда установили поэту надгробный памятник, и последний — в 1842 году. Наталья Николаевна в 1844 году вышла замуж за генерала Петра Ланского. Впоследствии она встречалась с Дантесом в поместье своей сестры Александры Николаевны, в замужестве Фризенгоф. Наталья Николаевна умерла 26 ноября 1863 года в Петербурге.

В России первый памятник Пушкину (и вообще поэту) был поставлен лишь в 1880 году в Москве. Тогда были произнесены знаменитые пушкинские речи Достоевского, Тургенева и Островского. Сейчас памятник стоит на месте, который называется Пушкинской площадью.

Если вам посчастливится там побывать в 7 часов вечера, вам может показаться, что все влюбленные города встречаются у памятника поэту. Хотя бы на миг, перед свиданием, они берут частичку его любовной энергии, его тепла, мудрости, страсти и силы. Конечно, есть и более прозаическое объяснение: его статуя стоит прямо над развязкой трёх самых загруженных линий метро. Но, чувствуется, это не просто совпадение, что влюбленные с цветами приходят именно туда, где стоит Пушкин. Не случайно он стоит над центральными артериями города, в сердце России, в сердце Москвы, где он родился и женился, на маленьком холме. Может, даже не случайно, когда его переносили из-за строек, монумент оказался развернут почти спиной к Кремлю. Пушкин как бы отворачивается от этого великого средоточия власти, предпочитая печально вглядываться в непрерывный поток простых людей, проходящих через самый переполненный во всем мире «Макдональдс».

Как поэт (и пускай только американский поэт), я привязан душой к Пушкинской площади; она мне принесла много личного счастья. Но мало таких истинно спокойных, душевных мест на земле, как кладбище в Святогорском монастыре, где Пушкин покоится возле матери и где:

Стоит широко дуб над важными гробами,
Колеблясь и шумя...

Такое умиротворение и любовь, кажется, живут в этом месте — такая благодать, такое достоинство! Ведь кладбище — место для тихой скорби и безмолвных раздумий... Я стоял у его могилы. Там вместе с горем ощущаешь на самом деле какое-то удивительное тепло, необъяснимую легкость в сердце и несказанное утешение.

Словно великая душа — «душа в заветной лире» — нашла там, хотя бы от Матери-Природы, наконец, ту материнскую, вечно преданную, вечно-женственную любовь, которую всегда искала.

И хоть бесчувственному телу
Равно повсюду истлевать,
Но ближе к милому пределу
Мне все б хотелось почивать.

И пусть у гробового входа
Младая будет жизнь играть,
И равнодушная природа
Красою вечною сиять.

Осень 2003   Джулиан Лоуэнфэлд

АЛФАВИТНЫЙ УКАЗАТЕЛЬ ПРОИЗВЕДЕНИЙ ПУШКИНА В КНИГЕ

Адели («Играй, Адель...»)	651
Анчар («В пустыне чахлой и скупой...»)	282
Арион («Нас было много на челне...»)	274
«Беги, сокройся от очей...» (Вольность. Ода)	132
Бесы («Мчатся тучи, вьются тучи...»)	362
«Близ мест, где царствует Венеция златая...»	402
«Бог помочь вам, друзья мои...» (19 октября 1827 г.)	284
Борис Годунов (Сцена XIII)	248
«Брожу ли я вдоль улиц шумных...»	440
Буря («Ты видел деву на скале...»)	156
«Буря мглою небо кроет...» (Зимний вечер)	220
В альбом Сосницкой	124
«В еврейской хижине лампада...»	162
«В крови горит огонь желанья...»	228
«В отдалении от Вас...» (Ек. Н. Ушаковой)	288
«В пустыне чахлой и скупой...» (Анчар)	282
«В степи мирской, печальной и безбрежной...» (Три ключа)	292
«В те дни, когда мне были новы...» (Демон)	198
Веселый пир («Я люблю вечерний пир...»)	639
«Весна, весна, пора любви...»	302
Виноград («Не стану я жалеть о розах...»)	158
«Вновь я посетил...»	422
«Во глубине сибирских руд...» (Послание в Сибирь)	278
Вода и вино («Люблю я в полдень воспаленный...»)	614
Возрождение («Художник-варвар кистью сонной...»)	324
Вольность. Ода («Беги, сокройся от очей...»)	132
Воспоминание («Когда для смертного умолкнет шумный день...»)	322
«Всей России притеснитель...» (На Аракчеева)	128
«Все в ней гармония, все диво...» (Красавица)	384
«Высоко над семьей гор...» (Монастырь на Казбеке)	346
«Город пышный, город бедный...»	310
Гречанке («Ты рождена воспламенять...»)	160
«Дар напрасный, дар случайный...» (26 мая 1828 г.)	320
19 октября («Роняет лес багряный свой убор...»)	238
19 октября 1827 («Бог помочь вам, друзья мои...»)	284
Делибаш («Перестрелка за холмами...»)	352
Демон («В те дни, когда мне были новы...»)	198
Дориде («Я верю: я любим; для сердца нужно верить...»)	126
Евгений Онегин. Роман в стихах.	446
Египетские ночи («Поэт идет, открыты вежды...»)	428
Желание славы («Когда, любовию и негой упоенный...»)	214
Заклинание («О, если правда, что в ночи...»)	194
«Зима. Что делать нам в деревне? Я встречаю...»	340

Зимнее утро («Мороз и солнце; день чудесный!..»)	230
Зимний вечер («Буря мглою небо кроет...»)	220
Зимняя дорога («Сквозь волнистые туманы...»)	332
«Зорю бьют ...из рук моих...»	350
«Играй, Адель...»	651
(Из Пиндемонти) («Не дорого ценю я громкие права...»)	436
«Итак, я жил тогда в Одессе...»	116
К*** («Нет, нет, не должен я, не смею, не могу...»)	388
К***(«Я помню чудное мгновенье...»)	232
К Чаадаеву («Любви, надежды, тихой славы...»)	144
«Каков я прежде был, таков и ныне я...»	298
Калмычке («Прощай, любезная калмычка!..»)	344
«Когда в объятия мои...»	374
«Когда для смертного умолкнет шумный день...»(Воспоминание)	324
«Когда за городом, задумчив, я брожу...»	430
«Когда, любовию и негой упоенный...» (Желание славы)	214
«Когда порой воспоминанье...»	326
Красавица («Все в ней гармония, все диво...»)	384
«Любви, надежды, тихой славы...» (К Чаадаеву)	144
«Люблю я в полдень воспаленный...» (Вода и вино)	614
Мадонна («Не множеством картин старинных мастеров...»)	368
Медный всадник. Пролог.	304
«Миг вожделенный настал: окончен мой труд многолетний...» (Труд)	444
«Мне не спится, нет огня...»	316
«Мне скучно, бес...» (Сцена из Фауста)	216
«Мой голос для тебя и ласковый и томный...» (Ночь)	182
«Мой друг, забыты мной следы минувших лет...»	164
«Мой первый друг, мой друг бесценный!..» (И.И. Пущину)	276
Монастырь на Казбеке («Высоко над семьею гор...»)	346
«Мороз и солнце; день чудесный!..» (Зимнее утро)	230
«Мчатся тучи, вьются тучи...» (Бесы)	362
На Аракчеева («Всей России притеснитель...»)	128
На Булгарина. Эпиграмма. («Не то беда,что ты поляк»)	290
На Воронцова. Эпиграмма.(«Полу-милорд, полу-купец...»)	656
«На холмах Грузии лежит ночная мгла...»	372
«Наперсница волшебной старины...»	110
«Напрасно я бегу к Сионским высотам...»	434
«Нас было много на челне...» (Арион)	274
«Не дай мне Бог сойти с ума...»	404
«Не дорого ценю я громкие права...» (Из Пиндемонти)	436
«Не множеством картин старинных мастеров...» (Мадонна)	368
«Не пой, красавица при мне...»	348
«Не стану я жалеть о розах...» (Виноград)	158
«Не то беда,что ты поляк» (Эпиграмма)	290
«Нет, нет, не должен я, не смею, не могу...» (К***)	388

«Нет, я не дорожу мятежным наслажденьем...»	382
«Ночной зефир...»	186
Ночь («Мой голос для тебя и ласковый и томный...»)	182
Няне (« Подруга дней моих суровых...»)	300
«О, если правда, что в ночи...» (Заклинание)	194
«Октябрь уж наступил — уж роща отряхает...» (Осень)	414
Осень («Октябрь уж наступил уж роща отряхает...»)	414
«Отцы пустынники и жены непорочны...»	432
Паж, или пятнадцатый год («Пятнадцать лет мне скоро минет...»)	114
Памятник («Я памятник себе воздвиг нерукотворный...»)	442
Певец («Слыхали ль вы за рощей глас ночной...»)	108
«Перестрелка за холмами...» (Делибаш)	352
«Погасло дневное светило...»	148
«Под небом голубым страны своей родной...»	190
«Подруга дней моих суровых...» (Няне)	300
«Подъезжая под Ижоры...»	338
«Поедем, я готов; куда бы вы, друзья...»	330
«Пока не требует поэта...» (Поэт)	406
«Полу-милорд, полу-купец...» (На Воронцова. Эпиграмма)	656
«Пора, мой друг, пора! Покоя сердце просит...»	390
«Последняя туча рассеянной бури!..» (Туча)	354
Поэт («Пока не требует поэта...»)	406
«Поэт! Не дорожи любовию народной...» (Поэту)	412
«Пред испанкой благородной...»	188
Предчувствие («Снова тучи надо мною...»)	356
Признание («Я вас люблю — хоть я бешусь...»)	236
Приметы («Я ехал к вам: живые сны...»)	336
Пророк («Духовной жаждою томим...»)	410
«Простишь ли мне ревнивые мечты...»	396
«Прощай, свободная стихия!..» (К морю)	200
Птичка («В чужбине свято наблюдаю...»)	166
И. И. Пущину («Мой первый друг, мой друг бесценный!..»)	276
«Пятнадцать лет мне скоро минет...» (Паж, или пятнадцатый год)	114
«Ревет ли зверь в лесу глухом...» (Эхо)	408
«Редеет облаков летучая гряда...»	154
«Роняет лес багряный свой убор...» (19 октября)	238
«Сват Иван, как пить мы станем...»	224
«Свободы сеятель пустынной...»	280
«Сижу за решеткой в темнице сырой...» (Узник)	196
Сказка о царе Салтане (фрагмент)	376
«Сквозь волнистые туманы...» (Зимняя дорога)	332
«Слыхали ль вы за рощей глас ночной...» (Певец)	108
«Снова тучи надо мною...» (Предчувствие)	356
Сожженное письмо («Прощай, письмо любви, прощай! Она велела...»)	212
Стихи, сочиненные ночью во время бессонницы	316

Сцена из Фауста («Мне скучно, бес...»)	216
Талисман («Там, где море вечно плещет...»)	210
Телега жизни («Хоть тяжело подчас в ней бремя...»)	334
Три ключа («В степи мирской, печальной и безбрежной...»)	292
Труд («Миг вожделенный настал; окончен мой труд многолетний...»)	444
Тургеневу («Тургенев, верный покровитель...»)	138
Туча («Последняя туча рассеянной бури!..»)	354
«Ты рождена воспламенять...» (Гречанке)	160
Узник («Сижу за решеткой в темнице сырой...»)	196
«У лукоморья дуб зеленый...» (Пролог, «Руслан и Людмила»)	226
«Умолкну скоро я. Но если в день печали...»	166
Ек. Н. Ушаковой («В отдалении от вас...»)	288
«Хоть тяжело подчас в ней бремя...» (Телега жизни)	334
«Храни меня, мой талисман...»	1
Цветок («Цветок засохший, безуханный...»)	318
«Чем чаще празднует Лицей...»	358
«Что в имени тебе моем?..»	370
«Что смолкнул веселия глас?..» (Вакхическая песня)	294
Элегия («Безумных лет угасшее веселье...»)	438
Эхо («Ревет ли зверь в лесу глухом...»)	408
«Я вас любил: любовь еще, быть может»	314
«Я вас люблю — хоть я бешусь...» (Признание)	236
«Я верю: я любим; для сердца нужно верить...» (Дориде)	126
«Я возмужал среди печальных бурь...»	392
«Я думал, сердце позабыло...»	386
«Я ехал к вам: живые сны...» (Приметы)	336
«Я люблю вечерний пир...» (Веселый пир)	639
«Я памятник себе воздвиг нерукотворный...»	442
«Я пережил свои желанья...»	164
«Я помню чудное мгновенье...» (К***)	232
Dis-moi, porquoi l'Escamoteur	633
Mon Portrait (Vous me demandez mon portrait)	112

INDEX OF TITLES AND FIRST LINES

A country winter. What's to do here?	341
A dried out flower, without fragrance	319
A drizzly day's fizzed out; a drizzly night's dull haze	209
A green oak tree's by a cove curving (Prologue, Ruslan and Lyudmila)	227
A lantern in a Jewish hovel	163
Alas! Say why is she so shining	153
A Little Bird ("Though exiled, I observe, still heeding")	171
A lot of us were on that skiff (Arion)	275
Although at times the burden's heavy (The Cart of Life)	335
A Message to Siberia ("Deep in your dark Siberian mine")	279
A savage artist, brushstrokes drooping (Rebirth)	325
A wondrous moment I remember (To ***)	233
Arion ("A lot of us were on that skiff")	275
Autumn ("October has arrived. The grove's already shaking")	415
A wondrous moment I remember (To ***)	233
A Winter Evening ("Snowstorm, gloom-filled, heavens drowning")	223
A Winter Morning ("It's frost and sunshine–wondrous morning!–")	231
A Winter Road ("Through a mist that's waving, rolling")	333
Bacchanalian Hymn ("How comes it that joy lost its voice?")	295
Back when, to me all things shone newly (The Demon)	199
Beauty ("She is all harmony, all marvel")	385
Begone, and vanish from my sight (Ode to Liberty)	133
Beneath the light blue skies of her own native land	191
Bound for your homeland's distant shoreline	193
By a noble señorita	189
Clouds are racing, clouds are writihing (Demons)	363
Confession ("I love you so–though it's distress–")	237
Dawn drums sound...from my hand tips...	351
Deep in your dark Siberian mine (A Message to Siberia)	279
Delibash ("Shots ring out beyond the hillocks")	353
Demon, I'm bored (Scene from Faust)	217
Demons ("Clouds are racing, clouds are writhing")	363
Deliver me, my talisman	1
Elegy ("The faded gaiety of past years' frenzies")	439
Epigram on Arakcheyev ("Persecuting all of Russia")	129
Epigram on Bulgarin ("There's nothing wrong with being Polish")	291
Eugene Onegin, Chapter 8 (Unpublished verses, Chapter VIII)	117
Eugene Onegin (Excerpts)	447
Exegi Monumentum ("I've built myself a monument")	443
Farewell, dear pleasant Kalmyk maiden! (To a Kalmyk Girl)	345
Farewell, farewell, free force of nature! (To the Sea)	201
Farewell, letter of love, farewell! It was her order (The Burnt Letter)	213
For one last time, my friend so tender	185
For you the gods but briefly will (To my Friends)	123
Foreboding ("Once again the black clouds gather")	357
Fragment from Onegin's Journeys ("And so, I lived then in Odessa")	173
From Egyptian Nights ("The poet walks...his eyes are open")	429

From Pindemonte ("I do not value much those rights....")	437
From The Tale of Tsar Saltan	377
Gift so futile, gift so random (May 26, 1828)	321
God help you all, my dear, dear friends (October 18, 1827)	285
Grapes ("No, I'm not going to mourn the roses")	159
Half a milord, half merchant, he:	50
Have you not heard his voice through groves at night (The Bard)	109
Have you seen, perched upon a cliff (The Storm)	157
High o'er mountain family (The Monastery of Mount Kazbek)	347
How comes it that joy lost its voice? (Bacchanalian Hymn)	295
I am fond of evening feasts	34
I came back again	423
I can't sleep, fire out, no light (Written on a sleepless night)	317
I do not value much those rights...(From Pindemonte)	437
I have outgrown my aspirations	165
I love you so — though it's distress (Confession)	237
I loved you once, and still, perhaps, love's yearning	315
If in thick woods a wild beast roars (The Echo)	409
If not for something murky gnawing	395
If, perhaps, life should deceive you	271
If they send me far from you (To Yekaterina Ushakova)	289
I'm glad to see you, lonely barren nook	139
Imprisoned, I'm caged in a dungeon that's dank (The Captive)	197
I will fall silent soon. But if, on days of sadness	167
In fearsome desert, barren, dead (The Poison Tree)	283
In lonesome wasteland freedom sowing	281
In mournful storms I have become a man	393
In the Album of the Actress Sosnitskaya	125
In vain I seek to flee and climb up Zion's heights	435
Invocation ("Oh, if it's true that in the night")	195
I rode towards you, and waking dreams (Superstition)	337
I thought my heart had long forgotten	387
It's frost and sunshine–wondrous morning!– (A winter morning)	231
It's time, my friend, it's time! For peace the heart is calling	391
Ivan, dear coz' , if we start drinking	225
I will fall silent soon. But if, on days of sadness	167
In vain I seek to flee and climb up Zion's heights	435
I've built myself a monument (Exegi Monumentum)	443
Labor (Upon Completing Eugene Onegin)("Finally, now the time's come")	445
Let's leave, I'm ready now! Wherever you, my friends	331
Madonna ("Of all the great old masters' paintings, few indeed")	369
May 26, 1828 ("Gift so futile, gift so random")	321
May God forbid I go insane	405
My blood is blazing with desire	229
My confidante of magical old times	111
My fifteenth year I'll soon be reaching (The Page)	115
My friend, I have forgot all trace of passing years	169
My friend through my travails, woes hardest (To Nanny)	301

My voice, when meant for you, affectionate and yearning (Night)	182
My Portrait ("My portrait you demand")	113
My very first, my priceless friend (To Ivan Ivanovich Pushchin)	277
Near lands where sovereignty of golden Venice rules	403
Night ("My voice, when meant for you, affectionate and yearning")	182
Night's soft breeze	187
No, I do not hold dear that pleasure so rebellious	383
No, I'm not going to mourn the roses (Grapes)	159
No, no, it isn't right, I cannot, I don't dare	389
October 19th ("The forest casts its scarlet garments off")	239
October 19th, 1827 ("God help you all, my dear, dear friends")	285
October has arrived. The grove's already shaking...(Autumn)	415
Ode to Liberty ("Begone, and vanish from my sight")	139
Of all the great old masters' paintings, few indeed (Madonna)	369
Of foreign lands an inexperienced lover	131
Of love, and hope , and quiet glory (To Chaadayev)	145
Oh, beauty, do not sing to me	349
Oh, blessed he picked with choice capricious	313
Oh, if it's true that in the night (Invocation)	195
Oh, spring, oh spring, oh time of love	303
Once again the black clouds gather (Foreboding)	357
Our hermit fathers and our nuns blessed and blameless	433
O very last cloud of the storm that has scattered (The Cloud)	355
Persecuting all of Russia (Epigram on Arakcheyev)	129
Play on, Adele (Adele)	45
Poet! Care not for love through fame, now or hereafter (To the Poet)	413
Prologue, Ruslan and Lyudmila ("A green oak tree's by a cove curving")	227
Prologue, The Bronze Horseman	305
Rebirth ("A savage artist, brushstrokes drooping")	325
Remembrance("When to most mortals sounds of noisy day do fade")	323
Round Izhora I was riding	339
Scene from Faust ("Demon, I'm bored")	217
Scene XIII from Boris Godunov	249
She is all harmony, all marvel (Beauty)	385
She loves me! I believe! The heart must keep believing (To Dorida)	127
Shots ring out beyond the hillocks (Delibash–The Turkish Captain)	353
Sometimes when moody reminiscence	327
Snowstorm, gloom-filled, heavens drowning (A Winter Evening)	223
Superstitions ("I rode towards you, and waking dreams")	337
The Bard ("Have you not heard his voice through groves at night)	109
The Burnt Letter ("Farewell, letter of love, farewell! It was her order")	213
The Captive ("Imprisoned I'm caged in a dungeon that's dank")	197
The Cart of Life ("Although at times the burden's heavy")	335
The Cloud("O very last cloud of the storm that has scattered!")	355
The Country ("I'm glad to see you, lonely barren nook")	141
The day's last gleam fades out, is disappearing	149
The Demon ('Back when, to me all things shone newly")	199
The Echo ("If in thick woods a wild beat roars")	409

The faded gaiety of past years' frenzies (Elegy)	439
The Flower ("A dried out flower without fragrance")	319
The flying wisps of clouds are thinning, scattering far	155
The forest casts its scarlet garments off (October 19th)	239
The last late flowers are more dear	269
The Monastery of Mount Kazbek ("High o'er mountain family")	347
The more we do commemorate	359
The Page ("My fifteenth year I'll soon be reaching")	115
The Poet ("Until the poet by Apollo")	407
The poet walks...his eyes are open (From Egyptian Nights)	429
The Prophet("With thirsting soul wracked, worn and thin")	411
The Poison Tree ("In fearsome desert, barren, dead")	283
The Storm ("Have you seen, perched upon a cliff")	157
The Talisman ("Where the ocean comes careening")	211
The way I used to be, that way I still am now:	299
There's nothing wrong with being Polish (Epigram on Bulgarin)	279
Three Springs (In this world's plain that stretches sad and endless)	293
Though exiled, I observe, still heeding (A Little Bird)	171
Through a mist that's waving, rolling (A Winter Road)	333
To *** ("A wondrous moment I remember")	233
To Adele	45
To a Greek Girl ("You have been born to set afire")	161
To a Kalmyk Girl ("Farewell, dear pleasant Kalmyk maiden!")	345
To Chaadayev ("Of love, and hope anf quiet glory")	145
To Dorida ("She loves me! I believe! The heart must keep believing")	127
To Ivan Ivanovich Pishchin (My very first, my priceless friend)	277
To My Friends ("For you the gods but briefly will")	123
To Nanny ("My friend through my travails, woes hardest")	301
To Princess Golitsyna, sent with an Ode to Liberty ("A simple child...")	139
To the Sea ("Farewell, farewell, free force of nature")	201
To the Poet (A Sonnet)("Poet! Care not for love through fame....")	413
To Turgenev ("Turgenev, the protector faithful")	139
To Yekaterina Nikolayevna Ushakova ("If they send me far from you")	289
Town so gorgeous, town of beggars	311
Until the poet by Apollo (The Poet)	407
Upon the Georgian hills there lies the haze of night	373
What is there in my name for you?	371
When full of love and bliss I felt complete elation (Wish for Glory)	215
When in the grasp of my embrace	375
When past the city gates in wistful thought I roam	431
When through the noisy streets I wander	441
When to most mortals sounds of noisy day do fade (Remembrance)	323
Where the ocean comes careening (The Talisman)	211
Will you forgive my jealous reverie	397
Wish for Glory ("When full of love and bliss I felt complete elation")	215
With thirsting soul wracked, worn and thin (The Prophet)	411
Written on a sleepless night ("I can't sleep, fire's out, no light")	317
You have been born to set afire (To a Greek Girl)	161

ОБ АВТОРЕ

Джулиану Лоуэнфелду посчастливилось родиться в семье, которая с малых лет прививала ему любовь к прекрасной поэзии, читая ему вслух стихи. Почитание русской литературы передавалось в семье из поколения в поколение. Прадедушка Джулиана, Рафаэль Левенфельд, был корреспондентом немецкой газеты «Berliner Tagesblatt» в России, являлся первым переводчиком произведений Льва Толстого на немецкий, и автором его литературной биографии «Разговоры о Толстом с Толстым», а также основателем прославленного Шиллеровского Театра в Берлине. Сто лет спустя правнук Рафаэля Джулиан стал изучать русскую литературу в Гарварде и стажировался в ЛГУ, затем закончил юридический факультет Нью-Йоркского Университета и стал практикующим судебным адвокатом. Его специализации — авторское право и федеральные дела. Он продолжает изучать русскую литературу с помощью известного литературоведа Надежды Семеновны Брагинской.

В числе недавних работ Джулиана — сценарий и партитура музыкальной пьесы «Благодарение», лирико-драматическое исследование о первой любви, сложных семейных отношениях и достижении совершеннолетия. В процессе работы находятся «Musings» (книга стихов и размышлений), одноактная черная комедия «Кафка для начинающих», а также книга ироничных современных сказок «Волшебный Уолкман». Джулиан еще написал более пятидесяти песен. В 2002 году его переводы с испанского двух пьес аргентинского философа-писателя Хулио Кортасара «Прощай Робинзон» и «До Пехуахо — ничего» были поставлены офф-Бродвейской нью-йоркской театральной компанией Steps Theatre Company.